INSPIRE / PLAN / DISCOVER / EXPERIENCE

JAPAN

JAPAN

CONTENTS

DISCOVER 6

EXPERIENCE TOKYO 78

EXPERIENCE JAPAN 146

NEED TO KNOW 326

Left: Sake barrels at Meiji Jingu Shrine, Tokyo
Previous page: Oarai Isosaki Shrine, Northern Honshu
Front cover: Arashiyama bamboo grove, Kyoto

DISCOVER

The glowing lights of Nagasaki

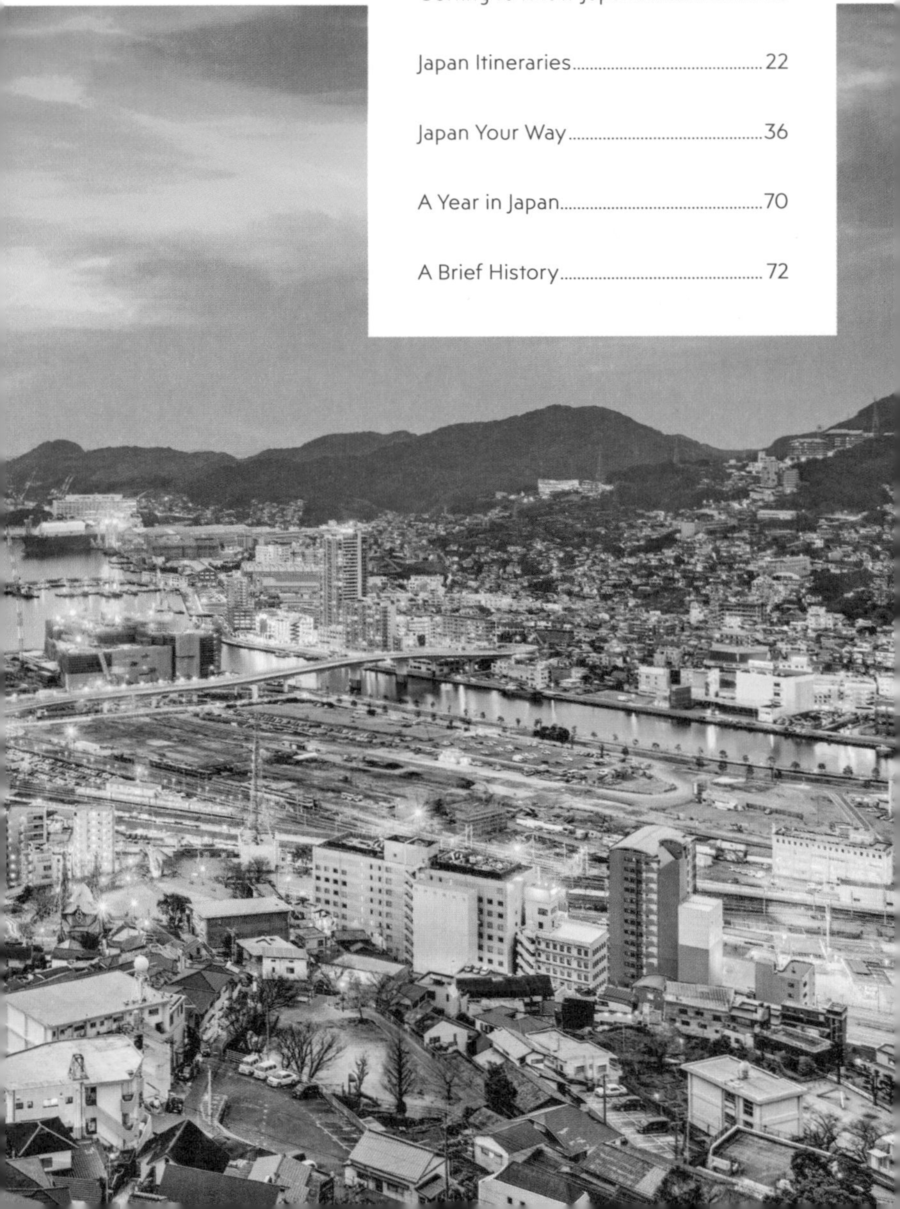

WELCOME TO JAPAN

Konnichiwa from one of the most fascinating countries on earth. Japan is a land of contrasts – of tranquil Zen gardens and steaming *onsen*, teeming crowds and robot restaurants – and it has charmed visitors for centuries because of it. Whatever your dream trip to Japan includes, this DK Eyewitness travel guide is the perfect companion.

1 A statue of the Buddha at Eikan-do Temple, Kyoto.

2 Neon lights of Tokyo's frenetic Akihabara.

3 A delicate plate of sushi.

4 Kiyomizu-dera Temple, surrounded by fall foliage.

Formed of thousands of scattered islands, Japan's impossibly varied landscape stretches 1,900 miles (3,000 km) from the edge of Siberia in the north to tropical Okinawa in the south. In between, you'll discover the snow-covered slopes of Hokkaido, majestic Mount Fuji, the otherworldly Arashiyama bamboo grove, and much more besides. This is a land of eternal natural beauty, as well as the yearly flowering and falling of ethereal cherry blossoms.

Japanese efficiency is no myth – these islands may be some of the most densely populated on the planet, but the country's thronging cities really do run like clockwork. Tokyo, the capital, where it sometimes feels that the only constant is change, is a science-fiction movie brought to life, with its cosplaying locals, cat-filled cafés, and psychedelic neon street scenes. To the west,

the ancient capital of Kyoto – the yin to Tokyo's yang – with its gilded shrines and graceful geisha, is a heritage wonderland, and – whisper it – a cosmopolitan city. And don't forget Osaka, where proud locals, a chaotic downtown and vibrant food scene meet under the enormous shadow of the city's giant castle.

Even with its unparalleled rail networks, Japan can still overwhelm with the sheer number of unmissable sites on offer. We've broken the country down into easily navigable chapters, with detailed itineraries, expert local knowledge and colorful, comprehensive maps to help you plan the perfect visit. Whether you're staying for a few days, weeks or longer, this DK Eyewitness guide will ensure that you see the very best Japan has to offer. Enjoy the book, and enjoy Japan.

REASONS TO LOVE
JAPAN

An avant-garde capital that pulsates with quirky cosplayers and raucous karaoke bars, hovering trains that rocket through awe-inspiring countryside, engrossing traditions, and an obsession with etiquette – what's not to love?

1 FAST TRAINS

When Japan launched the *shinkansen* (bullet train) in 1964, they left the rest of the world behind. Silently speeding at 200 mph (320 km/h), you'll feel as if you're in the future.

STAYING IN A RYOKAN *2*

These guesthouses provide the ultimate Japanese experience. Don a *yukata* (kimono), indulge in a communal bath, and savor a home-cooked meal, washed down with plenty of sake.

3 CELEBRATING OTAKU

Once an offensive term for a superfan, more and more people are calling themselves *otaku*. Explore the world of manga, anime, and cosplay in Tokyo's Akihabara *(p118)*.

4 RIOTOUS FESTIVALS

Don't let its introvert reputation fool you – Japan hosts some raucous celebrations. Expect loin-cloth-clad revelers, sumo wrestlers, and tantalizing scents drifting from stalls *(p70)*.

FANTASTICAL CASTLES 5

From the imposing fortresses of the Warring States period, such as Kumamoto Castle *(p274)*, to Himeji-jo's graceful donjon *(p224)*, Japan's castles seem straight out of a fairy tale.

SIPPING SAKE 6

Made from a large-grain rice and *koji* (similar to yeast), sake gets its rich flavor from its unique fermentation process. Hot in winter, or cold in summer, it's the perfect thirst quencher *(p65)*.

HISTORIC KYOTO 7
With 1,600 Buddhist temples and more UNESCO-listed World Heritage Sites than any other city on earth, majestic Kyoto is an absolute must for any culture vulture *(p180)*.

CHERRY BLOSSOM SEASON 8
Each spring, as the cherry blossom front sweeps northward, the Japanese population indulges in one of its all-time favorite pastimes: *hanami* – picnicking under blooms.

9 ZEN GARDENS
Some think that the rocks represent islands, while others believe that they symbolize emotional obstacles. Search for your own meaning in these mysterious gardens *(p48)*.

10 RELAXING IN AN ONSEN

As one of the most active volcanic regions in the world, in Japan, *onsen* are everywhere you look. Soak away your troubles in one of these bubbling pools *(p61)*.

SAVORING SUSHI 11

You'll find this dish on the menu at swanky Michelin-starred eateries and neighborhood dives. Get your chopsticks at the ready to sample sushi at its most authentic *(p140)*.

KARAOKE NIGHTS 12

Everyone from giggling teens to suit-clad businessmen belt out tunes in soundproof booths. Grab your earplugs, have your song at the ready, and enjoy the ultimate singalong.

EXPLORE
JAPAN

This guide divides Japan into nine color-coded sightseeing areas, as shown on this map. Find out more about each area on the following pages.

OKINAWA

Kyushu

Yaku

East China Sea

Amami

OKINAWA
p282

Okinawa

Miyako

Ishigaki

0 km	200
0 miles	200

N ↑

Sea of Japan (East Sea)

Toyama
Kanazawa
Takayama

Tottori

Izumo

WESTERN HONSHU
p210

KYOTO
p180

Nagoya

Hiroshima
Okayama
Osaka
Matsusaka

Takamatsu

Kokura
Ube
Matsuyama
SHIKOKU
p246
Wakayama

Fukuoka

Kochi

Nagasaki
Kumamoto

KYUSHU
p260

Kagoshima
Miyazaki

0 kilometers	150
0 miles	150

N ↑

Yaku

GETTING TO KNOW
JAPAN

Made up of four main islands – Honshu, Hokkaido, Kyushu, and Shikoku – and several thousand smaller ones, Japan is a land of buzzing metropolises, rural seaside villages, and much more besides. Becoming familiar with each region will help when planning your trip to this sprawling country.

TOKYO

PAGE 78

Japan's capital may be rooted in the past but it is also a vision from the future. Traditional low-slung houses sit beside sleek skyscrapers, and historic Ueno Park is a short walk away from frenetic, neon Akihabara. This city really comes alive after dark, when serious-faced businessmen and giggling teenagers caterwaul in karaoke booths, and the glowing lanterns outside cozy, hole-in-the-wall *izakaya* (pubs) tempt passersby. On top of this, Tokyo's restaurants have garnered more Michelin stars than any other city in the world, but there also many cheap eats to sniff out here.

Best for
That world-famous relentless buzz

Home to
Ginza, Ueno Park, and more

Experience
Everything from watching a sumo tournament to dining at the bizarre Robot Restaurant

CENTRAL HONSHU

PAGE 148

Although it is home to the charming cities of Kamakura and Kanazawa, Central Honshu is best known for its breathtaking scenery. This stunning region, where you'll find both Mount Fuji and the sprawling Japanese Alps, is the perfect destination for those who yearn to explore the great outdoors. Despite being well connected, parts of Central Honshu are still remote enough to have kept their traditional rural lifestyles, buildings, and festivals, making it seem far away from Tokyo.

Best for
Getting lost in nature

Home to
Yokohama, Kamakura, Mount Fuji and the Fuji Five Lakes, Takayama, Kanazawa

Experience
Watching snow monkeys relax in the hot pools outside of Nagano

KYOTO CITY

PAGE 180

To truly understand Japan, you must spend time in its old imperial capital, where scores of the country's famous monuments are preserved within a lively modern city. Kyoto is home to graceful parasol-carrying geisha, beguiling temples and towering bamboo groves. Life here is still largely tied to nature's rhythms. *Kyo-ryori*, Kyoto's celebrated cuisine, for example, makes much of seasonality, and the city's exquisite gardens go through striking seasonal transitions, from fall's bright-red maple leaves to spring's blush-pink cherry blossom.

Best for
Traditional temples

Home to
Nijo Castle, Fushimi Inari-taisha Shrine

Experience
A tour of the wooden-clad district of Gion

$\rightarrow$

WESTERN HONSHU

PAGE 210

Osaka, western Japan's largest city, is the cultural counterweight to the economic dominance of Tokyo. With its unique dialect, rough-and-tumble streets, and superlative foodie scene, it's one of Japan's unmissable cities. Away from Osaka, Western Honshu has many allures, including heavenly Himeji-jo Castle and thought-provoking Hiroshima, as well as some of the country's most stunning scenery. The Otorii gate of Miyajima, which seems to float above the waves, is a must-see for any visitor, while Mount Yoshino is the best place to walk beneath pink blooms during sakura season.

Best for
Cherry blossom

Home to
Nara, Osaka, Kobe, Himeji-jo Castle, Hiroshima Peace Memorial Park, Miyajima Island, and Horyu-ji Temple

Experience
Watching the diving women searching for pearls in the water surrounding the Mikimoto Pearl Island

PAGE 246

SHIKOKU

Isolated for centuries, Shikoku still feels like a backwater, and is all the more charming for it. The least explored of the Japanese islands, it offers a glimpse of the country as it used to be. The charming castle town of Matsuyama, with its clattering trams and ancient hot springs, is a great base from which to explore the island, while the more adventurous might attempt to master the famous 745-mile- (1,200-km-) long 88 Temple Pilgrimage.

Best for
Rural charm

Home to
Benesse Art Site Naoshima

Experience
Walking the historic 88-Temple Pilgrimage, which white-robed pilgrims believe atones for the worst transgressions

KYUSHU

PAGE 260

Active volcanoes, rolling grasslands, bubbling hot springs, and outgoing locals combine to give this island a very different feel to the rest of the archipelago. City-wise, bustling Fukuoka and beautiful Nagasaki are two of Japan's most cosmopolitan metropolises, showcasing Kyushu's historic role as Japan's gateway to the rest of the world. The menu on the island reflects this cultural melting pot: unctuous Hakata ramen or crisp lotus roots satisfy hungry tummies, while *shochu*, made from sweet potatoes, leaves a fiery taste.

Best for
Steaming onsen

Home to
Fukuoka, Nagasaki

Experience
A soak in the outdoor hot springs of Sakurajima, an active volcano

→

OKINAWA

Approximately 1,000 miles (1,600 km) south of Tokyo lies a tropical paradise. Okinawa's pristine beaches, spectacular diving, and slower pace of life have made it the favorite Japanese holiday destination. Although it could be easy to just flop on the sand here, the islands reward a deeper look. Naha, the main city, is a heady mix of refined civilization and neon glitz. Here, traditional red-tiled Okinawan houses, topped with ceramic *shisa* lions, stand alongside pulsating karaoke bars. Outside the city, you'll find poignant war memorials, sacred groves, and brimming craft stores to explore.

Best for
Rest and relaxation

Home to
Beautiful beaches

Experience
Awamori, the local tipple made by distilling fragrant rice into a powerful liquor

NORTHERN HONSHU

This part of Japan's largest island is steeped in myth and legend. Home to sacred mountains, dense forests, and vibrant folk traditions, Tohoku – as the Japanese call it – is a rugged and remote wonderland. The region overflows with literary connections, most famously to the haiku poet Basho, who chronicled his intrepid journey into the region in *The Narrow Road to the Deep North*. These days, with easy transport to the capital, this epic book title no longer holds true, and this region is as well connected as anywhere else in the country.

Best for
Literature and folk traditions

Home to
Nikko

Experience
A powerful performance of taiko *drumming on Sado Island*

PAGE 314

HOKKAIDO

The northernmost of Japan's major islands, and the country's largest prefecture, Hokkaido is a land of fire and ice. Characterized by fertile plains, perfect skiing conditions, and looming volcanoes, this spectacular island sometimes feels like a different world. The gateway to Hokkaido, Hakodate is famed for its bounteous morning market, supplied by the fertile seas that surround the island, while Sapporo – the capital – is best known for the intricate ice sculptures that take over the city during its annual Snow Festival.

Best for
Winter sports

Home to
Boundless national parks

Experience
Snowboarding on the powder-covered pistes of Niseko Ski Resort

←

1 Exhibits at
Intermediatheque.

2 The Fushimi Inari-
taisha Shrine.

3 The entrance to Ginza Six.

4 Stylish shoppers in
Tokyo's Harajuku District.

A land of dramatic contrasts, Japan rewards visitors who have the luxury of time. This itinerary is the perfect introduction to the country.

2 WEEKS
in Japan

Day 1

Start in Tokyo, getting your bearings by jumping aboard the Nihonbashi loop of the free Hinomaru Limousine sightseeing bus (www.hinomaru.co.jp). Get off at Nihonbashi Muromachi 1-Chome stop for Japanese paper-making at Ozu Washi (www.ozuwashi.net), followed by lunch at Mitsukoshi's huge food hall (p110). Next, walk to the Imperial Palace (p112). If the weather is good, check out the gardens; otherwise, the free Intermediatheque museum will keep you entertained (www.intermediatheque.jp). For dinner, try Edomae – the original Tokyo-style sushi – at Yoshino Sushi Honten (3-8-11 Nihonbashi), followed by a nightcap at the bar at the top of the Mandarin Oriental Hotel, overlooking the neon-lit city (www.mandarinoriental.com).

Day 2

Once dismissed as a clubbing hotspot, Roppongi (p90) has fast developed a reputation as a cultural hub. Purchase the ATRo Saving ticket and spend the day exploring the Roppongi Art Triangle; the Mori Art Museum, which specializes in contemporary art, is up first. Pause for lunch at Afuri (afuri.com), famed for its delicately scented ramen, before continuing your whistle-stop art tour at the National Art Center and the Suntory Museum of Art. Stick around Roppongi as the evening draws in; there's no place better for a night on the town.

Day 3

Today you'll meet Tokyo's quirky side. Start on the brash and bustling Takeshita-dori in Harajuku (p94); packed with trendy boutiques and vintage stores, it'll easily absorb your morning. Indulge your sweet tooth at Marion Crepes for lunch (www.marion.co.jp), then take the metro to Ikebukuro for more pop culture madness on Otome Road. Be sure to call into Animate (www.animate.co.jp) and take tea at Swallowtail, the butler café (www.butlers-cafe.jp). Round off your dive into Tokyo's subcultures at the Robot Restaurant (www.shinjuku-robot.com).

Day 4

Rise and shine before the dawn for an early morning visit to the Toyosu Fish Market (p138). Copy the locals and power up on some early morning ramen, before hitting the shopping mecca of Ginza (p106). Ginza Six is the district's largest shopping complex, which even has a Noh theater in its basement – buy a happy hour ticket before 1:30pm to see part of one of the plays staged here (kanze.net). After browsing the shops for the rest of the afternoon, arrive early (no reservations) at Sushi no Midori Ginza (www.sushinomidori.co.jp) for a sushi dinner.

Day 5

Board the *shinkansen* to Kyoto. After arriving in under 2.5 hours at the striking Kyoto Station (p189), make your way to To-ji Temple (p188) for an introduction to Kyoto's religious heritage. Marvel at the 1,001 goddess statues in Sanjusangen-do Temple (p189), then grab a snack at Tsuruki Mochi Hompo Shichijo (561 Nishinomoncho). Next, head to the Fushimi Inari-taisha Shrine (p186), where a tunnel of torii leads to great views over the city. Return to central Kyoto come evening for a riverside stroll and dinner at Gyoza Hohei (p195).

→

Day 6

Delve into Kyoto's past at the Imperial Palace *(p195)*, learning its history on a free tour. At lunchtime, make a beeline to bustling Nishiki Market to fuel up before embarking on the Philosopher's Walk *(p208)*. It ends at Nanzen-ji Temple *(p194)*, where you can enjoy a traditional *matcha* tea. Round off your day sampling different sakes at the Jam Sake Bar *(p192)*.

Day 7

Spend your final morning in Kyoto at the Kitano Tenman-gu Shrine *(p198)* and the glittering Kinkaku-ji *(p199)*. Grab a bento for lunch from Kyoto Station, before boarding the train to Osaka *(p218)*. Head into the lively Dotonbori area of downtown Osaka for dinner and drinks – Bar Dragon *(p221)* is a top option.

Day 8

Spend the morning exploring Osaka Castle *(p218)*. Sample marinated eel at Sumiyaki-Unagi Uoi Tengo *(www.sumiyaki-unagi.com)* for lunch, then continue learning about the city's history at the 6th-century Shitenno-ji Temple *(p221)*. As the sun sets, leave the past behind and head to the top of the sleek Conrad Osaka – with epic city views, this is the perfect cocktail spot.

Day 9

Start by exploring Osaka's subterranean National Museum of Art *(p219)*, then make your way to Michelin-starred Kashiwaya *(www.relaischateaux.com)* for lunch in a traditional tearoom-style setting. Next, head to the distinctive Umeda Sky Building for panoramic views from its Kuchu Teien Observatory *(p220)*. In the evening, explore the retro charms of the Shinsekai district, famed for its narrow lanes and old-school bars.

Day 10

Spend today in Nara *(p214)*, just an hour's train ride from Osaka. Pick up picnic supplies near the station before heading to Nara Park to visit Todai-ji Temple *(p216)*.

5

1 The West Gate at Osaka's
Shitenno-ji Temple.

2 A stall at Nishiki Market.

3 Colorful signage in
Osaka's Shinsekai district.

4 Kobe's Maritime Museum
and Port Tower.

5 Benesse House at the
Benesse Art Site Naoshima.

After lunch, explore the shops and *machiya* (merchant homes) in the Naramachi district before returning to Osaka.

Day 11

Journey 30 minutes from Osaka to Kobe *(p222)*. Start by walking up Kitano-zaka to Kitano-cho and touring the European-style villas. No trip to Kobe would be complete without trying its famed beef, so order it for lunch at Steak House Garaku *(www. steakhouse-garaku-kitano.jp)*. Spend the afternoon sampling sake at the Ginjo Brewery *(p223)*, then take a sunset walk around the harbor to admire the striking Port Tower and Maritime Museum. Head to the city's lively Chinatown for dinner.

Day 12

From Kobe take the *shinkansen* to Okayama *(p236)*, famous for its beautiful Koraku-en Garden. The garden is close to Okayama's castle, as well as the city's museums, so there's plenty to fill the morning. After lunch catch a ferry to the Benesse Art Site Naoshima *(p250)* – an art-filled island.

Spend the night at stylish Benesse House, enjoying artfully presented *kaiseki* (small plates) for dinner.

Day 13

Rise early for a morning exploring Naoshima's museums, before heading back to Okayama and taking the *shinkansen* to Hiroshima. Have lunch at Okonomiyaki Nagata-ya *(www.nagataya-okonomi.com)*, then pay your respects at the monuments and museum in the Hiroshima Peace Memorial Park *(p228)*. Oysters are a Hiroshima staple – try them for dinner at Kakifune Kanawa *(www.kanawa.co.jp)*.

Day 14

Discover Hiroshima's forward-thinking attitude at the Hiroshima Museum of Art *(www.hiroshima-museum.jp)* and Hiroshima Orizuru Tower. After slurping some slippery noodles at Bakudanya *(2-12 Shintenchi)*, fly back to Tokyo. If you have the energy, go bar hopping in Shimokitazawa, or the narrow alleyways of Golden Gai *(p96)*.

←

1 Shibuya Crossing, one of the busiest crosswalks in the world.

2 The vermilion Tokyo Tower in Shiba Park.

3 Tuna being prepared at the Toyosu Fish Market

4 Shoppers at one of the stalls that line the street up to Senso-ji Temple.

5 DAYS
in Tokyo

Day 1

Start with the Shibuya Crossing *(p92)* to catch a glimpse of one of the city's most iconic sights. After enjoying a ramen lunch at Ichiran *(en.ichiran.com)*, ride the Yamanote line to Yoyogi and make a beeline through Yoyogi Park *(p96)* to Meiji Jingu Shrine *(p86)*. Stroll the leafy avenues, before continuing to Takeshita-dori in Harajuku *(p94)*, an epicenter for youth fashion. In the evening, rent a karaoke booth and belt out some classic hits – Shibuya's Karaoke Kan *(karaokekan.jp)* featured in *Lost in Translation*.

Day 2

Make your way to Shiba Park *(p118)* and take the elevator to the top of the Tokyo Tower for stunning city views. Continue the morning with a stroll through the park, exploring Zojo-ji Temple before a fresh tuna lunch at nearby Itamae Sushi *(itamae.co.jp)*. Spend the afternoon browsing the huge stores of nearby Ginza; for traditional items, check out Mitsukoshi in Nihonbashi *(p110)*. Have a pick-me-up at legendary hole-in-the wall bar MOD *(3-4-12 Ginza)* before an *unagi* (eel) dinner at Takashimaya *(p110)*, or a Kabuki show at the Kabuki-za Theater *(p114)*.

Day 3

Set your alarm for an early jaunt to the Toyosu Fish Market: the tuna auctions kick off at 5:30am *(p138)*. Spend the rest of the day exploring the artificial island of Odaiba *(p145)*, pausing for a lunch of battered octopus balls at the Odaiba Takoyaki Museum *(p143)*. Call in at the seven-story Diver City Mall to explore the amazing array of shops and see the giant robot statue, then marvel at the technology displays in the National Museum of Emerging Science and Innovation *(p145)*. For dinner, head to Shin-Toyosu Station for a barbecue at Wild Magic – The Rainbow Farm *(wildmagic.jp)*.

Day 4

You could spend days exploring all the sites that Ueno Park *(p126)* has to offer, but today settle for a visit to the Honkan building at the Tokyo National Museum *(p128)* for an introduction to Japanese art. After lunch at Yamabe Okachimachi *(p128)*, walk to the splendid Senso-ji Temple complex *(p132)*. Cross over the Sumida river and visit the Tokyo Skytree *(p135)* for uninterrupted panoramic views of the city, before heading to the tangled lanes of Asakusa *(p133)* for dinner at Nakasei, a tempura restaurant that has been going strong since 1870 *(nakasei.biz)*.

Day 5

Embrace your inner *otaku* at the myriad manga stores and cafés in Ikebukuro *(p142)*, one of Japan's cosplay capitals. Be treated like royalty at Swallowtail, Ikebukuro's famous butler café *(www. butlers-cafe.jp)*, then head to the Sky Circus at Sunshine 60 for an out-of-this-world virtual reality experience. Afterwards, stroll to Jiyugakuen Myonichikan for a tour of Frank Lloyd Wright's "House of Tomorrow" *(2-31-3 Nishiikebukuro)*. Round off your day in *otaku* paradise at the ultimate geek attraction – the Robot Restaurant, which is 20 minutes away on the Saikyo line *(www.shinjuku-robot.com)*. Here, your dinner will be accompanied by a bizarre robot-themed burlesque show.

←

1 The modern cityscape of Yokohama, with Mount Fuji in the background.

2 The famous Giant Buddha in Kamakura.

3 A skier competing on the slopes of Nagano.

4 Shopping at a stall selling fresh fish at Wajima's early morning market.

5 DAYS
in Central Honshu

Day 1

Begin your tour in the buzzing young city of Yokohama *(p152)* at the world-class Yokohama Museum of Art. When you've finished browsing the collection, and are ready for lunch, head to the atmospheric streets of Chinatown to try some *nikuman* (steamed buns) – Edosei *(192 Yamashitacho)* serves the best. Next, join the locals in praying for prosperity at the Kanteibyo Temple, then catch a bus to the beautiful Sankeien Garden. Head back into the city for a *katsu* dinner at Katsuretsu An *(katsuretsuan.co.jp)*, followed by a stroll along the waterfront. End the day with a ride on the ferris wheel for glittering views.

Day 2

Catch a train to historic Kamakura *(p154)*, famed for its hillside temples. Start at the Tsurugaoka Hachiman-gu Shrine, then walk to the waterfront to enjoy the city's seaside vibe. After lunch at one of the waterfront eateries, check out the iconic Great Buddha, pausing to cool down with some *kakigori* (shaved ice) if the weather is warm, then take the 40-minute train ride from Hase Station to Enoshima. This island's enchanting beaches are ideal for a lazy afternoon. Enoshima's specialty is *shirasu* (fresh whitebait) – try it at Tobiccho Sandoten *(tobiccho.com)* before heading back to Kamakura.

Day 3

Nagano *(p174)* is nearly three hours away on the train so set off early. Make your first stop Zenko-ji Temple, where you walk through a dark passage in search of the "key to paradise." Once you've found it,

reward yourself with some tasty soba noodles at Uzuraya *(3229 Togakushi)*. Spend the rest of the day on the slopes or hiking, depending on the season. Either way, indulge in a relaxing dip in one of Nagano's *onsen* before dinner. Splash out on a meal at Fujiya Gohonjin *(www.thefujiyagohonjin. com)*, or enjoy budget-friendly ramen at Misoya *(1362 Minaminagano)*.

Day 4

Catch the *shinkansen* to Kanazawa *(p164)*. This city is renowned for its sushi, so be sure to sample some at Honten Kaga Yasuke, near the station *(www.spacelan. ne.jp/~kagayasuke)*. Stroll around Omicho market, the old Higashi-chaya geisha district, and magnificent Kenroku-en Garden to discover why Kanazawa is called "little Kyoto". Be sure to leave enough time to make the three-hour bus ride to Wajima *(p176)*. Check into Wajima Yashio, a *ryokan* with ocean views and tasty treats for dinner *(www.wajima-yashio.com)*.

Day 5

Wajima is famed for its morning market along Asaichi-dori, near the port. Seek out local seafood delicacies, before walking to the Wajima Nuri Kaikan *(wajimanuri.or.jp/ kaikan/file12.html)* to learn about the city's famous lacquerware. Head back toward the market for a seafood lunch at Naruse *(2-16 Kawaimachi)*, then spend the afternoon sampling sake at Hiyoshi Sake Brewery. Finish in time to catch the bus from Banbacho to the Shiroyone Senmaida rice fields for a picturesque rural sunset. Return to Wajima and, after another top meal, relax in the *onsen* at your *ryokan*.

←

 The glittering exterior of the Golden Pavilion.

② The approach to Kiyomizu-dera Temple.

③ Locals cycling along the streets of Kyoto.

④ One of the delicious dishes served at Kikunoi.

With its easily navigable grid layout, Kyoto rewards exploration on foot or by bicycle. Rentals are commonly available, and many hotels provide bicycles to their guests for free.

2 DAYS

in Kyoto

Day 1

Morning Start your trip at Ryoan-ji Temple *(p200)*. This extensive temple serves as a mausoleum for several emperors, but its crowning glory is its Zen garden, an ideal place to relax and reflect. The complex also houses a tofu restaurant called Ryoanji Yudofu, where visitors can drop in for a *shojin-ryori* meal – traditional Buddhist vegan cooking.

Afternoon The park surrounding Ryoan-ji Temple offers a number of walking trails, which are particularly lovely in autumn and spring. After exploring these, cycle the short distance to the Kinkaku-ji Temple *(p199)*. This is one of Japan's most famous sites, and you cannot fail to be enchanted by its golden silhouette. Koto, which is next to the temple, hosts traditional tea ceremonies *(www.teaceremony-kyoto.com)*.

Evening Join a walking tour of the evocative Gion district *(p192)*. Tours start every night at 6pm in front of the Gion Omoide Museum *(www.getyourguide.com)*. Be sure to book a table for a late dinner afterwards at Kikunoi *(kikunoi.jp)*. Run by the famed chef Yoshihiro Murata, this eatery is renowned for its *kaiseki*, a decadent multi-dish meal of reimagined traditional plates. Round off your night with a tasting course at the Jam Sake Bar *(p192)*, where the staff will be delighted to walk you through the nuances of Japan's national drink.

Day 2

Morning Spend your morning exploring Nijo Castle *(p184)*, the former home of the Tokugawa shoguns. Listen out for the squeaking "nightingale floors," designed to protect the occupants from assassins by making a noise when anyone walks on them. For lunch, a good option is Hyoto *(hyoto.jp)*, which serves *kaiseki*-style bento boxes and *shabu-shabu* (hotpot) at Kyoto Station and Shijo Station.

Afternoon Cycle to Kiyomizu-dera Temple *(p191)* for spectacular views over the city. The approach to the temple along the steep and busy lanes of the charming Higashiyama district is part of the fun, but it might be wise to park your bike before the start of the hill. The many shops and restaurants in the area have been catering to tourists and pilgrims for centuries – seek out local specialties such as sweets, pickles, and Kiyomizu-yaki pottery.

Evening A gentle five-minute cycle ride away is Pontocho Alley *(p191)*, one of the most atmospheric streets in the city. It runs parallel to the broad gravel path of the Kamo River, a popular place for a nighttime stroll. For dinner, eat at the world famous Kichikichi *(p195)*, home to Japan's most celebrated maker of *omurice* (you'll need to book in advance). Grab a drink afterwards at Hello Dolly, a jazz bar known for its impressive collection of vinyl LPs *(hellodolly.hannnari.com)*.

←

1 Todai-ji, the historic Buddhist temple in Nara.

2 The famous Otorii gate of the Itsukushima Shrine on Miyajima Island.

3 Skeletal roof of the A-Bomb Dome, Hiroshima Peace Memorial Park.

4 Visitors in Osaka's Kuromon Ichiba market.

5 DAYS

in Western Honshu

Day 1

Begin your trip at Osaka's grand castle (*p218*); tours take in the excellent collection of art and weaponry. For lunch, head south to the Namba area for Kuromon Ichiba market, a foodie hotspot. Travel back into the city center to check out some cutting-edge Japanese fashion at the Hankyu department store (*www.hankyu-dept.co.jp*), before exploring the eye-catching National Museum of Art. In the evening, take a relaxing dip in one of the baths at Spa World (*p220*). For dinner, head to Bar Dragon (*p221*), a lively bar near Osaka's famous Dotonbori canal district.

Day 2

Take a one-hour train ride to the ancient city of Nara (*p214*). Instead of leaving the station, first make the short train journey to Horyu-ji Temple (*p232*) to see the oldest wooden building in Japan. Head back to central Nara for an *unagi* (eel) lunch at Edogawa (*43 Shimomikadocho*), then take a stroll through Nara Park. Huge wooden guardians mark the entrance to Todai-ji Temple, home to the towering Great Buddha (*p216*) – see if you can squeeze through the hole behind him to be blessed with everlasting luck. Choose Kura (*16 Komyoincho*) for dinner, an *izakaya* (pub) housed in a traditional art storehouse.

Day 3

After a 2.5-hour train journey from Nara, you'll be greeted on arrival in Himeji by the breathtaking Himeji-jo fortress (*p224*). Explore the main donjon and the verdant grounds of the castle, before having a late lunch at Wabisuke (*2 Zaimokucho*),

an elegant restaurant by the moat. Next, catch a bus to the Shosha Ropeway to visit the 1,000-year-old Engyo-ji Temple. Then, head to Nadagiku Shuzo (*www.nadagiku.co.jp*), a sake brewery near Himeji Station. The brewery shuts at 6pm, but the restaurant, which specializes in tofu and *suminabe* (a type of hotpot cooked over charcoal), is open until 9pm.

Day 4

Catch the *shinkansen* to Hiroshima. Make your way to the Peace Memorial Museum (*p228*) to learn about the atomic bombing of the city in 1945, then pick up a bento box from Onigiri Nitaya (*www.nitaya.jp*) and spend lunchtime in quiet contemplation in the Peace Memorial Park (*p228*). After paying your respects at the park's poignant monuments, take the 45-minute ferry trip to Miyajima Island (*p230*) from the park's pier. Unwind in the *onsen* at Kurayado Iroha Ryokan, before enjoying the traditional meal prepared by your host (*miyajima-iroha.jp*).

Day 5

Rise early to view the world-famous Otorii of Itsukushima Shrine at high tide, when it seems to float on the sea. Explore the rest of the shrine at your leisure, then follow your nose to Kakiya (*www.kaki-ya.jp*) for a delicious lunch of fried oysters. Enjoy a moment of calm at the Daisho-in Temple nearby, then make the 90-minute hike up Mount Misen for spectacular panoramic views. Take the ferry back to Hiroshima in time for dinner at Okonomi Mura (*www.okonomimura.jp*), which serves delicious *okonomiyaki* (savory pancakes).

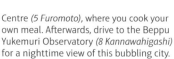

1

Although public transportation on the island is excellent, Kyushu is best explored by car, providing plenty of opportunity to head off the beaten path whenever temptation strikes.

7 DAYS
in Kyushu

Day 1

Start your trip in the modern city of Fukuoka (p264). First stop is the fascinating modern art collection at the Fukuoka Asian Art Museum. Your next port of call is Fukuoka Tower, a mere 25 minutes away by subway. Whizz to the top to admire the view, then head back down to ground level to visit the Fukuoka City Science Museum. Here, you can face the future and interact with almost 250 different robots. Round off your day with dinner at one of the many *yatai* (food stalls) on Nakasu, an island on the river that runs through the city center.

Day 2

Pick up your rental car and make the two-hour drive to Beppu (p271). Arrive in time for lunch – the *toriten* (chicken tempura) at Tokyoken (www.toyoken-beppu. co.jp) is an excellent option. In the afternoon, check out one of Beppu's hot spring resorts; Myoban Hot Spring, perched high above the city, is a nicely secluded option. Keep the temperature up in the evening at the Jigokumushi Kobo Steam Cooking

Centre (5 Furomoto), where you cook your own meal. Afterwards, drive to the Beppu Yukemuri Observatory (8 Kannawahigashi) for a nighttime view of this bubbling city.

Day 3

The attractive hot-spring town of Kurokawa (p276) is less than two hours' drive from Beppu. Check into the beautiful Fujiya *ryokan* (6541 Manganji), then spend the rest of the morning walking the main crater of Mount Aso (p276); tender beef from the Akaushi cattle that graze its slopes can be ordered for lunch at Imakin Shokudo (aso-imakin.com) in Aso Town. This afternoon, it's time for a spot of *onsen*-hopping around the town's many spas, before heading back to Fujiya in time for dinner.

Day 4

Set out early for Takachiho (p276), a town steeped in Japanese mythology. The surrounding area has some of the island's most dramatic scenery, making for a picturesque drive. Reach Kumamoto (p274)

1 *Yatai* food stalls on Nakasu Island in Fukuoka.

2 Rowing to the waterfall in Takachiho Gorge.

3 A road bridge between the Amakusa islands.

4 The impressive Suizen-ji Joju-en garden in Kumamoto.

in time for lunch at Aoyagi *(aoyagi.ne.jp)*, a beautiful spot in which to enjoy the region's cuisine. Walk across the river to view Kumamoto's striking black castle, before making the short drive to Suizen-ji Joju-en, a superlative garden that re-creates sites from elsewhere in Japan. If you're feeling adventurous, try the local *basashi* (horse meat sashimi) at Iroha *(p277)* for dinner. Don't worry if it's not for you – there are plenty of other dishes to choose from.

Day 5

The islands of Amakusa, less than a two-hour drive away from Kumamoto, were once home to Kyushu's hidden Christian communities, who were driven out of the Shimabara Peninsula *(p275)*. Learn more about this at the Christian Museum in Amakusa City *(19-52 Funenoomachi)*, before lunch at Yakko Sushi *(76-2 Higashimachi)*. It's a 2.5-hour drive to Nagasaki *(p266)* through epic scenery, including a car ferry trip across the Hayasakiseto Strait. Once you've settled into your hotel, walk to Sumibi Yakitori Torimasa Ebisucho for some top-notch *yakitori (www.torimasa.net)*.

Day 6

Spend the morning exploring Dejima in Nagasaki harbor to learn about the Dutch, Portuguese and Chinese influences on the city. Continue this theme with a lunch of *champon* – a Chinese-style noodle soup – at Shikairou *(4-5 Matsugaemachi)*. Dedicate the afternoon to the affecting Atomic Bomb Museum and Peace Park, then make the short drive to Kagetsu *(p267)* for fusion-style *shippoku*. After dark, park your car at the top of Mount Inasa and enjoy amazing views of the city.

Day 7

Head back to Fukuoka via the Saga Pottery Towns *(p280)*; Yobuko's morning market offers a selection of affordable ceramics. Once back in Fukuoka, return your hire car before slurping a "pork bone cappuccino" at Hakata Issou *(p265)*. Walk it off on a stroll to the Hakata Machiya Folk Museum, where you can watch a hypnotizing display of silk weaving. In the evening, go *yatai*-hopping on Nakasu Island again, resisting the temptation to go to the same stall as before.

Palatial Pads

Over the centuries, the imperial family's patronage led to the construction of impressive buildings across the country. Perhaps the most famous example is the Katsura Imperial Villa *(p203)*, which was originally built as a princely estate in the early 17th century. This elegant mansion has shaped what is commonly understood to be traditional Japanese architecture, but was also hailed as the ideal modernist prototype by Bruno Taut, the German architectural theorist, in 1937. Book a tour of the villa and other sights, including the Kyoto Imperial Palace *(p195)* and Shugaku-in Imperial Villa *(p204)*, through the Imperial Household Agency *(www. kunaicho.go.jp)*.

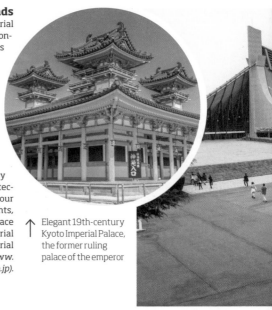

↑ Elegant 19th-century Kyoto Imperial Palace, the former ruling palace of the emperor

JAPAN FOR
ARCHITECTURE

Architecture is one of the most influential expressions of Japan's culture and creativity. Whether it's the elegant pagodas of the Tosho-gu Shrine, or the utopian optimism of the 20th-century Metabolist movement, the country's buildings encompass its multifaceted personality.

Modern Mountains

Roppongi is home to one of Japan's modern marvels of engineering - the Mori Tower. This cutting-edge skyscraper mitigates the risks posed by earthquakes with 192 fluid-filled shock absorbers. These semiactive dampers are filled with a thick oil and, as the tower begins to sway - as a result of tremor or high winds - the oil sloshes in the opposite direction to balance the structure. Another modern wonder in the capital is the Tokyo Skytree. Completed in 2012, and designed to evoke a traditional pavilion, the tower stretches 2,080 ft (634 m) above Tokyo. This latter-day pagoda is ostensibly a TV broadcasting tower, but also has restaurants and observation decks that offer tremendous views of the city's incredible skyline.

← The Tokyo Skytree piercing the clouds high above the vibrant cityscape

↑ The undulating exterior of Tokyo's cutting-edge Yoyogi National Gymnasium

Postwar Parks

Built for the 1964 Tokyo Olympics, the Yoyogi National Gymnasium in Yoyogi Park (p96) fused tradition with cutting-edge design, and symbolized the country's rebirth after the devastation of World War II. The architect Kenzo Tange also designed the Peace Memorial Museum in the Hiroshima Peace Memorial Park (p228). Along with the nearby A-Bomb Dome, it is an affecting memorial and symbol of peace. Join a community-led architectural walk of Hiroshima to understand how the city has reconciled with its tragic past (oa-hiroshima.org).

WHAT WAS METABOLISM?

Postwar reconstruction efforts in Japan's cities spawned new ideas about the future of urban planning and design. One of the most important of these was Metabolism. This movement came about during preparation for the 1960 Tokyo World Design Conference, and embraced the idea of modern cities in flux - constantly changing and adapting to meet the needs of their residents. This called for modular megastructures that could grow and shrink according to necessity. Although frustrated in their desire to build Tokyo anew, Metabolist devotees, such as Kenzo Tange and Kisho Kurokawa, exerted a major influence on the country's architecture. Check out Kurokawa's Nakagin Capsule Tower in Ginza (p106).

Sacred Structures

Shrines and temples are some of the most distinctive buildings in Japan. Common features to look out for include vermilion torii gates, troughs for ritual washing, and shimenawa, the straw rope with white zigzag paper strips that marks the boundary between the everyday and spirit worlds. Tosho-gu Shrine (p300) in Nikko symbolizes the power of the Tokugawa shogunate. Take a two-week tour to hear an expert unpack Japanese religious architecture (www. architecturaladventures.org).

The five-story pagoda at the entrance to Nikko's Tosho-gu Shrine

JAPAN
IN THE WINTER

While Japan is most often associated with its springtime cherry blossoms, winter is also a superlative time to visit. With perfect pistes, riotous festivals, and steaming hot springs – for people and primates – this season has something for everyone.

TOP 5 RELAXING ROTENBURO

Kita Onsen
 kitaonsen.com
Secluded bath in Tochigi, over 1,000 years old.

Ginzan Onsen
🅰 Obanazawa, Northern Honshu
Charming hot springs.

Yagen Onsen
🅰 Shimokita Peninsula, Northern Honshu
Free open-air pool.

Asahidake Onsen
🅰 Higashikawa, Hokkaido
Soak at the foot of the island's tallest peak.

Noboribetsu Onsen
🅰 Noboribetsu, Hokkaido
Eleven kinds of water.

A Good Soak

Sit in a steaming *rotenburo* (outdoor *onsen*), overlooking wintry surrounds, for the ultimate relaxing experience. Hokkaido, with its smoldering volcanoes, has more *rotenburo* than any other prefecture, but there are many more across the country. In Northern Honshu, there is even a bath that caters solely to monkeys. Red-faced macaques soak in the hot pools at the Jigokudani Monkey Park *(p174)*.

Hit the Slopes

Blessed with a mountainous landscape and some of the heaviest snowfall in the world, is it any wonder that Japan boasts some 600 ski resorts? Although the mountains might not compare to the scale of the Alps or the Rockies, the region of Hokkaido compensates by offering the most reliable ski season in the world, with certain resorts averaging 60 ft (18 m) of snowfall annually. The best-quality powder is arguably found in Niseko *(p319)*, where you can take advantage of the buoyant après-ski, as well as the excellent skiing and snowboarding conditions.

A snowboarder turning on a piste in Furano, one of Hokkaido's many resorts

EAT

Kotogaume

Nabemono, or *nabe* for short, is enjoyed throughout the cold winter months. Traditionally, this hotpot is eaten by groups sitting around the gas burner on which the dish bubbles. This Tokyo eatery, owned by a former sumo wrestler, is one of the best places to sample *nabe*.

🅰F4 🅰3-4-4 Kinshi, Sumida, Tokyo 🅲(03) 3624-7887 🅲L

¥¥¥

A little girl, crafted out of snow, at the Sapporo Snow Festival

A sculpture of a church, Sapporo Snow Festival

Relaxing in a *rotenburo* overlooking a lake in the Akan National Park

It's Snow Time!

Japan receives more snow for its latitude than any other country on earth, and the Japanese celebrate this epic snowfall with enthusiasm. The most famous snow festival is held in Sapporo *(p320)*, where hundreds of sculptures, crafted from ice and snow, punctuate the city. Look around at night, when the sculptures of global landmarks and sci-fi characters are illuminated with neon lights. Step inside one of the ice huts – or *kamakura* – at the Yokote Kamakura Festival to enjoy a *mochi* (rice cake), chased down with warming *amazake* (low-alcohol sake).

Oodles of Noodles

In Japan, you're never far away from a steaming bowl of this much-loved staple. There are three main forms of noodle here: Chinese-style ramen wheat noodles, light soba (buckwheat noodles), and unctuous udon (white wheat noodles). Each region has their own twist; sample them all at the Shin-Yokohama Raumen Museum in Yokohama *(www. raumen.co.jp/english)*.

A serving of soba noodles with a side of tempura, a staple at Japanese tables

JAPAN FOR
FOODIES

The Japanese menu, featuring slippery noodles, hearty hotpots, and delicate tasting dishes, is about so much more than just sushi. Whether you're in the backstreets of Tokyo or the refined restaurants of Kyoto, here you can find the most memorable meals of your life.

Let's Roll!

There are hundreds, possibly even thousands, of different flavours and types of sushi, but at its most pure form, this delicacy is about two things: rice and fish. Chefs train for a lifetime before they can claim to master this dish. Don't let this put you off trying your hand at rolling your own. You could take a one-day class, but you'll learn more on Tokyo Sushi Academy's longer courses *(www.sushischool.jp)*.

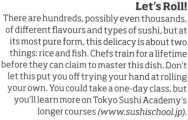

INSIDER TIP
Secret Tokyo Food Tour

Peek under the lid of local foodie scenes in Japan's biggest culinary cities on a foodie experience with Arigato Food Tours *(arigatojapan.co.jp)*. They will guide you through the warren of *izakaya* in Tokyo, the upmarket *kaiseki* scene in Kyoto, or Osaka during sakura season.

Eat the Streets

Downtown Fukuoka *(p264)* is full of *yatai*, glowing stalls providing hungry workers or revelers with late-night sustenance. While these stalls used to be common around Japan, the majority are now found in this bustling city. Follow your nose, and the smell of creamy *tonkotsu* ramen, to find spots, or discover the stalls most likely to have you shouting *"oishii"* on a tour with a local guide *(www.govoyagin.com)*.

→

Frying up Osaka's famous fried octopus balls, *takoyaki*, at a *yatai*

Season's Greetings

Visiting Japan during winter? *Nabemono* (hotpot) dishes will keep you warm. In spring, cherry-blossom ice cream is the perfect accompaniment for sakura spotting. Light noodles will cool you down in summer, while matsutake mushrooms are an autumn must.

←

A delicious swirl of cherry-blossom ice cream

←

Elevating Japanese dining to a fine art at Kikunoi in Kyoto

Delicate Dishes

Kaiseki, a tasting menu involving tens of delicate dishes, is the pinnacle of fine dining in Japan. Here, everything from the serving ceramics to the seasonality of the ingredients is taken into consideration. No trip would be complete without sampling this refined dining style. Eat on a budget in Tokyo at Kyoto Hyoki *(hyoki.jp/en)*, or splash out at Kikunoi *(kikunoi.jp)* in Kyoto, which is run by a third-generation *kaiseki* chef.

←

Showcasing the endless variety of sushi types, from *nigiri* to *maki*

Hiking the Heights

Pulling on walking boots and heading into the mountains is a popular pastime in Japan, and trails are easy to access and well-maintained. Our favorite is the three-day circuit through the Northern Japanese Alps from Kamikochi *(p175)*. Those looking for a once-in-a-lifetime experience can hike Mount Fuji, which, at 12,390 ft (3,776 m), is Japan's highest peak *(p158)*.

→

Hikers nearing the peak of Mount Fuji

JAPAN
OUTDOORS

Although Japan is one of the most densely populated countries in the world, over 70 per cent of its terrain is mountainous or forested. Such an untamed landscape offers a rich array of outdoor activities – a veritable nature playground for the adventurous.

TOP 3
MOUNT FUJI TRAILS

Mount Fuji is divided up into ten stages, with most hiking routes starting from the 5th stage, the last place accessible by vehicle.

Yoshida
Takes five to six hours from the 5th stage, and three to four hours down.

Subashiri
Over five hours up from the 5th stage, and three hours down.

Gotenba
The longest at seven to eight hours up from the 5th stage, followed by three hours down.

Snorkeling in Okinawa

This island nation provides plenty of opportunities to get up close to charming sea turtles, neon-colored clownfish, and flapping manta ray. The tropical island of Okinawa *(p282)* offers some of the best experiences – Cape Maeda's blue cave is one of the most popular spots. Odo Kaigan, near Gyokusendo Cave *(p288)*, is a more off-the-beaten-path option. Set in shallow water, just off the beach, this coral reef is perfect for families.

→

Snorkeling with a turtle in the tropical waters off Okinawa

Camping in Yakushima

Spend the night in a fairy-tale setting of gnarled tree trunks and moss-covered rocks at this UNESCO Biosphere Reserve. Jerry's campsite offers bicycles, snorkeling gear, and even the chance to try beekeeping *(www.eu-guesthouse-in-yakushima.net)*. You can learn more about Yakushima's unique fauna and flora on a private hiking tour *(www.yakushimaexperience.com)*.

$\rightarrow$

The atmospheric ancient forest of Yakushima

Surfing in Miyazaki

As you might expect from a country formed of thousands of islands, Japan offers waves aplenty. The year-round consistency of its swell has made Miyazaki, on Kyushu, a surfer's paradise. Kisakihama – a big beach to the south of the city – is one of the most popular places to ride the waves. Book a lesson at one of the local surf schools to learn the secret to riding the waves. On Shikoku, the area around Kochi *(p254)* offers an array of surfing spots that cater to all abilities.

$\leftarrow$

A surfer preparing to hit the waves from the beach in Miyazaki

$\uparrow$ Fly fishing in Hokkaido's Akan National Park

Fly Fishing in Hokkaido

Unsurprisingly for a nation that prizes its sushi, you will see plenty of fresh fish across the country. Try your hand at catching your own in Hokkaido, where crystal-clear rivers and flawless lakes are home to salmon and trout. One of the most spectacular places to fish is the majestic Akan National Park *(p322)*.

Built for speed,
the *shinkansen* at ↑
Shin-Osaka Station

JAPAN
ON A BUDGET

Billed as one of the most expensive countries in the world, Japan can be surprisingly affordable. Savvy visitors can go far using reasonably priced public transport, while low-cost fast food and happy hours make evenings a pleasure.

Cheap Eats

Vending machine restaurants offer affordable and filling food in the cities. Insert some yen into the slot, select the meal you want, and your change and ticket will pop out of the machine. Give this ticket to the staff at the counter, and receive a steaming bowl of ramen or a piled plate of fluffy rice. Yoshinoya, the oldest fast-food chain in Japan, has served up *gyudon* – a hearty dish of rice, beef and onion – since 1899 *(www.yoshinoya.com)*. If you're out and about, lunch at a *conbini* (convenience store) is a great way to save yen.

→

Eating *gyudon* at a communal table at a Yoshinoya in Tokyo

Smart Travel

Buses are an inexpensive way of getting around Japan. Long-distance buses often have reclining seats and footrests, making them comfortable and practical. If travelling overnight, you'll even save the cost of a hotel. Savvy train travelers should buy a Seishun 18, which permits anyone, of any age, unlimited rides on local and rapid JR trains over five days apart from during school holidays *(www.jreast. co.jp/e/pass/seishun18.html)*. For those who want to travel faster and further, the multi-day Japan Rail Pass allows unlimited journeys on any public transportation run by JR, including the bullet train *(japan railpass.net)*.

← The friendly-looking Asakusa sightseeing panda bus

STAY

9h nine hours Capsule
A "smart sleep" system in a high-end capsule.

⌂ 2-9-4 Kajicho, Chiyoda-ku, Tokyo 101-0044 Ⓦ ninehours.co.jp

---

The Millennials
Beer and coffee come with the capsule.

⌂ 235 Yamazaki-cho, Nakagyo-ku, Kyoto-shi Kyoto 604-8032 Ⓦ themillennials.jp

---

Book and Bed Fukuoka
Sleep in bunks hidden between bookshelves.

⌂ PARCO, 2-11-1 Tenjin, Chuo-ku, Fukuoka 810-0001 Ⓦ bookandbed tokyo.com

Entertainment for Less

Hitomaku-mi – or single-act – tickets are the perfect way to see Kabuki for less. One act at Tokyo's Kabuki-za Theater *(p114)* could last anything from 15 minutes to an hour. If you'd rather be the performer, make a beeline for a karaoke spot for a night of cheap but highly entertaining and ultra-Japanese fun. Karaoke Kan and Karaoke no Tetsujin are cheap and popular chains, while Karaoke Uta Hiroba includes soft drinks in the price.

→

Actor Nakamura Baigyoku performing Kabuki at Kabuki-za Theater

Today's Voice

Haruki Murakami is arguably Japan's most famous contemporary novelist. Fans of *Norwegian Wood* (1987) should visit DUG in Tokyo (*www.dug.co.jp*), the bar in Shinjuku where Toru Watanabe sinks whiskeys with sodas. In Takamatsu (*p253*), discover why Nakata, protagonist of *Kafka on the Shore* (2002), described the city as "udon central."

←

A still from a television adaptation of Murakami's novel *Norwegian Wood*

JAPAN ON
PAGE AND SCREEN

With its awe-inspiring scenery and unique ways of life, it's little wonder that Japan has captured the imagination of so many great writers and filmmakers. Follow the trail of your favorite books and movies to see the sights behind the set and pen.

TOP 5 ESSENTIAL JAPANESE FILMS

Late Spring (1949)
Looks at the relationship between a widowed father and his daughter.

Rashomon (1950)
Different characters give conflicting versions of events in this thriller.

Tampopo (1985)
A "ramen" version of a spaghetti Western.

Spirited Away (2001)
The tale of a little girl who is magicked into the spirit world.

Shoplifters (2018)
Palme-d'Or-winning story of a poor family that must shoplift to survive.

Be Spirited Away

For many, the quintessential Japanese filmmaker is Hayao Miyazaki, cofounder of Studio Ghibli. Step into the animator's imagination at Tokyo's Ghibli Museum (*p143*), with its recreated sets, original sketches, and show reels of his films. For full immersion, why not visit one of the real-life spots that inspired Miyazaki's fantastical worlds? The bathhouse in *Spirited Away* is said to be modeled on Dogo Onsen Honkan in Matsuyama (*p256*).

Windows into the Past

Written in the early 11th century by Murasaki Shikibu, a lady-in-waiting at the imperial court, *The Tale of Genji* is thought to be the oldest work of fiction in the world. Visit the room where Shikibu began to write this historic romance on a moonlit night in 1004 at Ishiyama-dera Temple in Otsu, near Kyoto. Japan is also home to another ancient art form – the haiku. Learn more about these concise poems at Tokyo's Basho Memorial Museum *(1-6-3 Tokiwa)*, dedicated to the masterful Matsuo Basho. You can also retrace part of his travelogue *The Narrow Road to the Deep North* by climbing up Mount Haguro *(p308)*. As you walk the forest path, surrounded by towering trees, it is easy to see how Basho was inspired to write his meditative verses. And at the end of your trip, why not summarize your travels in your own haiku?

Illustration depicting Lady Murasaki writing *The Tale of Genji* ↑

← A still from Hayao Miyazaki's Oscar-winning animated movie *Spirited Away*

Through International Eyes

For many people, *Lost in Translation* (2003) perfectly renders the realities of being a foreigner in Tokyo. Visit the New York Bar at the top of the Park Hyatt Tokyo *(p89)* to recreate the most iconic moments from Sofia Coppola's film. Wes Anderson fans, meanwhile, should take a boat trip to Gunkanjima from Nagasaki *(www.yamasa-kaiun.net/en)*. As well as being the inspiration for *Isle of Dogs* (2018), this abandoned industrial island also featured in the 2012 James Bond film *Skyfall*.

← Exploring the wonderful Ghibli Museum in Tokyo

Scarlett Johansson and Bill Murray in *Lost in Translation* ↑

Paradise Gardens

Introduced to Japan by Buddhist monks during the Heian period, a Paradise Garden is designed to evoke the Pure Land, or Buddhist paradise. You can easily imagine the Buddha meditating on an island in one of the gardens' lotus ponds. Byodo-in Temple in Uji *(p240)* is one of the most famous examples, while Motsu-ji Temple's garden in Hiraizumi *(p306)* makes use of "borrowed landscape" - trees or mountains outside the garden that appear to be part of it.

IKEBANA

The practice of using flowers as temple offerings originated in the 7th century, but formalized flower arranging, or *ikebana*, didn't take hold until the late 15th century. Nowadays, it is seen as a meditative art. Arrangements are supposed to be created in silence, to allow the designer to observe the beauty of nature and gain inner peace.

The Phoenix Hall and lotus pond in Byodo-in Temple's garden in Uji ↑

JAPAN'S
GARDENS

Reflecting the Shinto love of nature and the Buddhist ideal of paradise, Japan's gardens may seem like heaven on earth. From strolling in Western-style parks to meditating among curious rock formations in a Zen garden, there are plenty of ways to appreciate these outdoor spaces.

Zen Gardens

Looking to be more mindful? Find a *karesansui* (Japanese rock garden) and focus on one of the stones, seemingly floating in a sea of raked gravel. Kyoto is home to some of the best, including Ryoan-ji Temple *(p200)* - where the plain earthen walls enhance the abstract arrangement of the stones - and Daisen-in Temple *(p198)*. Kyoto Garden Experience *(www.kyoto gardenexperience.com)* offers private tours and the chance to access gardens usually barred to the public.

←

Visitors soaking up the peaceful atmosphere at Ryoan-ji Temple in Kyoto

TOP
3
**GARDENS
IN JAPAN**

Kenroku-en
One of Japan's "three
great gardens," this
park in Kanazawa is
equally breathtaking
in every season (p165).

Kairaku-en
Located in Mito, the
second of the "three
great gardens" is at its
most spectacular when
its 3,000 plum trees
blossom in February
and March.

Koraku-en
The last of the "three
great gardens," this
picturesque stroll
garden in Okayama is
unusual for its spacious
lawns (p236).

Stroll Gardens

The landscape comes to life
on a walk through one of
Japan's stroll gardens, as
vistas are concealed and
revealed with every step.
Suizen-ji Joju-en (p274) is
one of the country's finest,
while the garden of the
Katsura Imperial Villa
(p203) replicates famous
Japanese landscapes. Tokyo's
Rikugi-en Garden (p144) was
inspired by famous poems.

→

The undulating landscape
of the Suizen-ji Joju-en
garden in Kumamoto

Tea Gardens

To reach a teahouse for the tea ceremony,
you must first pass through a *roji*. Lined
with sweet-smelling moss, this garden
is designed to resemble a mountain trail,
leading from reality into the magical
world of the teahouse.
Head to Kenroku-en
Garden (p165) or the Ise
Shrine (p244) to take part
in this unique ritual.

←

The secluded
surrounds of
a teahouse

Horse Around

Perfected in the 12th-century *yabusame* (horseback archery) involves an archer galloping down a 837-ft- (255-m-) long track, controlling his horse with his knees, while shooting an arrow at three targets. Witness this feat at the Tsurugaoka Hachimangu Reitaisai *(p70)* in Kamakura, held each September. The inspired can attempt to master this art in Ibaraki *(www.govoyagin.com)*.

$\rightarrow$

Showcasing the art of *yabusame* at the Kamakura Festival

JAPAN FOR
SAMURAI STORIES

While samurai may be a thing of the past, the legend around these mythical and honorable warriors has not been forgotten. Step into the world of this ancient military elite by visiting their old haunts or trying your hand at mastering skills, from sword fighting to archery on horseback.

TOP 5 SAMURAI MOVIES

Seven Samurai (1954)
Farmers hire samurai to fight against bandits stealing their crops.

Yojimbo (1961)
A samurai convinces two competing crime lords to hire him.

Harakiri (1962)
Conflict arises over the practice of ritual suicide, seppuku.

Samurai Rebellion (1967)
A samurai risks death to save his son's wife.

The Twilight Samurai (2002)
A reluctant samurai is forced to fight.

Fight Club

A samurai's sword (*katana*) was said to be his soul – naturally, these weapons could only be made by expert craftsmen. See swords on display at The Japanese Sword Museum in Tokyo *(p144)* or check out the Seki Traditional Swordsmith Museum *(visitseki.jp)*.

$\rightarrow$

A model in samurai regalia, clutching a prized sword

Silent Assassins

While samurai were military nobility, dressed in elaborate suits of armor, ninja were mercenaries, clothed in all black. The samurai - ruled by elaborate codes of honor - looked down on the ninja, who specialized in espionage, sabotage, and guerilla warfare. Experience the world of these dark assassins for yourself at the Koka Ninja Village, where the brave are put through their paces in a ninja training class *(p233)*. Alternatively, watch the experts at work at the Ninja Museum of Igaryu *(p235)*.

↓ The dark arts of the ninja, on display at Koka Ninja Village

Looking up at the ↑ towering fortress walls of Kumamoto Castle

Capture the Castle

Forget about the fairy-tale Himeji-jo or the domineering structure at Osaka - the mightiest fortress is Kumamoto *(p274)*. Alas, this castle wasn't as impenetrable as hoped: it was ravaged during the 1877 Satsuma Rebellion. Currently undergoing reconstruction due to damage sustained during the 2016 earthquake, this fortress can still be viewed from the outside.

The Last Samurai

As warfare changed, the samurai transformed from mounted archers to master swordsmen, and finally to desk-bound bureaucrats. Find out about their evolution at the Tokyo National Museum *(p128)*, which has a superb collection of weapons and armor. Delve deeper into the story at the Edo-Tokyo Museum *(p144)*, where the samurai and their society are explained through life-size models, dioramas, and interactive exhibits.

→

Ornate Buddha statue on display at the Tokyo National Museum

Rainy-Day Activities

When the weather outside is frightful, head into an amusement arcade. Often located near major train stations, these flashing alleys are a great place for kids to burn off excess energy. The country's big game companies, such as Sega and Capcom, churn out new titles for these arcades, keeping young and old gamers entertained. For a family day out on a rainy day, head to the man-made island of Odaiba *(p145)* in Tokyo, which is home to amusement arcades, theme parks, and family-friendly museums.

→

Odaiba's Giant Sky Wheel, an iconic structure on the island

JAPAN FOR
FAMILIES

Japan is a great place for a family holiday. The people are friendly, the crime rate is low, and the public transportation system is easy to use. With a huge mix of attractions and activities, you won't fail to keep the kids entertained.

Make-Believe Worlds

Creative cosplay is a great way to introduce children to Japanese culture. Kids will love dressing up as samurai, ninja, daimyo and geisha *(www.toei-eigamura.com)*, and reliving the days of yore at the epic Toei Kyoto Studio Park. For rather more contemporary culture, the Ghibli Museum *(p143)* immerses visitors in the worlds of *Totoro, Princess Mononoke,* and *Spirited Away.* Don't miss the life-sized robot from *Castle in the Sky* that dominates the rooftop garden.

←

Children playing on the "Cat Bus" at the interactive Ghibli Museum

Active Fun
Japan's clean, fast, and affordable public transportation system provides ready access to the Japanese countryside. The densely forested mountains, lush green of rice paddies, and pristine beaches are ideal natural playgrounds. Take the kids to Niseko's slopes for some of Japan's best skiing *(p319)*, or to learn to surf *(p43)* in the waves of Miyazaki.

←

Family enjoying the snow on the nursery slopes of Niseko

Theme Parks
Children will clamor to visit Tokyo Disneyland, home to Mickey Mouse and his pals. Here you can ride hair-raising roller coasters, and have your photo taken with one of Disney's iconic characters *(www.tokyodisneyresort.jp)*. If you only have time for one of the parks, choose Tokyo DisneySea for its under-the-sea theme. To explore the worlds of some of your favorite movies, head to Universal Studios *(p220-21)* in Osaka or, for a wackier experience, go to Huis Ten Bosch, near Nagasaki *(p269)*. Occupying a seafront plot the size of Monaco, this vast park re-creates a 17th-century Dutch town, with windmills, canals, and narrow houses.

→

Posing in front of the iconic Disneyland Castle

Kimono Dragons

A kimono-clad *geiko* is an enduring image of Japan. For a peek at this nonpareil apparel, check out the fabulous silks at the Itchiku Kubota Art Museum *(p158)*. Then create your own at the Nagamachi Yuzen Silk Center *(p164)*.

A trio of women elegantly dressed in colorful silk kimonos

JAPAN FOR
TRADITIONAL CRAFTS

Hailed as "Living National Treasures," Japan's *shokunin*, or artisans, venerate tradition, continuity, and attention to detail. Across the country you can visit workshops and markets brimming with hand-turned pottery, delicately painted silks and exquisitely crafted paper – and even design your own.

TOP 5 OTHER CRAFTS

Origami
Folding paper into unexpected treasures.

Shodo
The art of calligraphy arrived in Japan from China in AD 600.

Bonsai
Carefully pruned, perfectly formed tiny trees.

Ikebana
Beautiful flower arrangements originally used as offerings.

Kodo
An "art of refinement" – the practice of appreciating incense.

Dyeing to Meet You

For centuries, strict sumptuary laws restricted all but the wealthiest from wearing certain colors and fabrics, such as silk. Learn more about the history at Kyoto's Little Indigo Museum *(shindo-shindigo.com)*. Get a feel for creating your own textiles at the Mingei Iyo Kasuri Kaikan in Matsuyama *(p256)*, or scour flea markets for vintage pieces.

Take a Leaf Out of Their Book

The Genda Shigyo company has been handcrafting paper since 771 and in Kyoto since 794. Visit the ancient store to admire the *mizuhiki* – twisted paper ribbons. Give the tradition a go: head to Ozu Washi in Tokyo *(p23)* to pour a mixture of bark and water into a sieve, before sifting to form a perfect piece of paper. Just like panning for gold.

$\rightarrow$

A traditional paper craftsman working in his studio

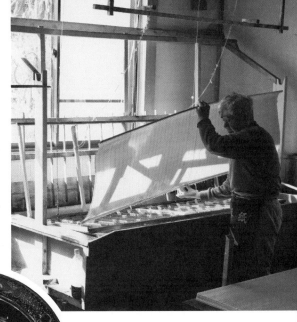

Lustrous Lacquerware

Made from the sap of the urushi tree, lacquer is durable, waterproof, and shiny - the perfect varnish. Lacquerware is as ornate as it is resilient. The birthplace of this craft, Wajima is the perfect place to try your hand at designing your own *(p176)*. At the Wajima Kobo Nagaya workshop, you can engrave a set of chopsticks and talk to experienced artisans about their work *(4-66-1 Kawai-machi)*.

$\leftarrow$

Sumptuous lacquerware plate inlaid with pearl

Seize the Clay

In the 16th century, advanced techniques from Korea revolutionized Japan's ceramics industry. Kyushu – on the Korea Strait - has since been Japan's greatest ceramics producer. Hop between ancient workshops and laden market stalls in the Saga pottery towns *(p280)*. At Rokuro-za in Arita, take to the potter's wheel to mold your own masterpiece *(1-30-1 Izumiyama)*.

$\leftarrow$

Hand-wringing freshly dyed silk at a textile plant's dye workshop

$\rightarrow$

Spinning clay by hand at a Kyushu potter's workshop

The Inspiring Island

One of the country's most atmospheric islands, Sado is studded with wooden villages bleached gray from wind and salt *(p307)*. Despite its bleak appearance, this island has inspired some of Japan's greatest art forms. It was here that *taiko* drumming truly took off. Feel the beat as you strike one of these massive drums at the Sado Island Taiko Center *(www.sadotaiken.jp)*.

→

The windswept landscape of Senkaku Bay on the island of Sado

Did You Know?

Only 430 of Japan's 6,852 islands are inhabited.

JAPAN
OFF THE BEATEN PATH

Japan is endlessly fascinating, and taking a trip to the country feels like a journey off the beaten path even when you're surrounded by crowds. But, beyond the well-worn tourist trail between Kyoto and the capital, there are nearly 7,000 islands to explore, with myriad sites to experience.

The secluded Kominato Beach on Chichijima, Ogasawara Islands ↑

Galapagos of the Orient

Located 620 miles (1,000 km) south of Tokyo, the UNESCO-protected Ogasawara Islands are an unspoiled Eden. This isolated archipelago, made up of over 30 tropical and subtropical islands, is home to countless endemic species, from tiny Bonin white-eye birds and jewel-like tiger beetles to the elusive Bonin flying fox.

Land of the Diving Women

These days, the tiny island of Hegura, located off the coast of Ishikawa, is best known as a paradise for bird-watchers. In the 1960s, however, it was made famous by the Italian anthropologist Fosco Maraini when he published his photographic book about the *ama* (diving women) of the island. Amazingly, some of the same women that he photographed still work on the island during summer. The last survivors of a dying tradition, they can be seen sorting seaweed and diving for abalone.

← The famous *ama* (diving women) of Hegura island hauling a net

The Hidden Christians

When Christianity was banned at the end of the 16th century, many believers fled to Amakusa, a series of islands between Kumamoto and Nagasaki. Here, the community lived in secrecy for more than 300 years, disguising their faith under a veil of Buddhism. The Christian Museum in Amakusa City *(p35)* displays Buddhist statues, with crucifixes carved into their backs, as well as images of the Virgin Mary that were made to look like Kannon, the Buddhist goddess of Mercy. Explore Amakusa by boat to see why these mist-shrouded islands made the perfect hiding place *(www. seacruise.jp/cruise-english)*.

→ One of the elegant churches found in the Amakusa Islands

Quirky Nights

As twilight hits, Japan's dark side is unleashed. Ghosts and ghouls join handcuffed diners at Lock Up in Shinjuku *(www.lock-up.jp)*, while writhing women and robo-pandas dance to *taiko* techno at Tokyo's Robot Restaurant *(p27)*. Order a bento box, grab a drink, and enjoy the spectacular show.

→

Diners ensconced in shell-shaped chairs at the Robot Restaurant

JAPAN
AFTER DARK

When the sun sets, Japan's streets transform under bright neon lights. From deliciously dingy dive bars to psychedelic robot cabaret, frenetic nightclubs to chilled out live music events, the country's heady nightlife is not to be missed.

Japan Live!

Music lovers flock to Tokyo to hear everything from mellow guitarists to roaring punk bands. Try Shimokitazawa Three for the next big thing *(www.toos.co.jp/3)*, while AKB48 Theater in Akihabara *(www.akb48.co.jp)* is the place for sickly sweet J-Pop. Outside the capital, Osaka Muse is altogether more gritty *(osaka.muse-live.com)*.

←

Jazz drummer on a cabaret stage tapping out a beat

Dive Deep

The shabby alleys and arcades of Tokyo's Golden Gai are home to some of the country's moodiest dive bars (p96). Hidden within this warren-like area is Albatross (www. alba-s.com), a legendary drinking den frequented by artists, students, expats, and salarymen, who chat away into the night. In Osaka, seek out a *tachinomiya*, such as Bar Dragon (p221), and rub shoulders with Japan's Everymen. Tucked into the gaps in the cityscape, these modest "standing bars" are as authentic as can be.

→

Tending a busy
bar in Tokyo's
Shibuya district

Join the Club

Fans of electro-funk, techno, or house music, look no further – Japan's got you covered. The stand-out venue of Tokyo's Shibuya district (p100) is Womb, an enormous club throbbing across four floors (www.womb.co.jp), while Sound Museum Vision keeps the party pumping (www. vision-tokyo.com). Dance till dawn at Nagoya's sprawling ID Café (www.idcafe. info), or join the crowds at Osaka's Club Joule (club-joule.com).

←

Sound Museum
Vision in Tokyo's
Shibuya district

 INSIDER TIP
Take a Cruise

Osaka's glittering lights and the extravagant signage of seemingly countless bars and restaurants are best seen at night. Take a night cruise (www. ipponmatsu.co.jp) along the canal to suss out where to go, or find out on foot with a night walk (www.magical-trip.com), hopping from *izakaya* to *izakaya*.

LGBT+ Venues

Ni-chome, in Shinjuku, has the highest concentration of gay bars in the world. Take a nighttime tour with OutAsia Travel to discover the best of the 300 bars on offer (outasiatravel.com). In Osaka, head to Frenz Frenzy Rainbow Haven for a night of karaoke (8-14 Kamiyamacho).

↑

Costumed
partygoers
atop a float
at Tokyo's
Pride march

Embark on a Pilgrimage

Japan's rich religious tradition has left the country peppered with numerous pilgrimage routes. The most famous is the 88-Temple Pilgrimage (p258). On this journey around Shikoku, Buddhist devotees follow a circuit shaped like a mandala. At around 745 miles (1,200 km) long, it can take between 30 and 60 days to complete; get a taster by walking a section of the course.

Buddhists walking part of the 88-Temple Pilgrimage around Shikoku

JAPAN FOR
WELLNESS

If you're looking for a little rest and relaxation, there's nowhere better than Japan. Whether it's chilling out in hot springs or trying "forest bathing," becoming a pilgrim or immersing yourself in temple life, this tranquil country offers endless ways to maximize your wellbeing.

Time in a Temple

The country's Buddhist heritage has imbued it with a deep spirituality. Find inner peace by staying at a tranquil temple. Secluded from the modern world, visitors can fully immerse themselves in an often silent Buddhist community. Sacred Mount Koya (p234) is home to over 50 temples, with lodgings, where visitors can meditate, sample traditional *shojin ryori* (vegan) cuisine, and soak in hot springs.

Test the Waters

Soak away any aches and pains at one of Japan's many *onsen* – devotees claim that these hot springs have a number of health-giving properties, including the alleviation of neuralgia. For those of a metaphysical mindset, *shinrin-yoku*, or "forest bathing," might be just the ticket. This new age practice is said to reduce blood pressure and increase "energy flow."

→

People relaxing in an outdoor *onsen* at dusk

Find Your Ikigai

There's much to be said for the Japanese concept of *ikigai*, or reason for being, for aiding mindfulness. Infuse each day with meaning by trying an activity such as Zen gardening at the Kyoto University of Art and Design *(www.jghh.jp/center)* or learning the art of *washoku* (Japanese cuisine) at the Tsukiji Cooking School in Tokyo *(tsukiji-cooking.com)*.

←

A man carefully tending his garden

Eat Yourself Well

The traditional Japanese diet of fish and fermented foods has been linked to the country's longevity, giving you an excellent excuse to devour more of Japan's delicious fare. In Tokyo, take a cookery class at Mayuko's Little Kitchen *(www.mayukos-littlekitchen.com)* to learn how to make this mouthwatering cuisine yourself, or find out how fermentation can improve your health with a visit to the traditional miso factory at the Kyushu Yufuin Folk Art Village in Yukuin *(p270)*.

↑ Monks outside Kongobu-ji Temple on Mount Koya

→

A delicious bowl of mouthwatering homemade ramen

▽ Cosplay Central

Cosplay, where people dress as their favorite comic book characters, is huge in Japan, thanks to its love of manga and anime. Expect to see locals in the streets in costume, especially in Tokyo's Harajuku (p94), Ikebukuro (p142), and Akihabara (p118) districts. While Akihabara is geared toward men, female fans might prefer Ikebukuro, where stores focus on series popular with women.

△ Gotta Catch 'Em All

Japan is the birthplace of Pokémon, and wannabe trainers will love visiting the Pokémon Center Mega Tokyo in Ikebukuro (p142). Packed full of colorful merchandise, from sweets to pillows, it's *the* place to pimp your Pokédex.

JAPAN FOR
POP CULTURE

It might be renowned for its timeless traditions, but Japan is also home to a fascinatingly futuristic pop culture. From quirky anime to cute cat cafés, kitsch karaoke bars to quick-witted robots, the country's eclectic culture has taken the rest of the world by storm.

△ Bubblegum Pop

Born in the 1990s, Japan's kitschy J-pop – known for its focus on bubblegum pop, catchy tunes, and wacky outfits – has spawned many imitators, including K-pop. Sing along to hits from AKB48 or SMAP at a karaoke booth, or visit Karaoke Kan (karaokekan.jp), the popular chain featured in *Lost in Translation*, to warble with the locals.

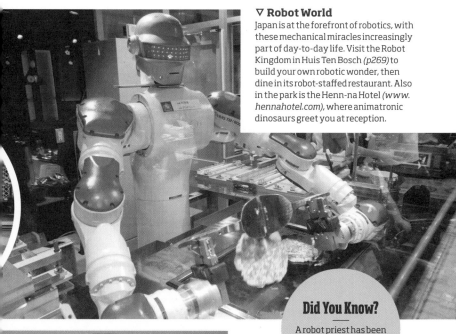

▽ Robot World

Japan is at the forefront of robotics, with these mechanical miracles increasingly part of day-to-day life. Visit the Robot Kingdom in Huis Ten Bosch *(p269)* to build your own robotic wonder, then dine in its robot-staffed restaurant. Also in the park is the Henn-na Hotel *(www.hennahotel.com)*, where animatronic dinosaurs greet you at reception.

Did You Know?

A robot priest has been developed to recite mantras at funerals.

▽ Fashion Forward

Renowned as one of the most influential areas in the fashion world, Harajuku's Takeshita-dori is populated by stalls selling an eye-watering array of outfits *(p94)*. Spy black "Gothic Lolita" dresses, leather "visual kei" skirts, and 1950s-style "rockabilly" headbands – all items beloved by the area's quirky Harajuku girls *(p95)*. After finding the perfect outfit here, transform yourself into a living anime character at a *purikura* (photo booth). These machines offer hundreds of different editing options, with stickers, filters, and more.

△ Sticking to a Theme

Sparking a global craze for cat cafés, Japan's eateries cater to every predilection. Take tea with a feline friend at Calico Cat Café *(catcafe.jp)* or sink your teeth into Dracula-themed treats at the Vampire Café in Ginza *(6-7-6 Ginza)*. Giant merchandise retailer Animate runs several theme cafés in Tokyo *(cafe.animate.co.jp)*. The venues change their theme regularly, with each one dedicated to a different anime.

Get a Grape

While legend has it that the first wine grapes were grown in Japan as early as AD 718, local wine did not win acclaim overseas until recently. The country's signature grape, Koshu, is mainly grown in the lush mountains of Yamanashi Prefecture; tours and tastings are offered at most of the 90 vineyards here, but Sadoya *(www.sadoya.co.jp)*, is a particular favorite.

→

Furano wine flavored with lavender, produced in northern Hokkaido

JAPAN
RAISE A GLASS

From flavorful sake to refreshing beer, ceremonial *matcha* tea to biting whisky, the Japanese drinks cabinet is overflowing with tasty tipples. Alongside these classic beverages, there are surprising new additions, drawing on international influences. Don't miss these must-drinks.

TOP 5 TEAS IN JAPAN

Matcha
These powdered green tea leaves are used in everything from ice cream to noodles.

Sencha
While the green tea used in *matcha* is grown in the shade, Sencha is reared in the full sun.

Hojicha
This green tea has less caffeine than others.

Mugicha
Chilled barley tea is popular in summer time.

Genmaicha
Made from green tea and brown rice, this is used to settle stomachs.

Hopping Mad

Japan's big four – Kirin, Asahi, Sapporo, and Suntory – are known around the world, as are a number of craft breweries. For a hopping good time, visit the Sapporo Beer Garden and Museum *(p320)* to learn about the history of beer, and to sample some delicious brews.

→

On Japan's northernmost island, Sapporo entices visitors in from the cold

💬 INSIDER TIP
Hit the Cider Trail

Japanese cider is on the march – check out the cider trail in Niigata to taste the latest addition to Japan's drinks menu *(www.pommelier.net)*.

Neat Drinks

Nursed in dimly lit bars across the world, Japanese whiskies – often award-winning – are firmly on the taste buds of the whisky world. See where the magic happens at noted brand Suntory's distillery and museum in Yamanashi *(www.suntory.com)*.

↓ Award-winning Ichiro, one of Japan's smallest distilleries

↑ A girl practicing the elaborate ritual of a tea ceremony

Traditional Tea

Japanese monks brought tea to Japan after traveling to China in the 6th century. Since then, tea has become a quintessential part of local culture. It is sipped everywhere, from Tokyo's cool cafés to elaborate tea ceremonies in temple gardens *(p197)*. Wazuka, near Kyoto, is a beautiful land of undulating tea bushes. Pick your own leaves at one of these plantations, before sampling different teas alongside traditional Japanese sweets at Kyoto Obubu Tea Farms *(obubutea.com)*.

For Goodness' Sake

Traditionally served in small ceramic cups, sake is Japan's national drink. Made from rice, water, and yeast and served at a variety of temperatures, it's the perfect accompaniment to Japanese food. There are hundreds of breweries, each producing unique flavors. Visit all the best breweries with Sake Tours *(www. saketours.com)*.

→ Colorfully decorated barrels of sake stacked up in Tokyo

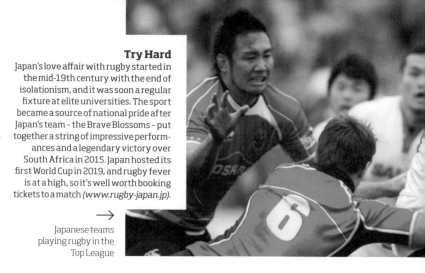

Try Hard

Japan's love affair with rugby started in the mid-19th century with the end of isolationism, and it was soon a regular fixture at elite universities. The sport became a source of national pride after Japan's team – the Brave Blossoms – put together a string of impressive perform- ances and a legendary victory over South Africa in 2015. Japan hosted its first World Cup in 2019, and rugby fever is at a high, so it's well worth booking tickets to a match *(www.rugby-japan.jp)*.

→

Japanese teams playing rugby in the Top League

JAPAN FOR
SPORTS FANS

Japan's sporting calendar is packed with both quintessential traditional offerings, such as sumo and kendo, and Western games like baseball. Experience the energy and excitement for yourself by mingling with locals at a baseball game or a sumo match, or just hanging out in a good sports bar.

No Kendo

Kendo, a traditional style of fencing using bamboo swords, traces its roots back to the samurai. Take a lesson, visit an armorer, or eat with the professionals on a tour with Samurai Trip *(www.samuraitrip07.com)*.

→

Competitors fighting kendo-style with bamboo swords

Hit a Home Run

Baseball was imported to Japan from the US during the early Meiji period, and almost immediately gained popularity among amateur athletic clubs and universities. During World War II, there was a shortage of players and it was seen as a corrupting American influence. It is now the most watched and played sport in the country. Housed in Tokyo Dome – the home stadium of the Yomiuri Giants – the Baseball Hall of Fame and Museum displays a fascinating array of memorabilia *(www. english.baseball-museum.or.jp)*. Try out your swing at the Shinjuku Batting Centre *(2-21-13 Kabukicho)*.

← Yomiuri Giants fans at the Tokyo Dome

DRINK

MLB Cafe Tokyo
This shrine to baseball is packed with memorabilia.

◉ F4 ⬛ 1-3-61 Kouraku, Bunkyo ⬜ mlbcafe.jp/en

Golden Ball Café
Watch live international sport or play darts here.

◉ E8 ⬛ 7-14-5 Roppongi, Minato ⬜ golden ballcafe.com

Legends Sports Bar
Burgers and craft beer accompany the games.

◉ F4 ⬛ 3-16-33 Roppongi, Minato ⬜ legendsports.jp

RINGS OF GLORY

The 1964 Summer Olympics and Paralympics in Tokyo symbolized Japan's rebirth after World War II. Many Japanese people see the 32nd Olympiad, which was postponed in 2020 because of COVID-19, as a similarly significant and renewing event, marking the end of the difficult few decades. Despite controversies and a major redesign, the huge New National Stadium promises to be a monument to match those from the last Olympics. Hire a bike, and cycle around Yoyogi Park *(p80)* to admire some of the original 1964 venues that will be used once again at the 32nd games.

↑ Sumo wrestlers and a *gyoji* (referee)

Want Sumo This?

The rituals around sumo may be complicated, but the rules are simple: the first to exit the ring, or touch the ground with any part of his body besides his feet, loses. Tokyo's Ryogoku Kokugikan venue hosts three grand tournaments a year, and tickets go on sale a month in advance *(www.sumo.or.jp/EnTicket)*. For a taste of life in a *beya* – where the wrestlers live – try some *chankonabe* (a hotpot commonly known as "sumo stew") at a restaurant in Ryogoku *(p144)*. Many of these eateries are run by ex-sumo.

Modern Masters

Immerse yourself in Tokyo's vibrant contemporary art scene at the Mori Art Museum *(p91).* Located in the Mori Tower, it features constantly rotating exhibitions. At the extraordinary Benesse Art Site Naoshima – Japan's "art island" – visitors can walk among Yayoi Kusama's iconic, spotty sculptures and Tadao Ando's concrete masterpieces *(p250).*

 ←

The impressive *Pumpkin* by Yayoi Kusama at Benesse Art Site Naoshima

JAPAN FOR
ART LOVERS

Art has long been one of the country's most successful exports, with the world clamoring over ukiyo-e prints and screen paintings for hundreds of years. Now, a host of exciting museums and innovative contemporary artists are stealing some of the spotlight from these traditional art forms.

 INSIDER TIP
Arty Stay

Palace Hotel Tokyo offers bespoke tours of the capital for art fans, led by art historians. You can take in the world-class museums, browse for pieces, and visit some offbeat galleries *(www.en. palacehoteltokyo.com).*

Traditional Scenes

To understand how Japan fuses traditional art with modern design, visit Tokyo's Nezu Museum *(p92).* Designed by award-winning architect Kengo Kuma, it showcases over 7,400 works of Japanese and East Asian art, including *Irises,* an exquisite screen painting by Ogata Korin (c 1701–05). Another site for traditional art in the capital is the Tokyo National Museum *(p128).* Seek out the museum's haunting collection of Noh masks for a fleeting glimpse into one of Japan's most idiosyncratic traditional art forms.

Striking Sculptures

The Hakone Open-Air Museum *(p169)* displays works by Rodin, Miro, and Picasso, as well as one of the world's largest collections of Henry Moore. The Kirishima Open-Air Museum, on Kyushu, is home to sculptures by Gormley, Turrell, Kapoor, and Yayoi Kusama *(www.open-air-museum.org)*.

↑ Emil-Antoine Bourdell's *Hercules the Archer* at the Hakone museum

Asian Art

The Fukuoka Asian Art Museum *(p265)* showcases some of the continent's most daring artists. Spanning the early 20th century to the present, the collection includes everything from traditional oil paintings to video art. For a deep dive into contemporary Asian art, check out the Lee Ufan Museum at Benesse Art Site Naoshima *(p250)*.

← The entrance to the Fukuoka Asian Art Museum

Fantastic Photography

As Hiroshi Sugimoto is known for his long-exposure shots of seascapes and structures, it is appropriate that his Odawara Art Foundation Enoura Observatory juts out over Sagami Bay *(www.odawara-af.com/en)*. This eccentric museum features a minimalist exhibition space, a teahouse, and an outdoor No theater.

→

Hiroshi Sugimoto's Odawara Art Foundation Enoura Observatory

↑ *Irises* by Ogata Korin (c 1701–05), at the Nezu Museum, Tokyo

A YEAR IN JAPAN

Japan's seasons are a source of national pride, each one bursting with its own beauty and traditions, and dictating cuisine, fashion, and social events. The springtime sakura blossoms are well known, but there are countless highlights to discover whenever you visit.

Spring

From late March to early April, the brief but beautiful sakura season brings with it the bittersweet feeling known as *mono no aware*: awareness of the impermanent. But this feeling is soon forgotten with riotous festivals, including Buddha's birthday, Aoi Matsuri in Kyoto and Sanja Matsuri – Tokyo's wildest festival, featuring parades, dancing, and music.

1. Blush pink cherry blossom in Sakitama Kofun Park, Saitama Prefecture

Summer

The tinkling of *furin* (cooling wind chimes), the relentless humming of cicada, sighs of *"Atsui!"* ("It's hot!") – these are the sounds of summer in Japan. This is the best season to explore outside the cities, so join a traditional rice-planting festival in the paddies, hang a wish on a tree during

MICRO-SEASONS

The traditional Japanese calendar was split into 24 seasons, each broken down into micro-seasons. Some of these have a poetic ring, like *kasumi hajimete tanabiku* (February 24–28), when mist begins to linger, and *higurashi naku* (the evening call of cicadas) in August.

Tanabata Matsuri, or visit the Fuji Five Lakes to enjoy the cooler mountain air. This is also the time to climb Mount Fuji during its short open season (July to September).

2. Planting rice during the Isobe-no-Omita festival in June

Autumn

Striking a similar note as spring's sakura, *koyo* (red leaves) come to the fore in fall. Bursts of red and gold brighten city streets, but many people make a trip to the mountains to enjoy the seasonal colors. Nikko is one of the best options, as the beautiful scenery is accompanied by the Shuki Taisai Grand Autumn Festival in mid-October, with impressive displays of *yabusame* (horseback archery).

3. Riding a cable car high above Nikko's fall foliage

Winter

Winter is a time of traditions both old and modern. Christmas has been adopted as an annual date night, whereas New Year's is a time for friends and family. January's Coming of Age Day is an important milestone for young people, who dress in traditional clothes for festive ceremonies. For the rest of the season, there are *rotenburo* (outdoor hot springs), skiing and snow sculptures at Sapporo's festival.

4. Snow sculpture at Sapporo Snow Festival, and (inset) skiing at Niseko Ski Resort

FLOWER EVENTS

Plum Blossom Viewing
Blossoming plum trees - called *ume* - signal the start of spring in February.

Cherry Blossom Viewing
Crowds picnic under the pink blossoms in parks and gardens in April.

Fall Leaves
Red maples, russet fall leaves, and yellow ginkgoes bloom in parks and Edo-period gardens in late November.

Chinese Lantern Plant Fair
This popular fair, held at Tokyo's Senso-ji Temple in July, sells a distinctive plant with lantern-shaped fruit.

3

4

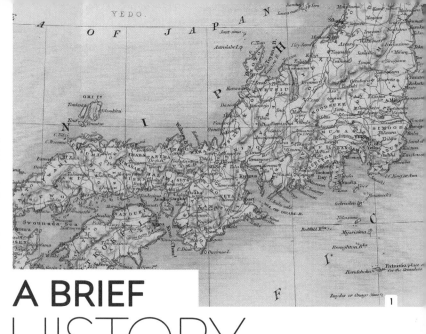

A BRIEF
HISTORY

Japan's history is characterized by its separation, both geographically and politically, from the Asian continent. When centuries of isolationism ended in the 19th century, the country embraced new technologies, and today Japan is a world leader in everything from fashion to robotics.

The Emergence of Japan

Japan's first inhabitants arrived over 40,000 years ago, possibly via land bridges from the Asian continent. The Jomon hunting and gathering society emerged around 14,500 BC, and from 300 BC to AD 300 the Yayoi people spread from Kyushu to Honshu and Shikoku. In the west of Japan, between 538 and 710, a local clan – the forebears of today's imperial family – began to consolidate its power. It was during this period that Buddhism and Chinese writing arrived in the islands, and a system of laws based upon Confucianism and Chinese legal standards was established.

[1] A map showing the prefectures of Japan.

[2] Yayoi-period dwellings in Yoshinogari Park.

[3] Murasaki Shikibu, author of *The Tale of Genji*.

[4] An illustration of the Mongol invasion in 1281.

Timeline of events

300 BC– AD 300

Methods of farming, metalwork, and pottery reach Japan from the continent.

794

Heian-kyo (Kyoto) becomes the capital, which it remains until 1868.

823

Kukai, an advocate of Shingon Buddhism, is made head of To-ji Temple.

239

Queen Himiko sends an envoy to the Wei kingdom in China.

710

Heijo-kyo (Nara) is made capital the capital of Japan.

From Nara to Heian

Beginning with the establishment of an imperial capital in 710, the Nara period saw spectacular literary, artistic, architectural and religious advances. The era ended with the relocation of the capital to Heian-kyo (Kyoto) in 794. There, Chinese influences blended with native Japanese elements in painting, calligraphy, poetry and prose. After the collapse of the Chinese Tang dynasty in 907, Japan began to distance itself from its neighbor and developed a culture that was more distinctly Japanese.

Kamakura Period

In 1185, the elegant world of the Heian court was shattered by the struggle between the Taira and Minamoto warrior clans. The result was the establishment of Japan's first shogunate – rule by warriors – and power shifted from the imperial court to Kamakura, near modern Tokyo. The Mongols launched two invasion attempts in 1274 and 1281, both of which were halted by the weather, leading the Japanese to coin the term *"kamikaze"* – divine wind. In 1333, the Kamakura shogunate collapsed after the emperor Go-Daigo attempted to reassert imperial control.

PERIODS OVERVIEW

Jomon 14,500–300 BC
Yayoi 300 BC–AD 250
Yamato 250–710
Nara 710–794
Heian 794–1185
Kamakura 1185–1333
Muromachi 1333–1568
Momoyama 1568–1603
Tokugawa (Edo) 1603–1868
Meiji 1868–1912
Taisho 1912–1926
Showa 1926–1989
Heisei 1989–2019
Reiwa 2019–present

c 1000

The Tale of Genji - possibly the world's oldest novel - is written by court lady Murasaki Shikibu.

1274

The first Mongol invasion attempt lands in Kyushu.

1333

The Kamakura shogunate collapses.

1087

Emperor Shirakawa abdicates and becomes first cloistered emperor.

1180–85

Minamoto clan defeats the Taira and establishes Kamakura shogunate.

Warring States Period

After years of civil war, the Muromachi shogunate emerged victorious in 1336. Whereas Kamakura had existed in equilibrium with the imperial court, the Muromachi took over the remnants of the imperial government. Rebellions followed and, in 1467, the Onin War broke out, leaving Kyoto devastated and effectively ending the national authority of the shogunate. For the next century, Japan was racked by debilitating warfare between increasingly autonomous samurai sections. Nobunaga Oda – a daimyo (feudal lord) who rose through military ranks in the provinces – set out to unify the nation, but died unsuccessful in 1582. Nobunaga's deputy, a former peasant named Hideyoshi Toyotomi, continued the work of unification. To achieve this, he set about destroying as many of the country's castles and forts as he could and confiscating weapons belonging to farmers. After Hideyoshi died, daimyo from eastern and western Japan fell into dispute and sent their samurai, led by Ieyasu Tokugawa and Mitsunari Ishida respectively, to battle in Sekigahara. Ieyasu Tokugawa emerged victorious in 1600 and subsequently founded the Tokugawa shogunate in 1603.

① General and statesman Nobunaga Oda.

② Statue of Hideyoshi Toyotomi outside Osaka.

③ The landing of Commodore Perry.

④ The Great Kanto Earthquake of 1923.

Did You Know?

The Japanese imperial family were believed to have succeeded from the sun goddess, Amaterasu.

Timeline of events

1467
The devastating Onin War begins, destroying much of Kyoto.

1603
Ieyasu Tokugawa establishes the Tokugawa shogunate.

1633
The *sakoku* (closed country) policy begins. Most foreign nationals are barred.

1641
Only the Dutch and Chinese are allowed access to Japan.

1707
Last eruption of Mount Fuji.

The Edo Era and the Meiji Restoration

Peace was achieved by forcing the daimyo to reside every other year in Edo (Tokyo), the new seat of the shogunate. While Kyoto remained the official capital, Edo greatly eclipsed it in size. Japan isolated itself from the rest of the world until 1853, when the American naval officer Commodore Perry challenged Japan's refusal to enter into international relations. Weakened by internal unrest, the shogunate could only accede to Perry's demands. Imperial power was restored in 1868, and Japan swiftly embraced Western technology under Emperor Meiji. Tokyo became the capital and seat of the emperor, the samurai class was abolished and the first prime minister was appointed in 1885. Conscription was introduced to create a modern fighting force, which proved effective with victories in the Sino-Japanese War of 1894–5 and the Russo-Japanese war of 1904–5. During the subsequent Taisho era, party politics flourished, suffrage was extended and new labor laws were enacted, but World War I, the 1918 Rice Riots, the Great Kanto Earthquake of 1923, and the repressive Peace Preservation Laws challenged this liberal atmosphere.

↑ A portrait of Emperor Meiji, instrumental in the modernization of Japan

1853

US naval officer Commodore Matthew Perry anchors in Edo Bay.

1854

The Kanagawa Treaty between the US and Japan is signed.

1868

Imperial power is restored and Tokyo becomes the capital.

1894

The First Sino-Japanese War begins.

1905

The Russo-Japanese War ends with the Treaty of Portsmouth.

1

2

World War II

Following the end of the Taisho era, hardliner army officers began assassinating moderates in an attempt to manipulate Japan's policies. These militarists believed that seizing land from China and Russia would secure raw materials and improve national security. By 1937, the country was embroiled in a war with China that estranged it from the rest of the world. When the US cut off Japan's access to oil, Tokyo made the decision to attack Pearl Harbor in Hawaii, in December 1941. American bombers decimated Japanese cities in retaliation, but the military government refused to surrender. In August 1945, the US dropped atomic bombs on Hiroshima and Nagasaki, and the Soviet Union entered the Pacific War. Emperor Hirohito ordered the cabinet to sue for peace and the US occupied Japan.

An Economic Bubble

By 1952, when the American occupation finally ended, Japan was beginning to find its feet. A new atmosphere of freedom unleashed a creative shockwave that saw intense innovation in art, film, literature and architecture. The country profited

↑ A newspaper reporting surrender of the Japanese in World War II

Timeline of events

1932
Young naval officers assassinate the prime minister and attempt a coup.

1933
Japan withdraws from the League of Nations.

1941
Japan enters World War II.

1945
Atomic bombs are dropped on Hiroshima and Nagasaki.

1964
The first journey is made by *shinkansen* (bullet train).

further from the Korean War, as it supplied the US forces with vehicles and technology. Industrial production surged and exports, such as cars and electronics, made Japan one of the world's richest nations. It all came to a screeching halt in 1992, however, when the economic bubble that inflated real estate and stock market prices burst. Decades of stagnation followed.

Japan Today

In March 2011, Northern Honshu was hit by an earthquake with a magnitude of 9.0, resulting in a tsunami. The disaster caused problems at four of the nuclear reactors at the Fukushima Daiichi Power Plant, leading to radioactive contamination and a continued loss of confidence in the government. In 2012, Shinzo Abe was elected prime minister after promising to put an end to deflation but, due to a rise in sales tax, Japan entered another recession just two years later. The Japanese economy has also been hampered by a workforce that is both aging and declining – between 2010 and 2018 the population had shrunk by about 1.3 million people. Yet Japan remains prominent on the world stage as the host of events such as the postponed 2020 Olympics.

[1] Japanese troops on the march in 1939.

[2] The Hiroshima Peace Memorial.

[3] A *shinkansen* in Tokyo.

[4] People praying for the victims of the 2011 earthquake.

Did You Know?

The average delay of a *shinkansen* (bullet train) is only 30 seconds.

1997
Economic recession in Southeast Asia, spreading to Japan

1989
Emperor Hirohito (Showa) dies; his son, Akihito, assumes his role.

2011
Major earthquake and tsunami causes destruction to Honshu.

2020-
Olympic and Paralympic Games postponed due to COVID-19.

2019
Emperor Naruhito ascends the throne; Reiwa era begins.

EXPERIENCE
TOKYO

The frenetic Shibuya Crossing

EXPLORE
TOKYO

This section divides Tokyo into three
sightseeing areas, as shown on this map,
plus an area beyond the center.

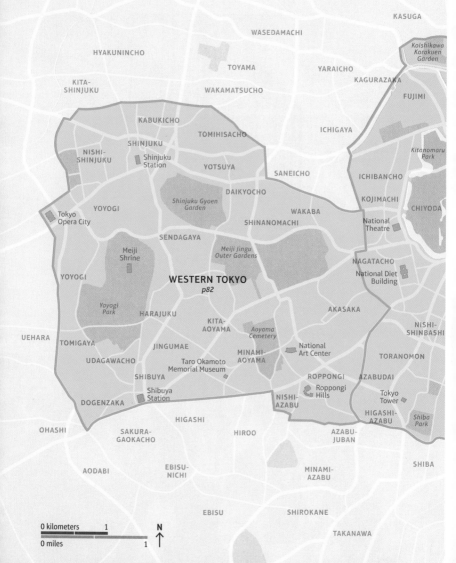

SUGAMO

SENGOKU

OTSUKA

KOHINATA

KASUGA

WASEDAMACHI

Koishikawa
Korakuen
Garden

HYAKUNINCHO

TOYAMA

YARAICHO

KAGURAZAKA

FUJIMI

KITA-
SHINJUKU

WAKAMATSUCHO

KABUKICHO

TOMIHISACHO

ICHIGAYA

SHINJUKU

NISHI-
SHINJUKU

Shinjuku
Station

YOTSUYA

SANEICHO

Kitanomaru
Park

ICHIBANCHO

KOJIMACHI

CHIYODA

DAIKYOCHO

Tokyo
Opera City

YOYOGI

Shinjuku Gyoen
Garden

WAKABA

SHINANOMACHI

National
Theatre

SENDAGAYA

Meiji
Shrine

Meiji Jingu
Outer Gardens

NAGATACHO

National Diet
Building

YOYOGI

WESTERN TOKYO
p82

Yoyogi
Park

HARAJUKU

AKASAKA

NISHI-
SHINBASHI

UEHARA

TOMIGAYA

KITA-
AOYAMA

Aoyama
Cemetery

JINGUMAE

MINAMI
AOYAMA

National
Art Center

TORANOMON

UDAGAWACHO

Taro Okamoto
Memorial Museum

ROPPONGI

AZABUDAI

SHIBUYA

Shibuya
Station

Roppongi
Hills

Tokyo
Tower

DOGENZAKA

NISHI-
AZABU

HIGASHI-
AZABU

Shiba
Park

HIGASHI

OHASHI

SAKURA-
GAOKACHO

HIROO

AZABU-
JUBAN

AODABI

EBISU-
NICHI

MINAMI-
AZABU

SHIBA

EBISU

SHIROKANE

TAKANAWA

0 kilometers   1

0 miles   1

N
↑

TABATA

NISHI-
NIPPORI

MINAMI-
SENJU

SUMIDA

HIGASHI-
NIPPORI

MINOWA

SENDAGI

Yanaka
Cemetery

KIYOKAWA

TSUTSU
MIDORI

NEGISHI

SENZOKU

YANAKA

UENO-
SAKURAGI

IRIYA

IMADO

HIGASHI-
MUKOJIMA

NEZU

Tokyo
National Museum

Tokyo Metropolitan
Museum of Art

MATSUGAYA

ASAKUSA

MUKOJIMA

NISHIKATA

HONGO

Ueno
Park

Senso-ji
Temple

Tokyo
Skytree

INARICHO

NORTHERN TOKYO
p122

AZUMABASHI

NARIHIRA

UENO

KOTOBUKI

YUSHIMA

TAITO

MISUJI

HONJO

KURAMAE

SOTOKANDA

ISHIWARA

MISAKICHO

ASAKUSA-
BASHI

KAMEZAWA

KINSHI

KANDA

IWAMOTOCHO

RYOGOKU

KOTOBASHI

UCHI-
KANDA

TATEKAWA

Imperial
Palace
Grounds

OTEMACHI

HAMACHO

SARUE

CENTRAL TOKYO
p102

NIHONBASHI-
NINGYOCHO

TAKABASHI

Imperial
Palace

YAESU

Imperial
Palace
Plaza

MARUNOUCHI

NIHONBASHI

KIYOSUMI

SENGOKU

Tokyo
International Forum

SHINKAWA

Hibiya
Park

SHINTOMI

EITAI

FUYUKI

TOYO

GINZA

MINATO

UCHISAI-
WAICHO

AKASHICHO

JAPAN

TSUKIJI

SHINBASHI

SHIBA-
DAIMON

Hama Rikyu
Garden

KAIGAN

TOYOMICHO

HARUMI

TOKYO

Mirror-encased escalator at Tokyu Plaza Omotesando Harajuku mall

WESTERN TOKYO

Shinjuku and Shibuya, the dual centers of Western
Tokyo, three stops apart on the Yamanote line,
began to boom only after the 1923 earthquake
and the extension of the Tokyu Toyoko line, linking
the capital and Yokohama, in 1932. Despite its short
history, the area still has stories to tell, from
Hachiko – the dog who faithfully waited for his
owner outside Shibuya Station every day from
1923 to 1935 – to the US occupation of Yoyogi
Park, or Washington Heights as it became known,
between 1945 and 1964. The park remained on the
world stage for the 1964 Summer Olympic Games.

This part of the city is new Tokyo – all vitality
and energy, fast-paced, constantly changing, and
challenging the more traditional pleasures of
Central and Northern Tokyo. When the Imperial
Japanese Army moved to Roppongi in 1890, the
area became a nightlife hot spot, and this reputation
was only reinforced with the influx of expatriates
after World War II. Today, Roppongi still has a
vibrant nighttime scene, with its cosmopolitan
bars and clubs, but its modern galleries and sleek
urban redevelopments have also made it a popular
place to hang out during the day. On top of this,
Shibuya, along with neighboring Harajuku and
Minami-Aoyama, have been the epicenters of
both young and haute-couture Japanese
fashion since the 1980s.

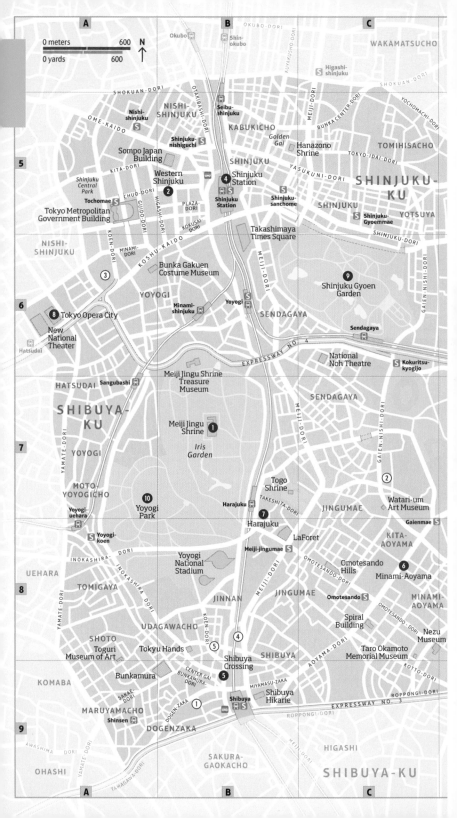

WESTERN TOKYO

Must Sees
1 Meiji Jingu Shrine
2 Western Shinjuku
3 Roppongi

Experience More
4 Shinjuku Station
5 Shibuya Crossing
6 Minami-Aoyama
7 Harajuku
8 Tokyo Opera City
9 Shinjuku Gyoen Garden
10 Yoyogi Park
11 Akasaka

Eat
1 Maruhachi
2 Den

Drink
3 New York Bar

Stay
4 Sequence Miyashita Park
5 The Millennials Shibuya

❶
MEIJI JINGU SHRINE

明治神宮

📍 B7 🚩 1-1 Yoyogikamizonocho, Shibuya 🚇 Harajuku
🕐 Treasure Museum and Annex: 10am–4:30pm Fri–Wed;
Naien inner precinct: dawn–dusk daily (times vary
seasonally) 🌐 meijijingu.or.jp/english

For Tokyo's residents, the lush grounds of Meiji Jingu
Shrine are a welcome green lung in the heart of this
hectic city. Take a stroll through its beautiful grounds,
stocked with some 120,000 trees, learn more about
the imperial family through the artifacts on display
in the museums, and soak up traditional Shinto life.

Originally built in 1920, Meiji Jingu Shrine was
destroyed during World War II in an air raid, but
was rebuilt in 1958. Controversially, the shrine
was rededicated to Emperor Meiji (1852–1912),
rather than a *kami* (spirit), contravening the
imperial family's renunciation of divinity in
1946. At the Treasure Museum and its annex,
which require an admission charge, visitors
can see items belonging to the imperial family,
including gorgeous kimonos, lacquerware, and
furniture. Don't miss the shrine's inner precinct
(Naien), said to have been designed by Emperor
Meiji for his wife. Here, a teahouse overlooks a
pond stocked with water lilies and carp. To the
right of the pond, a path leads to the beautiful
Minami-ike Shobuda (iris garden).

Guiding Spirit

One of the most striking sights at Meiji Jingu
Shrine is the huge wall of sake barrels. While
the barrels on display are empty, they are
loaded with meaning. Sake is supposed to
facilitate the connection with the gods and in
the oldest Japanese texts "miki," the old word
for sake, is written with the characters for "god"
and "wine." Shinto shrines pray for the brewers'
prosperity and, in turn, the breweries donate
sake for the shrines' rituals and ceremonies.

THE MEIJI EMPEROR

Having succeeded to
the throne in 1868 at
just 14 years of age,
the Meiji Emperor set
out to modernize Japan.
During his reign, the
Diet was founded, the
industrial revolution
took place, and the
country emerged vic-
torious from conflicts
with China, Korea,
and Russia.

📷 PICTURE PERFECT
Here Comes the Bride

Fortunate visitors may catch a glimpse
of a traditional Shinto wedding taking
place at the shrine. Take a picture of the
bride in her magnificent wedding kimono
(from a respectful distance), as she
shelters under a red parasol accompanied by a procession of priests.

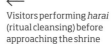
Visitors performing *harai* (ritual cleansing) before approaching the shrine

→
Admiring the huge wall of empty sake barrels, marked with the name of the breweries they were made in, at the entrance to the shrine

↑ Visitors at the Minami-shin Mon, the gate to Meiji Jingu Shrine's inner sanctuary

2

WESTERN SHINJUKU

西新宿

B5 **Shinjuku** **S** Shinjuku

Most of Tokyo's skyscraper office blocks (and some of its most expensive land) are clustered just to the west of Shinjuku Station. About 250,000 people work here each day, creating endless bustle. Many of western Shinjuku's hotels, and some office blocks, have top-floor restaurants with views of the city.

In 1960 the government designated Shinjuku a *fukutoshin* ("secondary heart of the city"), and in 1991, when the city government moved into architect Kenzo Tange's massive 48-story Metropolitan Government Offices, many started calling it *shin toshin* (the new capital). Tange's building was dubbed "tax tower" by those outraged at its US$1 billion cost. Away from the skyscrapers, the neighborhood's western side has rustic, off-beat corners, including the retro Omoide Yokocho *(1-2 Nishishinjuku)*, a narrow alleyway full of cozy bars and restaurants.

↑ Observation deck on the 45th floor of the Tokyo Metropolitan Government Offices

Did You Know?

Shoppers spend over ¥1.3 trillion in Shinjuku's stores every year.

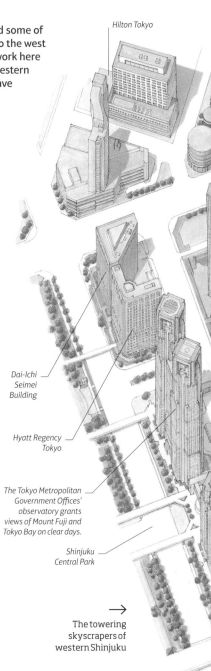

Hilton Tokyo

Dai-Ichi Seimei Building

Hyatt Regency Tokyo

The Tokyo Metropolitan Government Offices' observatory grants views of Mount Fuji and Tokyo Bay on clear days.

Shinjuku Central Park

→ The towering skyscrapers of western Shinjuku

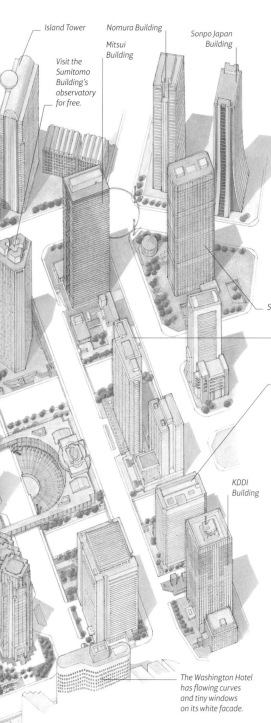

Island Tower

Visit the Sumitomo Building's observatory for free.

Nomura Building

Mitsui Building

Sonpo Japan Building

Shinjuku Center Building

Keio Plaza Hotel

The Monolith Building has a pleasant courtyard garden on the north side.

KDDI Building

The Washington Hotel has flowing curves and tiny windows on its white facade.

Must See

DRINK

New York Bar

The Park Hyatt Tokyo hotel will be forever linked to Sofia Coppola's 2003 film *Lost in Translation*. There is no better spot in Tokyo than this iconic bar to order a whisky soda while gazing out at Tokyo's twinkling lights.

📍 A6 🏢 52 Fl, Park Hyatt Tokyo, 3-7-1-2 Nishishinjuku, Shinjuku 🌐 hyatt.com/en-US/ hotel/japan/park-hyatt-tokyo/tyoph

↑ The distinctive Sonpo Japan Building, with its graceful curving base

Overlooking the city from the Rooftop Sky Deck on Mori Tower ↑

ROPPONGI

六本木

⦿E9 🚇Minato 🚇Roppongi

Roppongi is where Tokyo's grown-ups come to play. Once famous for its dissolute nightlife, it has been transformed by major art galleries and huge developments. Today, Roppongi is a draw for its culture, shopping, entertainment, and clubbing scene.

---

①

Roppongi Hills

🏠6-10-1 Roppongi, Minato
🌐roppongihills.com

This commercial and residential complex, opened in 2003, is one of the largest developments of its kind in Japan. The mix of restaurants, bars, cafés, shops, museums, and entertainment venues all bound together in a cutting-edge architectural vision, make it easy to spend an entire day in this complex. The area is full of outdoor art installations and green areas that complement the indoor artistic spaces.

Roppongi Hills has a cosmopolitan vibe and it is a popular nightlife and shopping spot for Tokyo's international community.

②

Mori Art Museum

🏠Roppongi Hills Mori Tower, 6-10-1 Roppongi, Minato
🕐10am–10pm daily (to 5pm Tue) 🌐mori.art.museum

Immerse yourself in a visit to the Mori Art Museum, located in the Mori Tower. This is one of three art spaces that comprises the "Roppongi Art Triangle," along with the National Art Center Tokyo and the Suntory Museum of Art. It features constantly rotating exhibitions, with a focus on contemporary pieces and the postwar avant-garde. It is an influential presence within Japan's art scene, renowned for showcasing the hottest artists, such as Takashi Murakami and Leandro Erlich. The Mori Tower has several other attractions worth visiting. The Mori Arts Center Gallery hosts short-term exhibitions on various themes, from historical figures to manga and anime. Tokyo City View and Rooftop Sky Deck – the tower's two observation areas – offer panoramas over the capital, with the latter also hosting parties on the open-air rooftop.

---

③

Nogi Shrine

🏠8-11-27 Akasaka, Minato
🕐Early–6pm daily
🌐nogijinja.or.jp

Nogi Shrine is dedicated to General Nogi Maresuke – a hero in Imperial-era Japan – and his wife. When Emperor Meiji died in 1912, the couple demonstrated their loyalty on his funeral by committing the ritual, suicide act of *seppuku* (disembowelment). Despite the violent nature of their end, this shrine is a beautiful place. The Nogi family's 19th-century house still remains in Nogi Park. It is open to visitors on the eve and anniversary of the couple's death on September 12–13, and can be seen in the gardens throughout the year. There is also a flea market held in the shrine's grounds on the fourth Saturday of each month (weather permitting).

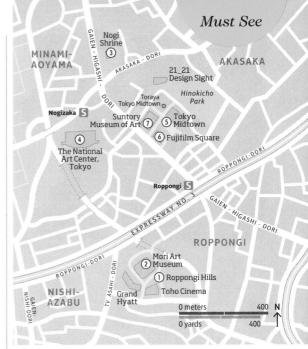

The National Art Center, Tokyo

 7 22-2 Roppongi, Minato
 Times vary, check website nact.jp

The National Art Center, Tokyo (NACT) was built in 2007 to reinvent Roppongi as something more than a nightlife hub. The work of Kisho Kurokawa, the rippling glass facade of the building was inspired by waves and hills. One of Japan's largest exhibition spaces, the NACT does not have a permanent collection of its own, but focuses entirely on temporary exhibitions, artist associations' displays, and educational programs. Check their website to see what exhibitions are currently on.

Tokyo Midtown

 9-7-1 Akasaka, Minato
 tokyo-midtown.com

Completed in 2007, this high-rise development helped spur Roppongi's transformation into a chic district for shopping, entertainment, and art. Similar to the nearby Roppongi Hills, Tokyo Midtown is full of stores, eateries, and museums in the Galleria, Plaza and Midtown Tower buildings, and is bordered to the northeast by Hinokicho Park. This park is located on the former site of the gardens belonging to the lords of the Hagi clan, and harks back to the time when Roppongi was covered in cypress trees (*hinoki*).

Opposite the park is the 21_21 Design Sight gallery, a collaboration by architect Tadao Ando and fashion designer Issey Miyake, with the goal to enrich everyday life through the beauty of thoughtful design. The exhibits change regularly, and the museum store is like a gallery of its own.

Fujifilm Square

 9-7-3 Akasaka, Minato
 10am-7pm daily
 fujifilmsquare.jp

For a fun, free activity in Roppongi, check out this gallery space by the Fuji company. The Photo Salon showcases photos from the Japanese Meiji era to the present day, while Touch Fujifilm lets visitors try out all the latest cameras and tech.

Suntory Museum of Art

 Tokyo Midtown Galleria, 9-7-4 Akasaka, Minato
 10am-6pm Wed-Mon
 suntory.co.jp/sma

The third and final point of the Roppongi Art Triangle is inside the Tokyo Midtown Galleria. Here, the Suntory Museum of Art showcases the collection of the Suntory company, which has amassed a fortune producing whisky and beer. The exhibits focus on older works and traditional crafts, hosting a series of changing exhibitions on textiles, glass, lacquerware, and ceramics.

Embracing the traditional spirit of the exhibits, the museum hosts tea ceremonies every other Thursday, in a tranquil and traditional tea ceremony room with tatami mat floors. Advance online reservations are not available, so be sure to buy your ticket early on the day (available from 10am at the museum's reception desk).

PICTURE PERFECT
Not so Itsy Bitsy

Head to the Mori Art Museum to see Louise Bourgeois's spider-like *Maman*. At a terrifying 30 ft (9 m) tall and 33 ft (10 m) wide, the bronze statue is the stuff of nightmares. Pose next to one of the sculpture's towering legs to show the perspective.

↑ Commuters on the platform at Shinjuku, the busiest train station in the world

EXPERIENCE MORE

Shinjuku Station
新宿駅

◉B5 🚇Shinjuku
🚃🚇🚌Shinjuku

With over two million people passing through each day, Shinjuku Station is considered the world's busiest train station. On the Yamanote and Chuo line platforms during the morning rush hour (about 7:30–9am), staff are employed to push those last few commuters on to the train.

A major stop on both the JR and metropolitan subway systems, Shinjuku Station is also the starting point for trains and buses into the suburbs. Steep home prices have forced people farther out of the city, and a commute of at least an hour is standard. An entire industry has come up around commuters, including stand-up eateries serving meals to those with a long ride ahead.

It's easy to lose your way in this maze of seemingly identical passages between the lines. These passages connect to department stores, so it's possible to spend the day window-shopping in Shinjuku without spending a moment on the streets.

Shibuya Crossing
渋谷スクランブル

◉B9 🏠2-2-1 Dogenzaka, Shibuya 🚃🚇🚌Shibuya

If visitors had to pick one defining view of Tokyo, the bustling Shibuya Crossing would be a leading contender. Also known as the Shibuya Scramble, the crossing is located outside the major transportation hub of Shibuya Station, which sees around 2.4 million passengers pass through it each day. At peak times, more than 2,500 people cross the road from five different directions each time the light goes green.

This area is where Japan's youth come to party, and the overwhelming mass of billboards, bright lights, and enormous television screens blaring out commercials has made the crossing the defining image of the city. The cafés and restaurants that look down at the intersection from the buildings that surround it often feel almost as frenetic as the Shibuya Scramble itself, as hundreds of people vie for window space to try to photograph the crossing.

Minami-Aoyama
南青山

◉C8 🚇Minato
🚃Gaienmae, Omotesando, Nogizaka, Aoyama-itchome

Favored by artists, writers, and young entrepreneurs, this district lies between the large Aoyama Cemetery and Shibuya. Aoyama-dori, the wide street running through it, is famous for its boutiques.

Located on Gaien-Nishi-dori is the **Watari-Um**, also known as the Watari Museum of Contemporary Art. Exhibits are by international and Japanese artists, and change regularly.

 PICTURE PERFECT
Walk this Way

The upper floor of the glass-fronted Starbucks at Shibuya Tsutaya is the perfect place to get a shot of the famous Shibuya Crossing – the busiest intersection in the world. Grab a coffee before making a beeline for the second floor, where the window seats offer great views of the madness below.

Did You Know?

Tokyo's crows know how to use tools and can recognize human faces.

Back on Aoyama-dori, turn left at the Omotesando junction for the **Nezu Museum**, which has a collection of Japanese, Chinese, and Korean art. A very different museum is found a few blocks away. The **Taro Okamoto Memorial Museum** houses the peculiar works of this post-war sculptor. The figures have crudely realized faces and tapering plant-like tendrils. A short walk from here is Kotto-dori, another fashionable street full of antique shops selling scrolls, paintings, and porcelain; notable cafés, boutiques, and shops are also springing up here.

Return to Aoyama-dori, near the Omotesando junction toward Shibuya, and the next landmark is the white, geometric **Spiral Building**, which owes its name to the large spiral ramp inside. It was designed by Fumihiko Maki in 1985, and is one of the most popular places in Minami-Aoyama. There is nothing in it that can't be described as hip and trendy (*torendi* in Japanese), and that includes most of the people. Attractions include the Spiral Hall, used for exhibitions and performances, an Italian café, a French restaurant, a stationery and housewares boutique, and a beauty salon.

Head eastward toward the Nogizaka subway station for the **Aoyama Cemetery**, Japan's first public necropolis, and probably its most exclusive. A number of high-profile people

→

An upscale boutique near Omotesando, in Minami-Aoyama

are buried here, including former prime minister Shigeru Yoshida and famed novelist Yukio Mishima. This tranquil spot is also a popular place to view cherry blossoms.

Watari-Um

3-7-6 Jingumae, Shibuya ⏲11am-7pm Tue–Sun (to 9pm Wed) 🌐 watarium.co.jp

Nezu Museum

6-5-1 Minamiaoyama, Minato ⏲10am–5pm Tue–Sun 🌐 nezu-muse.or.jp/en

Taro Okamato Memorial Museum

6-1-19 Minamiaoyama, Minato ⏲10am–6pm Wed–Mon 🌐 taro-okamoto.or.jp/en

Spiral Building

5-6-23 Minamiaoyama, Minato 🌐 spiral.co.jp

Aoyama Cemetery

2-32-2 Minamiaoyama, Minato ☎ (03) 3401-3652 ⏲24 hours daily

STAY

Sequence Miyashita Park

A stylish Shibuya hotel, with everything from dormitories to suites.

📍B8 6-20-10 Jingumae, Shibuya 🌐 sequencehotels.com/miyashita-park

¥¥¥

The Millennials Shibuya

Free beer is served for one hour every evening at this sociable capsule hotel.

📍B8 1-20-13 Jinnan, Shibuya 🌐 the-millennials-shibuya-shibuya-ku-jp.book.direct/en-gb

¥¥¥

 7

Harajuku
原宿

Q B7 **A** Shibuya **R** Harajuku **S** Meiji-jingumae

Harajuku Station was the main station for the 1964 Tokyo Olympic village and that concentration of international culture had a great impact on the area, attracting the young and innovative of Tokyo. Today Harajuku remains a center for fashion from high-end international stores to bargain boutiques.

Takeshita-dori, a narrow alley between Meiji-dori and Harajuku Station, is the place to find what's hot in teen fashion and culture. Sundays bring the biggest crowds. Prices range from cheap to outrageous, as do the fashions.

Starting from the Harajuku Station end, about 200 yards (180 m) down, a left turn leads up some stairs to Togo Shrine, founded for Admiral Togo, the commander who defeated the Russian fleet in the Battle of Tsushima, which was part of

the Russo-Japanese War. It was a huge naval victory, the first of an Asian country over a Western one. Admiral Togo remains a hero in Japan, and his shrine has a beautiful garden and pond. Located a few blocks east of the shrine is **Design Festa Gallery**. This Postmodern, bohemian gallery focuses on future-generation artists and has a design-themed café-bar.

Running parallel to, and south of, Takeshita-dori is the sophisticated Omotesando. With its wide, tree-shaded sidewalks and dozens of boutiques showcasing top fashion designers and brands such as Celine, Fendi, and Dior, this is one of the best places to stroll in Tokyo.

As you walk from Harajuku Station, just before the intersection with Meiji-dori, off to the left, you will see a street leading to the **Ota Memorial Museum of Art**, which houses one of the best collections of ukiyo-e prints *(p131)* in Japan. A vivid image of a Kabuki actor portraying a superhero in the classic *aragoto* style by

Sharaku and a masterful program of a memorial Kabuki performance by Hiroshige are among many familiar works. There is a small restaurant and a shop selling prints and other ukiyo-e-related souvenirs.

To the left down Meiji-dori is LaForet, a fashion mecca, with more than 150 boutiques. It is particularly good for women's casual wear, stocking everything from high-end labels, such as Vivienne Westwood, to local indie brands.

Leading off Omotesando, just before the pedestrian bridge, a narrow lane to the left is lined with boutiques of

---

 PICTURE PERFECT
Japan in the Mirror

Quirky Tokyu Plaza Omotesando Harajuku, a multistory shopping complex in the heart of the district, is accessed via a mirror-encased escalator *(p82)*. Snap a kaleidoscope-like image from the top as you exit.

> **Takeshita-dori, a narrow alley between Meiji-dori and Harajuku Station, is the place to find what's hot in teen fashion and culture. Sundays bring the biggest crowds.**

← Crowds on neon-lit Takeshita-dori, in Harajuku

up-and-coming designers and gives a good idea of residential life in this upscale area. Cat Street, to the right, is also quiet and a good place to find affordable creations by local designers and vintage pieces.

Farther up the hill from the footbridge on the left is Omotesando Hills. This huge complex is home to boutiques such as Jimmy Choo, and specialist luxury-goods stores, as well as many brand stores such as UGG Australia. Over the pedestrian bridge to the right is the Oak Omotesando Building. This shopping zone has an impressive glass facade and houses luxury brands, such as Coach and Emporio Armani, as well as Japan's first Nespresso boutique. Just before the Oak Omotesando Building is the vermilion-and-white Oriental Bazaar, a collection of shops full of real and fake antiques and good handicrafts, ideal for souvenirs.

Design Festa Gallery
🏠 3-20-18 Jingumae, Shibuya
🕙 11am-8pm daily 🌐 design festagallery.com

Ota Memorial Museum of Art
♿ 🏠 1-10-10 Jingumae, Shibuya 🕙 10:30am-5:30pm Tue-Sun 🔁 Check website for exhibit changes and details 🌐 ukiyoe-ota-muse.jp

Tokyo Opera City
東京オペラシティー

🚇 A6 🏠 3-20-2 Nishi-Shinjuku, Shinjuku 🚉 Hatsudai 🌐 operacity.jp

This towering skyscraper is home to Tokyo's impressive music and theater complex. On the first floor of the building, you will find two main halls. One of these is primarily used for Japanese classical music and theater, while the second is a vast opera hall with a soaring vaulted roof that stages large-scale opera recitals. Performances are frequent – check the calendar on Opera City's website for up-to-date listings, and book your tickets in advance.

On top of the two halls, there are 54 floors, mostly housing company offices. The first three floors are accessible to the public, however, and house an art gallery, shops, and restaurants, which are worth investigating before or after the opera. The expansive NTT Intercommunication Center occupies the fourth floor. This is one of Tokyo's primary centers for modern interactive art. The 53rd and 54th floors of the buildings hold dozens of swanky restaurants and bars, some of which offer panoramic views of the city.

HARAJUKU STYLE

Harajuku has been a mecca for Tokyo teens since at least the mid-1990s, when disparate fashion subcultures would gather near the former Olympic Park to shop and show off. Around that time, a magazine called *FRUiTS* would feature portraits of young people in zany outfits, popularizing the idea of Tokyo as a hub for teen fashion. A number of mainstream brands, such as Uniqlo, moved into the district, transforming it into a tourist hot spot. In 2017, the print edition of *FRUiTS* ceased publication. Nevertheless, one Sunday a month, devotees gather for the Harajuku Fashion Walk to relive the glory days.

Springtime sakura (cherry blossoms) in Shinjuku Gyoen Garden

11

Akasaka
赤坂

 E7 🚇 Minato 🚉 Akasaka, Akasaka-Mitsuke

With the Diet Building (p116) and many government offices just to the east, Akasaka is a favorite place for politicians to socialize. The roads are often dotted with limousines ferrying men and women to the exclusive establishments here.

About 200 yards (180) along Aoyama-dori from Akasaka-Mitsuke Station is **Toyokawa Inari Shrine** (also called Myogon-ji). With its red lanterns and flags, and dozens of statues of foxes (traditional messengers of Inari, a Shinto rice deity), this is a pleasant place to linger for a while.

9

Shinjuku Gyoen Garden
新宿御苑

 C6 🏠 11 Naitomachi, Shinjuku 🚇🚉 Shinjuku ⏰ Tue–Sun; times vary, check website for details 🌐 env.go.jp/garden/ shinjukugyoen/english

Like many of Japan's gardens, Shinjuku Gyoen was once an Edo-era lord's residence. After serving as an imperial family property, it became a public park shortly after World War II. Since then, it has developed into a vast group of gardens, featuring traditional Japanese, French, and English landscaping styles. There are also lawns that are ideal for a picnic in spring, when cherry blossoms make this a prime *hanami* (cherry blossom-viewing) spot.

10

Yoyogi Park
代々木公園

 A7 🚇 Shibuya 🏠 Harajuku, Sangubashi 🚉 Yoyogi-koen

For almost three decades the park filled with an array of performers and bands every Sunday. These events were stopped in the mid-1990s, supposedly owing to worries about the rise in criminal activities and maintaining public order. Weekends are still a good time to visit – for the occasional flea markets and an array of annual events, such as international food festivals and Earth Day. At the park entrance you can still see members of the *zoku* (fashion tribes) who used to perform here, including punks, goths, hippies, and break-dancers.

Kenzo Tange's two Olympic stadiums, the landmark structures in Yoyogi Park, were completed in 1964 for the Tokyo Olympics. They were renovated for the postponed 2020 Tokyo Olympics, when they will be used as handball venues, as well as for wheelchair rugby and badminton in the Paralympics. The impressive curves of the shell-like structures are achieved with steel suspension cables.

EATING IN GOLDEN GAI

Situated north of Shinjuku Gyoen Garden, the Golden Gai area retains a shabby charm that is fast disappearing in the increasingly slick and tidy modern city. In this labyrinth of dark alleys and backlit acrylic signs, there are more than 200 tiny bars and restaurants to choose from. But don't head over too early – nothing opens before 9pm. Plus, there's no rush, as the fun goes on all night.

TOP 5 SYMBOLIC ANIMALS

Fox
Messengers of Shinto god Inari, fox statues are found at shrines.

Cranes
Cranes represent longevity. Japanese folklore says that they live for 1,000 years.

Tanuki
Sculptures of these Asian raccoon dogs represent good luck.

Cats
The *Maneki-neko* (beckoning cat) is thought to bring luck, wealth, and prosperity.

Koi
Carp symbolize faithfulness and marriage in Japan.

Back past the station and over the moat, there's a building that you may recognize from the James Bond film *You Only Live Twice* (1967). This is the luxurious **Hotel New Otani**. On the 17th floor is THE SKY revolving restaurant, which serves Japanese, Chinese, and Western cuisine (diners can choose the ingredients and the chefs prepare it on the spot), and offers stunning views. It has a 17th-century Japanese garden, which is free to enter. To the west of the hotel is a surprising Tokyo landmark: the **Akasaka Palace** (also known as the State Guesthouse), which was modeled after European palaces. Built in 1909 as an imperial residence, it is now used by visiting VIPs.

South of Akasaka-Mitsuke Station is the Hie Jinja Shrine, built in 1478. Shogun Ietsuna moved it here in the 17th century to buffer his castle. In mid-June, the Sanno Matsuri is celebrated here with a grand procession of 50 *mikoshi* (portable shrines) and people dressed in costumes of the Heian era (794–1185).

Toyokawa Inari Shrine

🏠 1-4-7 Motoakasaka, Minato 🕐 5am–7:30pm daily 🌐 toyokawainari.jp

Hotel New Otani

🏠 4-1 Kioicho, Chiyoda 🌐 newotani.co.jp

Akasaka Palace

♿ 🏠 2-1 Motoakasaka, Minato 🕐 10am–5pm Thu–Tue 🌐 geihinkan.go.jp

The approach to Toyokawa Inari Shrine, lined by dozens ↓ of fox statues *(inset)*

EAT

Maruhachi
The food served at this friendly *izakaya* can be washed down with *shochu* (sweet potato and rice liquor) or *awamori* (made from long-grain rice).

📍 B9 🏠 2-10-12 Dogenzaka, Shibuya 📞 (03) 3476-5729

¥¥¥

Den
Chef Zaiyu Hasegawa crafts beautiful dishes. Order the "Dentucky Fried Chicken."

📍 C7 🏠 2-3-18 Jingumae, Shibuya 🕐 L & Sun 🌐 jimbochoden.com

¥¥¥

A SHORT WALK
EASTERN SHINJUKU

Distance 1.5 miles (2.5 km) **Time** 45 minutes
Nearest subway Shinjuku Station

Eastern Shinjuku is where Tokyoites come to play.
The area has been a nightlife center from as early as
the Edo period, when it was the first stop on the old
Tokaido road to Kyoto. Since Shinjuku Station opened
in the 1880s, the area's entertainments have been
targeted at mainly male commuters en route back
to the suburbs. Amusements are focused in the tiny
bars of Golden Gai, and in the red-light district of
Kabukicho. Daytime attractions include several art
galleries, a tranquil shrine, and some of Tokyo's best
department stores. A late-afternoon stroll as the
neon starts to light up will take in both the highbrow
and dark sides of this fascinating, bustling area.

Did You Know?

Despite its name,
a Kabuki theater
was never built
in Kabukicho.

*Instantly recognizable
by its huge TV screen,*
Studio Alta *is a popular
place for meeting up or
just hanging out.*

Seibu-
shinjuku

CINECITY
SQUARE

OTAKIBASHI-DORI

GINZA-DORI

KABUKICHO

CHUO-DORI

START

MOA 2ND ST

MOA CHUO

Studio
Alta

MOA 3RD

FINISH

Shinjuku
Station

Blue Bottle
Coffee

**Blue Bottle
Coffee** *is a
convenient stop.*

| 0 meters | 150 |
| 0 yards | 150 |

N

↑ Flashing advertisements on the exterior
of Studio Alta shopping complex

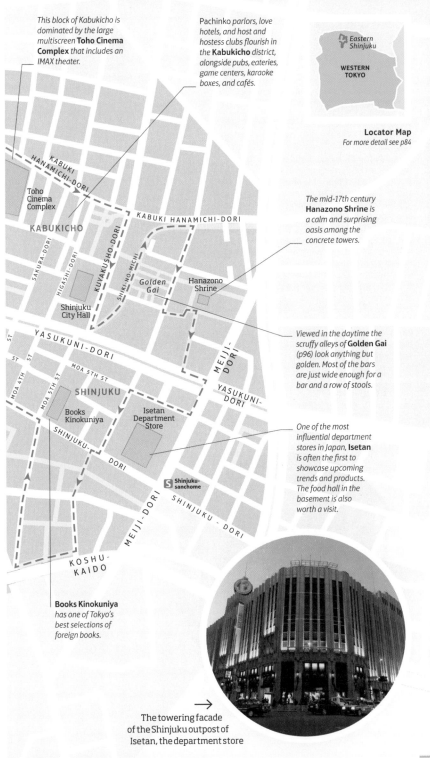

This block of Kabukicho is dominated by the large multiscreen **Toho Cinema Complex** that includes an IMAX theater.

Pachinko *parlors*, love hotels, and host and hostess clubs flourish in the **Kabukicho** district, alongside pubs, eateries, game centers, karaoke boxes, and cafés.

Eastern Shinjuku

WESTERN TOKYO

Locator Map
For more detail see p84

The mid-17th century **Hanazono Shrine** is a calm and surprising oasis among the concrete towers.

Viewed in the daytime the scruffy alleys of **Golden Gai** (p96) look anything but golden. Most of the bars are just wide enough for a bar and a row of stools.

One of the most influential department stores in Japan, **Isetan** is often the first to showcase upcoming trends and products. The food hall in the basement is also worth a visit.

Books Kinokuniya has one of Tokyo's best selections of foreign books.

→ The towering facade of the Shinjuku outpost of Isetan, the department store

KABUKI HANAMICHI-DORI

Toho Cinema Complex

KABUKICHO

KABUKI HANAMICHI-DORI

SAKURA-DORI

HIGASHI-DORI

KUYAKUSHO-DORI

SHIKI-NO-MICHI

Golden Gai

Hanazono Shrine

Shinjuku City Hall

YASUKUNI-DORI

MEIJI-DORI

YASUKUNI-DORI

MOA 4TH ST

MOA 5TH ST

MOA 5TH ST

SHINJUKU

Books Kinokuniya

Isetan Department Store

SHINJUKU-DORI

S Shinjuku-sanchome

SHINJUKU - DORI

MEIJI-DORI

KOSHU-KAIDO

A SHORT WALK
SHIBUYA

Distance 2 miles (3 km) **Time** 45 minutes
Nearest subway Shibuya Station

Shibuya has been the *sakariba* (party town) for Tokyo's youth since the 1930s, when the Tokyu Toyoko Line made the area a key terminal between the capital and Yokohama, and the first facades featured rockets streaking across the sky. Today, it still feels out of this world and cutting edge, and this is where you'll find the latest in fashion and music. Shibuya's continuing expansion has been spurred by the appetites of the increasingly affluent youth of the world's third-biggest economy. Due to their demands, the area, which lies to the northwest of Shibuya Station and south of Yoyogi Park, is a mix of trendy boutiques, fashionable department stores, and record shops. On top of these commercial enterprises, a stroll through the area will also take you past a couple of interesting museums, as well as the multifaceted Bunkamura cultural center. Once you've explored Shibuya, head into the adjoining area of Dogen-zaka, where you'll find a jumble of sloping streets and alleyways lined with nightclubs, bars, and love hotels.

Bunkamura is a popular site for rock and classical concerts, but also shows movies, and houses an art gallery and theater.

INOKASHIRA-DORI

SHOTO

Bunkamura

*Live musicians perform at **Tsutaya O-East** every night.*

Tsutaya O-East

Yosano Akiko Monument

*The **Yosano Akiko Monument** immortalizes the famous poet.*

← Nighttime traffic on an expressway in Shibuya

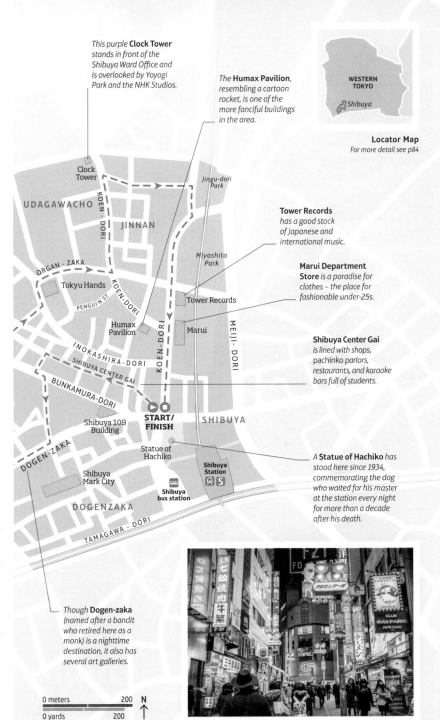

This purple **Clock Tower** stands in front of the Shibuya Ward Office and is overlooked by Yoyogi Park and the NHK Studios.

The **Humax Pavilion**, resembling a cartoon rocket, is one of the more fanciful buildings in the area.

Locator Map
For more detail see p84

WESTERN TOKYO

Shibuya

Tower Records has a good stock of Japanese and international music.

Marui Department Store is a paradise for clothes – the place for fashionable under-25s.

Shibuya Center Gai is lined with shops, pachinko parlors, restaurants, and karaoke bars full of students.

UDAGAWACHO

KOEN-DORI

JINNAN

Clock Tower

ORGAN-ZAKA

Tokyu Hands

PENGUIN ST

KOEN-DORI

Humax Pavilion

INOKASHIRA-DORI

SHIBUYA CENTER GAI

BUNKAMURA-DORI

Shibuya 109 Building

DOGEN-ZAKA

Shibuya Mark City

DOGENZAKA

Jingu-dori Park

Miyashita Park

Tower Records

Marui

MEIJI-DORI

KOEN-DORI

START/ FINISH

SHIBUYA

Statue of Hachiko

Shibuya Station

Shibuya bus station

TAMAGAWA-DORI

A **Statue of Hachiko** has stood here since 1934, commemorating the dog who waited for his master at the station every night for more than a decade after his death.

Though **Dogen-zaka** (named after a bandit who retired here as a monk) is a nighttime destination, it also has several art galleries.

| 0 meters | 200 |
| 0 yards | 200 |

N ↑

↑ Strolling Shibuya's busy central shopping street, neon-lit Center Gai

CENTRAL TOKYO

Situated to the north and west of the Sumida River, this area has been at the heart of Tokyo since the shogun Ieyasu Tokugawa built his castle and capital where the Imperial Palace still stands today. When Ieyasu Tokugawa moved his military center here in 1590, it was surrounded by swamp and marshland. Once filled in, the area that became Ginza – "the silver place" – attracted tradesman and merchants. Destroyed by a series of disasters, including a devastating fire in 1872, the Great Kanto Earthquake of 1923, and the Allied bombing in World War II, the area has reinvented itself several times over, but has always remained true to its history as the center of Tokyo.

The area's continuing importance is evident in the Hibiya business district and cosmopolitan Marunouchi, home to the Tokyo International Forum. Ginza and Nihonbashi remain as thriving and prosperous today as they were back in the Edo period (1603–1868), offering a mix of department stores and chic side-street boutiques.

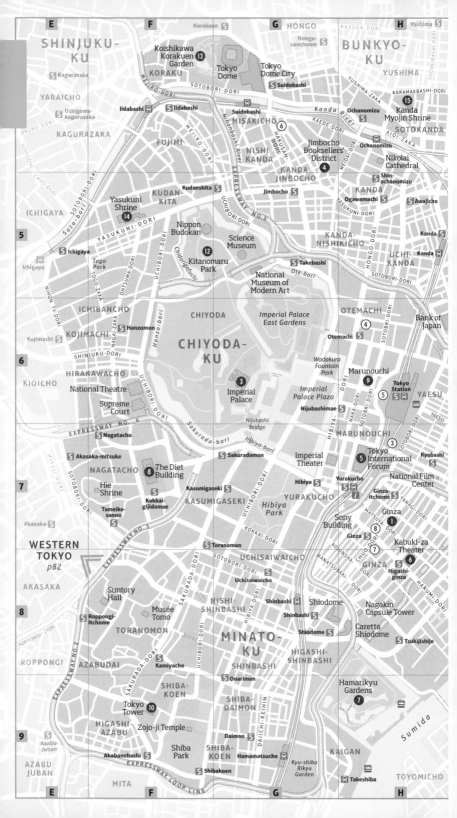

CENTRAL TOKYO

Must Sees

1. Ginza
2. Nihonbashi
3. Imperial Palace

Experience More

4. Jimbocho Booksellers' District
5. Tokyo International Forum
6. Kabuki-za Theater
7. Hamarikyu Gardens
8. The Diet Building
9. Marunouchi
10. Tokyo Tower
11. Akihabara
12. Kitanomaru Park
13. Koishikawa Korakuen Garden
14. Yasukuni Shrine
15. Kanda Myojin Shrine

Eat

1. Takashimaya
2. Sushi Shin
3. Rokurinsha

Stay

4. Aman Hotel
5. Hotel Niwa Kanda
6. Tokyo Prince Hotel

Shop

7. Ginza Six
8. Ginza Wako

❶
GINZA

銀座

◉ H7 Ⓐ Chuo Ⓢ Ginza, Yurakucho

Tokyo must count as the single greatest city to shop in the world, and Ginza is its Mayfair, Fifth Avenue, and Avenue Montaigne rolled into one. Tiny shops selling traditional crafts mix with trendy galleries and sprawling department stores for an unrivaled shopping experience.

The sophisticated neighborhood of Ginza, with its tree-lined avenues and broad pedestrianized streets, has a more cosmopolitan feel than many other parts of Tokyo. The area was destroyed by a devastating fire in 1872 and the newly restored imperial government commissioned Irish architect Thomas Waters to rebuild Ginza in red brick – the height of fashion at the time. The area has never looked back and its leafy streets are now home to some of the smartest boutiques and chicest restaurants that the capital has to offer. These include the gargantuan Ginza Six, which focuses on the latest fashion trends, and Ginza Wako, a traditional department store dating from the 1940s. Known as Brand Street, Chuo-dori is home to some of Japan's most prestigious shopping, ranging from department stores such as Matsuya to international fashion boutiques, including Dior, Gucci, Louis Vuitton, and Prada.

SHOP

Ginza Six
Home to over 240 stores, Ginza Six is the biggest shopping complex in the area. Inside this mammoth building, you'll find big international names, including Céline and Dior.

◉ H8 Ⓐ 6-10-1 Ginza, Chuo ⏰ 10:30am–8:30pm daily Ⓦ ginza6.tokyo

Ginza Wako
With its distinctive clock tower, Wako has been a hard-hitting presence on Ginza's shopping scene for decades. Known for its range of watches, jewelry, chocolate, and porcelain, it's a great place to browse.

◉ H7 Ⓐ 4-5-11 Ginza, Chuo ⏰ 10:30am-7pm daily Ⓦ wako.co.jp

← Fashion-forward retail concessions in the foyer of Ginza Six

PICTURE PERFECT
Capsule Capture
A short walk from the south end of Chuo-dori is the Nakagin Capsule Tower, a rare example of Japanese Metabolism (p37). Take a picture of this modular building, seemingly built out of washing machines, from across the street.

↑ Walking past the stylish window displays of Chanel on Chuo-dori

Did You Know?
—
The irregular windows on the Mikimoto Ginza2 building aim to mimic the ocean's surface.

The striking exterior of Mikimoto Ginza2, a jewelry and cosmetics store ↑

A SHORT WALK
GINZA

Distance 1 mile (2 km) **Time** 30 minutes
Nearest subway Yurakucho Station

Ever since Thomas Waters rebuilt the area in red brick back in the 19th century, Ginza (p106) has been Japan's epicenter of Western influences and all things modern, and it is still one of Tokyo's great commercial centers. Tiny shops selling traditional crafts mix with galleries and landmark department stores, offering a huge variety of shopping options. Wander Ginza's leafy streets, and take a moment to pop into the many department stores to check out glitzy food halls, where gleaming cabinets display tempting delectables. Some of these mammoth stores even house their own art galleries.

Did You Know?

On Saturdays, Sundays and public holiday afternoons, Chuo-Dori street is closed to traffic.

The second floor of the **Gallery Center Building** houses exclusive galleries showcasing Japanese and Western art and an auction house on the fifth floor.

The **Asahi Building** contains a traditional kimono shop, silversmiths, and several boutiques.

Namiki-Dori is lined with boutiques such as Gucci, Dior, Louis Vuitton, and Cartier.

Hankyu Men's department store focuses on men's fashion, with a mix of Japanese and international labels.

Yurakucho Station

Hankyu Men's

START/ FINISH

Sukiyabashi Park

Sony Showroom

TOKYO EXPRESSWAY

Gallery Center Building

SOTOBORI-DORI

SUKIYA-DORI

MIYUKI-DORI

SONY-DORI

Asahi Building

KOJUNSHA-DORI

NAMIKI-DORI

NISHI-GOBANGAI-DORI

↑ The facade of the Bulgari store on Chuo-Dori

0 meters 150
0 yards 150
N ↑

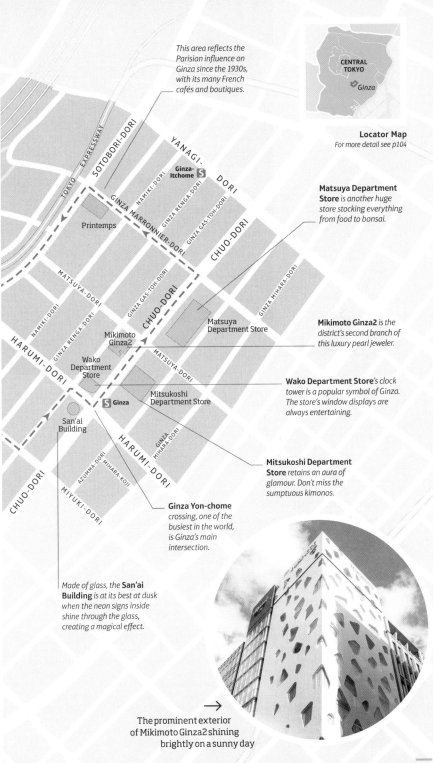

This area reflects the Parisian influence on Ginza since the 1930s, with its many French cafés and boutiques.

CENTRAL TOKYO

Ginza

Locator Map
For more detail see p104

Matsuya Department Store *is another huge store stocking everything from food to bonsai.*

Mikimoto Ginza2 *is the district's second branch of this luxury pearl jeweler.*

Wako Department Store's *clock tower is a popular symbol of Ginza. The store's window displays are always entertaining.*

Mitsukoshi Department Store *retains an aura of glamour. Don't miss the sumptuous kimonos.*

Ginza Yon-chome *crossing, one of the busiest in the world, is Ginza's main intersection.*

Made of glass, the **San'ai Building** *is at its best at dusk when the neon signs inside shine through the glass, creating a magical effect.*

SOTOBORI-DORI
TOKYO EXPRESSWAY
YANAGI-DORI
GINZA MARRONNIER-DORI
NAMIKI-DORI
GINZA RENGA-DORI
GINZA GAS-TOH-DORI
CHUO-DORI
Ginza-Itchome S
Printemps
MATSUYA-DORI
NAMIKI-DORI
GINZA RENGA-DORI
GINZA GAS-TOH-DORI
CHUO-DORI
Mikimoto Ginza2
Matsuya Department Store
GINZA MIHARA-DORI
HARUMI-DORI
Wako Department Store
MATSUYA-DORI
Mitsukoshi Department Store
S Ginza
San'ai Building
HARUMI-DORI
GINZA MIHARA-DORI
CHUO-DORI
AZUMA-DORI
MIHARA-KOJI
MIYUKI-DORI

→ The prominent exterior of Mikimoto Ginza2 shining brightly on a sunny day

EAT

Takashimaya

The recipe for the sauce used at Takashimya eel shop has not been altered since the eatery opened in 1875. What's more, this venerable restaurant doesn't just serve up any old eel to its discerning clientele. Only the Kyosui *unagi*, a slow-growing and richer flavored sub-species of the fish, will be found in the kitchen here. A bento option for takeout is available.

 J6 🏠 11-5 Nihonbashikobunachō, Chuo 🕙 Sun 🌐 takashimaya.info

→

Coredo Muromachi illuminated during spring blossom time

❷

NIHONBASHI

日本橋

📍 J6 🏠 Chuo 🚆🚇 Tokyo 🚇 Nihonbashi, Mitsukoshimae 🕙 Tokyo Stock Exchange: 9am–4:30pm Mon–Fri 🌐 Tokyo Stock Exchange: jpx.co.jp

The mercantile and entrepreneurial center of Edo and Meiji Tokyo, Nihonbashi has been the city's traditional commercial hub for centuries. It is here, amid the ultramodern streets and buildings, that you will find some of the oldest continuously operating businesses in the world, including dozens of bank headquarters, huge department stores, and smaller traditional stores.

Home to both the Bank of Japan and the Tokyo Stock Exchange, which has an observation deck, Nihonbashi feels as if it is at the center of the city. The district is named after the famous bridge, immortalized in Hokusai's prints of great processions passing over on their way into the shogun's city. The Edo era still feels within touching distance in this densely packed district and, to this day, Nihonbashi remains the center for traditional Japanese small-scale crafts in the city. Kimono-makers, embroiderers, and even toothpick whittlers still sell their wares here. One former kimono shop is Mitsukoshi.

Founded in 1673, this labyrinthine complex was Japan's first department store, and serves as a monument to consumption. A newer addition to the neighborhood is the Coredo Muromachi complex. Its three buildings are home to fashion and interior design boutiques, as well as traditional delis, sweet shops, bars, and restaurants.

Although trading in the Tokyo Stock Exchange was computerized in 1999, this is still a great place to see the importance of commerce in the capital. The visitors' observation deck overlooks the trading floor.

Did You Know?

In Japan, distances are measured from Nihonbashi Bridge.

⌐1¬ Nihonbashi Bridge is decorated with statues of symbolically powerful animals, including lions and dragons.

⌐2¬ The main hall of Mitsukoshi is crowned with a statue of the Goddess of Sincerity.

⌐3¬ Although cherry trees can only be found along Edo Sakura-dori, Nihonbashi celebrates the flowering of sakura with many events, including light shows.

IMPERIAL PALACE

皇居

📍 G6 🏠 1-1 Chiyoda, Chiyoda 🚃 Tokyo Ⓢ Nijubashi, Otemachi 🕐 Imperial Palace: Jan 2, Feb 23; East Gardens of the Imperial Palace: times vary, check website for details 🌐 kunaicho.go.jp

The residence of the emperor of Japan, the Imperial Palace is a modern, working castle at the heart of Tokyo. In a city where everything can feel to be in a permanent state of flux, the palace and its grounds form a green thread of continuity with the capital and Japan's past.

Following the Meiji Restoration in 1868, Japan's imperial family moved from Kyoto to Tokyo. Edo Castle, the former home of the Tokugawa shoguns, was commandeered for the emperor and rechristened the Imperial Palace. None of the main buildings from this period remain today, but the moats, walls, entrance gates, and guardhouses bear testament to this martial past. Most of the palace was destroyed during World War II, but it was rebuilt in the same style. Popular sights include Nijubashi – two bridges that form an entrance to the inner palace grounds – and the luxuriant East Gardens. The grounds feature both Japanese- and Western-style gardens and the foundations of the castle's former keep. Visitors are only able to enter the Imperial Palace on two days each year, but guided tours of the grounds are available throughout the rest of the year (10am & 1:30pm Tue–Sat; registration begins an hour before each tour).

> **In a city where everything can feel to be in a permanent state of flux, the palace and its grounds form a green thread of continuity.**

↑ An entrance to the East Gardens of the Imperial Palace

💬 **INSIDER TIP**
Poetry at the Palace

Utakai Hajime (poetry reading) is held in the Imperial Palace every New Year's Day. There is a record of the event having taken place as early as 1267. Today it is attended by the emperor and broadcast live on TV.

↑ Browsing through stalls selling secondhand books in Jimbocho Booksellers' District

↑ The imposing Kyuden, the main building of the Imperial Palace

EXPERIENCE MORE

❹

Jimbocho Booksellers' District
神保町古本屋街

📍 G4 🏛 Chiyoda
Ⓢ Jimbocho

Three of the country's great universities – Meiji, Chuo, and Nihon – started out in this area in the 1870s and 1880s, and soon booksellers sprang up selling both new and used books. At one time as many as 50 per cent of Japan's publishers were based in this district.

Although only Meiji and Nihon universities are still in the area, dozens of bookshops, remain – including several selling ukiyo-e prints – all of them clustered around the junction of Yasukuni-dori and Hakusan-dori. For books in English language on Eastern subjects, try Issei-do or Kitazawa Books; for ukiyo-e prints, visit Oya Shobo – all are located on the south side of Yasukuni-dori, walking away from Hakusan-dori.

The change in the economic status (as well as pastimes and priorities) of Tokyo's university students is evident in Jimbocho Booksellers' District. Shops selling surf- and snowboards have cropped up everywhere, and music shops selling electric guitars now seem as numerous as the bookshops.

Did You Know?

The Japanese word *"tsundoku"* means "to buy more books than you can ever read."

The enormous, sleek interior of the Tokyo International Forum ↑

INSIDER TIP
Market Days

The best time to visit the Tokyo International Forum is on the first or third Sunday of the month when the Oedo Antique Market – the largest in Japan – takes over the forecourt with overflowing stalls.

Kabuki-za Theater
歌舞伎座

📍H8 🏠4-12-15 Ginza, Chuo 🚇Higashi-Ginza
🌐kabuki-za.co.jp

Tokyo's principal theater for Kabuki opened in 1889 during the reign of Emperor Meiji as part of Kabuki's shift from daytime entertainment for the masses in Asakusa to a more high-brow art form.

The theater has witnessed numerous incarnations over the years, but still employs traditional Japanese design. It was almost destroyed in the Allied bombing of 1945, and was rebuilt in 1951, only to be demolished yet again in 2010. The theater reopened in 2013, and now enchanting performances, including dance, historical plays and updated Kabuki plays take place here most evenings.

Tokyo International Forum
東京国際フォーラム

📍H7 🏠3-5-1 Marunouchi, Chiyoda 🚇Yurakucho, Tokyo 🚇Yurakucho, Tokyo, Ginza 🕐7am-11:30pm daily 🌐t-i-forum.co.jp

Designed by the renowned American-based architect Rafael Viñoly, and completed in 1996, the International Forum is one of downtown Tokyo's most distinctive buildings. A bustling cultural center, it is made up of two buildings: a curved glass atrium soaring 200 ft (60 m) into the sky, and a white, cube-like structure housing four halls (with the largest able to seat 5,012). A tree-shaded courtyard separates the two, while glass walkways provide an overhead link. The interior of the huge atrium is filled with natural light and has a ceiling resembling a ship's hull. There are plenty of shops, cafés, restaurants, and food trucks, as well as conference rooms, all supported by state-of-the-art facilities. Free internet access available in the entrance lobby.

The entrance to the much-reconstructed Kabuki-za Theater →

↑ The hero of a Noh performance fighting a masked demon

JAPANESE TRADITIONAL THEATER

Four major types of traditional theater are still performed regularly in Japan: Noh, Kyogen, Kabuki, and Bunraku. Originating in Shinto rites, Noh became more ritualistic and ceremonial, before splintering into different forms designed to entertain the masses.

NOH

First performed by Kan'ami Kiyotsugu (1333–84), Noh is a restrained but powerful theatrical form. One or two masked characters appear on the bare stage at a time, and perform slow, choreographed actions (kata) to music.

KYOGEN

This form evolved from comic interludes devised as relief from the demanding nature of Noh. A down-to-earth, colloquial form, its characters highlight human foibles. Rather than masks, the actors wear distinctive yellow tabi socks.

↑ Elaborately dressed Kabuki performers on stage

KABUKI

If Noh is stark, Kabuki is flamboyant and colorful. Elaborate make-up replaced Noh masks, and a curtain allowed set changes. Although Kabuki was founded by a woman, all actors are now male, and female roles are played by highly skilled onnagata.

BUNRAKU

Elaborately dressed 4-ft- (1.2-m-) high puppets are manipulated by a puppeteer and his two assistants. Shamisen music accompanies the action, and a narrator both tells the story and speaks all the parts.

↑ A Bunraku puppet striking a ceremonial bell

← A stream running through the charming, tree-filled Hamarikyu Gardens

7 ⌖

Hamarikyu Gardens
浜離宮庭園

⊙ H9 ⌂ 1-1 Hamarikyuteien, Chuo ⊞ Shinbashi ⊜ Shiodome ⊜ ⊙ 9am–5pm daily ⊠ tokyo-park.or.jp/teien/en/hama-rikyu

Situated where the Sumida River empties into Tokyo Bay, this 62-acre (25-hectare) garden dotted with colorful and fragrant plants like camellia and azalea was built in 1654 as a retreat for the shogun's family, who also hunted duck here. The garden has had an illustrious history. The US president Ulysses S. Grant stayed in a villa in the gardens during his visit in 1879 and sipped green tea in Nakajima teahouse.

The garden grounds surrounding the duck ponds are still a pleasant, uncrowded place to stroll and unwind, although all of the original teahouses and villas, trees, and vegetation burned down after a devastating bombing raid on November 29, 1944. But Nakajima teahouse has been faithfully rebuilt, appearing to float over the large pond. Green *matcha* tea and Japanese sweets are available here.

INSIDER TIP
All Aboard!

The Tokyo Cruise floats along the Sumida River from the Hamarikyu Gardens to Asakusa in northern Tokyo. In a spaceship-like boat, you will pass under bridges, take in the city's soaring skyscrapers, and see people relaxing in waterside parks. Cruise tickets include entrance to the Hamarikyu Gardens. Near Asakusa there are long boats for lantern-lit evening cruises *(www.suijobus.co.jp/en)*.

8 ⟨M⟩

The Diet Building
国会議事堂

⊙ F7 ⌂ 1-7-1 Nagatacho, Chiyoda ⊜ Nagatacho, Kokkai-Gijidomae ⊙ 8am–5pm Mon–Fri (by reservation) ⊠ sangiin.go.jp

Completed in 1936, the Diet Building houses the legislature of the Japanese government, originally established as the Imperial Diet in the Meiji era. Tours (in Japanese only) cover the impressive interior, including the Diet chamber, where you can see the deliberations of Diet members, and the extravagantly decorated rooms formerly used by the emperor for official functions.

Nearby, you'll find Central Tokyo's only Western-style park, Hibiya Park. Its location, close to the political centers of Kasumigaseki and the Diet Building, makes it a favorite

→ The imposing entrance to Tokyo Station, in Marunouchi

place for public protests, especially on May Day. The large bandstand in the center is also occasionally used for concerts.

 9

Marunouchi
丸の内

♥H6 **🏛**Chiyoda **🚇🚉**Tokyo

During the Edo era, this district earned the name "Gambler's Meadow" as its isolation made it an ideal place to gamble secretly. In the Meiji period the army used it, selling it in 1890 to Mitsubishi. The arrival of the railway increased the desirability of this barren wasteland as a business site, and after the 1923 earthquake, many other firms moved here.

Tokyo Station, designed by Kingo Tatsuno and completed in 1914, is supposedly based on the design of Amsterdam's Centraal Station. Its dome was damaged in the 1945 air raids and subsequently replaced by the polyhedron there today. The original reliefs adorning the domes above the north and south exits are worth a look. Opposite the station's south gate, you will find the shopping mall KITTE, with the **Tokyo City-i** information center on the first floor.

Did You Know?
During the Edo period, some of Japan's most powerful feudal lords resided in Marunouchi.

The English-speaking staff here, including Pepper the robot, offer advice and help to visitors.

For those interested in traditional Japanese arts and crafts, the **Idemitsu Museum of Arts** showcases the vast art collection of Sazo Idemitsu, the founder of one of Japan's largest oil companies. The regularly changing exhibits display astonishing examples of Japanese calligraphy and paintings, as well as Japanese and Chinese ceramics.

Tokyo City-i
🏛2-7-2 Marunouchi, Chiyoda
🕐8am–8pm daily
🌐en.tokyocity-i.jp

Idemitsu Museum of Arts
 🏛3-1-1 Marunouchi, Chiyoda **🕐**10am–4pm Tue–Thu, Sat & Sun (to 7pm Fri) **🌐**idemitsu-museum.or.jp

---

STAY

Aman Hotel
A glamorous high-rise hotel, with a hot tub in each room.

♥H6 **🏛**1-5-6 Otemachi, Chiyoda **🌐**aman.com

 ¥¥¥

The Tokyo Station Hotel
Next to Tokyo Station, this luxury hotel is an oasis of calm and peace.

♥H6 **🏛**1-9-1 Marunouchi, Chiyoda **🌐**thetokyostationhotel.jp

¥¥¥

Hotel Niwa Kanda
This hotel blends the look of a traditional Japanese inn with contemporary touches.

♥G4 **🏛**1-1-16 Kanda Misakicho, Chiyoda **🌐**hotelniwa.jp

 ¥¥¥

⑩

Tokyo Tower
東京タワー

📍 F9 🏠 4-2-8 Shibakoen, Minato 🚇 Akabanebashi 🕐 9am-11pm daily 🌐 tokyotower.co.jp

The Tokyo Tower was erected partly as a symbol of Japan's postwar boom, and as the sole broadcasting tower for the Kanto region. Two observation decks – the Main Deck at 492 ft (150 m) and the Top Deck at 820 ft (250 m) – offer views of Tokyo Bay, nearby districts of Shimbashi and Ginza, and Mount Fuji.

As a lofty symbol of the city, it may have been usurped by Tokyo Skytree (p135), but Tokyo Tower is worth a visit for the views, as well as for the cafés and shops in "Foot Town," the building at the tower's base.

To the east of Tokyo Tower extends Shiba Park, at the center of which lies **Zojo-ji Temple**, the Tokugawa family temple. It was founded in 1393, and Ieyasu Tokugawa moved it here in 1598 to protect his new capital. The present-day temple dates from 1974; nearby are the rebuilt Daimon (big gate)

JAPAN'S OTAKU (GEEK) CULTURE

Otaku is the Japanese term for people with obsessive interests, particularly in anime and manga, but also cameras, cars, pop stars, or electronics. Although originally a pejorative, like the English word "geek," an increasing number of people now self-identify as *otaku*. The subculture began in the 1980s, coinciding with the anime boom, as changing social mentalities led a section of Japanese society to consider themselves outcasts.

and the Sanmon (great gate), built in 1622, and the oldest wooden structure in Tokyo.

Zojo-ji Temple
🏠 4-7-35 Shibakoen 🕐 9am-5pm daily 🌐 zojoji.or.jp

⑪

Akihabara
秋葉原

📍 H4 🏠 Chiyoda 🚇 Akihabara

Also known as Akiba, Akihabara is the unofficial capital of some of Japan's beloved exports: electronics, video games, and anime. Tokyo's "Electric Town" reinvents itself every 15 to 20 years. During the postwar years it was a ramshackle market popular for its cheap radio sets, before changing to meet the demand for TVs and washing machines – so much so that as much as 10 per cent of all household appliances sold in Japan were bought here. In the 1980s, the district's major chain stores moved to the suburbs and the focus of Akiba's products moved away from household appliances to the new home computer craze.

As many people were also into video games, manga, and

anime, *otaku* (geek) culture began to find its way into Akiba, and by the late 1990s the community had found a home here. Today, Akihabara is a geek capital known around the world. As for the old "electronic heart" of the district, it has survived to this day, with many tiny stores still selling household appliances and gadgets of all kinds.

⑫

Kitanomaru Park
北の丸公園

📍 F5 🏠 1-1 Kitanomarukoen, Chiyoda 🚇 Kudanshita, Takebashi 🕐 24 hours daily

A former ground for the Imperial Palace Guard, this beautiful area became a park in 1969. Before entering, keep Tayasumon gate on your left, and walk straight to reach Chidorigafuchi (the west moat), one of Tokyo's most beautiful cherry-blossom viewing spots. Rowboats can be rented here.

Within Kitanomaru, there are a number of buildings. Near Tayasumon gate is the Nippon Budokan. Built for the 1964 Olympics martial arts competition, it is now used mostly for rock concerts. A short walk on is the **Science Museum**.

↑ Vibrantly colored neon signs lighting up the streets of Akihabara

People rowing on a moat and *(inset)* strolling in Kitanomaru Park during cherry-blossom season

The fun interactive exhibits include virtual bike rides and electricity demonstrations (explanations are in Japanese).

Five minutes beyond, over a main road and left down the hill, is the **National Museum of Modern Art**. The permanent collection comprises Japanese works from the 1868 Meiji Restoration to the present day; visiting exhibits are often excellent. Nearby is the National Museum of Modern Art's **Crafts Gallery**. Inside this 1910 Neo-Gothic brick building is an exquisite collection of modern workings of traditional Japanese crafts – pottery, lacquerware, and damascene (etched metal artifacts). Some pieces are for sale.

Science Museum
2-1 Kitanomarukoen, Chiyoda 9:30am–4:50pm Thu–Tue jsf.or.jp

National Museum of Modern Art
3-1 Kitanomarukoen, Chiyoda 10am–5pm Tue–Sun (to 8pm Fri & Sat) momat.go.jp

Crafts Gallery
1-1 Kitanomarukoen, Chiyoda 10am–5:30pm Tue–Sun momat.go.jp/cg

13

Koishikawa Korakuen Garden

小石川後楽園

F4 1-6-6 Koraku, Bunkyo Korakuen 9am–5pm daily tokyo-park.or.jp/teien/en/koishikawa

Korakuen, meaning "garden of delayed pleasure," is one of Tokyo's best traditional stroll gardens. Construction started in 1629 and finished 30 years later. Exiled Chinese scholar Zhu Shunsui helped design the Engetsukyo (full-moon) Bridge, a stone arch with a reflection resembling a full moon. Tsukenkyo Bridge, a copy of a bridge in Kyoto, is striking for the contrast between its vermilion and the surrounding deep-green forest.

The garden recreates larger landscapes in miniature, including Rozan, a Chinese mountain, and Kyoto's Oikawa River. In the middle of the pond is Horai island, a beautiful composition of stone and pine trees.

EAT

Sushi Shin
In the Mandarin Oriental, this Michelin-starred sushi restaurant offers a stunning view of the Tokyo skyline.

H6 2-1-1 Nihonbashi Muromachi, Chuo mandarinoriental.com

¥¥¥

Rokurinsha
Try the *tsukemen* at this popular ramen spot, where noodles are served separately and dunked into a thickened broth.

H7 1-9-1 Marunouchi, Chiyoda (03) 3286-016

¥¥¥

⑭ Yasukuni Shrine
靖国神社

🇶 F5 🏠 3-1-1 Kudankita, Chiyoda 🅂 Kudanshita 🕐 Mar-Oct: 6am-6pm daily; Nov-Feb: 6am-5pm daily 🇼 yasukuni.or.jp/english

The 2.5 million Japanese soldiers and civilians who have died in war since the Meiji Restoration in 1878 are enshrined at Yasukuni Jinja (Shrine of Peace for the Nation). It is a sobering place to visit.

Until the end of World War II Shinto was the official state religion, and the ashes of all who died in war were brought here regardless of the families' wishes. Controversially, the planners and leaders of Japan during World War II and the colonization of China and Korea are also enshrined here, including wartime prime minister Hideki Tojo.

Beside the shrine is the **Yushukan**, a museum dedicated to the war dead. Many exhibits put a human face on Japan at war: under a photo of a smiling young officer is a copy of his last letter home, and there are mementos of a nurse who died from overwork.

THE YASUKUNI CONTROVERSY

Since 1869, Yasukuni has honored the souls of those who have died in the service of Japan. The shrine is a place of remembrance for millions of Japanese who lost relatives fighting for their country. Among these, however, are about 1,000 war criminals from World War II. The perception that these souls are being honored has made Yasukuni a site of enormous controversy among Japan's neighbors who suffered greatly during the war as a result of their actions.

Still, romanticized paintings of Japanese soldiers in Manchuria and displays of guns, planes, and even a locomotive from the Thai-Burma Railway may be troubling to some.

Yushukan

 🕐 9am-4:30pm daily

⑮ Kanda Myojin Shrine
神田明神

🇶 H4 🏠 2-16-2 Sotokanda, Chiyoda 🅁🅂 Ochanomizu 🕐 24 hours daily 🇼 kanda myoujin.or.jp

Kanda Myojin is more than 1,200 years old, although the present structure is a reproduction built after the 1923 earthquake. The gate's guardian figures are tight-lipped archers: Udaijin on the right and Sadaijin on the left. Just inside the compound on the left is a big stone statue of Daikoku, one of the *shichi-fuku-jin* (seven lucky gods). Here, as always, he is sitting on top of two huge rice bales.

The vermilion shrine itself and its interior, all lacquer and gold, are very impressive. Early morning is the best time to glimpse the Shinto priests performing rituals. The Kanda Matsuri, celebrated in mid-May in odd numbered years, is one of the greatest and grandest of Tokyo's festivals – come early and be prepared for crowds.

Behind the main shrine is a **museum** containing relics from the long history of Kanda Myojin.

Museum

 🕐 9am-4pm daily

The *akane* (a special shade of vermilion) exterior of Kanda Myojin Shrine ↑

↑ The brightly colored main hall of Kanda Myojin Shinto Shrine in Tokyo's Chiyoda district

SHINTO

Japan's oldest religion, Shinto's core concept is that deities, *kami*, preside over all things in nature, be they living, dead, or inanimate. Today, there are few pure Shintoists, but *jinja* (shrines) still line waysides and Shinto rituals are observed alongside Buddhist practices.

SACRED GATES

The approach to the *jinja* transports worshippers from the secular to the sacred world. Vermilion torii often line the path, symbolizing gateways, and red-bibbed stone foxes stand guard at Inari Shrines. Inside the shrine's main complex, a *shimenawa*, a rope made of twisted rice straw, hangs over entrances to ward off evil and sickness.

HAIDEN AND HONDEN

At the *haiden*, or hall of worship, devotees pull on a bell rope, toss money into a box, clap twice to summon the resident *kami*, then stand in silent prayer for a few moments. The *kami* is believed to live in the shrine's *honden* (main sanctuary), but usually only the head priests are permitted to enter this hallowed space.

KANNUSHI

The Shinto priesthood *(kannushi)* tended to be passed down through families, and some of these dynasties *(shake)* are still connected with certain shrines. Usually dressed in white and orange robes, the *kannushi* perform purification ceremonies and other rituals.

CHARMS AND VOTIVE TABLETS

Good-luck charms, called *omamori*, are sold at shrines across Japan. Common themes relate to fertility, luck in examinations, general health, or safety while driving. The charm itself might be written on a piece of paper or thin wooden board and tucked into a cloth bag, which can be worn next to the body or placed somewhere relevant. Do not open the bag to read the charm or it will not work! Prayers or wishes can also be written on *ema* boards *(above)* and hung at the shrine.

→

A cloth bag containing a paper *omamori*

NORTHERN TOKYO

The northern districts of Ueno and Asakusa contain what remains of Tokyo's old Shitamachi (low city). Once the heart and soul of culture in Edo, Shitamachi became the subject of countless ukiyo-e woodblock prints. Merchants and artisans thrived here, as did Kabuki theater. As a consequence of this liberal atmosphere, the Yoshiwara red-light district moved to near Asakusa in the 17th century after the Great Fire of Meireki in 1657. By 1893, there were over 9,000 women living and working in this raucous area.

One of the last great battles in Japan took place in Ueno in 1868, when Emperor Meiji's forces defeated the Tokugawa shogunate. In 1872, Dr Anthonius Baudin, a Dutch military doctor, observed the area's natural beauty and successfully petitioned for the land to be turned into one of Japan's first public parks, rather than the proposed army hospital and cemetery. In 1876, Ueno Park was registered as Japan's oldest park. The park became a haven for art and thought, hosting the first and second National Industrial Exhibitions in 1877 and 1881 respectively, and becoming home to the Tokyo National Museum in 1882.

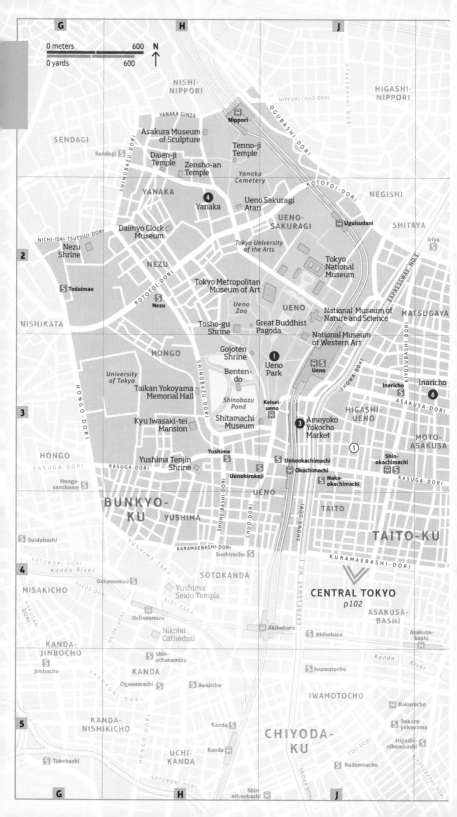

NORTHERN TOKYO

Must Sees
1 Ueno Park
2 Senso-ji Temple

Experience More
3 Ameyoko Yokocho Market
4 Yanaka
5 Tokyo Skytree

6 Inaricho and Kappabashi-dori

Eat
① Yamabe Okachimachi

Shop
② Kamata
③ Ganso

People enjoying *hanami* picnics under the cherry blossoms in Ueno Park ↑

❶

UENO PARK

上野公園

📍J3 🏠5-20 Uenokoen, Taito 🚃Uguisudani, Ueno 🚇Ueno

Erupting in a riot of pink cherry blossoms every spring, it is little wonder that Ueno Park, one of Tokyo's most beautiful green spaces, has figured in so many woodblock prints and stories. As well as its epehemeral, natural beauty, the park is home to a diverse array of permanent attractions, ranging from modern art museums to tranquil temples.

① Shitamachi Museum

🏠2-1 Uenokoen, Taito
🕐9:30am–4:30pm Tue-Sun 🌐taitocity.net/zaidan/shitamachi

Set on the shores of the Shinobazu Pond, this museum is dedicated to preserving the spirit and artifacts of Shitamachi Tokyo, the area around the Sumida River that was historically home to the lower classes. The 50,000 exhibits here include fascinating recreations of Edo-era shops, traditional toys, tools, and photographs, all donated by Shitamachi residents.

② Tokyo Metropolitan Art Museum

🏠8-36 Uenokoen, Taito
🕐9:30am–5:30pm daily
🚫1st and 3rd Mon of month
🌐tobikan.jp/en

Opened in 1926, this was the first public art museum in Japan, set up with the aid of a donation from industrialist Keitaro Sato. Today, houses an eclectic mix of Japanese and Western art. Entry is free, but there are admission fees for some special exhibitions, which in recent years have included a retrospective on the work of Norwegian painter Edvard

Munch (1863–1944), a look at Ukiyo-e woodblock prints, and shows featuring local artists.

③ National Museum of Nature and Science

🏠7-20 Uenokoen, Taito
🕐9am–5pm Tue-Sun
🌐kahaku.go.jp

Located in the northeast corner of Ueno Park, this museum is easy to spot from the life-sized model of a blue whale outside its entrance. Inside, the dinosaur exhibits are just as striking. Spread across four floors, the museum also has permanent exhibitions dedicated to topics such as the history and nature of Japan's islands, Japanese inventions from the Edo era onwards, and the Earth's origins.

④ National Museum of Western Art

🏠7-7 Uenokoen, Taito
🚫For renovations until 2022 🌐nmwa.go.jp

The fabulous NMWA was established in 1959 with the private collection of Japanese

Shinobazu Pond dominates the southernmost part of Ueno Park. The pond is split into three sections, with a temple located on the small island at its center. One of the sections is set aside for boating, another functions as a habitat for cormorants and migrating birds, and the third is covered in lotuses, which bloom in July.

Kiyomizu Kannon-do Temple

🏠 1-29 Uenokoen, Taito
🕐 9am-5pm Sun-Fri
🌐 kiyomizu.kaneiji.jp/english

Tokyo's oldest temple, Kannon-do was constructed during the early years of the Tokugawa shogunate as part of the Kan'ei-ji Temple complex, which at its peak included 68 structures

spread across what is now Ueno Park. Its signature feature is the "moon pine tree", cultivated to form a circle with its branches, and depicted in Hiroshige's famed Ukiyo-e series *100 Famous Views of Edo.*

> 💬 INSIDER TIP
> ## Sakura Spotting
>
> Some 1,000 sakura (cherry blossom) trees grow in Ueno Park. Over a brief period every spring, more than 2 million people visit the park for *hanami* (cherry blossom-viewing) picnics. To find out the best time to sit beneath the blossoming trees for your own *hanami* picnic, check the sakura forecast online *(sakura.weathermap.jp).*

businessman and art collector Kojiro Matsukata at its core. It features pre-18th-century paintings by Van Cleve, Van Ruysdael, and Rubens, as well as 19th- to early 20th-century pieces by Gaugin, Monet, Renoir, and Van Gogh.

Tosho-gu Shrine

🏠 9-88 Uenokoen, Taito
🕐 Mar-Sep: 9am-5:30pm daily; Oct-Feb: 9am-4:30pm daily 🌐 uenotoshogu.com

Built in the memory of Ieyasu Tokugawa in 1627, Tosho-gu Shrine is anything but subtle, featuring intricate carvings and gold foil. Mid-April to mid-May is the best time to visit, when the peony garden, which you must pay to enter, is in bloom. The shrine tends to be busiest around exam times, when students come here to pray for academic success.

Shinobazu Pond

🏠 5-20 Uenokoen, Taito
🕐 24 hours daily

With a circumference of 1 mile (2 km), the picturesque

The exterior of Honkan, the main building of the Tokyo National Museum

1 The Western-style works of Seiki Kuroda, including *Lakeside* (1897), are displayed in the Kuroda Memorial Hall.

2 The Gallery of Horyu-ji Treasures displays a collection of items from the temple, including rare statues dating from the 7th to 8th centuries.

3 The Honkan gallery has examples of ukiyo-e (woodblock prints), including these 14th-century portraits of the 36 Immortals of Poetry.

Must See

Heiseikan

Gallery of Horyu-ji Treasures

Honkan

Hyokeikan

Ueno Park

Toyokan

Locator Map
For more detail see p124

EAT

Yamabe Okachimachi

Instead of having lunch at one of the museum's pricey restaurants, head here for tasty *tonkatsu* (breaded pork).

◎ J3 **⌂** 6-2-6 Ueno **☎** (03) 5812-8076

¥ ¥ ¥

⑧

TOKYO NATIONAL MUSEUM

東京国立博物館

◎ J2 **⌂** 13-9 Uenokoen, Taito **ⓡⓢ** Ueno **◔** 9:30am–5pm Tue–Sun (to 9pm Fri & Sat) **ⓦ** tnm.jp

Seven buildings in the northeast corner of Ueno Park make up one of Tokyo's finest museums. Displaying everything from kimonos to archaeological finds, it provides an intriguing insight into Japan's history and culture.

More than 110,000 items make up the Tokyo National Museum's collection – the best assembly of Japanese art in the world – and the displays change frequently, with about 4,000 of these exhibits on public view at any one time. The museum also stages temporary exhibitions, covering art from around the world. If you only have a couple of hours to spare, stick to the second floor of the Honkan gallery. With audio guides, tours, and good signage in English, it's a great introduction to Japanese heritage. Those with the luxury of more time can explore the museum's other buildings, admiring ancient statues, Chinese ceramics and Impressionist paintings at their leisure.

Did You Know?

The Tokyo National Museum is the oldest museum in Japan.

A wooden statue of a Shinto deity on display in the Honkan gallery ↑

Exploring the Galleries

The Honkan is the museum's main building, housing Japanese art from ancient finds to modern masters. To its east is the Toyokan, housing non-Japanese Eastern art. The 1909 Beaux-Arts Hyokeikan is usually closed to the public and opens only for special exhibitions. Behind it is the Gallery of Horyu-ji Treasures, containing stunning objects from Horyu-ji Temple, near Nara, and the Heiseikan, which hosts exhibitions of archaeology. Access to all of the museum's buildings is included in the cost of one admission ticket, so set out to explore as much of this expansive museum as possible.

INSIDER TIP
Appy Travels

Download the Tohaku Navi app for six free guided tours around the museum. Choose which one you want to go on based on your interests.

A folding screen by Shuki Okamoto on display in the Honkan gallery ↑

TOP 4 UNMISSABLE EXHIBITS

Ukiyo-e
The Honkan has many poetic woodblock prints, dating from the 17th to 19th centuries.

Gilt Bronze Buddhas
Don't miss the collection of statues, all 12-16 inches (30-40 cm) tall, in the Gallery of Horyu-ji Treasures.

Korean Art
Ancient Korean pieces, some dating from the Bronze Age (100 BC to AD 300), are displayed in the Toyokan.

Haniwa Figures
From warriors to horses, you'll find charming examples of these clay figures in the Heiseikan.

Museum Galleries

Honkan

▷ Spanning two floors, the gallery is arranged chronologically to show the development of Japanese art from Jomon-era (from 10,000 BC) clay figures to 19th-century ukiyo-e woodblock prints depicting everything from landscapes to scenes from pleasure houses *(right)*. In between is everything from calligraphy and tea utensils to armor, as well as textiles used in Noh and Kabuki. The first floor is themed, with stunning exhibits of sculpture, lacquerware, swords, and Western-influenced modern art. The gallery is best navigated by working your way counterclockwise.

Toyokan

Opened in 1968, the Toyokan displays an excellent and eclectic collection of Asian art that ranges from textiles to ceramics. Many of the exhibits are from China and Korea – a consequence of these countries' historic ties with Japan. On the first floor, you'll find beautiful Buddhist statues, while the second floor houses sculptures from India, as well as artifacts from Egypt and the Middle East. A collection of Chinese art spans the third and fourth floors, and the final floor is dedicated to the history of Korea, including the rise and fall of the country's kings.

Heiseikan

Built in 1993 to commemorate the wedding of the Crown Prince – now Japan's 126th emperor – the Heiseikan houses major temporary exhibitions and a superb collection of Japanese archaeological artifacts, with items from 10,000 BC onward. The highlight of this collection is undoubtedly the Haniwa figures. Literally meaning "clay ring," Haniwa is used to describe earthenware sculptures that were made for 4th- to 7th-century tombs and were thought to protect the dead. The gallery also houses Jomon-period (14,500-300 BC) finds, including *dogu*, ceramic figures with bulging eyes.

Gallery of Horyu-Ji Treasures

◁ When the estates of Horyu-ji Temple *(p232)* near Nara were damaged during the Meiji reforms, the impoverished temple gave a number of its treasures to the imperial family in exchange for money to finance its repairs. Over 300 of those priceless treasures *(left)*, including rare and early Buddhist statues, masks used for Gigaku dances, and beautifully painted screens, are housed in this modern gallery, designed by Yoshio Taniguchi.

Kuroda Memorial Hall

Dedicated to Seiki Kuroda (1866-1924), this building displays the Western-style artist's oil paintings, sketches and other works. There is also a collection of letters from the painter, giving a greater insight into Kuroda's life and times.

2 🛍️

SENSO-JI TEMPLE
浅草寺

📍L3 🏠2-3-1 Asakusa, Taito 🚈Asakusa, Tobu-Asakusa 🚇Asakusa
⏰Main Hall: 6am–5pm daily (from 6:30am Oct–Mar); Nakamise-dori:
9:30am–7pm daily (individual store hours vary) 🌐senso-ji.jp

Popularly known as Asakusa Kannon, this is Tokyo's most sacred and spectacular temple, as well as the city's oldest. Although the buildings are impressive, it is the people following their daily rituals that make this place so special.

In AD 628, two fishermen pulled a small gold statue of Kannon, the Buddhist goddess of mercy, from the Sumida River. First, their master built a shrine to Kannon, then, in 645, the holy man Shokai built a temple to her. Senso-ji's fame, wealth, and size grew until Ieyasu Tokugawa bestowed upon it a large stipend of land. When the Yoshiwara pleasure quarter moved nearby in 1657, the temple became even more popular. Senso-ji survived the Great Kanto Earthquake of 1923 but not Allied bombing during World War II. Its main buildings are therefore relatively new, but follow the original Edo-era layout. Today, incense still wafts through the air, and people teem along the wide shopping avenue, Nakamise-dori, leading to the temple.

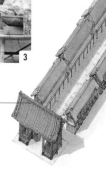
The Garden

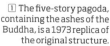

① The five-story pagoda, containing the ashes of the Buddha, is a 1973 replica of the original structure.

② Built of reinforced concrete in 1964, the two-story Hozo-mon gate has a treasure house upstairs holding a number of 14th-century Chinese sutras.

③ One of the shops lining the expansive Nakamise-dori selling souvenirs and traditional foods.

The Kaminari-mon, or "Thunder Gate," is topped by guardian statues of Fujin (right) and Raijin (left), which have elderly heads and young bodies.

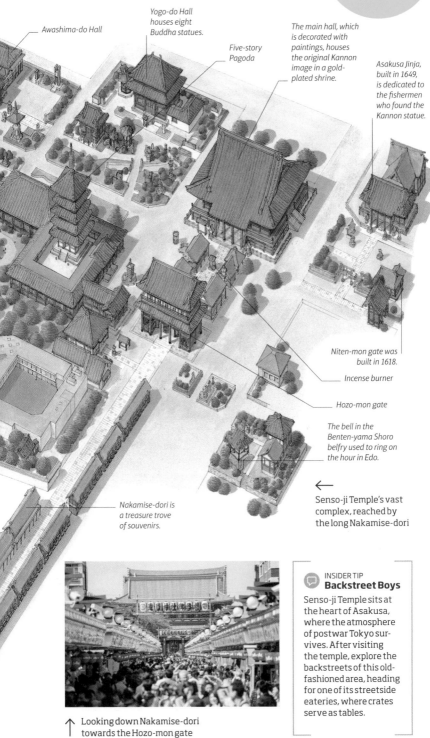

Awashima-do Hall

Yogo-do Hall houses eight Buddha statues.

Five-story Pagoda

The main hall, which is decorated with paintings, houses the original Kannon image in a gold-plated shrine.

Asakusa Jinja, built in 1649, is dedicated to the fishermen who found the Kannon statue.

Niten-mon gate was built in 1618.

Incense burner

Hozo-mon gate

The bell in the Benten-yama Shoro belfry used to ring on the hour in Edo.

← Senso-ji Temple's vast complex, reached by the long Nakamise-dori

Nakamise-dori is a treasure trove of souvenirs.

↑ Looking down Nakamise-dori towards the Hozo-mon gate

INSIDER TIP
Backstreet Boys

Senso-ji Temple sits at the heart of Asakusa, where the atmosphere of postwar Tokyo survives. After visiting the temple, explore the backstreets of this old-fashioned area, heading for one of its streetside eateries, where crates serve as tables.

EXPERIENCE MORE

❸ Ameyoko Yokocho Market
アメヤ横丁

📍J3 🏠4-9-14 Ueno, Taito
🚇Okachimachi, Ueno
🚊Ueno, Ueno-Okachimachi

One of the great bazaars in Asia, Ameyoko is a place where almost anything is available – and almost always at a discount. In Edo times, this was the place to come and buy *ame* (candy). After World War II, black-market goods – such as liquor, cigarettes, chocolates, and nylons – started appearing here, and *ame* acquired its second meaning as an abbreviation for American (*yoko* means "alley"). An area of tiny shops packed under the elevated train tracks, Ameyoko is no longer a black market, but still the place for bargain foreign brands. Clothes and accessories are concentrated under the tracks, while foods, including a huge range of seafood, line the street that follows the tracks.

---

❹ Yanaka
谷中

📍H2 🏠Taito 🚇Nippori

This quiet area is rewarding to wander through because it survived the Great Kanto Earthquake of 1923 and Allied bombing of World War II. It preserves something of the feel of old Shitamachi, with tightly packed houses set in narrow alleys, and traditional food stalls selling rice crackers and old-fashioned candy.

The large Yanaka Cemetery is a must-see in cherry-blossom season. Inside is Tenno-ji, a temple with a large bronze Buddha dating from 1690. To the west of Tenno-ji Temple lies the **Asakura Museum of Sculpture**, home of sculptor Fumio Asakura (1883–1964). On the second floor is a delightful room full of his small statues of one of his favorite subjects – cats – but the garden is the real highlight, with its traditional composition of water and stone.

To the north, Yanaka Ginza, the neighborhood's shopping street, has traditional stores and family-run places to eat. Hidden amid the neighborhood's old backstreets, along with several trendy cafés and bars is **SCAI the Bathhouse**, a leading contemporary art gallery set in a former public bathhouse. Located a short walk away from here is the understated **Daimyo Clock Museum** where 100 Edo-era clocks are lovingly preserved and presented.

SHOP

Kamata

Made in Kappabashi, Kamata's famous knives are crafted from the same metal and to the same principles as samurai swords. A must for all keen chefs.

📍K3 🏠2-12-6 Matsugaya, Taito
🌐kap-kam.com

Ganso

This Kappabashi store stocks *sanpuru* (plastic food), seen in Japanese restaurant windows. Ganso also sells kits with which you can make your own fake food.

📍B2 🏠3-7-6 Nishiasakusa, Taito
🌐ganso-sample.com

> **JAPANESE FUNERAL CUSTOMS**
>
> When a Japanese person dies, the body is brought back home to spend one final night on his or her own futon. The next morning, it is taken to the service. At the wake, guests offer gifts of money and, after the cremation, the family use a special pair of chopsticks to pick the bones out and transfer them to an urn. Remembrance ceremonies are held in the following years on the anniversary of the death.

Asakura Museum of Sculpture

♿ 🏠7-18-10 Yanaka, Taito
📞(03) 3821-4549 ⏰9:30am-4:30pm Tue-Wed & Fri-Sun

SCAI the Bathhouse

🏠6-1-23 Yanaka, Taito
⏰ Noon-6pm Tue-Sat
🌐scaithebathhouse.com

Daimyo Clock Museum

♿ 🏠2-1-27 Yanaka, Taito
📞(03) 3821-6913 ⏰Jan 15-Jun 30 & Oct 1-Dec 24: 10am-4pm Tue-Sun

↑ Unassuming entrance to the Asakura Museum of Sculpture

5

Tokyo Skytree
東京スカイツリー

M3 1-1-2 Oshiage, Sumida Tokyo Skytree, Oshiage 8am-9:45pm tokyoskytree.jp

At 2,080 ft (634 m), this is the tallest structure in Japan. Its main function is broadcasting, but the Skytree also hosts a large mall, aquarium, planetarium, and restaurants. The Tembo Deck, at 1,150 ft (350 m) above ground level, offers 360-degree views across Tokyo. Another viewing deck, Tembo Galleria, is the highest observation deck in Japan at 1,475 ft (450 m). On a clear day you can see as far as Mount Fuji.

6

Inaricho and Kappabashi-dori
稲荷町とかっぱ橋通り

K3 Taito Inaricho, Tawaramachi

Inaricho is the Tokyo headquarters for wholesale religious goods. Small wooden boxes to hold Buddhas and family photos, paper lanterns, bouquets of brass flowers *(jouka)*, Shinto household shrines, and even prayer beads can be found here.

Kappabashi-dori, named after the mythical water imp *(kappa)* who supposedly helped build a bridge *(bashi)* here, is Tokyo's center for kitchenware and a source of the *sanpuru* (plastic food) you'll see displayed in almost every restaurant window across Japan. Although the "food" is for sale, prices are much higher than for the real thing.

→ Slender silhouette of the Tokyo Skytree, towering above the city's skyline

BEYOND THE CENTER

Must See

❶ Toyosu Fish Market

Experience More

❷ Gotoh Museum
❸ Japan Folk Crafts Museum
❹ Ikebukuro
❺ Toden Arakawa Line
❻ Ebisu
❼ Sengaku-ji Temple
❽ Ghibli Museum
❾ Rikugi-en Garden
❿ Ryogoku
⓫ Odaiba

Greater Tokyo, home to an astonishing 35 million people, is by far the biggest urban area on the planet. The districts beyond the center of Tokyo are some of its most characteristic – whether they are the new pop cultural hot spot of Ikebukuro, the manmade islands of Tokyo bay, or the hip neighborhoods of Ebisu, Daikanyama, and Meguro on the west side. Here, too, you will find some of the city's most exciting developments, such as Toyosu, the location of one of Tokyo's largest shopping malls and the vast fish market. Nearby, futuristic Odaiba and its surrounds are a breath of fresh air from the frenetic inner city.

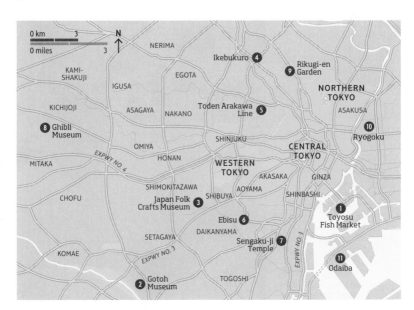

TOYOSU FISH MARKET

豊洲市場

🏠 6-6-2 Toyosu, Koto 🚇 Shijo-mae 🕐 5am–5pm Mon–Sat

The largest market of its kind in the world and the beating heart of Japan's gastronomic culture, the Toyosu fish market turns over some 1,200 tons of seafood every single day. Most visitors come here not to buy fish, but to soak up vibrant market life and to eat fantastic seafood.

After years of delays, this state-of-the-art fish market opened in 2018 in Toyosu, just 1 mile (2 km) away from the previous site at Tsukiji. Sleeker and less chaotic than its predecessor, Toyosu's purpose-designed layout eliminates previous tensions between tourists and market traders. Head to the observation deck to watch the daily tuna auction (book in advance). It takes place from 5:30am and lasts up to an hour, with huge fish laid out in long rows for buyers. While visitors are not able to purchase directly from the market, many sushi vendors that plied their trade in the shadow of the old Tsukiji market have also made the move over to Toyosu, providing hungry visitors with some of the freshest sushi imaginable.

TUNA FISH SUPPLIES

Toyosu specializes in *maguro* (tuna) from as far away as New Zealand and the North Atlantic. The Japanese consume about 30 per cent of the annual global 1.7 million-ton tuna catch, and eat 80 per cent of it raw, as sashimi, which requires the best cuts of fish. The Pacific Ocean's south blue fin tuna, a favorite for sashimi, is declining steadily in spite of efforts to manage numbers. The Japanese fishing industry has come under a great deal of scrutiny, with other governments exerting pressure on Japan to keep an eye on its activities.

→

Bustling stalls laden with fresh fish in the Toyosu Fish Market

1 Market traders can be seen slicing fish using a huge knife requiring two people. Cutting the fish in this way serves to demonstrate its freshness to potential buyers.

2 Buyers browse tuna fish before bidding on them.

3 As well as fish, Toyosu's traders sell fruit and vegetables, such as wasabi, in a designated area.

Did You Know?

The tuna auction area is cooled down to almost 0° C (32° F) - bring a sweater!

↑ A skilled chef preparing different kinds of sushi at a restaurant in Tokyo

SUSHI AND SASHIMI

Newcomers to Japan are often both fascinated and intimidated by these ubiquitous dishes. While sashimi denotes sliced fillets of raw fish served without rice, there are several different types of sushi (usually written with the suffix "-zushi") in which cold, lightly sweetened and vinegared rice is topped or wrapped up with raw fish or other items, such as pickles or cooked meat.

NIGIRI-ZUSHI

Thin slices of raw fish are laid over molded fingers of rice with a dab of wasabi in between. Dip it in soy sauce, and consume in one mouthful.

CHIRASHI-ZUSHI

The "scattered" style involves a colorful combination of toppings, including fish, chunks of omelet, and vegetables, artfully arranged on a deep bed of cold rice.

MAKI-ZUSHI

"Rolled" sushi is very familiar outside Japan. Rice is combined with slivers of fish and other morsels, and rolled up in a sheet of toasted seaweed (nori).

SASHIMI

Sliced fillets of fresh uncooked fish may be served alone. Sashimi is delicate and creamy, and the only accompaniments should be soy sauce, wasabi, daikon (radish), and a shiso leaf.

POPULAR FISH IN JAPAN

Of the 3,000 or so varieties of fish eaten in Japan, the most common are maguro (tuna), tai (sea bream), haze (gobies), buri (yellowtail), saba (mackerel), crustaceans such as ebi (shrimp) and kani (crab), and fish that are usually salted such as sake (salmon) and tara (cod). You'll find these fish on menus and market stalls all year round, but some fish are seasonal treats. In spring, the ayu (sweet-fish) – a river fish traditionally caught by trained cormorants – is enjoyed. Katsuo (skipjack tuna) is available in spring and summer, unagi (eel) in midsummer, and sanma (saury) in the fall. Winter, meanwhile, is the time for dojo (loach), anko (angler fish), and fugu (blowfish), prized for its delicate flavor but also feared for deadly toxins in its liver and ovaries.

EXPERIENCE MORE

Gotoh Museum
五島美術館

📍 3-9-25 Kaminoge, Setagaya-ku 🚇 Tokyu Denentoshi line from Shibuya Stn to Futago-Tamagawa, then Tokyu Oimachi line to Kaminoge Stn ⏰ 10am–5pm Tue–Sun 🌐 gotoh-museum.or.jp

Set in a pleasant hillside garden, this museum showcases the private collection of the late chairman of the Tokyu Corporation, Keita Gotoh. He was originally attracted to Buddhist calligraphy, particularly that of 16th-century priests. His collection contains many examples of this work, called *bokuseki*. Also included are ceramics, calligraphy, paintings, and metalwork mirrors; items are changed several times a year. The museum's most famous works, however, are scenes

Did You Know?

Keita Gotoh was a school teacher before he entered the world of business.

from 12th-century scrolls of *The Tale of Genji*, painted by Fujiwara Takayoshi, which have been designated National Treasures. They are shown once a year, usually in "Golden Week" (April 29–May 5). The museum is closed during summer maintenance, when exhibitions change over, and on New Year's Day.

Japan Folk Crafts Museum
日本民芸館

📍 4-3-33 Komaba, Meguro-ku 📞 (03) 3467-4527 🚇 Komaba-Todaimae Stn, Keio Inokashira line ⏰ 10am–4:30pm Tue–Sun

Known to the Japanese as Mingeikan, this small but excellent museum was set up by art historian Muneyoshi Soetsu Yanagi. The museum building, designed by Yanagi and completed in 1936, uses black tiles and white stucco outside. The criteria for inclusion in the museum's collection are that the object should be the work of an anonymous maker, produced for daily use, and representative of the region from which it comes.

Items ranging from woven baskets to ax sheaths, iron kettles, pottery, and kimonos present a fascinating view of rural life. There are also themed exhibits, such as 20th-century ceramics or Japanese textiles, and a room dedicated to Korean Yi-dynasty work. A small gift shop sells fine crafts and some books.

DRINK

Belg Aube Toyosu
A café with a good range of Belgian beers and European dishes such as Iberico ham, duck confit, and, of course, mussels.

📍 LaLaport Toyosu 1F, 2-4-9 Toyosu, Koto 📞 (03) 6910-1275

Hops125
One of Tokyo's most exciting craft beer venues, Hops125 features an array of local and international beers, with more than ten on tap at any time.

📍 1-21-18 Ebisu, Shibuya 📞 (03) 3447-1496

Spring Balley Brewing
The beers on tap at this cool brewpub include everything from crisp pils and IPAs to experimental fruit beers.

📍 Log Road Daikanyama, Daikanyamacho, Shibuya 📞 (03) 6416-4960

← Exterior of the Japan Folk Crafts Museum, designed by its art-historian founder

4

Ikebukuro
池袋

🏛 Toshima 🚇Ⓢ Ikebukuro

Ikebukuro has become one of Japan's most popular *otaku* (geek) districts. Here, you'll find the flagship store for the country's biggest anime goods retailer – Animate – as well as several locations of their Animate Cafe, where the anime-themed decor, menu, and exclusive merchandise change every few months.

While Tokyo's most famous geek district Akihabara (p118), is more popular with men, Ikebukuro is frequented more by women, as many of the stores in the area focus on media with a large female fanbase. The district even has a butler café (*www.butlers-cafe.jp*) in place of Akihabara's typical maid versions.

But even non-*otaku* will enjoy exploring this lively leisure district, which is full of shops, arcades, bars, and restaurants. There's also the incredible **Sunshine City** mall, which has an aquarium, observation deck, and amusement park, plus a long list of stores and restaurants. With all of this activity, the Ikebukuro district has firmly earned a spot on the map of cool Tokyo highlights.

Sunshine City
🏛 3-1 Higashiikebukuro
🕐 Times vary, see website
🌐 sunshinecity.jp

5

Toden Arakawa Line
都電荒川線

Ⓢ Many stations

In 1955, 600,000 people a day were riding the dozens of tram lines that crisscrossed the city. Now the 8-mile (13-km) Toden Arakawa Line is one of only two that remain, along with the privately owned Tokyu Setagaya line. The others were eliminated as old-fashioned in the modernization for the 1964 Olympics.

The Toden Arakawa Line runs from Waseda in the west to Minowabashi in the east and costs ¥170 for each trip. Near the Waseda end of the line is the quiet stroll garden of Higo-Hosokawa Teien. There are few outstanding sights en route, but the pleasure of this tram ride lies in seeing a quieter, residential side to Tokyo. Near the Arakawa Yuenchi-mae stop, past tightly packed houses, is a modest amusement park, Arakawa Yuen Amusement Park (closed for renovations until 2021). Opposite the Arakawa Nanachome stop is Arakawa Nature Park.

↑ A tram trundling along the Toden Arakawa Line at night

6

Ebisu
恵比寿

🏛 Shibuya 🚇Ⓢ Ebisu

The completion of Yebisu Garden Place, a commercial and residential center, in the mid-1990s brought this area to life. The **Tokyo Photographic Art Museum**, to the right of the entrance, has a permanent collection of work by Japanese and foreign photographers. The center has a Mitsukoshi store, numerous boutiques, two cinemas, a theater, and restaurants. To the left of Mitsukoshi is the small **Yebisu Beer Museum** containing exhibits and videos about beer worldwide and in Japan.

Tokyo Photographic Art Museum
♿ 🏛 1-13-3 Mita, Meguro
🕐 10am–6pm daily
🌐 topmuseum.jp

↑ The illuminated entrance gate to the Sunshine City mall, with its numerous restaurants and shops

Did You Know?

The Ebisu district was named after the Yebisu Beer brand.

Yebisu Beer Museum
 4-20-1 Ebisu, Shibuya ⏰11am–6pm Tue–Sun (last adm for tours 5:10pm) 🌐sapporobeer.jp/english/brewery/y_museum

---

7 Sengaku-ji Temple

Sengaku-ji Temple
泉岳寺

📍2-11-1 Takanawa, Minato Ⓢ Sengaku-ji ⏰Museum: 9am–4:30pm (to 4pm Oct–Mar) 🌐sengakuji.or.jp

This is the site of the climax of Japan's favorite tale of loyalty and revenge, retold in the play *Chushingura* and many movies. Lord Asano was sentenced to death by seppuku

(disembowelment) for drawing his sword when goaded by Lord Kira. Denied the right to seek revenge, 47 of Asano's retainers (or ronin), led by Oishi Kuranosuke, plotted in secret. In 1702, they attacked Kira's house and beheaded him, presenting the head to Asano's grave at Sengaku-ji Temple. They in turn were sentenced to seppuku and are buried here. Inside the temple gate is the well where the ronin washed Kira's head. Farther ahead on the right are the retainers' graves. Back at the base of the steps is a museum with artifacts from the incident, which you can visit for a fee.

8

Ghibli Museum
三鷹の森ジブリ美術館

📍1-1-83 Shimorenjaku, Mitaka 🚉Mitaka ⏰10am–6pm Wed–Mon 🚫Dec 27–Jan 2 🌐ghibli-museum.jp

Japanese animation company Studio Ghibli is known across the world for its Oscar-winning anime – some of them charming coming-of-age

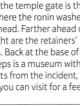

→ Statue of ronin leader Oishi Kuranosuke at Sengaku-ji

EAT

T.Y. Harbor
Serving up burgers, steaks, and crab cakes on the waterfront, T.Y. Harbor also brews its own beer.

📍2-1-3 Higashi-shinagawa, Shinagawa 🌐tysons.jp/tyharbor/en

Tokyo Ramen Kokugi-kan
Six ramen shops offering Sapporo-style miso ramen, Hakata-style *tonkotsu* (pork bone) ramen, and more.

📍Aqua City Odaiba 5F, 1-7-1 Daiba, Minato 📞(03) 3599-4700

Odaiba Takoyaki Museum
Seven different stalls dish up variations on the classic fried batter and octopus balls.

📍Decks Tokyo Beach, 1-6-1 Daiba, Minato 🌐odaiba-decks.com/en/takoyaki

tales, and others high fantasy epics. The studio's founder, Hayao Miyazaki, designed this museum with the aim of making fans feel as if they have stepped straight into the sets of *Princess Mononoke* (1997), *Spirited Away* (2001), and many more of his films. The museum features a whimsical children's playground, a cinema showing short films, and collections of original drawings from the famous films, as well as charming cafés and shops.

Tickets must be booked in advance online as none are available at the gate.

Rikugi-en Garden
六義園

🏠 6-16-3 Honkomagome, Bunkyo 🅰🅂 Komagome 🕒 9am–5pm daily 🌐 tokyo-park.or.jp/teien/en/rikugien

One of the finest Edo-era stroll gardens, Rikugi-en Garden was built by Yoshiyasu Yanagisawa, grand chamberlain of the fifth shogun, from 1695. The fine design recreates 88 landscapes in miniature from famous *waka* (31-syllable poems), so the vista changes every few steps. Sit on one of the many seats and enjoy the views while listening to songbirds overhead.

LIFE IN A SUMO STABLE

At the age of about 15, boys are accepted into a *beya*. Sumo society is supremely hierarchical, with newcomers serving senior wrestlers as well as cleaning and cooking for the entire *beya*. Junior practices may start at 4am. The day's single meal of *chanko-nabe*, a large stew, comes about noon, with juniors getting what the seniors leave. After, more work follows.

Ryogoku
両国

🏠 Sumida 🅰🅂 Ryogoku

A great entertainment and commerce center during the Edo era, Ryogoku is now a quiet place. However, it is still the best place to find the residents who have long made this district famous: sumo wrestlers. Many *beya* (sumo stables) are here, and it is not unusual to see the athletes walking the streets in *yukata* (light cotton kimonos) and *geta* (wooden sandals).

The Kokugikan sumo arena is also home to the **Sumo Museum**, which is lined with portraits of all the *yokozuna* (grand champions). Beside the stadium is the fascinating **Edo-Tokyo Museum**. Two zones trace everyday life in Edo and then Tokyo, as Edo was renamed in 1868. The exhibits have explanations in Japanese and English. The route around the museum starts by crossing a traditional arched wooden bridge, a replica of Nihonbashi. There are life-sized reconstructed buildings, plus scale-model dioramas showing everything from the house of a *daimyo* (feudal lord) to a section of Shitamachi. Models of the boats that once plied the Sumida River give an idea of

the river's significance. In the media section is a step-by-step example of how ukiyo-e wood-block prints *(p150)* were made.

The **Sword Museum** is full of fine Japanese swords, some dating from the 12th century. Also displayed are decorated hilts and old Japanese texts, illustrated with beautiful drawings, explaining the finer points of sword-making.

Opened in 2016, the **Sumida Hokusai Museum** is devoted to the ukiyo-e artist Katsushika Hokusai – perhaps most famous for his print *The Great Wave off Kanagawa*. The museum has an amazing array of Hokusai's art as well as videos and multilingual information about his life.

Sumo Museum
🏠 1-3-28 Yokoami, Sumida 🕒 10am–4:30pm Mon–Fri 🌐 sumo.or.jp

Edo-Tokyo Museum
♿ 🏠 1-4-1 Yokoami, Sumida 🕒 9:30am–5:30pm Tue–Sun 🌐 edo-tokyo-museum.or.jp

Sword Museum
♿ 🏠 1-12-9 Yokoami, Sumida 🕒 9:30am–5pm Tue–Sun 🌐 touken.or.jp/english

→

The distinctive bulk of the Tokyo Big Sight building, in Odaiba

↑ A bridge crossing a pond in the verdant Rikugi-en Garden

Sumida Hokusai Museum
 2-7-2 Kamezawa, Sumida ⏰9:30am–5:30pm Tue–Sun Ⓦhokusai-museum.jp

---

⑪
Odaiba
お台場

🅰Koto 🄯Odaiba-kaihinkoen 🚌From Asakusa 10:15am–4pm, every 40–50 mins

When the West began to force Japan to open up in the 1850s, the shogunate constructed a series of *daiba* (obstructions) across Tokyo harbor to keep foreign ships out. Odaiba (also known as Daiba), an island at the mouth of Tokyo Bay, takes its name from these. Odaiba is reached via the Yurikamome monorail, which

climbs a loop before joining Rainbow Bridge over Tokyo Harbor. Odaiba-Kaihinkoen, the first station, leads to Tokyo's only beach. Nearby is the Daisan Daiba Historic Park, with the remains of the original obstructions. A short walk west is Decks Tokyo Beach, with many restaurants and shops plus Joypolis, a Sega center full of the latest electronic games. In front of Decks is the station for water buses from Asakusa and Hinode Pier. Located in Aomi, the **National Museum of Emerging Science and Innovation**, better known as Miraikan, has interactive robots, biotechnology, and ecological exhibits. The Fuji TV building dominates the area.

At Aomi Station is the Palette Town development, including Venus Fort, a shopping mall, Mega Web's Toyota City Showcase, with driving simulators, and teamLab Borderless, which features interactive art projections. The Wanza Ariake building has shops and restaurants and is connected to Tokyo Big Sight Station, which takes its name from the Tokyo Big Sight conference center.

National Museum of Emerging Science and Innovation
🅰2-3-6 Aomi, Koto ⏰10am–5pm Wed–Mon 🚫Dec 28–Jan 1 Ⓦmiraikan.jst.go.jp

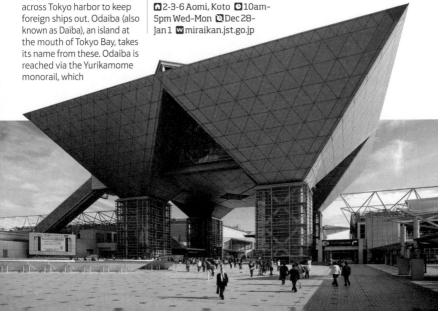

EXPERIENCE
JAPAN

Arashiyama bamboo forest, Kyoto

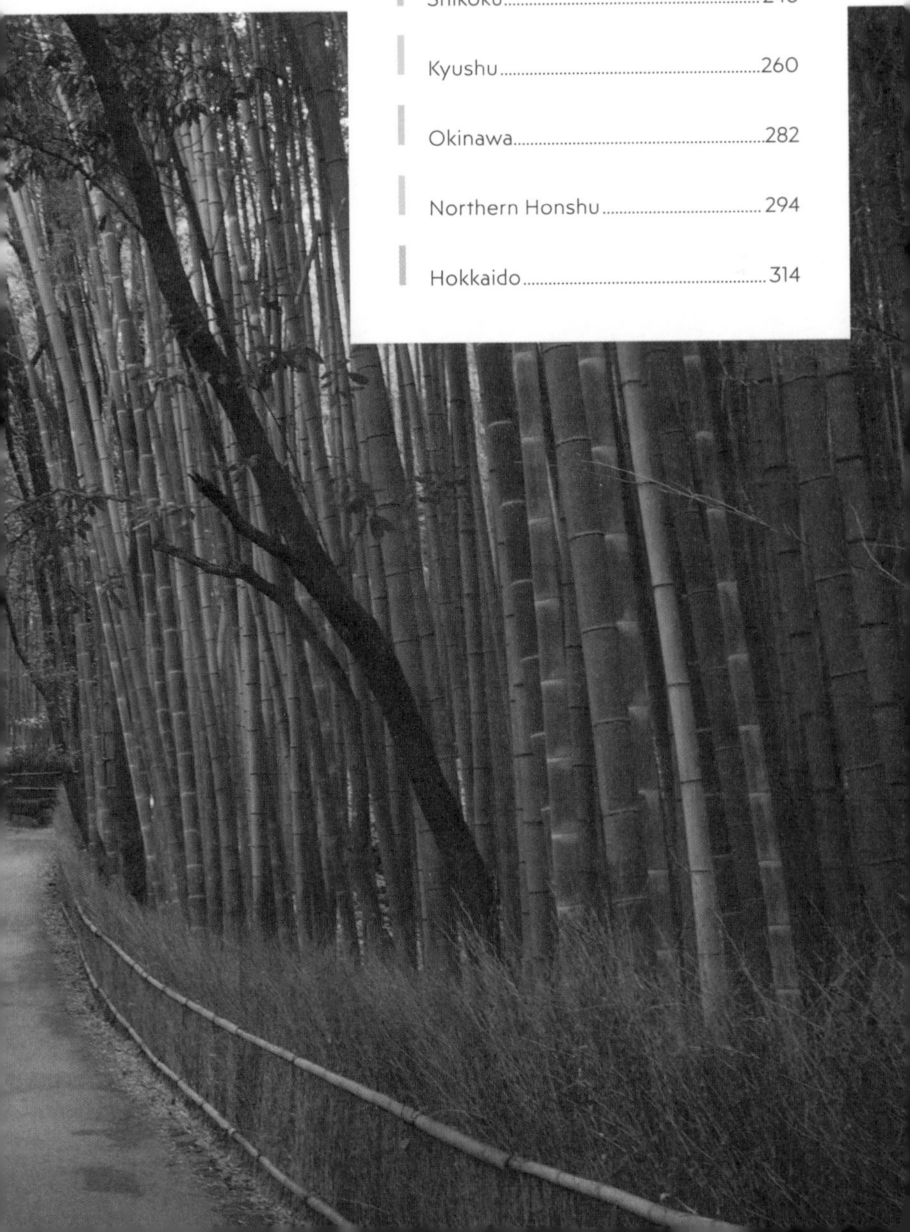

CENTRAL HONSHU

Lying between Kyoto and Tokyo's sprawling suburbs, Central Honshu epitomizes the contrasts of Japan today. Its densely populated coastal belt includes Yokohama and Nagoya, the country's second- and fourth-largest cities, while the interior contains its highest, wildest mountains, with Mount Fuji as well as the Northern and Southern Japanese Alps, with many peaks over 10,000 ft (3,000 m).

During the Edo period five post roads crossed the region, two of which – the Tokaido and the Nakasendo – linked Edo (Tokyo) and Kyoto. Feudal lords were required to spend half their time in Edo, so long processions traveled the roads, and checkpoints and post towns grew up along the route. The Tokaido ran via Yokohama, Hakone, and Shizuoka, while the Nakasendo headed inland through the Kiso Valley, and can still be walked. The settlements en route are relatively accessible, yet remote enough to remain unspoiled. The post towns of Kiso and the thatched villages of Shokawa offer Edo-period architecture, while Takayama and Chichibu attract thousands to their historic festivals, which originated in the 16th and 18th centuries respectively. The region's roots are also evident in the traditional crafts produced here: lacquerware in Takayama, Noto, and Kiso; carving in Kamakura; and *yosegi-zaiku* (Japanese marquetry) in Hakone. Until the 1970s, silkworms were raised in Shokawa and Chichibu, and silk is still dyed in Kanazawa.

WESTERN
HONSHU
p210

CENTRAL HONSHU

Must Sees

1. Yokohama
2. Kamakura
3. Mount Fuji and the Fuji Five Lakes
4. Takayama
5. Kanazawa

Experience More

6. Narita
7. Kawagoe
8. Hakone
9. Izu Peninsula
10. Nagoya
11. Shizuoka
12. Inuyama
13. Shokawa Valley
14. Gifu
15. Matsumoto
16. Nagano
17. Kamikochi
18. Chichibu-Tama-Kai National Park
19. Eihei-ji Temple
20. Noto Peninsula

↑ The modern skyline of Yokohama's Minato Mirai 21 district

①

YOKOHAMA

横浜

🅰F5 **🅰Kanagawa Prefecture** **🚇🚌🚢Yokohama** **ℹIn Yokohama Stn by west exit; www.yokohamajapan.com**

Japan's second-largest city, Yokohama has been a center for shipping, trade, foreign contact, and modern ideas since the mid-19th century. Formerly a small fishing village on the Tokaido road, it was made a treaty port in 1859; there followed an influx of foreign traders, making it the biggest port in Asia by the early 1900s.

①

Landmark Tower

🅰2-2-1 Minato Mirai **🚇🚈Yokohama, Sakuragicho** **🕙10am–9pm daily** **🌐yokohama-landmark.jp**

Landmark Tower is the focal point of the futuristic Minato Mirai 21 district, an area of redeveloped docks that is particularly lively at the weekend. Built in 1993, the tower is Japan's fourth-tallest structure at 971 ft (296 m). Reached by a super-fast elevator, traveling at 2,500 ft (750 m) per minute, the 69th-floor public lounge has a spectacular 360-degree view. Within the tower is the enormous Landmark Plaza

shopping mall, which houses a number of luxury brands, anime stores, and restaurants.

②

Yokohama Museum of Art

🅰3-4-1 Minato Mirai **🚇🚈Yokohama, Sakuragicho** **🕙10am–6pm Fri-Wed** **🌐yokohama.art.museum**

Yokohama's role as a meeting point between East and West means that it has long been a hub for the exchange of ideas. The Yokohama Museum of Art, designed by Kenzo Tange, celebrates this legacy with its impressive collection of modern art and photography. The museum is highly engaged

with Yokohama itself, and focuses on Japanese artists with connections to the city, including Shiko Imamura, Kanzan Shimomura, and Chizuko Yoshida.

③

NYK Maritime Museum

🅰3-9 Kaigandōri **🚈Bashamichi** **🕙10am–5pm Tue-Sun** **🌐nyk.com**

Founded in the 1880s, Nippon Yusen Kaisha (NYK) is one of the world's largest shipping companies. The quirky NYK Maritime Museum – with its exquisitely detailed model ships – celebrates the company's history and Yokohama's connection to the sea, showing how maritime commerce has revolutionized marine technology, trade, and politics.

> 🔍 HIDDEN GEM
> ### Oodles of Noodles
> True ramen obsessives should make a stop at Yokohama's cup noodle museum *(www.cupnoodles-museum.jp)*, where visitors can fry their own ramen and design their own cup.

④ Hikawa Maru

🏠 Yamashita Park Ⓢ Nippon Odori, Motomachi Chukagai 🕐 10am–5pm Tue–Sun 🌐 nyk.com

Originally built in 1930 as a cruise liner and light cargo ship, the Hikawa Maru spent World War II operating as a floating hospital and in its 30 years of service crossed the Pacific 254 times. The restored liner is now permanently docked in Yokohama, where visitors can stroll the decks, inspect the elegant wood-paneled cabins and soak up the Art Deco glamour of the lounge. Those who are technically minded will enjoy the opportunity to get close to the vessel's mighty engines.

Did You Know?

Japan's first railroad was constructed in 1872, connecting Yokohama to Tokyo.

⑤ Kantei-byo Temple

🏠 140 Yamashitacho Ⓢ Nippon Odori, Motomachi Chukagai 🕐 9am–7pm daily 🌐 yokohama-kanteibyo.com

Few sites better evoke Yokohama's cosmopolitan roots than Kantei-byo, the temple that has served as the heart of the city's Chinese community – the largest in Japan – for 150 years. This popular temple functions as a spiritual, cultural, and social hub, and is particularly atmospheric during Chinese New Year.

⑥ Yokohama Foreign General Cemetery

🏠 96 Yamatecho Ⓢ Motomachi Chukagai 🕐 10am–5pm Tue–Sun 🌐 yfgc-japan.com

Yokohama Foreign General Cemetery was founded in 1854 following the death of an American marine. Among the 4,500 tombs in the early 20th-century graveyard is that of Edmund Morel, the English engineer who helped build Japan's first railroads.

⑦   Sankei-en Garden

🏠 58 Honmokusannotani 🚌 Sankeien-iriguchi 🕐 9am–5pm daily 🌐 sankeien.or.jp

With its ponds, bamboo groves, rivers, and meandering trails, this hideaway transports visitors back to ancient Japan. Among the garden's architectural treasures is a 15th-century pagoda. Constructed in Kyoto, it was relocated to Sankei-en in 1914.

Opened to the public in 1906, the entire garden was once the home of Tomitaro "Sankei" Hara (1868–1939), a wealthy silk merchant. His personal lodgings – a sprawling complex featuring dozens of traditional tatami rooms, overlooking a private lawn – can be toured at the site.

↑ Visitors, under the cover of umbrellas, paying their respects to the Great Buddha

2

KAMAKURA

鎌倉

🅰F5 🚇Kanagawa Prefecture 🚉Kamakura, Kita-Kamakura 🚌 ℹAt Kamakura Stn; www.city.kamakura.kanagawa.jp/visitkamakura/en

A seaside town of temples and wooded hills, Kamakura was Japan's administrative capital from 1192 until 1333. Favored by artists and writers, Kamakura has numerous antique and crafts shops, and in cherry-blossom season and on summer weekends, it teems with visitors.

💬 INSIDER TIP
Getting Around

Some parts of the town are best explored on foot but, with so many hills, it's worth buying a one-day bus pass from Kamakura Station. The energetic can also rent a bicycle from here.

①

Great Buddha

🏠2-2-8 Hase 🚉Hase ⏰Apr-Sep: 8am-5:30pm daily; Oct-Mar: 8am-5pm daily 🌐kotoku-in.jp

The Great Buddha (Daibutsu) is Kamakura's most famous

> **Did You Know?**
> ――
> The Great Buddha has shock absorbers in its base to protect it from earthquakes.

sight. Cast in 1252, the bronze statue of the Amida Buddha is 44 ft (13.5 m) tall. Its proportions are distorted so that it seems balanced to those in front of it – this use of perspective may show Greek influence (via the Silk Road).

②

Hase-dera Temple

🏠3-11-2 Hase 🚉Hase ⏰Mar-Sep: 8am-5:30pm daily (Oct-Feb: to 5pm) 🌐hasedera.jp/en

Hase-dera Temple is home to 11-faced Kannon, bodhisattva of mercy. The Treasure House displays Muromachi-era

carvings of the 33 incarnations of Kannon. There is also a sutra repository; rotating the sutras is said to earn as much merit as reading them.

The 1264 bell is the town's oldest. Below it is a hall dedicated to Jizo, guardian of children, surrounded by countless statues to children who have died.

③

Myohon-ji Temple

🏠1-15-1 Omachi 🚉Kamakura ⏰9am-5pm daily 🌐myohonji.or.jp

On a hillside of soaring trees, this temple, with its unusually steep, extended roof, is the town's largest that belongs to the Nichiren sect. It was established in 1260, in memory of a 1203 massacre.

④
Tsurugaoka Hachiman-gu Shrine

📍 2-1-31 Yukinoshita
🚉 Kamakura 🕐 Shrine:
5am–9pm daily (Oct–Mar:
from 6am); Museum:
10am–4:30pm Tue–
Sun 🌐 tsurugaoka-
hachimangu.jp

Japan's Hachiman shrines
are dedicated to the god of
war; this one is also a guardian
shrine of the Minamoto (or
Genji) clan. Built in 1063 beside
the sea, it was moved here
in 1191. The approach runs
between two lotus ponds: the
Genji Pond has three islands
(in Japanese *san* means both
three and life) while the Heike
Pond, named for a rival clan,
has four (*shi* means both four

and death). The main shrine
was reconstructed in 1828 in
Edo style. By the ponds, the
Tsurugaoka Museum contains
a wealth of temple treasures.

---

⑤
Zuisen-ji Temple

📍 710 Nikaido 🚉 Ootono-
miya 🕐 9am–5pm daily
🌐 kamakurazuisenji.or.jp

This secluded temple is
known for its naturalistic

garden. Created in 1327
by the monk Muso Soseki,
it features a waterfall-fed
lake, rocks, and sand; a Zen
meditation cave is cut into
the cliff. Decorative narcissi
also bloom here in January,
and Japanese plum trees
blossom in February, making
it an idyllic natural
oasis even before
the cherry
trees bloom.

→

The *hongu* (main hall) of
the ornate Tsurugaoka
Hachiman-gu Shrine

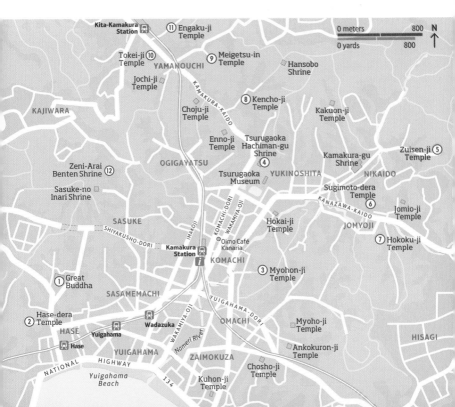

(6)
Sugimoto-dera Temple

🏠 903 Nikaido 🚌 Sugimoto Kannon 🕐 8am–4:15pm daily 🌐 sugimotodera.com

Founded in 734, this is the oldest temple in Kamakura and pleasantly informal. The softly thatched hall contains three wooden statues of 11-faced Kannon, protected by ferocious guardian figures at the temple gateway.

(7)
Hokoku-ji Temple

🏠 2-7-4 Jomyoji 🚌 Hokokuji 🕐 9am–4pm daily 🌐 houkokuji.or.jp

This Rinzai Zen temple was founded in 1334 and boasts a bamboo grove, which you can visit for a fee, as well as a rock garden. The temple's Sunday-morning *zazen* (meditation) sessions are open to all.

> Kencho-ji's beautiful rear garden is constructed around a pond supposedly in the shape of the kanji character for heart or mind.

(8)
Kencho-ji Temple

🏠 8 Yamanouchi 🚃 Kita-Kamakura 🕐 8:30am–4:30pm daily 🌐 kenchoji.com

Kencho-ji is the foremost of Kamkura's "five great" Zen temples and the oldest Zen training monastery in Japan. Founded in 1253, the temple originally had seven main buildings and 49 subtemples; many were destroyed in fires, but ten remain. Beside the impressive Sanmon (main gate) is the bell, cast in 1255, which has a Zen inscription by the temple's founder. The Buddha Hall contains a Jizo bodhisattva, savior of souls of the dead. Behind the hall is the Hatto, where public ceremonies are performed. The Karamon (Chinese gate) leads to the Hojo, used for services. Kencho-ji's beautiful rear garden is constructed around a pond supposedly in the shape of the kanji character for heart or mind. To the side of the temple, a tree-lined lane leads to subtemples and up steps to Hanso-bo – the temple's shrine.

(9)
Meigetsu-in Temple

🏠 1-8-9 Yamanouchi 📞 (0467) 24-3437 🚃 Kita-Kamakura 🕐 Jul–May: 9am–4pm daily; Jun: 8:30am–5pm daily

Known as the "hydrangea temple," Meigetsu-in is a small Zen temple with gardens. As

well as hydrangeas – which are at their peak in June – there are irises; these bloom in late May, when the rear garden, usually only tantalizingly glimpsed through a round window, is opened to the public.

↑ Inside the Butsunichian, the mausoleum of the founder of Engaku-ji Temple

⑩

Tokei-ji Temple

🏠1367 Yamanouchi ☎(0467) 22-1663 🚉Kita-Kamakura 🕗8:30am–4:30pm daily

This quiet little temple was set up as a convent in 1285, at a time when only men were allowed to petition for divorce. If a woman spent three years in a convent she could divorce her husband. Thus Tokei-ji was nicknamed the "divorce temple." In 1873 the law was changed to allow women to initiate divorce, and in 1902 Tokei-ji Temple became a monastery. It is still refuge-like, with gardens stretching back to the wooded hillside.

⑪

Engaku-ji Temple

🏠409 Yamanouchi 🚉Kita-Kamakura 🕗8am–4:30pm daily 🌐engakuji.or.jp

The largest of Kamakura's "five great" Zen temples, and set deep in trees, Engaku-ji Temple was founded by the Hojo regent Tokimune in 1282. An influential *zazen* (meditation) center since the Meiji era, it now runs public courses.

Although much of Engaku-ji was destroyed by the 1923 Kanto Earthquake, 17 of its more than 40 subtemples remain, and careful rebuilding has ensured that it retains its characteristic Zen layout *(p177)*. One of its highlights, in the Shozoku-in subtemple, is the Shariden, which houses the relics of the Buddha. Japan's finest example of Chinese Sung-style Zen architecture, it is open only at New Year but can be seen through a gate at other times. Farther on, the Butsunichian – the mausoleum of Engaku-ji's founder – serves *matcha* tea to visitors. This was the setting for Kawabata Yasunari's 1949 novel *Senbazuru* (*Thousand Cranes*).

←

The main gate to Hokoku-ji Temple, surrounded by bamboo

⑫

Zeni-Arai Benten Shrine

🏠2-25-16 Sasuke ☎(0467) 25-1081 🚉Kamakura 🕗8:30am–4:30pm daily

This popular shrine is dedicated to Benten, goddess of eloquence and the arts, one of the "seven lucky gods" of folk religion. Hidden in a niche in the cliffs, it is approached through a small tunnel and a row of torii. These lead to a cave spring where visitors wash coins in the hope of doubling their value.

Mount Fuji, framed by blossom and reflected in Lake Kawaguchi ↑

3

MOUNT FUJI AND THE FUJI FIVE LAKES

富士山と富士五湖

🅐 F5 🅠 Shizuoka & Yamanashi Prefectures 🅡 Fuji-san, Kawaguchi-ko, Gotenba, Mishima (Tokaido Shinkansen), Fujinomiya 🅑 Summer only, from all stations to the nearest 5th stage, also direct from Tokyo (Shinjuku bus terminal or Hamamatsu-cho) to Kawaguchi-ko, Gotenba, Lake Yamanaka 🅦 fujisan-climb.jp

At 12,390 ft (3,776 m), Mount Fuji (or Fuji-san) is Japan's highest peak by far, its near-perfect cone floating lilac-gray or snowcapped above hilltops and low cloud. A true Japanese icon, its silhouette is famed the world over.

Dormant since 1707, this volcano first erupted 8,000–10,000 years ago and its upper slopes are formed of loose volcanic ash, devoid of greenery. Until 150 years ago, Mount Fuji was considered so sacred that it was climbed only by pilgrims; women were not allowed until 1868. Today, the hiking trails, which are divided into ten sections – called stages – are tackled by a host of climbers. The Fuji Five Lakes, at the foot of the mountain, offer sports facilities and various attractions, including the Itchiku Kubota Art Museum.

 INSIDER TIP
Tips for Walkers

You can only climb from July to mid-September. To catch the sunrise, start at the 5th stage in the afternoon, sleep in a hut at the 7th or 8th stage, and rise early to finish the climb. Watch out for altitude sickness above the 8th stage.

→ Climbers around the torii (gate) at the mountain's summit

MOUNT FUJI IN ART

With its graceful, almost symmetrical form, its changing appearance with the seasons, and its dominance over the landscape, Mount Fuji has always been a popular subject for artists. The mountain features in various ukiyo-e, including Katsushika Hokusai's *Thirty-Six Views of Mount Fuji* (1830–32), above, and *Fifty-Three Stages of the Tokaido* (1833–4) by Hiroshige. In other arts, Mount Fuji is echoed in decorative motifs, for instance on kimonos, in wood carvings, and even in the shape of window frames.

↑ The Shiraito waterfalls on the Fujinomiya trail, a five-hour trek from the 5th stage

4

TAKAYAMA

高山

 E4 ⚑ Gifu Prefecture ⬜ Takayama 🛈 In front of JR station; www.hida.jp/english

Agriculturally poor but rich in timber, characterful Takayama has a centuries-long tradition of producing skilled carpenters. The city's isolated mountain location has meant the survival of its unspoiled Edo-period streets – today lined with tiny shops, museums, and eating places – while the pure water is ideal for brewing sake.

① Takayama Festival Floats Exhibition Hall

⬜ 178 Sakuramachi ☎ (0577) 32-5100 🕘 9am–5pm daily (Dec–Feb: to 4:30pm)

Takayama Festival dates from about 1690 and takes place twice a year: in spring, coinciding with planting, and in fall at harvest time. Both of these festivals involve processions of tall, lavishly decorated floats, guided by townspeople dressed in traditional costume.

Four floats also feature *karakuri* marionettes. This form of puppetry was invented in Edo (Tokyo) in 1617, and features mechanized dolls that perform traditional actions, such as pouring tea or bowing to the audience. These early robots feature in festivals all over Japan.

Between Takayama's two festivals, four of the floats are displayed in this hall next to the Sakurayama Hachiman-gu Shrine, along with photographs of the others. Intricately carved, they serve as evidence of Takayama's legendary craftsmanship. Once you've admired the floats, visit the gallery next door, which displays exquisite scale models of Nikko Tosho-gu Shrine (p300).

→
A float on display at the Takayama Festival Floats Exhibition Hall

↑ Walking through Sannomachi, the historic center of Takayama

② 🏛

Karakuri Museum

🏠 53-1 Sakuramachi
🕐 9:05am–4:25pm daily
🌐 takayamakarakuri.jp

Lion dances, to drive away wild animals and evil spirits, are integral to festivals such as Takayama's. This exhibition hall contains over 300 lion masks from all over Japan, as well as armor, screens, pottery, and coins. The highlight of any visit to the museum is watching a performance by the *karakuri* marionettes.

③ 🏛

Takayama Jinya

🏠 1-5 Hachikenmachi
🕐 8:45am–5pm daily
(Nov–Feb: to 4:30pm)
🌐 jinya.gifu.jp

This government office was built in 1615 for Takayama's lord, but in 1692 it was made the provincial office of the shogunate – the only one still in existence. The front of the building comprises waiting and meeting rooms; behind are the kitchens and living quarters of the governor's family. To one side is a jail, with a small array of torture instruments. The storehouses contain items relating to the rice-tax system.

④ 🏛

Hida Folk Village

🏠 1-590 Kamiokamotomachi
🕐 8:30am–5pm daily
🌐 hidanosato-tpo.jp/
english12.htm

Outside Takayama is Hida Folk Village, which contains over 30 examples of rural houses from the surrounding area, including a *gassho-zukuri* house from the Shokawa Valley. There are also reconstructed storehouses and a festival stage to explore here, and plenty of traditional crafts are on display. The buildings, located on a hillside that offers views of the Japanese Alps, are interesting both architecturally and for the human details that they reveal – such as the demands of a snowy climate or the life of a village headman.

> 💬 INSIDER TIP
> ### Cycling Tours
>
> A bicycle tour with Hida Satoyama (*www. satoyama-experience. com*) through the lush rice fields and charming avenues of Takayama gives a rare insight into rural Japan. Stopping off at natural hot springs, wooden farmhouses, orchards and farms, the 3.5-hour Takayama cycling tour travels along 14 miles (22 km).

> **Lion dances, to drive away wild animals and evil spirits, are integral to festivals such as Takayama's. This exhibition hall contains over 300 lion masks.**

A SHORT WALK
TAKAYAMA

Distance 1 mile (2 km) **Time** 30 minutes **Nearest train station** Takayama

With its unspoiled pedestrianized streets, Takayama's Sannomachi Quarter (Sanmachi-suji) is the perfect place to explore on foot. From 1692 to 1868 this area was under direct shogunate control as a source of timber, and the quality of the surrounding forests, as well as the famed skills of the town's carpenters,

are reflected in the buildings that line the streets. These old merchant houses reveal high, skylighted ceilings, wooden beams, and fireproof storage rooms. Many of them are still shops selling local crafts, making them the perfect spots to pause. There are several fascinating museums in this part of town, too.

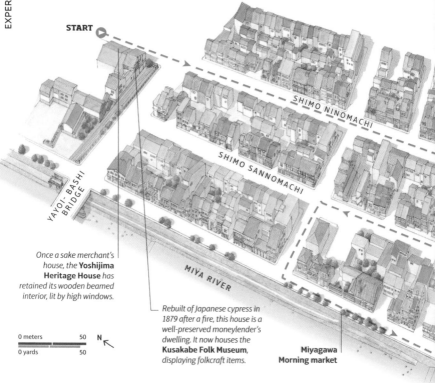

START

SHIMO NINOMACHI

SHIMO SANNOMACHI

YAYOI-BASHI BRIDGE

MIYA RIVER

Once a sake merchant's house, the **Yoshijima Heritage House** has retained its wooden beamed interior, lit by high windows.

Rebuilt of Japanese cypress in 1879 after a fire, this house is a well-preserved moneylender's dwelling. It now houses the **Kusakabe Folk Museum**, displaying folkcraft items.

Miyagawa Morning market

| 0 meters | 50 |
| 0 yards | 50 |

N

←

A merchant presenting his wares at a store on the Miya River

↑ Strolling through a charming street in the Sannomachi Quarter

The **Sannomachi Quarter** is an unusually large, intact area of Edo-period merchants' shops and houses, which are now home to specialty shops and sake brewers.

Hirase Sake Brewery has a tasting room where you can sample a variety of brews.

Hida Takayama Town Museum chronicles the town's history.

KAMI ICHINOMACHI

YASUGAWA-DORI

KAMI NINOMACHI

SAN-MACHI-DORI

KAMI SANNOMACHI

KAJI-BASHI BRIDGE

YANAGI-BASHI BRIDGE

IKEDA-BASHI BRIDGE

Some of the old houses of the Sannomachi Quarter overlook the fast-flowing **Miya River**.

⭘ **FINISH**

↑ A street lined with wooden buildings in the Higashi Chaya-gai district

5

KANAZAWA

金沢

🅰E4 🏠Ishikawa Prefecture ✈Komatsu 🚉Kanazawa 🌐visitkanazawa.jp

Wealth encouraged cultural development in this city. In 1583 the area, known as Kaga, passed from an egalitarian government under the Ikko Buddhist sect to the firm rule of the Maeda lords; while much of Japan was still unstable, Kaga had three centuries of peace and became the richest domain in the land. As a result, artists from Kyoto came and developed new styles here.

①

Nagamachi Samurai Quarter

Bisected by the picturesque Onosho Canal, this historic area of Kanazawa was once home to the city's samurai. Retaining its traditional earthen walled streets, this atmospheric neighborhood of waterways and winding lanes is located at the foot of Kanazawa Castle. Some of the former samurai houses and their gardens are open for public viewing.

At the end of the Edo era, many samurai were ruined by the collapse of the financial system. One such family was the Nomuras, who were forced to sell their home. While many others were simply torn down, the Nomura's house was bought by Hikobei Kubo, a wealthy businessman, who restored it. With its intricate woodwork, costly window-panes, and serene garden, **Nomura Family Samurai House** grants a rare insight into the day-to-day lives of the samurai. Visitors can even partake in a traditional tea ceremony for an extra charge.

Nomura Family Samurai House

 🏠1-3-32 Nagamachi 🚌 ⏰Apr–Sep: 8:30am–5:30 daily; Oct–Mar: 8:30am–4:30pm daily 🌐nomurake.com

②

Seisonkaku Villa

🏠1-2 Kenrokumachi ⏰9am–5pm Thu–Tue 🌐seisonkaku.com

The exquisite two-story Seisonkaku Villa adjoining Kenroku-en Garden was built in 1863 by Nariyasu Maeda, 13th lord, for his mother. Its lower floor houses formal receiving rooms, with walls coated in gold dust, and *shoji* paper doors with rare Dutch stained-glass insets. Upstairs is more informal and colorful. The house also features a famed 65-ft- (20-m-) long covered walkway known as the "horsetail corridor," which was engineered in such a way that no supporting beams hold up the roof.

🔍 HIDDEN GEM
Kimono Time

The Nagamachi Yuzen Silk Center exhibits this intricate material, which necessitates an 18-step dyeing process. For a fee, you can try your hand at silk painting and try on a kimono for size (*kagayuzen-club.co.jp*).

---

③

Ishikawa Museum of Traditional Arts and Crafts

⌂ 1-1 Kenrokumachi 🚌
🕐 9am-5pm daily 🗓 Apr-Nov: 3rd Thu of month; Dec-Mar: Thu 🌐 ishikawa-densankan.jp

At this tastefully laid-out museum, visitors can immerse themselves in the traditional crafts that the Ishikawa Prefecture is renowned for, including gorgeous Kutani pottery, silk painting, lacquerware, metalwork, gold leaf details, Japanese paper, and fireworks. Visitors are encouraged to interact with

Did You Know?

In winter, the city's mud walls are covered with straw mats to protect them from harsh weather.

↑ The beautiful and serene Kenroku-en Garden, its features blanketed in snow

the objects by making them themselves, and the museum hosts regular demonstrations by experienced traditional craftsmen. The shop on the first floor offers an assortment of pieces, all produced by local artisans and at reasonable prices.

For information about the demonstrations and hands-on experiences led by the experts, check the museum website.

④

Kenroku-en Garden

⌂ 1 Kenrokumachi 🚌
🕐 7am-6pm daily 🌐 pref.ishikawa.jp

Created by the Maeda family, Kenroku-en is one of Japan's "great three" gardens. Its name means "garden of six qualities:" spaciousness, seclusion, an air of antiquity, ingenuity, flowing water, and views.

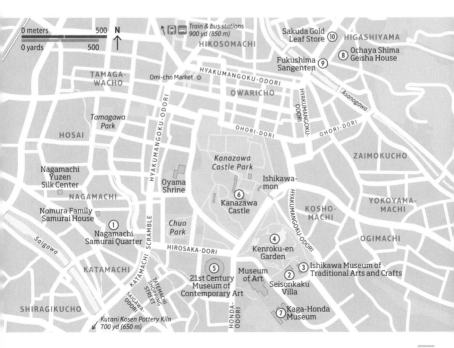

⑤
21st Century Museum of Contemporary Art

◨ 1-2-1 Hirosaka ▦
🕒 Exhibition Zone: 10am–6pm Tue–Thu & Sun, 10am–8pm Fri & Sat; Public Zone: 9am–10pm daily 🌐 kanazawa21.jp

This experimental museum was created by the architectural duo SANAA (Kazuyo Sejima and Ryue Nishikawa), who won the Pritzker Prize in 2010. The museum explores emerging new work in visual arts, design, craft, fashion, architecture, and film, particularly in relation to multiculturalism and transportation, technology, gender issues, and identity. The art on display encourages physical interaction from visitors and, as a result, it is particularly popular with families.

Olafur Eliasson's *Colour activity house* (2010) at the 21st Century Museum of Contemporary Art ↑

⑥
Kanazawa Castle

◨ Marunouchi ▦ 🕒 Mar–mid-Oct: 7am–6pm daily; mid-Oct–Feb: 8am–5pm daily 🌐 pref.ishikawa.jp

The size of Kanazawa Castle, one of the largest in feudal Japan, reflects the importance of its former residents, who were said to be the second most powerful family in Japan after the emperor's.

The Maeda clan began building their castle here in 1583, and the family resided for 14 generations, only leaving in 1869. The fortification was destroyed by fire in 1881, and only the armory and rear gate, Ishikawa-mon, survived. Restoration work has started, recreating the structures using original techniques. In the centre of the castle's park, visitors can access three large-scale reconstructions of the original buildings. Inside these structures are intricate models of the castle and displays showing the various architectural techniques used in the restoration.

⑦
Kaga-Honda Museum

◨ 3-1 Dewamachi ▦
🕒 Mar–Nov: 9am–5pm daily; Dec–Feb: 9am–5pm Fri–Wed 🌐 honda-museum.jp

Gain a glimpse into the history of feudal Japan through the artifacts belonging to the descendants of Masanobu Honda, an advisor to the Tokugawa shogun and the Maeda lord's highest vassal. This exhibition showcases a rare collection of military hardware, including exquisite armor and weaponry. Look out for the items connected to the samurai's mount, including a delicately lacquered saddle, stirrups with gold inlay, and imposing horse armor, which are said to be some of the finest examples in Japan. Also on display are curiosities such as fire-fighting attire, as well as wedding trousseaux belonging to women from the Maeda clan who married into the Honda family.

←
The reconstructed exterior of Kanazawa Castle, with its fortified walls

⑩ 🛍️
Sakuda Gold Leaf Store

📍 1-3-27 Higashiyama 🚌
🕐 9am–6pm daily
🌐 goldleaf-sakuda.jp

Despite Japan's reputation as the home of minimalism, gold leaf decorates everything from folding screens to chopsticks. For over 400 years, Kanazawa has been the center for gold leaf production, and the city still crafts over 98 per cent of the country's output. The city's humid climate is perfect for production because it minimizes the build-up of static electricity, which can tear the delicate sheets. At the Sakuda Gold Leaf Store, master craftsmen demonstrate how gold leaf is applied to all manner of traditional crafts. Here, you can take a tour of the factory, view the production process, and even try applying some of the gold leaf to an object of your choice.

Did You Know?
At Sakuda Gold Leaf Store, visitors can try a cup of tea with shimmering flecks of gold in it.

⑧
Ochaya Shima Geisha House

📍 1-13-21 Higashiyama 🚌
🕐 9am–6pm daily (Dec-Feb: to 5pm) 🌐 ochaya-shima.com

This museum is dedicated to preserving the history of Higashi Chaya-gai. Established in 1820, this was the grandest pleasure district outside Kyoto and Edo, and was frequented by rich merchants and nobility. The area still has old-fashioned street lamps and wooden-lattice windows, but these now hide elegant restaurants and crafts galleries.

At the center of the area, the Ochaya Shima Geisha House is still much the same as it was in the Edo era. On the upper floor are guest rooms with small stages where the geisha sang and danced for their customers, while downstairs are modest living quarters. The museum's collection displays items once used by the geisha who lived here, including tea ceremony utensils and musical instruments. After exploring the collection, you can relax with a cup of *matcha* here.

⑨
Fukushima Sangenten

📍 1-1-8 Higashiyama 🚌
🕐 10am–4pm Mon-Sat
🚫 2nd & 4th Sat of month; public hols 🌐 fukushima-sangenten.com

For those interested in traditional Japanese music, a visit to this shop where the Fukushima family have been hand-crafting three-stringed *shamisen (sangen)* since the early 20th century is a must. All geisha must master this instrument during their training and the haunting sound of the *shamisen* is one of the most evocative experiences in Japan. At Fukushima Sangenten, for a small fee, visitors can learn to play one of these instruments and see how they were made. Although the most traditional *shamisen* are crafted from cat and dog skin, they are now almost universally made from synthetic materials.

SHOP

Omi-cho Market
This 300-year-old market is home to about 170 stores, selling everything from fresh fish to flowers.

📍 50 Kamiomicho
🌐 ohmicho-ichiba.com

Kutani Kosen Pottery Kiln
The only surviving kiln in Kanazawa has been producing porcelain since the mid-19th century. Design your own piece at the Kutani Kosen Pottery Kiln, which can be shipped to you once it is fired.

📍 5-3-3 Nomachi
🌐 kutanikosen.com

EXPERIENCE MORE

Narita
成田

▲G4 ▲Chiba Prefecture
✈▣Narita ℹIn front of JR
station; www.nrtk.jp

A quiet little town, Narita is
worlds away from its nearby
bustling airport. The town's
main attraction is Narita-san
Shinsho-ji Temple, an interesting Esoteric Shingon-sect
temple founded in 940 and
dedicated to Fudo Myo-o,
Deity of Immovable Wisdom.
Several times daily, the priests
burn wooden sticks to symbolize extinguishing of earthly
passions. The streets are full
of traditional shops for the 12
million temple visitors a year.

Near Narita are over 1,000
ancient burial mounds (kofun);
the best are in the open-air
museum **Boso no Mura**.

Did You Know?

Narita is famous for its
eel restaurants, which
once served Edo lords
en route to Tokyo.

The **National Museum of
Japanese History** offers
a good survey of Japan.

Boso no Mura

▲1028 Ryukakuji, Sakae
☎(0476) 95-3333 ⌚9am-
4:30pm Tue-Sun

National Museum of
Japanese History

♿ ▲117 Jonaicho, Sakura
⌚Mar-Sep: 9:30am-5pm
Tue-Sun (Oct-Feb: to 4:30pm)
☒rekihaku.ac.jp

Kawagoe
川越

▲F4 ▲Saitama Prefecture
▣Kawagoe, Hon Kawagoe
ℹ24-9 Wakitamachi,
Kawagoe; www.koedo.or.jp

Nicknamed "Little Edo,"
Kawagoe preserves the
atmosphere of 19th-century
Edo (Tokyo) because of its
kura buildings. These clay-
walled structures have double
doors and heavy shutters.
About 30 kura remain today.
The **Kura-Zukuri Shiryokan**,
formerly a kura tobacconist,
is now a museum and gives
visitors the opportunity to
peek inside one of these old-
fashioned buildings. It also

displays historic machines.
Nearby, Toki-no-kane wooden
bell tower was built in 1624
to tell the time and warn of
fires. East of the kura streets
is Kita-in Temple, a Tendai-
sect temple which includes
the only extant rooms from
Edo Castle.

At one time, Kawagoe had
its own castle. Part of that
castle remains in the shape of
Honmaru Goten, the former
residence of the lord, with
many commodious rooms.

Kura-Zukuri Shiryokan

▲7-9 Saiwacho ☎(049) 222-
5399 ⌚9am-5pm Tue-Sun

Honmaru Goten

▲2-13-1 Kurawamachi
☎(049) 224-6015 ⌚9am-
5pm Tue-Sun

Hakone
箱根

▲F4 ▲Kanagawa
Prefecture ▣Hakone
Yumoto ℹ706-35 Yumoto,
Hakone; www.hakone.or.
jp/en/

Popular since the 9th century,
Hakone is a hilly hot-spring
town with scattered cultural
and natural attractions.

↑ Wandering past steaming sulfur vents in Owakudani valley, Hakone

YOSEGI-ZAIKU MARQUETRY

Originating in the 9th century, this type of marquetry looks like inlaid mosaic but in fact employs a very different technique. Strips are cut from planks of up to 40 varieties of woods and glued together to form patterned blocks, which are in turn glued into larger blocks. These are then either shaped with a lathe into objects like bowls, or shaved into sheets and used to coat boxes and purses.

The Hakone area extends across the collapsed remains of a huge volcano, which was active until 3,000–4,000 years ago, leaving a legacy today of hot springs and steam vents.

Although Hakone can be visited as a long day trip from Tokyo, it is worth an overnight stay. A convenient circuit of the main sights starts from the *onsen* town of Hakone-Yumoto, taking the Tozan switchback train up the hillside to **Hakone Open-Air Museum**, with its modern sculptures. Continue via funicular to **Hakone Art Museum**, which has an excellent Japanese ceramic collection and garden. Via the funicular and then a ropeway over the crest of the hill is the fascinating Owaku-dani ("valley of great boiling"), an area of sulfurous steam vents. This is an active volcanic zone, so sometimes the ropeway or sections of this area are closed to visitors for safety reasons. The ropeway continues to Lake Ashi, where replicas of historical Western-style boats run to Hakone-machi and Moto-Hakone. In clear weather

←

Old-fashioned street in Kawagoe, with *kura* buildings and Toki-no-kane bell tower

there are stunning views of Mount Fuji. At Hakone-machi is an interesting reconstruction of the **Seki-sho Barrier Gate**, a checkpoint that used to control passage on the Edo-period Tokaido road between Tokyo and Kyoto.

From Hakone-machi it is a short walk to Moto-Hakone. Located on a hilltop overlooking Lake Ashi, **Narukawa Art Museum** exhibits 1,500 artworks by modern Japanese masters, and has spectacular views of the surrounding mountains. Over a pass beyond Moto-Hakone is the Amazake-chaya teahouse, and Hatajuku village, known for *yosegi-zaiku*, a form of decorative marquetry.

Hakone Open-Air Museum

⊛ 🏠1121 Ninotaira 🕐9am–5pm daily 🔗hakone-oam.or.jp

Hakone Art Museum

⊛ 🏠1300 Gora 🕐9am–4:30pm Fri-Wed (Dec-Mar: to 4pm) 🔗moaart.or.jp/hakone

Seki-sho Barrier Gate

⊛ 🕐9am–5pm daily (Dec-Feb: to 4:30pm) 🔗hakonesekisyo.jp

Narukawa Art Museum

⊛ 🏠570 Motohakone 🕐9am–5pm daily 🔗narukawamuseum.co.jp

STAY

Hakone Kowakien Ten-yu

A luxurious spa resort in Hakone with an open-air *onsen* in each room.

🅰F4 🏠1297 Ninotaira, Hakone 🔗ten-yu.com

¥¥¥

Wakamatsu Honten

This 240-year-old inn, just a 15-minute drive from Narita airport, offers a slice of tradition.

🅰G4 🏠355 Honcho, Narita 🔗wakamatsuhonten.jp

¥¥¥

Ryokan Hakone Ginyu

Enjoy views over the Hakone mountains at this traditional *ryokan*.

🅰F4 🏠100-1 Miyanoshita, Hakone 🔗hakoneginyu.co.jp

¥¥¥

↑ Sunset over the harbor at Shimoda, on the Izu Peninsula

⑨ Izu Peninsula
伊豆半島

🅰 F5 🏯 Shizuoka Prefecture 🚆🚌 Atami, Ito, Shuzenji 🛈 Atami, Ito, and Shuzenji stations; www.exploreshizuoka.com

A hilly peninsula with a benign climate, Izu is popular for its many hot springs. A place of exile during the Middle Ages, in the early 1600s it was home to the shipwrecked English-man William Adams, whose story was the basis of the James Clavell novel *Shogun*.

Izu's east coast is quite developed, but the west has charming coves and fishing villages, such as Toi and Heda, offering delicious long-legged crabs and other seafood. The center is also relatively unspoiled, with wooded mountains and rustic hot springs, including Shuzenji *onsen* and a chain of villages from Amagi Yugashima to Kawazu. These latter were the setting for Yasunari Kawabata's short story *The Izu Dancer*, celebrated across Izu.

The whole region has become a popular area for cycling holidays, with its dynamic landscapes, and the many *onsens* (hot springs) making a great way to relax at the end of a day of cycling.

⑩ Nagoya
名古屋

🅰 E5 🏯 Aichi Prefecture ✈ Chubu Centrair 🚅 Nagoya 🛈 At Nagoya JR Stn; www.nagoya-info.jp/en

A major transportation hub for the region, Nagoya is a pleas-ant base. It rose to prominence in the 17th century as a Tokaido castle town, birthplace of feudal lords Nobunaga Oda and Hideyoshi Toyotomi. Japan's fourth-largest city and an industrial center, it was heavily bombed in World War II.

The city's Me-guru one-day sightseeing bus pass, or a bus-and-subway pass are good for exploring. **Nagoya Castle**, built

↑ Autumn leaves framing the elegant architecture of Nagoya Castle

in 1610–12 and one of the largest of the Edo period, was destroyed in a bombing raid in 1945; today's reconstruction has a top-floor observatory and exhibitions about the cas-tle. Though closed until 2022, the main keep is still worth a visit for the castle's exquisitely reconstructed Honmaru Palace.

A short bus ride east is the **Tokugawa Art Museum**, with Edo-period treasures, as well as a 12th-century illustrated handscroll of *The Tale of Genji*, part of which is exhibited each November. Reproductions of the scrolls are on display.

Nagoya Castle

♿ ⌚ 🏯 1-1 Hommaru Ⓢ Shiyakusho 🚌 Nagoya-jo Seimon-mae 🕐 9am–4:30pm daily 🌐 nagoyajo.city.nagoya.jp

Tokugawa Art Museum

♿ 🏯 1017 Tokugawacho 🚌 Tokugawaen Shindeki 🕐 10am–5pm Tue–Sun 🌐 tokugawa-art-museum.jp

11

Shizuoka
静岡

F5 Shizuoka Prefecture Shizuoka In JR station; www.visit-shizuoka.com

Settlement in this area goes back to AD 200–300. Once the retirement home of Ieyasu Tokugawa, Shizuoka is today a sprawling urban center, the city in Japan at greatest risk of a major earthquake – and probably the only place that is fully prepared.

The **Toro ruins** near the port have reconstructions of ancient buildings and an excellent interactive museum. The view from Nihondaira plateau, in the east of the city, to Mount Fuji and Izu is superb. Nearby is Kunozan Tosho-gu, one of the three top Tosho-gu shrines.

West of Shizuoka, Kanaya has one of Japan's largest tea plantations. Fields can be visited, and the **Fujinokuni Chanomiyako Museum** portrays tea lore. Nearby, the Oigawa steam railroad takes you to the South Alps.

Toro ruins
5-10-5 Toro (054) 285-0476 9am–4:30pm Tue–Sun

Fujinokuni Chanomiyako Museum
3053-2 Kanaya Fujimicho 9am–5pm Wed–Mon tea-museum.jp

12

Inuyama
犬山

E5 Aichi Prefecture Chubu Centrair Inuyama In front of W side of station; ml.inuyama.gr.jp/en

This quiet town sits on the Kiso River. The simple **Inuyama Castle**, built in 1537, is the oldest in Japan. It places more emphasis on defense than show, but is still graceful, with views across the river far below.

Outside Inuyama is **Meiji Mura**, a theme park with over 60 Meiji-era (1868–1912) buildings. Yaotsu, where Chiune Sugihara was born, is a train ride away. Japan's consul in Lithuania in World War II, Sugihara saved around 6,000 Jews using transit visas via Japan. He is commemorated by a monument and museum at the Hill of Humanity Park.

Inuyama Castle
65-2 Inuyama Kitakoken (0568) 61-1711 9am–4:30pm daily

Meiji Mura
20 mins by bus from Inuyama Stn 9:30am–5pm Tue–Sun (from 10am Aug; to 4pm Nov–Feb) Jan 21–Feb 25 meijimura.com/english

---

DRINK

ID Café
This vast nightclub in Nagoya's raucous Sakae district packs as many as 5,000 people on to its six dance floors.

E5 3-1-15 Sakae, Naka, Nagoya idcafe.info

Shooters
With over a dozen screens, this is Nagoya's largest sports bar and serves an array of American food and drinks.

E5 2-9-26 Sakae, Naka, Nagoya shooters-nagoya.com

7 Days Craft Kitchen
Close to Nagoya Station, this bar dispenses an excellent range of craft beer on draft.

E5 4-4-21 Meieki, Nakamura, Nagoya 7daysbrew.business.site

← A tourist boat on the Kiso River, overlooked by the charming Inuyama Castle

Gassho-zukuri houses in the pretty village of Ogimachi, in the Shokawa Valley

 13

Shokawa Valley
庄川渓谷

🅰E4 🏠Gifu and Toyama Prefectures 🚌From Nagoya, Takayama, Toyama, Shin-Takaoka, Kanazawa 🅸ml. shirakawa-go.org/en

A remote mountain region with unique thatched houses, the Shokawa Valley comprises two areas: Shirakawa-go (including Ogimachi) to the south and the five hamlets of Gokayama to the north. Under deep snow from December to March, the region was historically a refuge for the defeated and persecuted. Until the 1970s most families here produced silk, raising silkworms in *gassho-zukuri* thatched houses.

Of the original 1,800, fewer than 150 *gassho* houses remain. Three settlements – Ogimachi, Suganuma, and Ainokura – are World Heritage Sites. Every April–May, a few houses are re-thatched, one roof taking 200 villagers and volunteers two days. **Gassho-zukuri Minkaen Open-Air Museum** is the largest village, with 59 *gassho* houses. Suganuma has nine *gassho*

buildings. Ainokura is a hillside hamlet of 20 *gassho* houses (two open to visitors).

Gassho-zukuri Minkaen Open-Air Museum
 🏠2499 Ogimachi, Shirakawa-go 📞(05769) 6-1231 🕐Mar-Nov: 8:40am–5pm daily; Dec-Feb: 9am–4pm Fri-Wed

14

Gifu
岐阜

🅰E5 🏠Gifu Prefecture 🚉Gifu 🅸At JR station; www.visitgifu.com

Gifu Prefecture's main city is known for *ukai*, a tradition that involves using trained cormorants to catch fish. Nightly from mid-May to mid-October, except at full moon or when stormy, fishermen and their cormorants go out on torchlit boats; the birds dive for *ayu* (sweetfish) and trout, which they are prevented from swallowing by a ring around their necks.

On dry land, the town is known for the largest lacquer Buddha in Japan, at Shoho-ji Temple. Dating from 1832, it comprises a woven

bamboo frame covered with sutra-inscribed paper, then coated in clay and lacquered.

Gifu is also known for its unique cuisine, the result of its history as a center for trade.

 TOP 5 GIFU FOODS

Ayu
This fish is grilled over an open flame and served with just a sprinkling of salt.

Fuyu persimmons
A winter treat that tastes of dates, brown sugar, and cinnamon.

Hida beef
This high-quality beef is known for its marbling and a layer of fat.

Kuri kinton
Symbolizing wealth and usually eaten at New Year, this is a dish of candied chestnuts with mashed sweet potatoes.

Keichan
Chicken thighs stir-fried with cabbage and garlic soy sauce.

GASSHO-ZUKURI HOUSES

These houses are named for their steep thatched roofs, shaped like *gassho* ("praying hands"). Formed of a series of triangular frames on a rectangular base, the roofs are able to withstand heavy snow and shed rain quickly so that the straw does not rot. Generally three or four stories tall, the first floor of *gassho-zukuri* houses traditionally accommodated extended families of 20–30 people, who were all involved in silkworm cultivation. The upper floors housed the silkworms, permitting variations in light, heat, and air at different stages. To maximize ventilation and light, windows at both ends were opened to allow the wind through. Architectural details vary from village to village.

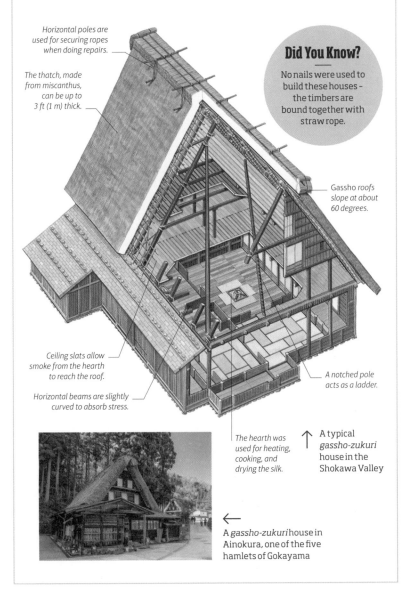

Horizontal poles are used for securing ropes when doing repairs.

The thatch, made from miscanthus, can be up to 3 ft (1 m) thick.

Did You Know?

No nails were used to build these houses – the timbers are bound together with straw rope.

Gassho *roofs slope at about 60 degrees.*

Ceiling slats allow smoke from the hearth to reach the roof.

Horizontal beams are slightly curved to absorb stress.

A notched pole acts as a ladder.

The hearth was used for heating, cooking, and drying the silk.

↑ A typical *gassho-zukuri* house in the Shokawa Valley

← A *gassho-zukuri* house in Ainokura, one of the five hamlets of Gokayama

15

Matsumoto
松本

A E4 **A** Nagano Prefecture
X A Matsumoto **i** At
JR station; www.visit
matsumoto.com/en

Despite being the gateway to the Japanese Alps, this city's main attraction is **Matsumoto Castle**. It has the oldest five-tiered keep in Japan (1593) and its walls and moat date from 1504. The top floor holds a shrine to the goddess of the 26th night who was thought to protect against fire and invasion.

Beside the keep is the Moon-Viewing Turret, added in the 1630s for aesthetic purposes. The castle admission includes entry to the Matsumoto City Museum in the grounds, which features local geography, wildlife, history, dolls, and tools.

Also in Matsumoto are the **Japan Ukiyo-e Museum**, an excellent collection of wood-block prints, and **Matsumoto Folkcraft Museum**, with folk art from Japan and across Asia; on the edge of the city, Utsukushigahara and Asama have pleasant hot springs.

North of Matsumoto, Hotaka is home to Japan's largest wasabi (horse-radish) farm.

Matsumoto Castle
⊗ **A** 4-11 Marunouchi
▥ Matsumoto-jo **Ⓞ** 8:30am–5pm daily **w** matsumoto-castle.jp

Japan Ukiyo-e Museum
⊗ **A** 2206 Shinkiri, Shimadachi **▥** Ukiyoe Hakubutsukan **Ⓞ** 10am–5pm Tue–Sun **w** japan-ukiyoe-museum.com

Matsumoto Folkcraft Museum
⊗ **A** 1313-1 Satoyamabe **▥** Mingeikan-mae **Ⓒ** (0263) 33-1569 **Ⓞ** 9am–5pm Tue–Sun

16

Nagano
長野

A E4 **A** Nagano Prefecture
A Nagano **i** At JR station;
www.go-nagano.net

Surrounded by low mountains, Nagano is a skiing center and was the main venue for the 1998 Winter Olympics. In town, the prime attraction is Zenko-ji Temple, a non-sect temple that has always been open to both women and men. Established in 670, it enshrines what is said to be Japan's oldest Buddhist image, an Amida triad brought from Korea in the 6th century. This is kept hidden, and a copy shown every six years.

The temple also has an underground passage

DOSOJIN STONES

These two jaunty stone figures are guardian deities of travelers. They are found at many roadsides in northern Nagano Prefecture, as well as at village boundaries. The pair are often depicted holding hands.

containing a "key to paradise:" touching the key is thought to bring happiness in the afterlife.

In nearby Obuse, the **Hokusai Museum** is devoted to artist Katsushika Hokusai (1760–1849), who stayed in the town as an old man. Farther into the mountains **Jigokudani Monkey Park**, reached by bus from Kanbayashi *onsen*, is famous for the wild macaques living around its hot pools.

Hokusai Museum
⊗ **A** 485 Obuse, Obusemachi
A Obuse **Ⓞ** 9am–5pm daily
w hokusai-kan.com

→ Walking over the Kappabashi bridge to cross the Azusa River, in Kamikochi

Jigokudani Monkey Park

 🚌15-minute bus from Yudanaka Stn 🕐Apr–Oct: 8:30am–5pm daily; Nov–Mar: 9am–4pm daily 🌐en. jigokudani-yaenkoen.co.jp

17

Kamikochi
上高地

🅰E4 📍Nagano Prefecture 🚉To Shin-Shimashima, then bus 🚌From Tokyo, Osaka, Kyoto, Hirayu *onsen* or Shin-Shimashima ℹ️Next to Kamikochi bus terminal; **www.kamikochi.org**

An alpine valley, Kamikochi lies in the southern part of the Chubu Sangaku (Northern Japanese Alps) National Park, at an altitude of 4,900 ft (1,500 m) and is a good hiking and climbing base. The valley is reached by a tunnel (open late April–early November); in July, August, Golden Week (first week of May), and on some weekends, private cars are banned. Japan's highest (after Fuji) and wildest mountains are in the Southern Alps, but the Northern Alps have more snow and impressive scenery. Mountain refuges allow hikes of several days from hut to hut, often via a hot spring.

A three-day route from Kamikochi takes in Mount Yari and Mount Hotaka – at 10,470 ft (3,190 m), the highest peak in the Northern Alps. Short hikes include the scree of Mount Yake, the only active volcano in the Northern Alps. In bad weather, walks are restricted to the valley floor by the Azusa River.

←

The moat surrounding Matsumoto Castle, built in the early 16th century

18

Chichibu-Tama-Kai National Park
秩父多摩甲斐国立公園

🅰F4 📍Tokyo, Saitama, Nagano, and Yamanashi Prefectures 🚉Seibu-Chichibu, Chichibu, Okutama, Mitake ℹ️Seibu-Chichibu Stn; **www.env.go.jp**

Chichibu-Tama-Kai National Park is a remote region of low mountains, stretching from the narrow valleys of Okutama in the south to the basin around Chichibu city in the north. The two parts of the park are separated by mountains, crossed only by a few hiking trails. Within the park, railroads reach a few spots, but travel is mostly by bus.

A silk-producing area until the early 1900s, Chichibu is now known for a pilgrim route linking 34 Kannon temples. To the north, at Nagatoro, the Arakawa River runs past rare schist rock formations.

In the Okutama area, Mount Mitake has a mountaintop shrine village, and the **Nippara Caves** are worth visiting.

Nippara Caves

 🚌760 Nippara, Okutama ☎(0428) 83-2099 🕐9am–5pm daily

EAT

Kobayashi
Matsumoto is famous for soba noodles, and this is one of the best places to enjoy them.

🅰E4 📍3-3-20 Ote, Matsumoto ☎(0263) 32-1298

Alps Gohan
This wholefood restaurant in Matsumoto offers patrons two daily-changing options.

🅰E4 📍3-7-5 Fukashi, Matsumoto 🌐alpsgohan.com

Fureai Yamabekan
Learn to make soba noodles for yourself with the help of experienced teachers at this Matsumoto eatery.

🅰E4 📍85-1 Satoya-mabe, Matsumoto ☎(0263) 35-9076

19

Eihei-ji Temple
永平寺

D4 ⏺Fukui Prefecture
🚉Eiheijiguchi, then bus
🌐daihonzan-eiheiji.com/en

Established in 1244, Eihei-ji Temple is one of the Soto Zen sect's two head temples and has been Japan's most active Zen meditation monastery since the late 16th century. In a classic rectilinear plan, its halls and covered corridors climb up the wooded mountainside. Soto Zen pursues gradual enlightenment by practicing meditation away from the real world; the monastery has about 50 elders and 250 trainees. The atmosphere is cheerful, yet life is austere, with no heating and a simple diet. In the Sodo Hall (to the left), each trainee has just one tatami mat for eating, sleeping, and *zazen* (meditation). Silence must be observed in the hall, as well as in the bath building and toilet. Laypeople wishing to experience the rigorous Soto Zen regime must book well ahead.

↑ The Jouyoumon gate of the Eihei-ji Temple, an important Soto Zen monastery

SHOP

Wajima Market
Each morning, the streets of Wajima ring out with the cries of the vendors at this market, which is said to be over 1,000 years old. Stalls sell fish brought in from the port, vegetables from the nearby farmland, and handicrafts like the famous Wajima lacquerware.

E3 ⏺1-115 Kawai-machi, Honmachidori, Wajima ⏰8am-noon, except 2nd & 4th Wed of month

20

Noto Peninsula
能登半島

E3-4 ⏺Ishikawa Prefecture 🚉🚌From Kanazawa ⓘIn the old Wajima train station; (0768) 22-1503

Projecting 45 miles (70 km) into the Japan Sea, Noto is a quiet region of fishing villages known for seafood and untouched traditions. The east coast and the sandy west coast near Kanazawa are quite developed, but the north and northwest are rocky and picturesque. Public transportation here is limited; bus and train are similar in time and cost, but the bus network is wider.

Wajima, a weathered fishing town, produces top-quality, durable lacquerware with at least 70 layers of lacquer. Nearby Hegura island is a stopping-off point for migratory birds. Located just east of Wajima, Senmaida is so famed for its "1,000" narrow rice terraces by the sea that it has been awarded heritage status by the Food & Agriculture Organization of the UN, while Sosogi's coast has unusual rock formations. Many summer festivals here feature demon-masked drummers and *kiriko* lanterns,

 PICTURE PERFECT
Sun Rice, Sunset

Shiroyone Senmaida comprises over 1,000 small rice paddies on the steep slopes leading down to the Noto Peninsula's rocky shoreline. Head here at sunrise or sunset for an atmospheric shot.

standing up to 50 ft (15 m) tall. Between events, drums are played at Wajima and Sosogi.

To the west, Monzen has the major Soji-ji Zen temple (partially open while undergoing restoration). In Hakui are the important Keta-taisha Shrine and a 2,000-year-old sumo ring – Japan's oldest, still used each September. Senmaida, Sosogi, and Monzen can be reached by bus from Wajima; Hakui by bus or train from Kanazawa.

Did You Know?

Wajima lacquerware is created by applying *nunokise* (cloth) onto the objects to be glazed.

THE LAYOUT OF A ZEN BUDDHIST TEMPLE

Designed to facilitate the path to enlightenment, Zen Buddhist temples transport worshippers from the earthly world to that of the Buddha.

Based on Chinese Sung-dynasty structures, Japanese Zen temples are usually set out in a straight line. The entrance is marked by a bridge over water, symbolizing the overcoming of earthly obstacles. The main buildings, including the Sanmon (main gate), Hatto lecture hall, Butsuden (Buddha Hall), meditation or study hall, and the abbot's and monks' quarters, are beautiful but natural looking. Often made of unpainted wood, they are intended to be conducive to emptying the mind of worldly thoughts, facilitating enlightenment.

↑ Kinkaku-ji (Golden Pavilion), a Zen Buddhist temple in Kyoto

↑ A serene statue of the Buddha in Engaku-ji Temple, Kamakura

TOP 5 ZEN BUDDHIST TEMPLES

Eihei-ji
The "temple of eternal peace" is a *daihonzan* (head temple) of the Soto Zen sect.

Kinkaku-ji
The Golden Pavilion is reflected in the pond at this Kyoto temple *(p199)*.

Engaku-ji
The most beautiful of Kamakura's five great Zen temples *(p157)*.

Ginkaku-ji
Despite its name, Kyoto's Silver Pavilion was never covered in silver foil *(p195)*.

Soji-ji
This *daihonzan* is one of the largest and busiest temples in Japan.

→

The layout of Engaku-ji Temple, a Zen Buddhist temple in Kamakura

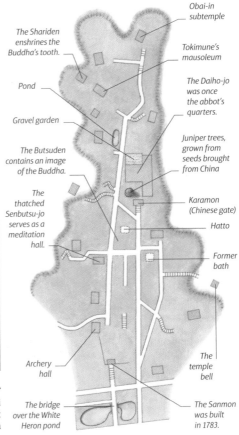

Obai-in subtemple

Tokimune's mausoleum

The Daiho-jo was once the abbot's quarters.

Juniper trees, grown from seeds brought from China

Karamon (Chinese gate)

Hatto

Former bath

The temple bell

The Sanmon was built in 1783.

The Shariden enshrines the Buddha's tooth.

Pond

Gravel garden

The Butsuden contains an image of the Buddha.

The thatched Senbutsu-jo serves as a meditation hall.

Archery hall

The bridge over the White Heron pond

Standing on one of the boulders in the Nezame-no-toko Gorge ↑

A DRIVING AND WALKING TOUR
KISO VALLEY TOUR

Distance 37 miles (60 km) **Stopping-off points** Narai, Magome, Tsumango **Difficulty** Trails and roads are well-maintained

The Kiso River runs through a picturesque mountain valley that was the route of the Nakasendo, one of the Edo-period post roads. Take a drive along this ancient route, stopping at the 11 charming post towns en route. Tsumago, Narai, and Magome, in particular, still retain much of that atmosphere, their narrow streets lined with wooden inns and stores. Parts of the old Nakasendo walking trail, especially between Tsumago and Magome, are as they were in the Edo days and can be followed past woods, farms, and milestones. More challenging hiking is found on nearby mountains such as Ontake.

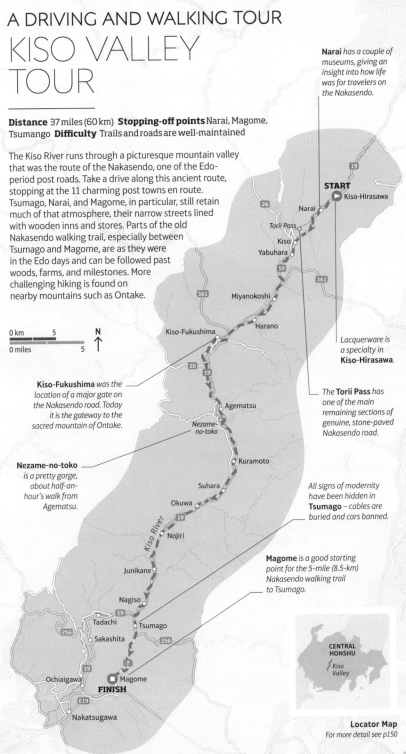

Narai has a couple of museums, giving an insight into how life was for travelers on the Nakasendo.

Lacquerware is a specialty in **Kiso-Hirasawa**.

The **Torii Pass** has one of the main remaining sections of genuine, stone-paved Nakasendo road.

Kiso-Fukushima was the location of a major gate on the Nakasendo road. Today it is the gateway to the sacred mountain of Ontake.

Nezame-no-toko is a pretty gorge, about half-an-hour's walk from Agematsu.

All signs of modernity have been hidden in **Tsumago** – cables are buried and cars banned.

Magome is a good starting point for the 5-mile (8.5-km) Nakasendo walking trail to Tsumago.

0 km   5
0 miles   5

N

START
Kiso-Hirasawa

Narai

Torii Pass

Kiso

Yabuhara

Miyanokoshi

Harano

Kiso-Fukushima

Agematsu

Nezame-no-toko

Kuramoto

Suhara

Okuwa

Nojiri

Junikane

Nagiso

Tadachi

Tsumago

Sakashita

Ochiaigawa

Magome

FINISH

Nakatsugawa

Kiso River

CENTRAL HONSHU

Kiso Valley

Locator Map
For more detail see p150

KYOTO CITY

Founded in 794 as Heian-kyo (capital of peace and tranquility), the city was modeled on the Tang Chinese city of Chang-an. Bounded on three sides by mountains and bisected by a river flowing north to south, the site was considered ideal by Emperor Kanmu's geomancers (people who practiced the art of divination by interpreting markings in the earth). As the population grew, however, hygiene was a problem, especially when the Kamo River flooded. A series of rituals and festivals came into being to placate the spirits responsible for plagues and other catastrophes, resulting in a tightly knit fabric of ritual and custom, mostly still observed.

Kyoto culture became an amalgam of several influences, of which the imperial court and nobility were the first and most important. Later came the samurai, patrons of Zen Buddhism, and the tea ceremony. Merchants were also influential, especially the silk weavers of Nishijin. The city was reduced to ashes at various times by earthquakes, fires, and the ten-year period of civil strife known as the Onin War (1467–77). During the Edo period (1603–1868), the balance of power shifted from Kyoto to Edo (Tokyo), and Kyoto eventually lost its status as capital in 1869. Despite this, Kyoto retains its refined, imperial air, while at the same time embracing all that comes with being a cosmopolitan 21st-century city.

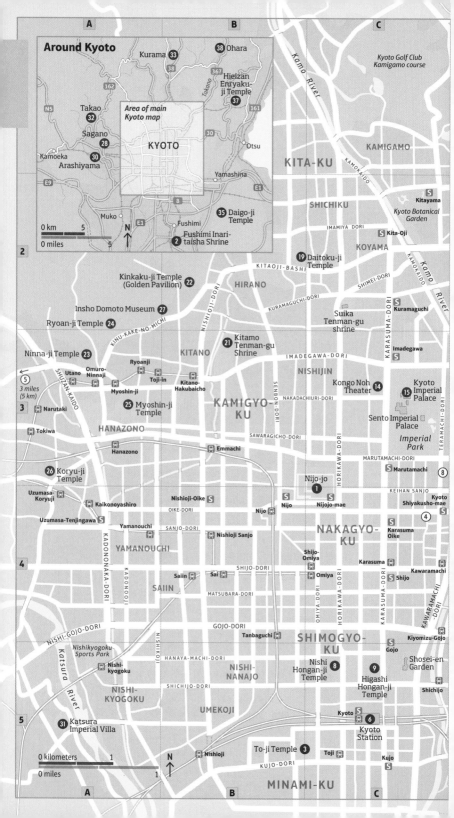

Around Kyoto

Kurama 33
38 Ohara 38
367 Hieizan
Enryaku-
ji Temple
37
161

Takao
32
Sagano
28
Kamoeka
Arashiyama 30

*Area of main
Kyoto map*

KYOTO

Otsu

Yamashina

162
N5
E9
30
8
E1

0 km   5
0 miles   5

Muko
Fushimi
Fushimi Inari-
taisha Shrine 2

Daigo-ji
Temple 35

N
E1

KITA-KU

Kyoto Golf Club
Kamigamo course

KAMIGAMO

KAMOKAIDO

Kitayama

Kyoto Botanical
Garden

SHICHIKU

IMAMIYA DORI

Kita-Oji

KOYAMA

Daitoku-ji 19
Temple

KITAOJI-BASHI

HIRANO

KITAOJI-DORI

Kuramaguchi

Kinkaku-ji Temple
(Golden Pavilion) 22

Insho Domoto Museum 27

Ryoan-ji Temple 24

KURAMAGUCHI-DORI

Suika
Tenman-gu
shrine

Imadegawa

SHIMEI-DORI

NISHIOJI-DORI

KARASUMA-DORI

KINU-KAKE-NO-MICHI

Kitamo
Tenman-gu
Shrine 21

KITANO

IMADEGAWA-DORI

Ninna-ji Temple 23

5
3 miles
(5 km)

SHIZAN-KAIDO

Utano
Omuro-
Ninnaji

Ryoanji

Toji-in

Kitano-
Hakubaicho

SENBON-DORI

NISHIJIN

NAKADACHIURI-DORI

Kongo Noh
Theater 14

Kyoto
Imperial
Palace 15

Kyoto
Imperial
Palace

Myoshin-ji

Myoshin-ji 25
Temple

**KAMIGYO-
KU**

Sento Imperial
Palace

TERAMACHI-DORI

Narutaki

Tokiwa

HANAZONO

SAWARAGICHO-DORI

Imperial
Park

Hanazono

Emmachi

MARUTAMACHI-DORI

Marutamachi 8

Koryu-ji 26
Temple

Uzumasa-
Koryuji

Kaikonoyashiro

Nishioji-Oike

Nijo-jo 1

HORIKAWA-DORI

KEIHAN SANJO

Kyoto
Shiyakusho-mae

Uzumasa-Tenjingawa

Yamanouchi

OIKE-DORI

Nijo

Nijo

Nijojo-mae

Karasuma
Oike 4

**NAKAGYO-
KU**

SANJO-DORI

Nishioji Sanjo

KADONONAKA-DORI

YAMANOUCHI

KADONOOJI

Saiin

Sai

SHIJO-DORI

Shijo-
Omiya

Karasuma

Kawaramachi

SAIIN

MATSUBARA-DORI

Omiya

OMIYA-DORI

Shijo

KARASUMA-DORI

KAWARAMACHI-DORI

GOJO-DORI

Tanbaguchi

**SHIMOGYO-
KU**

Kiyomizu-Gojo

NISHI-GOJO-DORI

Nishikyogoku
Sports Park

Nishi-
kyogoku

HANAYA-MACHI-DORI

**NISHI-
NANAJO**

Nishi
Hongan-ji 8
Temple

Gojo

Shosei-en
Garden

Katsura River

**NISHI-
KYOGOKU**

SHICHIJO-DORI

Higashi
Hongan-ji 9
Temple

Shichijo

NISHIOJI

UMEKOJI

Kyoto 6

Kyoto
Station

Katsura 31
Imperial Villa

N

Nishioji

To-ji Temple 3

KUJO-DORI

Toji

Kujo

MINAMI-KU

0 kilometers   1
0 miles   1

KYOTO CITY

Must Sees
1 Nijo-jo
2 Fushimi Inari-taisha Shrine

Experience More
3 To-ji Temple
4 Kyoto National Museum
5 Sanjusangen-do Temple
6 Kyoto Station
7 Chion-in Temple
8 Nishi Hongan-ji Temple
9 Higashi Hongan-ji Temple
10 Pontocho Alley
11 Kiyomizu-dera Temple
12 Gion
13 Nanzen-ji Temple
14 Kongo Noh Theater
15 Kyoto Imperial Palace
16 Ginkaku-ji Temple (Silver Pavilion)
17 Shoren-in Temple
18 Okazaki Park
19 Daitoku-ji Temple
20 Kamo Shrines
21 Kitano Tenman-gu Shrine
22 Kinkaku-ji Temple (Golden Pavilion)
23 Ninna-ji Temple
24 Ryoan-ji Temple
25 Myoshin-ji Temple
26 Koryu-ji Temple
27 Insho Domoto Museum
28 Sagano
29 Shisen-do Temple
30 Arashiyama
31 Katsura Imperial Villa
32 Takao
33 Kurama
34 Manshu-in Temple
35 Daigo-ji Temple
36 Shugaku-in Imperial Villa
37 Hieizan Enryaku-ji Temple
38 Ohara

Eat
1 Kichikichi
2 Gyoza Hohei

Drink
3 Jam Sake Bar

Stay
4 Tawaraya Ryokan
5 Hoshinoya Kyoto
6 Jam Hostel

Shop
7 Kyoto Handicraft Center
8 Ippodo

❶ 🖉 Ⓜ️ ▭

NIJO-JO

二条城

📍C3 🏠541 Nijojocho, Nakagyo 📞(075) 841-0096
🚈Nijojo-mae 🚌9, 12, 50, 101 🕐Oct-Jun: 8:45am-5pm daily; Jul-Aug: 8am-6pm daily; Sep: 8am-5pm daily
🚫Dec 26-Jan 3

Although it might not look like an impressive stronghold from the outside, the interior of Nijo-jo will not disappoint. Full of innovative defenses, and undeniably beautiful, it's a fascinating place to explore.

With few of the grand fortifications of other castles in Japan, Nijo-jo is instead best known for its unusually ornate interiors and "nightingale floors." This ingenious flooring is so called because it was designed to make bird-like squeaking sounds when walked upon, a warning of possible intruders. The complex was created by shogun Ieyasu Tokugawa (1543–1616), and symbolized the power and riches of the newly established Edo-based shogunate. Ieyasu's grandson Iemitsu commissioned the best Kano School painters for the reception halls, in preparation for an imperial visit. Ironically, in 1867 the last Tokugawa shogun resigned at Nijo-jo, in the presence of Emperor Meiji.

PAINTERS OF THE KANO SCHOOL

Kano artists came from a low-ranking samurai family, but grew to prominence in the 15th century for their Chinese-style land-scapes, figures, and bird and flower scenes. Nijo-jo has the largest Kano pieces ever executed. Among the motifs are life-size tigers crouching among bamboo groves, wild herons in winter, and frolicking peacocks.

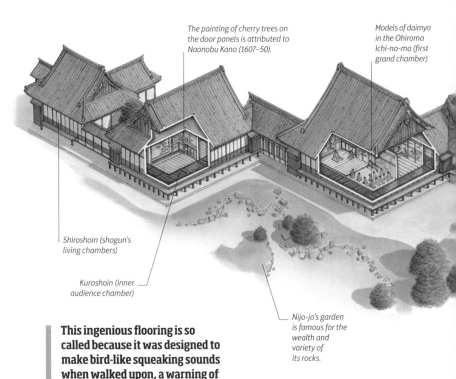

The painting of cherry trees on the door panels is attributed to Naonobu Kano (1607–50).

Models of daimyo in the Ohiroma Ichi-no-ma (first grand chamber)

Shiroshoin (shogun's living chambers)

Kuroshoin (inner audience chamber)

Nijo-jo's garden is famous for the wealth and variety of its rocks.

This ingenious flooring is so called because it was designed to make bird-like squeaking sounds when walked upon, a warning of possible intruders.

1 The Momoyama-period Karamon gate has a Chinese-style gable and gold-plated fixtures.

2 In the teahouse, visitors can take part in a traditional ceremony.

3 The castle's grounds are planted with a huge variety of cherry trees, which flower at different times between late March and mid-April.

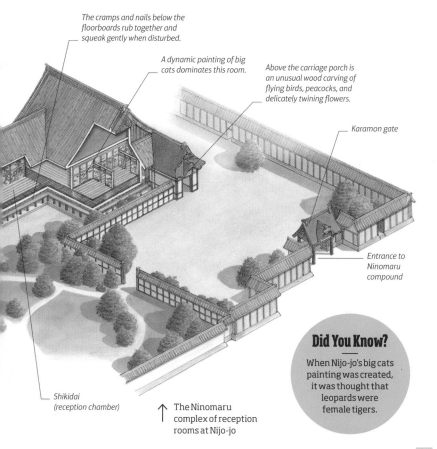

The cramps and nails below the floorboards rub together and squeak gently when disturbed.

A dynamic painting of big cats dominates this room.

Above the carriage porch is an unusual wood carving of flying birds, peacocks, and delicately twining flowers.

Karamon gate

Entrance to Ninomaru compound

Shikidai (reception chamber)

↑ The Ninomaru complex of reception rooms at Nijo-jo

Did You Know?

When Nijo-jo's big cats painting was created, it was thought that leopards were female tigers.

②

FUSHIMI INARI-TAISHA SHRINE

伏見稲荷大社

📍 B2 🏠 68 Yabunouchicho, Fukakusa, Fushimi 📞 (075) 641-7331
🚉 Fushimi-Inari, Inari 🕐 24 hours daily

This vast sprawling mountainside shrine complex with its thousands of bright red gates, meandering up the hills to the south of Kyoto City, is one of Japan's most striking sites.

Said to predate the founding of Kyoto, Fushimi Inari-taisha Shrine is an ancient wonder. Located in the ward of Fushimi – meaning "hidden water" – it is dedicated to Inari, the Shinto god of rice and sake (appropriate given that the area is Japan's second-largest producer of sake).

The thousands of vermilion torii that line the 2.5-mile- (4-km-) long trail from the main to the inner shrine were donated by ndividuals and companies, and their name and the date of donation is inscribed on the back of each gate. Larger gates can cost as much as a million yen to dedicate. The most impressive of these is the gargantuan Romon gate, which stands before the main shrine. It was donated in 1589 by Toyotomi Hideyoshi, the warlord responsible for the unification of the country.

INSIDER TIP
Hit the Streets

The streets around the shrine are worth exploring for their intriguing traditional architecture and bustling atmosphere. Keep an eye out for vendors selling roast sparrows on skewers. This traditional snack might not be for everyone as the bird is still very recognizable.

→ The stage, used for dance performances during yearly rituals at the shrine

← A red-collared statue of a fox – believed to be one of Inari's messengers – in the grounds of Fushimi Inari-taisha Shrine

Did You Know?

The function of a torii is to mark the boundary between the everyday and the sacred.

↑ Walking along the torii-lined path at Fushimi Inari-taisha Shrine

EXPERIENCE MORE

3

To-ji Temple
東寺

Q B5 **🏠** 1 Kujocho, Minami **🚌** 42 to Toji Higashimon-mae; 19 & 78 to Toji Minamimon-mae; 16 to Toji Nishimon-mae **⏰** Mid-Mar–mid Sep: 8am–5pm daily; mid-Sep–mid-Mar: 8am–4pm daily **W** toji.or.jp

Although it lacks the mossy beauty of many Kyoto temples, dusty To-ji (actual name Kyo-o-gokoku-ji) impresses by its history. Its Buddhas have been watching over the city ever since Kukai founded the temple in 794. The city's religious foundations were laid here, and echoes of bygone rituals seem to linger in To-ji's hallowed halls.

Kukai turned To-ji into the main headquarters of Shingon Buddhism. The sect's rituals relied heavily on mandalas, and in the Kodo (lecture hall), 21 statues form a mandala, at the center of which is Dainichi Nyorai, the cosmic Buddha who first expounded the esoteric teachings. About 1,200 years old, these and other major images were carved from single blocks of wood.

Statues of Yakushi Nyorai, the Buddha of healing, and his attendants Gakko and Nikko, are enshrined in the two-story Kondo (main hall). First built in 796, the present structure dates from 1603 and is considered a masterpiece. Rebuilt in 1644, To-ji's magnificent five-story pagoda – at 180 ft (55 m) the tallest wooden pagoda in Japan – has become a symbol of Kyoto. Inside are images of four Buddhas and their followers.

Northwest of the Kodo is the Miei-do or Taishi-do (great teacher's hall) where Kukai lived. It houses a Secret Buddha, a Fudo Myo-o image, shown on rare occasions, as well as an image of Kukai. A National Treasure, the graceful structure dates from 1380.

Kukai is remembered on the 21st of each month, when a flea market is held in the temple precincts. Many shoppers take time out for a brief pilgrimage to the Miei-do, where they offer money and incense, some rubbing the smoke onto whatever body part is troubling them.

THE BENTO BOX

A bento is a take-home meal in a compartmentalized box: office workers buy them for lunch, schoolchildren eat from them at their desk, and business travelers buy them at stations, such as Kyoto's, to enjoy with a beer on the bullet train. In its compartments there will typically be a portion of rice, a main serving of meat or fish, some vegetables, and pickles. But part of the charm of the bento is that anything goes. You may open a bento and find a small octopus or a tiny whole fish gazing up at you.

4

Kyoto National Museum
京都国立博物館

Q D5 **🏠** 527 Chayacho, Higashiyama **🚌** 100, 206 & 208 to Hakubutsukan Sanjusangendo-mae **⏰** 9:30am–6pm Tue–Sun **W** kyohaku.go.jp/eng

The city's National Museum was established in 1895 and is noted for its pictorial works, including Buddhist and ink paintings, textiles, and Heian-period sculptures. Special exhibitions are held in the Meiji-era brick building to the right of the entrance.

←

The five-story wooden pagoda in the grounds of To-ji Temple

→ The futuristic hall of Kyoto Station, an enormous glass-and-steel building

 ⑤

Sanjusangen-do Temple
三十三間堂

📍 D5 🏠 657 Sanjusangen-domawari, Higashiyama 📞 (075) 561-0467 🚉 Keihan Shichijo 🚌 100, 206, 208 to Hakubutsukan Sanjusangen-do-mae 🕐 Apr–mid-Nov: 8:30am–5pm daily; mid-Nov–Mar: 9am–4pm daily

Rengeo-in Temple, commonly known as Sanjusangen-do, induces an almost hallucinatory effect on its visitors who, once inside its elongated main hall, find themselves face to face with ranks of nearly identical Kannon (goddess of mercy) images – 1,001 of them, to be precise – all glimmering in the dark. Sanjusangen-do dates from 1164 and is the longest wooden structure in the world. Its name derives from the 33 (sanjusan) spaces between the building's pillars. The temple's main image of a 1,000-armed Kannon was carved in 1254 by Tankei at the age of 82. Upon its head are ten other heads, including a miniature image of the Amida Buddha. Stretching out on either side are 1,000 smaller images. Kannon was believed to have 33 manifestations, so the faithful would have invoked the mercy of 33,033 Kannons.

On the first Sunday in January the temple hosts an archery contest for young women, who shoot arrows from one end of the veranda of the main hall to the other.

---

⑥

Kyoto Station
京都駅

📍 C5 ℹ️ 2nd Flr main concourse, left from escalator; www.kyototourism.org

A sleek complex of soaring spaces, glass surfaces, and bleacher-like staircases, Kyoto's JR train station provides a futuristic entry to Japan's old imperial capital. Completed in 1997, the structure is the work of architect Hiroshi Hara, a former Tokyo University professor whose design triumphed in an international competition. Although it has been criticized for its refusal to incorporate traditional Japanese motifs in its design, the station is undeniably eye-catching. Thanks to its open-air spaces it also, ironically, resembles a traditional wooden Kyoto house: pleasant in summer, but drafty and cold in winter.

Within the station is a shopping area called The Cube, specializing in Kyoto craft items and food products.

STAY

Tawaraya Ryokan
Each room at this old *ryokan* has its own private garden.

📍 C4 🏠 278 Nakahakusancho, Nakagyo 📞 (075) 211-5566

¥ ¥ ¥

Hoshinoya Kyoto
Guests enter this luxury hotel on the Hozugawa River by boat. Soak in a deep cedar tub at the end of a long day.

📍 A3 🏠 11-2 Genrokuzancho, Nishikyo 🌐 hoshinoya.com

¥ ¥ ¥

Jam Hostel
A no-frills affair, this hostel offers communal dormitories with bunk beds, as well as a few private rooms.

📍 D4 🏠 170 Tokiwacho, Higashiyama 🌐 sakebar.jp

¥ ¥ ¥

Did You Know?

Chion-in Temple's Sanmon is the largest gate in Japan.

7

Chion-in Temple
知恩院

📍 D4 📫 400 Rinkacho, Higashiyama 🚃 Higashiyama 🚌 31, 46, 201, 203 to Chion-in-mae ⏰ 9am–4:30pm daily 🌐 chion-in.or.jp/en

The colossal Sanmon was built to proclaim the supremacy of Jodo-sect Buddhism, of which Chion-in Temple is the head-quarters. It also emphasized the authority of the Tokugawa shogunate, which funded the temple's restoration.

The well-endowed complex occupies the site where Honen, the founder of the Jodo sect, started to preach in 1175. It boasts a lavish founder's hall, a smaller hall enshrining an image of Amida Buddha, and elegant reception halls decorated with Kano School paintings. The Gongen-do

mausoleum enshrines the spirits of Ieyasu Tokugawa, his son Hidetada, and grandson Iemitsu. The temple also possesses a huge bell that is solemnly rung 108 times (once for each sin man is prone to commit) on New Year's Eve.

8

Nishi Hongan-ji Temple
西本願寺

📍 C5 📫 60 Horikawa-dori Hanayacho, Shimogyo 🚌 9, 28, 75 to Nishi Honganji-mae ⏰ May–Aug: 5:30am–6pm daily; Sep–Apr: 5:30am–5pm daily 🌐 hongwanji.kyoto/en

With their ornately carved transoms (panels above doors), massive flower-decked altars, and shimmering expanses of tatami matting, Kyoto's cavern-ous Hongan-ji temples testify to the power and popularity of the Jodo-Shinshu sect.

Nishi Hongan-ji Temple is rich in national treasures, but not all are always on view. They include the Shoin (study hall), with its lavishly decorated Shiroshoin and Kuroshoin compartments; Kokei no Niwa, a garden featuring cycad palms; two Noh stages, one of which is thought to

be the oldest Noh stage in existence; Hiunkaku, a large tea pavilion; and the Karamon, or Chinese gate. The Shoin is open twice a month, but dates vary (the Kuroshoin, however, is never shown). Hiunkaku can only be visited if a booking is made at least a day in advance, although this is not required on days when special events are held. A large donation is required if attending a tea ceremony or a Noh event at Hiunkaku.

9

Higashi Hongan-ji Temple
東本願寺

📍 C5 📫 754 Tokiwacho, Karasumadori Shichijo-agaru, Shimogyo 🚉 Kyoto ⏰ Mar–Oct: 5:50am–5:30pm daily; Nov–Feb: 6:20am–4:30pm daily 🌐 higashihonganji.or.jp

Higashi Hongan-ji's immense and lavish Goei-do gate is one of the first traditional structures visitors to Kyoto see as they head north out of Kyoto Station. The temple's Goei-do (founder's hall) dates

↑ Worshippers lighting incense sticks and praying at Kyoto's Chion-in Temple

from 1895 and claims to be the largest wooden structure in the world. The striking white plaster and gray-tile walls on the temple's northern side belong to the temple *kura*, or storehouse. Inside, there are many treasures.

Two blocks east of Higashi Hongan-ji proper is Shosei-en (nicknamed Kikoku-tei), a spacious garden owned by the temple. Poet-scholar Ishikawa Jozan (1583–1672) and landscape architect Kobori Enshu (1579–1647) are said to have had a hand in its design. Herons, ducks, and other wildlife find refuge here.

⑩ Pontocho Alley
先斗町通り

 D4 🚋 Kawaramachi
🚌 5, 17, 205 to Shijo-Kawaramachi

This charming alleyway is best appreciated after dusk, when it is reminiscent of an ukiyo-e print *(p131)*. Formerly a sandbar, the stretch of land began to be developed in 1670. The area flourished as an entertainment district and was licensed as a geisha quarter, a role it continues to play. Although neon and concrete are encroaching, the street largely remains the preserve of the traditional wooden *ochaya* – the type of teahouse where geisha entertain clients.

Pontocho is also home to the tiny Tanuki Shrine. In 1978 a fire broke out in Pontocho, taking the life of a geisha. Where it stopped, a ceramic *tanuki* (raccoon dog) was found shattered by the heat. Believing that the raccoon had sacrificed itself on their behalf, the residents built this little shrine to house its remains. Throw in a coin and a recorded message imparts such pearls of wisdom as "beware of fire." *Tanuki* statues have big testicles, symbolizing sacks of gold.

From the beginning of June to mid-September, many of Pontocho's riverside restaurants erect platforms, called *yuka*, over the canal running parallel to the Kamo River.

↑ The hilltop Kiyomizu-dera Temple, where visitors of all sects leave prayers *(inset)*

⑪ Kiyomizu-dera Temple
清水寺

 D4 🚋 294 Kiyomizu, Higashiyama 🚌 100, 206, 207 to Gojyozaka 🕐 6am–6pm or 6:30pm daily
🌐 kiyomizu dera.or.jp/en

While many other famous temples are the preserves of certain sects, Kiyomizu-dera seems to belong to everyone. For over 1,000 years, pilgrims have prayed to the temple's 11-headed Kannon image and drunk from its sacred spring. The main hall's veranda, a nail-less miracle of Japanese joinery, offers wonderful views of Kyoto. To see the temple itself, walk to the pagoda across the ravine, and you'll see why "to jump off Kiyomizu's stage" is the Japanese equivalent of the English "to take the plunge."

Gion
祇園

D4 **Gion-shijo** **100, 206 to Gion**

By turns tawdry and sublime, Gion is Kyoto's best-known geisha quarter, where Japanese men still come to revel in the company of professional geisha at private inns and teahouses found on the streets north and south of Shijo-dori, beside the Kamo River. Its history started in feudal times, with refreshment stalls catering to the needs of pilgrims and other visitors. These evolved into teahouses, or *ochaya*, fulfilling a variety of appetites. In the late 16th century, Kabuki theater moved from the Kamo riverbank, where it had started, into several venues just east of the river, furthering Gion's reputation as a playboy's paradise. One of these, Minami-za, still exists.

The Yasaka Shrine, whose striking two-story vermilion gate rises above the eastern end of Shijo-dori, was established in around 656 and originally called Gion Shrine.

Its deities protect from illness and, in 869, were paraded through the streets to stop an epidemic – the beginning of the famous Gion Matsuri. On New Year's Day, thousands flock here to pray for health and prosperity, while in early April crowds stream through its gates on their way to Maruyama Park, a cherry-blossom viewing site.

Gion's main shopping area is the stretch of Shijo between Yasaka Shrine and Shijo Bridge, which includes shops with expensive kimono accessories. On the southeast corner of Shijo and Hanamikoji is Gion's most famous *ochaya*, Ichiriki. Easily identified by its distinctive red walls, this teahouse is the setting of a scene in the Kabuki play *Chushingura*. Hanamikoji itself, a historically preserved zone, shows Gion at its classic, and classy, best. The restaurants and *ochaya* here are the haunts of politicians and company presidents, and are likely to turn a cold shoulder to people without a proper introduction. More accessible to tourists are the nearby Gion Corner and the Gion Kobu Kaburenjo venues.

Running east from Hanamikoji, north of Shijo, is Shinbashi, a street lined with discreet *ochaya*, and nary a neon sign to be seen. The average Gion-goer, however, is more likely to partake in karaoke with their colleagues in one of the gaudy, neon-lit buildings that populate the cluttered streets that make up the north-eastern part of the district, than to engage in geisha play at a prestigious *ochaya*.

DRINK

Jam Sake Bar
This bar boasts more than 30 different types of sake, organized by region, including many Kyoto specialties. Flights (tasters of different sakes) are available, and the staff speak English.

D4 **170 Tokiwacho, Higashiyama** **sakebar.jp**

← People walking through Gion, with the Yasaka Shrine in the background

GEISHA, GEIKO, AND MAIKO

Despite the fact that the profession, dating from the 17th century, is in decline and blurred by the activities of so-called *onsen* geisha and others who offer more sexual than classical arts, geisha still tread the streets of Kyoto. Known as *geiko* (children of the arts), their enclaves are Gion-kobu, Pontocho, Miyagawa-cho, and Kamishichi-ken.

A maiko's hair is her own, not a wig.

The white face and red lips are classic Japanese ideals of beauty.

GEIKO AND MAIKO COSTUME

Less polished than their *geiko* "sisters," *maiko*, apprentice geisha, are a Kyoto-only phenomenon. They wear their hair in a distinctive style, with ornamental hairpins, and sport a unique costume featuring a long, hanging *obi* (sash), tall *koppori* clogs, and an under-kimono with an embroidered collar. When becoming a fully fledged *geiko*, they exchange the embroidered collar for a white one in a transition known as *eri-kae*.

Under-kimono

PERFECT PERFORMANCES

Geisha's knowledge of traditional arts, skill at verbal repartee, and ability to keep a secret win them the respect, and some-times love, of their well-heeled male clients. The geisha world moves to the rhythm of the *shamisen*, a three-stringed instrument that originated in Okinawa. Poised and posture-perfect, the geisha dance to this eerie sound, sometimes using a fan as a prop. Geisha who choose not to specialize in dance will instead master the *shamisen* or another instrument, and play throughout their life.

Tabi socks

→

A maiko wearing her traditional costume before she becomes an accomplished *geiko*

Koppori clogs

INSIDER TIP
When to Visit

If you want to see geisha, the best time to visit Kyoto is April. Every day of this month, geisha in Gion-kobu stage performances, and the Miyagawa-cho district holds the Kyo Odori dance. For small-scale shows, head to Kamishichi-ken *(p199)* in the last two weeks of April for Kitano Odori.

↑ A geisha playing a *shamisen* with her teacher as another looks on

Nanzen-ji Temple
南禅寺

⑨ E4 ⑥ 86 Nanzenji Fukuchicho, Sakyo ⑤ Keage ⑫ 5 to Nanzen-ji-Eikan-do-michi ⓒ 8:45am–5pm daily (to 4:30pm Dec–Feb) ⑳ nanzenji.com

From its pine-studded outer precincts to the inner recesses of its subtemples, this quintessential Zen temple exudes an air of serenity. Since 1386, Nanzen-ji Temple has been the center of Kyoto's Gozan, or "five great Zen temples."

The Hojo (abbot's quarters) includes a small but exquisite dry garden attributed to Kobori Enshu (1579–1647), and Momoyama-period paintings, including the Tanyu Kano masterpiece *Tiger Drinking Water*. Nearby is a room overlooking a waterfall and garden, where a bowl of *matcha* (green tea) and a sweet can be enjoyed for a small fee.

The temple's colossal Sanmon, a two-story gate built

in 1628 to console the souls of those killed in the Summer Siege of Osaka Castle, is said to have been the hideout of Goemon Ishikawa, a legendary outlaw hero who was later boiled alive in an iron cauldron.

Three of Nanzen-ji's 12 subtemples are open to the public year-round. The most impressive, Konchi-in, boasts work by Kobori Enshu, featuring pines and boulders arranged in a tortoise-and-crane motif. Tenju-an has a dry garden and a small, lush stroll garden. Nanzen-in occupies the original site of Emperor Kameyama's villa. Restored in 1703, it faces a pond-centered garden backed by a wooded mountainside.

The red-brick aqueduct in front of Nanzen-ji Temple may seem incongruous, but for Japanese tourists this structure is one of Nanzen-ji's greatest attractions. Built in 1890, it formed part of an ambitious canal project to bring water and goods from neighboring Shiga Prefecture into the city. It was one of Meiji Japan's first feats of engineering.

Nanzen-ji Temple is synonymous with *yudofu*, boiled tofu, a delicacy best enjoyed during cold months. Specialty restaurants are located within the temple precincts.

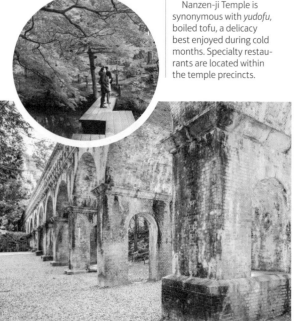

TOP 5 KYOTO SPECIALTIES

Yudofu
Kyoto is said to produce some of Japan's best tofu. *Yudofu* is soft tofu gently cooked in broth.

Kyo Tsukemono
Pickles made with just vinegar and salt.

Kyoto-style Sushi
Featuring preserved fish and vinegary rice.

Yatsuhashi
A soft, chewy, sweet cinnamon delicacy.

Yuba
The skin that forms on the surface of boiling soy milk is served with soy sauce, wasabi, and *ponzu* (citrus dressing).

Kongo Noh Theater
金剛能楽堂

⑨ C3 ⑥ Nakadachiuri-agaru, Karasuma-dori, Kamigyo ⑤ Imadegawa ⓒ Hours vary, check website for performance schedule ⑳ kongou-net.com

The Kongo Noh Theater across from the Imperial Palace grounds opened in June 2003, following its relocation from a site in Shijo Muromachi. During the Edo period (1603–1868) Noh was adopted as the official art of the warrior class, and the Kongo Theater has the longest history of regular use as a Noh stage in Japan; its players are particularly known for their agility and acrobatic feats. The theater incorporates several features

←

The aqueduct in front of Nanzen-ji Temple, whose grounds are perfect for walks *(inset)*

The bucolic setting of Ginkaku-ji Temple, also called the Silver Pavilion

from the earlier design, including the outdoor stage, pillars, and large acoustic earthenware jars. Regular performances are held at the theater, usually on the last Sunday of the month. Look out for exhibitions of Noh costumes and masks in the lobby.

Kyoto Imperial Palace
京都御所

📍C3 🚉3 Kyotogyoen Kamigyo Ⓢ Imadegawa ⏰9am–5pm Tue–Sun (to 4:30pm Mar & Sep; to 4pm Oct–Feb) 🚫Dec 28–Jan 4, public hols 🌐sankan.kunaicho.go.jp/english

With its stately pines and vistas of the Higashiyama, the Kyoto Imperial Palace Park (Kyoto Gyoen) is a spacious oasis in the heart of the city. On its grounds are the Imperial Palace (Kyoto Gosho) and Sento Imperial Palace (Sento Gosho), whose impressive stroll garden was built in 1 630. The Imperial Household Agency (Kunaicho), where tickets are issued for tours of the imperial structures as well as to Shugaku-in (p204) and Katsura villas (p203), is in the northwest corner. Remember to bring your passport.

At the southern end of the park is a delightful pond with an arched bridge. This is all that remains of one of several noble families' estates that occupied much of what is now parkland. From the bridge is an unobstructed view all the way north to the Kenreimon, the majestic gate in the middle of the south wall, which may be used only by the emperor.

Ginkaku-ji Temple (Silver Pavilion)
銀閣寺

📍E3 🚉2 Ginkakujicho Sakyo 📞(075) 771-5725 🚌5, 100, 203, 204 to Ginkaku-ji-michi ⏰Mar–Nov: 8:30am–5pm daily; Dec–Feb: 9am–4:30pm daily 🌐shokoku-ji.jp/ginkakuji

Ginkaku-ji Temple – actually, Jisho-ji; English nickname, Silver Pavilion – is considered by some to be an unequaled masterpiece of garden design; others find it overrated. But the important role the temple has played in Japanese culture is indisputable. Within its walls the tea ceremony, flower arrangement, and ink painting found new levels of refinement.

The temple was originally the mountain retreat of shogun Yoshimasa (1436–1490), who

is remembered for an artistic renaissance now referred to as Higashiyama culture. In tribute to his grandfather, who covered Kinkaku-ji Temple in gold leaf (p199), Yoshimasa had intended to finish his pavilion in silver. However, the ruinous Onin War thwarted that ambition. Minus its final coating, the graceful Silver Pavilion now shines with the patina of age.

EAT

Kichikichi
Enjoy chef Motokichi Yukimura's *omurice* (omelet on fried rice).

📍D4 🏠185-4 Zaimokucho, Sanjo Pontocho-dori Kudaru, Nakagyo 🌐kichikichi.com

Gyoza Hohei
This gem specializes in *gyoza*, fried dumplings.

📍D4 🏠373-3 Kiyomotocho, Higashiyama 🌐gyozahohei.com

17

Shoren-in Temple
青蓮院

📍 D4 🏠 69-1 Awataguchi Sanjobocho, Higashiyama Ⓢ Higashiyama 🚌 5, 46, 100 to Jingu-michi ⏰ 9am–5pm daily (see website for late openings) 🌐 shorenin.com

This aristocratic temple's symbol is its ancient camphor trees, whose 800-year-old gnarled limbs spread majestically on either side of the front gate. Shoren-in's grounds are beautifully landscaped, with a bright pond garden on one side and a mysterious, camphor-tree-shaded expanse of moss on the other. The teahouse in the garden has been rebuilt, the original having been burned in April 1993 by left-wing radicals protesting the Emperor's visit to Okinawa.

> Shoren-in's grounds are landscaped, with a bright pond garden on one side and a mysterious, camphor-tree-shaded expanse of moss on the other.

18

Okazaki Park
岡崎公園

📍 D3 🚌 5 or 100 to Kyoto Kaikan Bijutsukan-mae

Okazaki Park is home to museums, galleries, sports grounds, the municipal zoo, and Heian-Jingu, one of Kyoto's largest and newest shrines. Built in 1895, the shrine was intended to help boost the city's morale and economy – both of which were at a low ebb after Tokyo was made capital in 1868. With its vermilion pillars and green tiles, the shrine harks back to Tang Dynasty China. Its pond garden is famous for irises and a Chinese-style covered bridge.

The **National Museum of Modern Art** houses a superb collection of paintings by a school of Kyoto artists active during the Meiji and Taisho eras. Across the street is the venerable **Kyoto City KYOCERA Museum of Art**, which hosts exhibitions of European and American works. The **Kyoto International Exhibition Hall (Miyako Messe)**, hosts a variety of shows, while its basement museum presents scores of Kyoto crafts, including Kiyomizu-yaki porcelain.

National Museum of Modern Art
🎨 🏠 26-1 Okazaki Enshoji-cho, Sakyo ⏰ 9:30am–5pm Tue-Thu & Sun; 9:30am–8pm Fri & Sat 🌐 momak.go.jp

Kyoto City KYOCERA Museum of Art
🎨 🏠 124 Okazaki Enshoji-cho, Sakyo ⏰ 10am–6pm Tue-Sun 🌐 kyotocity-kyocera.museum

Kyoto International Exhibition Hall (Miyako Messe)
🏠 9-1 Okazaki Seishojicho, Sakyo ⏰ 7am–10:30pm daily 🌐 miyakomesse.jp

↑ Admiring works in the National Museum of Modern Art

↑ The beautiful gardens of Shoren-in Temple as seen from the teahouse

THE TEA CEREMONY

The point of the *chado* (the way of tea), in which whisked powdered *matcha* (tea), sometimes accompanied by a small sweet snack, is served by a host to a few invited guests, is summed up by the Buddhist notion "one lifetime, one meeting" *(ichigo, ichie)*.

TAKING THE TEA

Valued for its medicinal qualities, tea was imported from China in the 8th century. The nobility took to drinking it at lavish parties, and Shuko Murata (1422–1502) later developed the custom's spiritual aspects, which appealed to the samurai.

↑ Preparing the traditional tea utensils for a *chado* ceremony

The tea ceremony is a well-orchestrated series of events. First, you meet your fellow guests, before walking through the grounds of the teahouse, performing ablutions en route. Once you are inside the brightly lit room, you should compliment the features of the room, and the quality of the utensils, as you watch the tea being prepared. Only after bowing can you consume the *wagashi* (sweet) and tea.

In Kyoto, where the tea ceremony was developed, special rituals are put on for tourists, with commentary about the complex etiquette and Zen ideals.

↑ A well-presented tray with all the ingredients for a classic tea ceremony

> **INSIDER TIP**
> **The Perfect Matcha**
>
> To drink *matcha*, sit *seiza* (kneeling) on the tatami mat, bow to your host, then hold the tea with your right hand, and place it in the palm of your left. Turn the bowl clockwise about 90 degrees, raise it with both hands, and then empty the *matcha* in three gulps.

↑ Buddha statue in the Butsuden Hall of Daitoku-ji Temple

 19

Daitoku-ji Temple
大徳寺

📍 B2 🏠 53 Murasakino Daitoku-jicho, Kita 📞 (075) 491-0019 🚇 Kita-Oji 🚌 1, 12, 102, 204, 205, 206 to Daitoku-ji-mae ⏰ 9am–4:30pm daily

An air of eloquent restraint pervades the grounds of Daitoku-ji Temple. Founded in 1325, the temple prospered in the latter half of the 16th century, when it came under the patronage of warlords (and tea ceremony aficionados) Nobunaga Oda and Hideyoshi Toyotomi. Today, Daitoku-ji's subtemples, many with famous tearooms and jewel-like gardens, promote the ways of Zen and Tea.

Daisen-in, a subtemple, is famous for its Muromachi-period garden, while Koto-in features a grove of slender maples and a *roji* (tea garden). Zuiho-in, built in 1535 for a Christian daimyo (feudal lord), has a modern garden by Shigemori Mirei, with a crucifix made out of rocks. Ryogen-in, founded in 1502, has five gardens in different styles.

20

Kamo Shrines
上賀茂・下賀茂神社

📍 D2 🚌 4, 46, 67 to Kamigamo-jinja-mae; 4, 205 to Shimogamo-jinja-mae

At the northern reaches of the Kamo River, **Kamigamo Shrine** has probably existed since the 7th century, while **Shimogamo**, its southern counterpart, is a century older. Both are dedicated to the thunder deity. Set in sylvan Tadasu no Mori, Shimogamo has long played a role in ensuring the success of the rice harvest. The Aoi Festival features a procession between the shrines, horse races, and archery. Kamigamo Shrine is noted for its Haiden (worship) hall, rebuilt in 1628. In the vicinity are several *shake*, priests' residences. Of these, **Nishimura House** is open to the public.

DAISEN-IN GARDEN AT DAITOKU-JI TEMPLE

Mankind's relationship with nature, fate, and our place in the universe are all expressed in this dry-landscape design. For example, the "river of life" reemerges wider and deeper after being temporarily dammed, and the Takarabune ("treasure ship") stone glides serenely down, while the "turtle" stone tries vainly to swim upstream.

Kamigamo Shrine

🏠 339 Kamigamo Motoyama, Kita 📞 (075) 781-0011 ⏰ 5:30am–5pm daily

Shimogamo Shrine

🏠 59 Shimogamo Izumigawa-cho, Sakyo 📞 (075) 781-0010 ⏰ 6:30am–5pm daily

Nishimura House

🏠 1 Kamigamo Nakaojicho, Kita 📞 (075) 781-0666 ⏰ Mar 15–Dec 8: 9:30am–4:30pm daily

***

21

Kitano Tenman-gu Shrine
北野天満宮

📍 B3 🏠 931 Bakurocho, Kita 🚌 50, 101, 203 to Kitano Tenman-gu-mae ⏰ Apr–Sep: 5am–6pm daily; Oct–Mar: 5:30am–5:30pm 🌐 kitanotenmangu.or.jp

Always thronged with students praying for success in exams, Kitano Tenman-gu enshrines Heian statesman

→ Kinkaku-ji Temple, or the Golden-Pavilion, reflected in the lake waters

Sugawara no Michizane, or Tenjin-san, the deity of learning. Michizane's favorite tree, the plum (*ume*), is found throughout the grounds. On the 25th of each month, the shrine is the site of a bustling flea market, selling everything from Imari porcelains to nylon stockings.

Kamishichi-ken, an *ochaya* (teahouse) and bar-lined street running from Kitano Tenmangu to Imadegawa-dori, is Kyoto's oldest *geiko* (geisha) district. On February 25 the *geiko* conduct a tea ceremony in the shrine's orchard, and they perform dances for the public every spring and fall at the local theater.

Kinkaku-ji Temple (Golden Pavilion)
金閣寺

◙ B2 ⬚ 1 Kinkakujicho, Kita 🚌 12, 59, 101, 102, 204, 205 to Kinkaku-ji-michi ◷ 9am–5pm daily 🆆 shokoku-ji.jp/kinkakuji

A glimmering legacy of medieval Japan, Kinkaku-ji Temple (formal name Rokuon-ji) is known as the Golden Pavilion. It was built by the third Ashikaga shogun, Yoshimitsu (1358–1408), who, relinquishing his official duties (but not his hold on power), entered the priesthood at the age of 37. The temple originally served as his retirement villa. A fervent follower of the Zen priest Soseki, Yoshimitsu directed that the finished complex become a temple after his death, with Soseki as its superior.

The approach to the temple is along a tree-shaded path, which emerges into a bright garden facing the fabled pavilion. An exact replica of the original, which was destroyed by arson in 1950 (an event dramatized in Yukio Mishima's novel *The Temple of the Golden Pavilion*), the three-story structure is covered in gold leaf and topped by a bronze phoenix.

Mount Kinugasa serves as a backdrop to the stroll-type garden. The harmonious interplay of its various components makes it a superb example of Muromachi-period landscaping. Both pavilion and garden are especially exquisite after a snowfall.

🄾 PICTURE PERFECT
Going for Gold

Arrive at the Golden Pavilion as soon as it opens and head straight to the pond to get a shot of its golden silhouette reflected in the water. Use the surrounding maple trees to frame your shot.

23

Ninna-ji Temple
仁和寺

A3 **33 Omuro Ouchi, Ukyo** **(075) 461-1155** **Omuro-Ninnaji** **10, 26, 59 to Omuro Ninna-ji** **9am-5pm daily (to 4:30pm Dec-Feb)** **ninnaji.jp**

Ninna-ji Temple's colossal front gate serves as a reminder that this Shingon-sect temple used to be, until fires devastated it, a huge complex numbering up to 60 subtemples.

Completed by Emperor Uda in 888, until the Meiji Restoration (1868) Ninna-ji Temple was always headed by an imperial prince. The Kondo (main hall) and its wooden Amida image are National Treasures. Other sights include a five-story pagoda and a stand of dwarf cherry trees – the last of Kyoto's many sakura (cherry trees) to bloom.

Situated in the southwest of the precincts is the Omuro Gosho, a compound with a lovely Edo-period garden. On the mountain behind is the Omuro 88-Temple Pilgrimage, which reproduces in miniature the temples on Shikoku's 88-Temple Pilgrimage (p258). It takes about two hours to complete the full circuit.

↑ Visitors contemplating the rock garden and cherry trees in bloom at Ryoan-ji Temple

24

Ryoan-ji Temple
龍安寺

A2 **13 Ryoan-ji Goryonoshitacho, Ukyo** **Ryoanji** **59 to Ryoan-ji-mae** **Mar-Nov: 8am-5pm daily; Dec-Feb: 8:30am-4:30pm daily** **ryoanji.jp**

Founded in 1450, Ryoan-ji Temple is famous for its rock garden, a composition of white gravel and stones thought to be the ultimate expression of Zen Buddhism. Its riddles can be unraveled only by silent contemplation, something that the hordes of high-school students, not to mention the temple's recorded explanations, do little to facilitate. To avoid both, try to arrive just as the gates open.

The temple's lower pond garden should not be overlooked. Created before Zen arrived in Japan in the 12th century, its soft contours are in contrast to the spiritual rigors of the rock garden.

← Fearsome stone statue guarding the entrance to Ninna-ji Temple

25

Myoshin-ji Temple
妙心寺

A3 **64 Hanazono Myoshijicho, Ukyo** **Myoshin-ji, Hanazono** **10, 26 to Myoshin-ji Kitamon-mae** **9:10am-4:40pm daily (to 3:40pm Nov-Feb)** **myoshinji.or.jp**

Founded at the behest of retired Emperor Hanazono in 1337, destroyed during the Onin War, and rebuilt on a grand scale, this Rinzai-sect Zen temple complex boasts some 47 subtemples rich in Kano School paintings and other art objects. The main structures, aligned in a row in typically Zen fashion, include the Hatto (lecture hall), famous for a huge dragon painted by Tanyu Kano on its ceiling, and its bell, the oldest in Japan.

Subtemples normally open to the public include Keishun-in, with its four gardens and famous tea arbor, and Taizo-in, which has both a dry garden by Motonobu Kano (1476–1559) and a modern one by Kinsaku Nakane (1917–95). Taizo-in's prize possession is a famous example of Zen ink painting, Josetsu's *Catching a Catfish with a Gourd* (1413). Daishin-in has three gardens. Subtemples Reiun-in, which houses many Motonobu Kano works, and Tenkyu-in, noted for paintings by Sanraku Kano, are open on special days.

26

Koryu-ji Temple
広隆寺

Q A3 **🏠** 32 Uzumasa Hachiokacho, Ukyo **📞** (075) 861-1461 **🚉** Uzumasa-Koryuji **🚌** 11, 63, 66, 72, 73, 76 to Uzumasa Koryu-ji-mae **🕐** 9am–5pm daily (to 4:30pm Dec–Feb)

Koryu-ji Temple was founded in 603 by Korean immigrants. Among the impressive images in its Reihoden (treasure hall) is a Miroku Bosatsu (Buddha of the future) believed to have been brought to Japan from Korea in the 7th century. Kyoto's oldest image, the seated figure is known throughout the nation for its beatific smile. The temple's oldest structure, the Kodo, houses a 9th-century statue of the Amida Buddha.

27

Insho Domoto Museum of Fine Arts
堂本印象美術館

Q B2 **🏠** 26-3 Kamiyanagi-cho, Hirano Kita **📞** (075) 463-0007 **🚌** 12, 15, 50, 51, 52, 55, 59 to Ritsumeikan-daigaku-mae **🕐** 9:30am–5pm Tue–Sun **🚫** Dec 28–Jan 4

Along the road skirting the base of Mount Kinugasa lies the Insho Domoto Museum. It houses the impressive works of 20th-century *nihonga* master Insho Domoto (1891–1975). Often translated as "Japanese-style painting," *nihonga* is a fresco-like painting technique that utilizes mineral pigments.

SHOP

Kyoto Handicraft Center

This craft center north of Okazaki Park is a one-stop shop for local crafts, whether it's lacquer-ware, Kiyomizu pottery or simple origami paper. Learn how to make your own souvenir at a work-shop (also in English).

Q D3 **🏠** 21 Shogoin Entomicho, Sakyo **W** kyotohandicraft center.com

Ippodo

For more than 300 years, Ippodo has been selling Japanese teas. Here, at the main Kyoto store, there's a café and classes on how to prepare tea.

Q C4 **🏠** 52 Tokiwagicho, Nakagyo **W** ippodo-tea.co.jp/en/shop/kyoto.html

↑ Works by the artist Insho Domoto in the Kyoto museum dedicated to him

The vast pond in the garden of Tenryu-ji Temple, Arashiyama

28

Sagano
嵯峨野

📍A1 🚉Saga-Arashiyama 🚌28 or 91 to Daikaku-ji

Sagano's varied sights are by turn pastoral and poignant. Start exploring at Torii Moto, where a vermilion shrine gateway (torii) marks the beginning of a trail leading up to Mount Atago, abode of the fire divinity. Two thatched teahouses near the torii have been offering refreshment to pilgrims for centuries.

From the torii, head south to Adashino Nenbutsu-ji Temple. From the Heian to Edo periods, Adashino was a remote place where corpses were often disposed of. Established to offer solace for the souls of these forgotten dead, the temple gathered together their grave markers – rocks on which a likeness of the Buddha had been carved. The sight of row after row of these stone figures is strangely moving.

To the south is Gio-ji Temple, a tiny thatched nunnery. Known for the beauty of its fall foliage, the temple is bounded on one side by a magnificent stand of bamboo, while, to the front, slender maples rise from an emerald carpet of moss.

In central Sagano, the Jodo-sect's Seiryo-ji Temple houses an image of the Shakamuni Buddha reportedly brought to Japan in 987. Nison-in Temple has standing images of Amida and Shakamuni. The many maple trees on the temple's grounds attract large numbers of visitors in the fall. Charming Rakushi-sha (hut of the fallen persimmons) was the humble home of haiku poet Mukai Kyorai (1651–1704).

Secluded Nichiren-sect temple Jojakko-ji is on Ogura-yama mountain. A steep flight of stone steps leads to the temple from where there are great views of Kyoto and Mount Hiei.

29

Shisen-do Temple
詩仙堂

📍E2 📍27 Monguchicho, Ichijo-ji, Sakyo 📞(075) 781-2954 🚌5 or 8 to Ichijo-ji Sagarimatsu-cho ⏰9am–5pm daily

A samurai who had fallen out of favor with the shogunate, Jozan Ishikawa constructed this retirement villa below the Higashiyama mountains in 1641. A nearly perfect blend of building and garden, the hermitage (now a Soto-sect

Zen temple) retains the feel of a home. The garden is divided into two levels. The upper, best viewed from the main building's veranda, features a broad expanse of packed sand bordered by clipped azalea bushes. The lower level, which also makes use of areas of sand to add light and space, offers a fine view of the villa's tile-and-thatch roof and moon-viewing chamber.

30

Arashiyama
嵐山

📍A1 🚉Saga-Arashiyama, Hankyu Arashiyama 🚌11, 28 or 93 to Arashiyama Tenryu-ji-mae

Arashiyama has long held a special place in the hearts of the Japanese. At its center is timeless Togetsu-kyo, the

 GREAT VIEW
Bamboo Grove

Behind Tenryu-ji Temple is the fairy-tale-like Arashiyama Bamboo Grove, with its towering stalks. Visit during the Arashiyama Hanatoro in December, when the forest is bathed in an otherworldly green light every evening.

← Standing among the bamboo trees of Adashino Nenbutsu-ji Temple, Sagano

TOP 4

QUIRKY KYOTO MUSEUMS

Kyoto International Manga Museum
W kyotomm.jp
Home to about 300,000 manga and comic books.

Gekkeikan Okura Sake Museum
W gekkeikan.co.jp
This museum explores the history of sake brewing in Japan.

Nishijin Textile Center
W nishijin.or.jp
Focuses on the history of fabrics in the city. You can also try on kimonos.

Costume Museum
W iz2.or.jp
The place to see life-sized dolls dressed in beautiful traditional Japanese costumes.

graceful "moon-crossing" bridge. North of the bridge, mountainsides thickly forested with cherries and pines drop steeply to the river, which in summer becomes the stage for *ukai*, fishing done by firelight with trained cormorants. The narrow-gauge Torokko Train provides a different way of viewing the scenery.

Rinzai-sect temple Tenryu-ji was founded by the first Ashikaga shogun, Takauji, in 1339. The serene garden features a pond in the shape of the Chinese character *kokoro*, or "enlightened heart."

31

Katsura Imperial Villa
桂離宮

A5 **Katsuramisono** **Katsura** **33 to Katsura Rikyu-mae** **By appt only Tue-Sun; apply at Imperial Household Agency, sankan.kunaicho.go.jp/english**

Katsura Imperial Villa was built in 1620 by Hachijo no Miya Toshihito, an imperial prince, and later added to by his son. A sumptuous stroll garden (*p49*), Katsura is famous for the way in which its paths and stepping stones control the visitor's line of sight, resulting in a series

of ingeniously planned vistas. The scenic view from the Shokin-tei (pine zither) tea arbor replicates the scenery of Amanohashidate (*p238*). Many of the garden's scenic allusions are to places mentioned in the Chinese and Japanese classics. The tour includes the Shoka-tei (flower-viewing teahouse), then heads past the Shoi-ken (sense-of-humor teahouse), and on to the main villa, a set of halls poetically described as resembling a flock of geese in flight.

32

Takao
高雄

A1 **8 to Takao**

Esoteric mountain temples and pristine mountain scenery are Takao's main attractions. Jingo-ji Temple, founded in the 9th century, houses a wealth of national treasures including the Yakushi Nyorai (Buddha of healing). Set in an ancient cryptomeria forest, Kozan-ji Temple, founded in 774, has the look of an elegant estate.

Copies of the handscroll *Choju-Jinbutsu-giga* (frolicking birds and animals) are displayed in Kozan-ji's Sekisui-in hall, a brilliant example of Kamakura residential architecture.

33

Kurama
鞍馬

B1 **Kurama** **32 from Demachiyanagi Stn**

Famous as the abode of gods, demons, and super-heroes, Kurama was once an isolated village of foresters. Now a Kyoto suburb, it still retains an untamed feeling, a quality fully in evidence on the night of October 22, when the town celebrates its Fire Festival.

Kurama-dera, a Buddhist temple, was built in 770 to provide refuge for meditation. A gate marks the beginning of a mountain trail to the main temple buildings; the main hall offers splendid views of the Kitayama mountains. From the Reihokan (treasure hall) a path winds beneath towering cryptomeria trees to the village of Kibune, a collection of inns and teahouses alongside a stream.

EXPERIENCE Kyoto City

34 Manshu-in Temple
曼殊院

E2 | **42 Takenouchicho, Ichijo-ji, Sakyo** | **(075) 781-5010** | **5 to Ichijoji-Shimizu-cho** | **9am–5pm daily**

Even in spring and fall, when its cherries and maples draw the crowds, Manshu-in Temple maintains an atmosphere of repose. This Tendai-sect temple was restored in 1656 by the son of the prince who designed Katsura Imperial Villa (p203), and its elegant buildings call to mind those of the villa. The garden is composed of islands of rock and vegetation amid swaths of raked gravel, with the Higashiyama mountains forming a backdrop.

35 Daigo-ji Temple
醍醐寺

B2 | **22 Daigohigashiojicho Fushimi** | **Daigo** | **daigoji.or.jp**

The main draw at Daigo-ji Temple is subtemple **Sanbo-in**. Because Hideyoshi Toyotomi took a personal interest in restoring this after a visit in 1598, it contains some of the most representative works of art of the Momoyama period.

Did You Know?

Emperor Go-Mizunoo had 27 healthy children by six different women.

The lavish garden is noted for its many magnificent rocks, which were gifts to Hideyoshi from his daimyo (feudal lords).

The rest of Daigo-ji Temple is older and the graceful five-story pagoda, built in 951, is one of only two Heian-era pagodas in existence.

Sanbo-in
 Mar–Nov: 9am–5pm daily; Dec–Feb: 9am–4pm daily

36 Shugaku-in Imperial Villa
修学院離宮

E1 | **Yabuzoe, Shugaku-in** | **Shugaku-in** | **5, 31, 65 to Shugaku-in-rikyu-michi** | **By appt only Tue–Sun; apply at Imperial Household Agency, sankan.kunaicho.go.jp/english**

If Katsura Villa (p203) could be said to be yin, then Shugaku-in

could only be described as yang. While the former's garden, layered with literary and poetic allusions, is characterized by an inward-looking sensibility, spacious Shugaku-in might strike the viewer as extroverted.

Created by retired emperor Go-Mizunoo (1596–1680), the garden was a lifetime labor of love. Divided into three levels, each with a teahouse, the complex is imbued with a spirit of understated simplicity. Yet, a surprise awaits: the approach to the uppermost teahouse is designed so that the visitor is kept unaware until the very last minute of the panorama from the top of the Kitayama mountains, spread out as if an extension of the garden.

37 Hieizan Enryaku-ji Temple
比叡山延暦寺

B1 | **4220 Sakamoto Honmachi, Otsu, Shiga Prefecture** | **Yase-Hieizan-guchi, then cable car; or Hieizan Sakamoto, then cable car** | **hieizan.gr.jp/en**

A once mighty monastery fortress with 3,000 subtemples and thousands of sohei, or warrior monks,

 INSIDER TIP
Blossom Hunting

To have the cherry blooms to yourself during sakura season, try to get out and about before 8am to beat the crowds, or after 6pm, when the tour buses leave the city.

←

Fall foliage framing a graceful pagoda at Daigo-ji Temple

Hieizan today is but a shadow of its former self. Still, the solemnity of its isolated mountaintop setting and the grandeur of its remaining buildings make the trek here worthwhile.

Founded by the monk Saicho in 792, Hieizan became the main monastery of the Tendai sect. Although initially entrusted to protect the city from evil forces, the area itself became the bane of the capital. Emperor Go-Shirakawa (1127–92) once lamented that there were only three things beyond his control: the flooding of the Kamo River, the roll of the dice, and the warrior monks of Hieizan. In 1571, however, warlord Nobunaga Oda, angered by the temple's resistance to his authority, sent his army to attack the mountain. The complex was burned to the ground, and every man, woman, and child massacred.

The temple is divided into three distinct precincts. The Kokuho-den, a museum of treasures, is in the **east precinct** (Todo). Here, too, is the famous Konpon Chu-do, the inner sanctum, which enshrines a Healing Buddha

→
Lush gardens with fish-filled ponds *(inset)*, the serene setting for the Jakko-in Temple, Ohara

image said to have been carved by Saicho himself. Nearby Jodo-in (Pure Land Hall) is the site of Saicho's tomb.

In the Jogyo-do hall in the **west precinct** (Saito), monks chant an invocation called the *nembutsu*, while in the Hokke-do hall they meditate upon the Lotus Sutra, a central tenet of Tendai belief. Beyond these two buildings is the Shaka-do, the main hall of the west precinct.

Shuttle buses operate between these precincts, as well as to the lesser-known Yokawa precinct to the north.

East Precinct
⏱ Mar–Nov: 8:30am–4:30pm daily; Dec: 9am–4pm daily; Jan & Feb: 9am–4:30pm daily

West Precinct
⏱ Mar–Nov: 9am–4pm daily; Dec: 9:30am–3:30pm daily; Jan & Feb: 9:30am–4pm daily

38

Ohara
大原

🚩 B1 🚌 17 from Kyoto Stn

Known for its thatched farmhouses, delicious pickles, and other rustic charms, Ohara is also home to two famous temples. Set in an incomparably beautiful setting, Sanzen-in Temple's Amida Hall dates from 1148 and houses a meditating Amida Buddha. Its approach is lined with shops selling such local products as *shibazuke*, a pickle dyed purple with the leaf of the beefsteak plant. Across the valley is tiny Jakko-in Temple, where Kenreimon-in (1155–1213) lived. The sole survivor of the Taira clan, she prayed here for the souls of her son and kin killed by the Genji.

A SHORT WALK

EASTERN GION AND THE HIGASHIYAMA

Distance 1 mile (1.6 km) **Time** 20 minutes
Nearest station Gion-Shijo

For most of Kyoto's history, the area comprising the Higashiyama (Eastern Mountains) district lay outside the capital's official boundaries. As a result, it was always more secluded. Furthermore, being separated from the main city by the Kamo River, it was spared the fires that often ravaged Kyoto. Consequently, Higashiyama remains one of the city's most charming and unspoiled districts, making it a lovely place for a walk.

*The pleasant **Ishibe-Koji Lane**, with its discreet inns and teahouses, is an extension of the Gion entertainment district (p192). The exquisite wooden buildings with tiny gardens reflect the peaceful atmosphere of old Kyoto.*

*The elegant, five-story **Yasaka Pagoda** is all that remains of a Buddhist temple that once stood here.*

Yasaka Shrine
(p192) *oversees the religious rites of the city's main festival, the Gion Matsuri, in July.*

KACHO-MICHI

HIGASHIOJI-DORI

GIONMACHI KITAGAWA

Yasaka Shrine

START

GIONMACHI MINAMIGAWA

NE-NE NO MICHI

ISHIBE-KOJI LANE

HIGASHIOJI-DORI

Yasaka Pagoda

HOSHINOCHO

MATSUBARA DORI

GOJO-ZAKA

SHIMIZU NEW WAY

← The iconic levels of Yasaka Pagoda rising above the rustic streetscape of Higashiyama

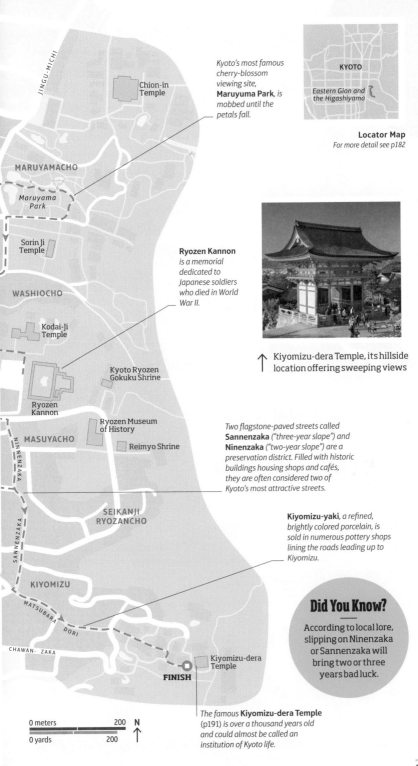

Kyoto's most famous cherry-blossom viewing site, **Maruyama Park**, is mobbed until the petals fall.

Locator Map
For more detail see p182

KYOTO

Eastern Gion and the Higashiyama

Chion-in Temple

JINGU-MICHI

MARUYAMACHO

Maruyama Park

Sorin Ji Temple

WASHIOCHO

Kodai-Ji Temple

Ryozen Kannon is a memorial dedicated to Japanese soldiers who died in World War II.

Kyoto Ryozen Gokuku Shrine

Ryozen Kannon

Ryozen Museum of History

Reimyo Shrine

NINNENZAKA

MASUYACHO

SANNENZAKA

SEIKANJI RYOZANCHO

KIYOMIZU

MATSUBARA DORI

CHAWAN-ZAKA

FINISH

Kiyomizu-dera Temple

↑ Kiyomizu-dera Temple, its hillside location offering sweeping views

Two flagstone-paved streets called **Sannenzaka** ("three-year slope") and **Ninenzaka** ("two-year slope") are a preservation district. Filled with historic buildings housing shops and cafés, they are often considered two of Kyoto's most attractive streets.

Kiyomizu-yaki, a refined, brightly colored porcelain, is sold in numerous pottery shops lining the roads leading up to Kiyomizu.

Did You Know?

According to local lore, slipping on Ninnenzaka or Sannenzaka will bring two or three years bad luck.

0 meters   200   N

0 yards   200   ↑

The famous **Kiyomizu-dera Temple** (p191) is over a thousand years old and could almost be called an institution of Kyoto life.

Did You Know?

Nanzen-ji is one of the most important temples of the Rinzai sect of Japanese Zen Buddhism.

Often heaving with tour groups, **Ginkaku-ji Temple**, the Silver Pavilion (p195) is set within a remarkable garden with ponds, a raked gravel garden, and pine trees.

GINKAKUJICHO

START

Ginkaku-ji Temple

SHISHIGATANI-DORI

Shishigatani Canal

Miroku-in Temple

JODOJI

Honen-in Temple

A short walk uphill, the **Honen-in** Jodo-sect temple, with its rustic, thatched gate and mounds of raked sand, is well worth a short detour.

Anraku-ji Temple

Reigan-ji Temple

SHISHIGATANI

Over a bridge to the east, **Otoyo-jinja Shrine** is one of a few small Shinto shrines among the great Buddhist foundations of the area.

Otoyo-jinja Shrine

SHISHIGATANI-DORI

Shishigatani Canal

Eikan-do Temple is a complex of buildings connected by corridors. It houses an Amida Buddha, and there are good views of Kyoto from the pagoda.

Koun-ji Temple

Kumano-Nyakuoji Shrine

Eikan-do Temple

NANZENJI

Rebuilt after the Onin War, most of **Nanzen-ji Temple** (p194) dates from the 17th century, apart from a Meiji-period aqueduct.

Sanmon

FINISH

Nanzen-ji Temple

0 meters		300
0 yards		300

N
↑

EXPERIENCE Kyoto City

A SHORT WALK
THE PHILOSOPHER'S WALK

KYOTO

The Philosopher's Walk

Locator Map
For more detail see p182

Distance 1.2 miles (2 km) **Time** 25 minutes
Nearest station Mototanaka

One of Kyoto's best-loved spots, the Philosopher's Walk follows a cherry-tree-lined canal meandering along the base of the scenic Higashiyama (Eastern Mountains) between Ginkaku-ji Temple south to Kumano-Nyakuoji Shrine, and connects with roads leading to the precincts of Nanzen-ji Temple. The pedestrian path is so-named because a Kyoto University philosophy professor, Nishida Kitaro (1870–1945), used it for his daily constitutional. A range of relaxed cafés, art and craft shops, restaurants, and boutiques are scattered along the scenic route. The path becomes a veritable promenade during the cherry and maple seasons, as couples from all over the Kansai region flock to enjoy its unspoiled nature blossoming before their eyes.

> 💬 INSIDER TIP
> **A Tranquil Path**
>
> For perfect harmony of peace and natural beauty, try an early morning walk among the petals. You'll find it easier to imagine Kitaro meditating along the canal without the crowds.

↑ Tranquil waters in the picturesque garden of Ginkaku-ji Temple

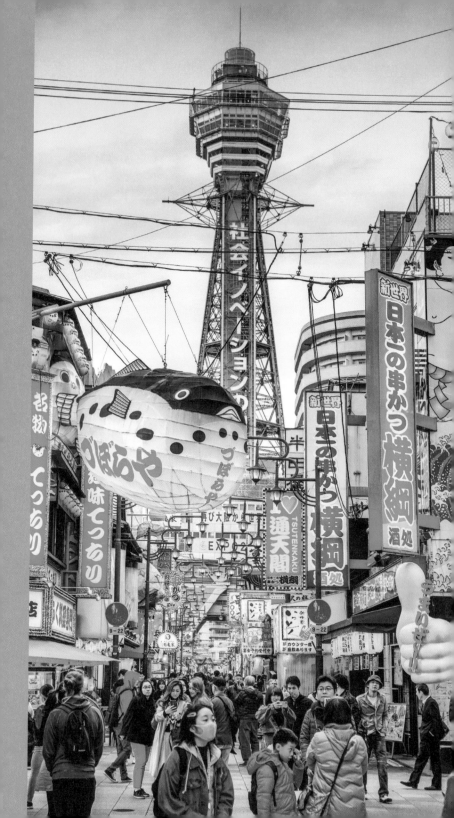

WESTERN HONSHU

The cultural heartland of the country, Western Honshu is where Japan's first imperial courts held sway, in an area called Yamato. The name Yamato refers to where heaven and earth divide, and also to the land founded by the mythical son of the gods, Emperor Jimmu. In the classical Japanese mind, Yamato is a holy place, a homeland, as the legendary Emperor Keiko expressed it in verse form almost two millennia ago, "whose trees and rocks, streams, and mountains house the gods."

Legend solidified into fact in the 4th century AD when a clan called Yamato expanded its kingdom in the region. Japan's first emperors, the Yamato rulers set up court on the Yamato Plain, the site of present-day Nara Prefecture, home to the graceful ancient city of Nara, with its quiet stroll gardens, the smell of lingering incense, and the reflections of winged pagodas in green ponds.

Despite this mystical history, this is not just a land of antiquity. Hiroshima, reborn after the devastating 1945 atomic bomb, the international port of Kobe, and Osaka are Western Honshu's great metropolitan centers.

WESTERN HONSHU

Must Sees

1. Nara
2. Osaka
3. Kobe
4. Himeji-jo Castle
5. Hiroshima Peace Memorial Park
6. Miyajima Island
7. Horyu-ji Temple

Experience More

8. Asuka Plain
9. Koka Ninja Village
10. Yoshino
11. Mount Koya
12. Kii Peninsula
13. Iga-Ueno
14. Okayama
15. Imbe
16. Kurashiki
17. Tottori Sand Dunes
18. Fukiya
19. Amanohashidate Sandbar
20. Lake Biwa
21. Uji
22. Matsue
23. Yamaguchi
24. Akiyoshi-dai Tablelands
25. Izumo
26. Iwakuni
27. Hagi
28. Tsuwano

↑ Children playing by a pond in the expansive Nara Park

NARA

奈良

△ D5 **🏠 Nara Prefecture** **🚆 Nara, Kintetsu Nara** **ℹ At former JR Nara Stn; www.visitnara.jp**

Founded in 710, Nara, then known as Heijo-kyo (citadel of peace), became one of Asia's most splendid cities. Avidly absorbing ideas from the mainland, the city became the grand diocese of Buddhism and the Far Eastern destination of the Silk Road. Having retained its natural beauty, Nara remains a symbol of tranquility.

① Nara Park

This 1,300-acre (502 ha) park is the cultural heart of the city, and it's where most of Nara's temples are located. Over 1,200 tame deer, regarded as messengers of the gods, roam the park.

② Kofuku-ji Temple

🏠 48 Noboriojicho **📞 (0742) 22-7755** **🕐 9am–5pm daily**

Few of the 175 buildings in this temple's original 669 complex remain. But even the reconstructions can lay claim to antiquity – the current five-story pagoda, burned to the ground five times, dates from 1426. The Treasure House has one of Japan's foremost collections of Buddhist art.

> 📷 **PICTURE PERFECT**
> **Oh Deer!**
>
> These hooved nomads have wandered Nara Park for centuries, nagging passersby for food. Grab your camera and stroll through the park to snap a shot or two of these beautifully photogenic critters.

③ Nara National Museum

🏠 50 Noboriojicho **🕐 9:30am–5pm Tue-Thu** **🌐 narahaku.go.jp**

Most of the exhibits in the Nara National Museum's collection, including Buddhist sculptures, paintings, and calligraphy, date from the Nara and Heian periods. The museum holds an annual exhibition in October and early November of treasures from the Shoso-in Treasure Repository, a storehouse in the Todai-ji Temple complex (p216) built to preserve Emperor Shomu's private collection of precious objects from all along the Silk Road.

④ Isui-en Garden

🏠 74 Suimoncho **🕐 9:30am–4:30pm Wed-Mon (Apr & May: to 5pm)** **🌐 isuien. or.jp/en**

This Meiji-era garden, with its many teahouses, is popular in spring for its plum, cherry, and azalea blooms, and in autumn for red maples.

⑤
Kasuga Taisha Shrine

📍160 Kasuganocho
🕐Apr-Sep: 6am-6pm daily;
Oct-Mar: 6:30am-5pm
🌐kasugataisha.or.jp

Originally built as the tutelary shrine of the Fujiwaras, who helped to establish Nara, Kasuga Taisha is one of the best-known Shinto sites. The original building was completed in 768 but, due to the strictures of purity and renewal governing Shinto beliefs, the structure had been rebuilt every 20 years until the end of the Edo era. The temple's lanterns are lit during festivals in February and August.

⑥
Shin-Yakushi-ji Temple

📍468 Takabatakecho
📞(0742) 22-3736 🕐9am-5pm daily

This temple was built by Empress Komyo (701–60) as an offering to the gods to help her husband recover from an eye disease. Some structures were rebuilt in the 13th century, but the main hall, the clay figures of the Healing Buddha, and the Twelve Heavenly Generals are originals.

⑦
Toshodai-ji Temple

📍13-46 Gojocho 🕐8:30am-5pm daily 🌐toshodaiji.jp

Founded in 759 by the blind Chinese sage and priest Ganjin, Toshodai-ji Temple is home to a stunning 18-ft- (5.5-m-) high Senju Kannon statue.

⑧
Yakushi-ji Temple

📍457 Nishinokyocho
🕐8:30am-5pm daily
🌐yakushiji.or.jp

Emperor Tenmu had this temple built for his wife's health, a gesture that seems to have worked as she outlived him. The temple's masterpiece is its east pagoda. Built in 730, it appears to have six levels, but three are roofs placed between the floors.

↑ The grand Golden Hall, the spectacular main hall of Shin-Yakushi-ji Temple

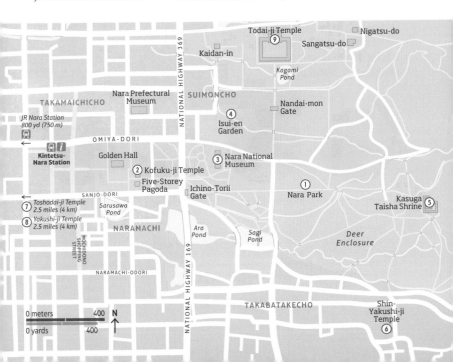

⑨ 🏯

TODAI-JI TEMPLE
東大寺

🏠 406-1 Zoshicho 🚌 Todaiji-Daibutsuden 🕐 Apr-Oct:
7:30am-5:30pm daily; Nov-Mar: 8am-5pm daily
🌐 todaiji.or.jp

The construction of Todai-ji Temple was ordered by Emperor Shomu ostensibly to house Nara's Great Buddha image but also to consolidate the position of the city as the capital and a powerful center of Buddhism.

This temple is the headquarters of the Kegon school of Buddhism. A World Heritage Site, Todai-ji Temple consists of the Great Buddha hall (Daibutsuden), and subtemples, halls, pagodas, and gates of exceptional historical and architectural interest. The most impressive building is undoubtedly the Great Buddha Hall. It was rebuilt twice and the current structure, completed in 1709, is only two-thirds of the original size. Despite this fact, it is still reputedly the largest wooden building in the world. Natural disasters have also failed to diminish the scale of the seated figure inside. At 53 ft (16 m) high, it is the world's largest bronze image of the Buddha. Behind the Buddha is a small hole bored into a large wooden pillar. A popular belief holds that if you can squeeze through the hole you will be protected from bad things happening to you in the future.

Entrance

> **Natural disasters have also failed to diminish the scale of the seated figure inside. At 53 ft (16 m) high, it is the world's largest bronze image of the Buddha.**

The Great Buddha Hall ↑
with the towering statue
inside, at Todai-ji Temple

Timeline

743

▲ The construction of the temple is ordered by Emperor Shomu and the first incarnation of the Great Buddha is cast.

1692

▲ After fires and earthquakes dislodged previous versions, the current head of the Great Buddha is cast and has remained in place ever since.

1709

▲ The current Great Buddha Hall is constructed after an earthquake.

1994

▲ International names, including Bob Dylan, Jon Bon Jovi, INXS, and Joni Mitchell, perform at the temple for four nights in May during the Great Music Experience.

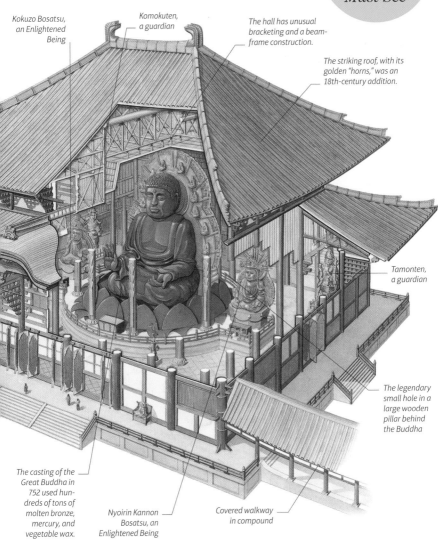

Kokuzo Bosatsu, an Enlightened Being

Komokuten, a guardian

The hall has unusual bracketing and a beam-frame construction.

The striking roof, with its golden "horns," was an 18th-century addition.

Tamonten, a guardian

The legendary small hole in a large wooden pillar behind the Buddha

The casting of the Great Buddha in 752 used hundreds of tons of molten bronze, mercury, and vegetable wax.

Nyoirin Kannon Bosatsu, an Enlightened Being

Covered walkway in compound

Walking towards the striking Great Buddha Hall at Todai-ji Temple ↑

INSIDER TIP
Spring Clean

Time your visit with Todai-ji Ominugui. Roughly translating as "Wiping Down the Great Buddha," this ceremony takes place on the morning of August 7. Up to 120 priests, wearing white robes and straw sandals, abseil down the Buddha's face, dusting as they go.

2

OSAKA

大阪

 D5 Osaka Prefecture Kansai, 22 miles (35 km) S; Itami, 6 miles (10 km) N Osaka, Shin-Osaka In JR Osaka Stn, Central exit; www.osaka-info.jp

Hideyoshi Toyotomi encouraged traders from all over Japan to settle in Osaka in the 16th century, and by the early 1900s it was an industrial powerhouse. Nowadays, the nondescript skyline is being replaced with galleries, futuristic living spaces, and exciting Postmodernist architecture, while the city's nightlife and culinary predilections attract fans from far and wide.

Osaka Museum of History

4-1-32 Otemae Tanimachi-Yon-Chome 9:30am–5pm Wed-Mon mus-his.city.osaka.jp

This modern museum uses life-size reconstructions, miniature models, and video presentations to bring to life the history of Osaka from ancient times to the modern day. Its most notable exhibits are objects excavated from the 7th-century Naniwa Palace, which once stood on this site. On the 10th floor there is a model of the Daikokuden, the main building of the palace, and excavations in the basement and on the adjacent archaeological site reveal the intriguing remains of warehouses and palace walls.

Of special interest to young children is the Resource Center on the eighth floor. Here, kids can complete a jigsaw puzzle using ancient pottery pieces or play with Bunraku puppets.

2

Osaka Castle

1-1 Osakajo Osakajo-koen Tanimachi-Yonchome 9am–5pm daily osakacastle.net/english

The present main donjon, dating from 1931, is smaller than the castle completed by Hideyoshi in 1586 but still gives some idea of the power and majesty of the original. The largest castle in the country at the time that it was built, Osaka-jo's turbulent history began when it was besieged and destroyed by the Tokugawa shogunate in 1615. The castle was rebuilt only to be struck by lightning a few years later, and then the remains were burned down in a fire in 1868. Only some ancillary buildings, including the Tamon tower and the impressive Otemon gate, have survived from the Tokugawa period.

The modernized lower floors of the main keep displays a collection of armor and memorabilia connected with Hideyoshi. Ride the elevator up to the eighth floor of the donjon – you'll be rewarded with great views over the city.

one of the world's finest collections of Oriental ceramics. The display comes from the Ataka Collection. Computer-regulated, light-sensitive rooms highlight the surfaces of the items. A few of the Japanese pieces are National Treasures.

↑ The futuristic curved exterior of the National Museum of Art

④ 🍴 🛍

National Museum of Art

🏠 4-2-55 Nakanoshima
🚇 Watanabebashi
🕐 10am–5pm Tue–Sun
🌐 nmao.go.jp

The entrance of the National Museum of Art, made from curved steel and extending high above the building itself, was designed to invoke both the strength and the flexibility of bamboo – the ancient building material. The collection inside is equally awe-inspiring, with works by Western artists such as Picasso, Cézanne, Miró, and Warhol, as well as ancient Chinese treasures and modern Japanese art. Check out the museum's website for a list of upcoming exhibitions.

↑ Beautiful Osaka Castle, framed by golden fall foliage

③ 🏛 📷 🛍

Museum of Oriental Ceramics

🏠 1-1-26 Nakanoshima
🚇 Naniwabashi
Ⓢ Yodoyabashi
🕐 9:30am–5pm Tue–Sun 🌐 moco.or.jp

With over 1,000 items of mostly Chinese and Korean origin, this museum houses

> 💬 INSIDER TIP
> **Hot Ticket**
>
> The city center is served by a user-friendly loop system called the JR Kanjo Line. Visitors who intend to cover a lot of sightseeing ground will benefit from buying a one- or two-day pass that offers unlimited travel on subways, trams, and local train lines.

Must See

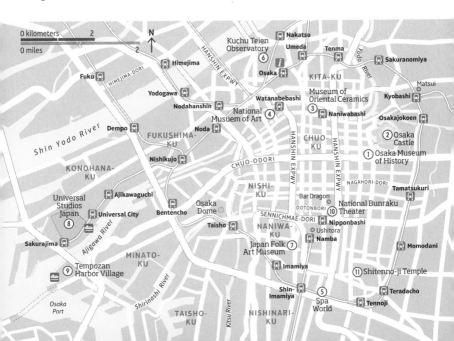

Spa World

🏠 3-4-24 Ebisuhigashi 🚉 Shin-imamiya 🚇 Dobutsuenmae line ⏰ 24 hours daily; some areas have different hours 🌐 spaworld.co.jp/english

Built to cater for up to 5,000 people at any time, Spa World offers an amazing bathing experience, with the water coming from springs almost 3,000 ft (900 m) underground. The complex is divided into zones representing bathing customs of various countries around the world, such as China and Turkey. There are also stone saunas representing eight countries, including Finland, Russia, Iceland, and Korea.

Adding a family friendly side is an amusement pool with a collection of water slides, plus a pool area for small children.

Away from the water, the dining area features a number of restaurants serving Osakan favorites such as *okonomiyaki* and *kushikatsu* (fried skewers).

Kuchu Teien Observatory

🏠 1-1-88 Oyodonaka 🚉 Osaka 🚇 Umeda ⏰ 9:30am–10:30pm daily 🌐 skybldg.co.jp/en

This futuristic structure, reached by taking an exposed glass escalator to the 39th floor, is not for those who suffer from vertigo or fear of being caught in high places in earthquake-prone regions. The observatory, sited 576 ft (173 m) above ground, straddles the twin towers of Hara Hiroshi's Umeda Sky Building. Views of Osaka from the top are incredible. There are also

↑ Walking toward the twin towers housing the Kuchu Teien Observatory

high-tech displays and a virtual-reality game center here, but neither can really compete with the panoramas.

Japan Folk Art Museum

🏠 3-7-6 Nambanaka 🚉🚇 Namba 🚋 Nihon-teien-mae 🔒 For restoration work; check website for details 🌐 nihon-kogeikan.or.jp

An outstanding collection of traditional folk arts and crafts is housed in this museum. It offers a superb introduction to regional handicrafts centering on textiles and fabrics, ceramic ware, bamboo, toys, and more.

---

⑧

Universal Studios Japan

🏠 2-1-33 Sakurajima 🚉 Universal City ⏰ Hours vary, check website for details 🌐 usj.co.jp/web/en/us

This theme park aims to attract people of all ages and is fast becoming a major landmark of Osaka. There are nine themed areas, as well as live entertainment throughout the site. Among the attractions are the Hollywood Premiere Parade, Hollywood Magic, and, in the "New York" area, a St. Patrick's Day Celebration. The Wizarding World of Harry Potter, meanwhile, features a state-of-the-art Harry Potter and the Forbidden Journey™ ride.

The latest addition is Minion Park, inspired by *Despicable Me*.

Tempozan Harbor Village

📍 1-1-10 Kaigandori 🚇 Osaka-ko; hours vary, check website ⏰ Daily 🌐 kaiyukan.com/language/eng

Begun as a reclamation program in the 1830s, this waterfront project in Osaka Port is the new face of an older, Edo-period landfill. The enormous Tempozan Ferris Wheel, once the world's tallest at 371 ft (113 m), offers passengers panoramic views of the entire city of Osaka, the ocean, and mountains. The ferris wheel can hold up to 480 passengers in its 60 cars. At night the illuminated wheel is a popular date venue for the locals.

As well as a Legoland Discovery Center and the mammoth Osaka Aquarium Kaiyukan, the village is also home to the Tempozan Marketplace – a large center for restaurants and shopping.

National Bunraku Theater

📍 1-12-10 Nippon-bashi 🚇 Nipponbashi 🌐 ntj.jac.go.jp

Japan's main venue for Bunraku puppet dramas, the National Bunraku Theater can be spotted by the colorful banners hanging outside. Shows take place every January, April, June, July, August, and November, and headsets are available for foreign visitors.

Shitenno-ji Temple

📍 1-11-18 Shitennoji 🚇 Shitennoujimae Yuhigaoka 📞 (06) 6771-0066 ⏰ Daily

Prince Shotoku ordered the construction of the original temple here in 593, and the complex is considered to be the birthplace of Japanese Buddhism. The temple was destroyed many times by fire, and the current concrete buildings date from 1965. As exact copies of the originals, however, they are of interest to visitors wishing to know more about early Buddhist architecture. The best time to visit the temple is on the 21st and 22nd of every month, when an excellent flea market is held on the site.

DRINK

Matsui

This *tachinomi* offers a beer, five *kushikatsu* (deep-fried) or *yakitori* (grilled) skewers, and an appetizer for only Y1,000 until 5pm.

📍 3-5-1 Higashinodamachi 📞 (06) 6353-3106

Ushitora

An affordable and friendly bar, Ushitora is the perfect place to relax after a tiring day exploring the city.

📍 15-19 Nanbasennichimae 📞 (06) 6632-7830

Bar Dragon

Located right in the heart of Osaka's iconic, riverside Dotonbori district, this friendly and lively bar offers local sake from the Kansai region.

📍 2-1-3 Dotonbori 📞 (06) 6210-2910

←

The vermilion Saidaimon (West Gate) at the entrance to Shitenno-ji Temple

3

KOBE

神戸

△D5 **△**Hyogo Prefecture **✈**Kobe, 5 miles (8 km) SE; Kansai 43 miles (70 km) S **🚄**Shin-Kobe, Kobe **🛈**In front of JR Sannomiya Stn; www.feel-kobe.jp

Kobe has been a center of international trade since the 8th century and is today home to a large expatriate community, giving it a cosmopolitan and multicultural flair. The city hit the headlines in 1995 when a huge earthquake struck, but there is little evidence of the disaster now, so effectively has the city been rebuilt. The downtown area is famous for its nightlife, while Kobe beef is renowned around the world.

Did You Know?

Kobe beef only comes from the black wagyu cows of Hyogo Prefecture.

("southern barbarian") at first referred to foreigners who arrived from the south, mainly the Portuguese. Later it was applied to all Europeans.

1

Chinatown

△1-3-18 Sakaemachidori **🚄**Motomachi

The city's 14,000 or more Chinese residents have turned this quarter (Nankin-machi) into a lively and colorful slice of Kobe life. Approached via four large gateways, the central plaza, Nankin Park, is bordered by Chinese restaurants and trinket shops, and is filled with street vendors. The park has statues representing the 12 animals of the Chinese astrological calendar.

2

Kobe City Museum

△24 Kyomachi **🚄**Motomachi **🕐**Hours vary, check website **🌐**kobecitymuseum.jp

This museum covers the history of the city from its origins to its reconstruction after the 1995 earthquake. There is an intriguing display of objects retrieved from the Old Foreign Settlement and a scale model of the area. The museum also has the world's top collection of 16th-century Nanban art. The word Nanban

3

Kitano-cho

△12-min walk N of Sannomiya Stn **🚄**Sannomiya

Wealthy foreign traders and diplomats built homes in this area after Kobe became one of Japan's major international ports at the start of the Meiji period. Over 20 of these beautifully preserved homes, many in the Gothic Victorian style, are open to the public. The area, which suggests fin-de-siècle European elegance to many Japanese people, is considered one of Kobe's more fashionable districts.

↑ Cosmopolitan Kobe's eye-catching skyline at sunset

THE GREAT HANSHIN EARTHQUAKE

At 5:46am on January 17, 1995, the Great Hanshin Earthquake struck Japan, its epicenter 10 miles (16 km) beneath the Akashi Strait near Kobe. The tremor lasted almost a minute and measured 6.9 on the Moment Magnitude scale. The quake and aftershocks killed over 6,000 inhabitants and destroyed over 100,000 buildings.

④
Meriken Park

⌂ 2-2 Hatobacho
Ⓜ Motomachi

Meriken Park's name comes from the Meiji-era rendition of "American." From the park you will see the distinctive outline of the Kobe Maritime Museum, which has a roof designed like the sails of a ship and houses displays on the city's role as a port. For a good overview of the area climb the Kobe Port Tower on Naka Pier.

⑤ 🚶
Kiku-Masamune Shuzo Kinenkan

⌂ 1-9-1 Uozakinishimachi, Higashinada Ⓜ Minami Uozaki ⊙ 9:30am–4:30pm daily

Although most of the best breweries were razed during the earthquake, reconstruction and preservation of the few

left has been going on at a furious pace, and it is possible once again to visit some of Kobe's best-known producers. The Kiku-Masamune Shuzo Kinenkan museum offers an insight into the art of making sake. Although the brewery's storehouses perished in the quake, the watermill cottage survived and now houses a small but interesting display of brewing utensils.

DRINK

Hamafukutsuru Ginjo Brewery

At this brewery and shop, visitors can take a tour to watch the fermenting process and also try a selection of sakes in a tasting.

⌂ 5-min walk from Hanshin Uozaki Stn
⊙ 10am–5pm Tue–Sun
🖥 hamafukutsuru.co.jp

Shin-Kobe Station 0.6 miles (1 km)

③ Kitano-cho

0 meters 500 N
0 yards 500

PEARL STREET

KITANO-ZAKA

FLOWER ROAD

Ikuta Shrine

KITANO

Sannomiya S

Sannomiya

Kobe Kokusai Kaikan

Sorakuen Garden

NAKAYAMATE-DORI

IKUTA SHINMICHI

TOR ROAD

KOIWAWA

MOTOMACHI-DORI

IKUTA ROAD

Sannomiya-Hanadokei-Mae

FLOWER ROAD

Kencho-Mae S

Motomachi S

Kyukyoryuchi-Daimarumae S

URAMACHI-DORI

Kobe City Hall

SUNSET-DORI

OLD FOREIGN SETTLEMENT

Kiku-Masamune Shuzo Kinenkan 4 miles (6.5 km) ⑤

Chinatown ①

Kobe City Museum ②

MEIKEN RD

KYOMACHI

Hamafukutsuru Ginjo Brewery 5 miles (8 km)

Kobe Station 0.6 miles (1 km)

KAIGAN-DORI

SAKEMACHI-DORI

Minatomoto-machi S

HANSHIN EXPRESSWAY 3

HAMATE BYPASS

Kobe Port Tower

Kobe Maritime Museum

Kobe Harbour

④ Meriken Park

4 ⌖

HIMEJI-JO CASTLE

姫路城

🅐 D5 🅞 Hyogo Prefecture 🅡 Himeji 🅞 9am–4pm daily (to 5pm May–Aug)
🅦 himejicastle.jp

Better known as Shirasagi-jo, the "white egret castle," Himeji-jo resembles a bird taking flight, with its plastered walls stretching either side of the main donjon. For many people its military architecture, ameliorated by these graceful aesthetic lines, qualifies Himeji-jo as the ultimate samurai castle.

The castle's main donjon was developed by Terumasa Ikeda in 1609, transforming a modest military stronghold into a symbol of the Tokugawa shogunate's newly consolidated power. With its undulating dormer and Chinese gables, the tower is undeniably beautiful, but it was also built to withstand attack. Angled chutes set at numerous points in the walls enabled stones, boiling oil, and water to be dropped on the heads of any invaders. On the roof, dolphin-like *shachi-gawara* motifs were thought to protect the donjon from fire, while the portholes, in the shape of circles, triangles, and rectangles, were used by musketeers and archers.

Originally an armaments store, the interior remains largely unadorned and houses exhibits relating to castle life. The Museum of Weaponry displays samurai arms and armor, as well as guns and pouches of gunpowder, introduced to Japan by the Portuguese in the 16th century. The uppermost chamber offers panoramas on four sides over Himeji, but the main donjon's exterior is far more awe-inspiring than its stark interior.

↑ Samurai armor in the Museum of Weaponry

↑ A *shachi-gawara* statue on the roof of the main donjon

> **Better known as Shirasagi-jo, the "white egret castle," Himeji-jo resembles a bird taking flight, with its plastered walls stretching either side of the main donjon.**

1333
△ Akamatsu Norimura builds a fort in a strategic location on top of a hillock at Himeji.

1600
△ Battle of Sekigahara, after which Terumasa Ikeda is rewarded with Himeji-jo.

1609
△ The five-story donjon is completed.

1749
△ Tadazumi Sakai and descendants live in the castle until the Meiji Restoration of 1867.

Did You Know?

The main donjon appears to have five floors, but it actually has six.

The main donjon of Himeji-jo Castle standing on a hill high above the city ↑

Exploring the Complex

Built on a high bluff, Himeji-jo Castle, the grandest of Japan's 12 remaining feudal castles, dominates the city of Himeji, and is a designated UNESCO World Heritage Site. Its cinematic potential was exploited by Akira Kurosawa in his 1985 film *Ran*, a Japanese retelling of Shakespeare's *King Lear*. But the tranquil grounds and graceful buildings seem a world away from both the castle's feudal past and the modern city that it overlooks. The verdant complex is crowned by its famed donjon, but it is also blessed with undulating walls, moats, and baileys. Although these aspects were once defensive, they now serve as the perfect setting for taking a stroll, spotting cherry blossoms, or even practicing tai chi.

Vanity Tower – the abode of Princess Sen (1597–1667) and other women – was locked each night under guard.

West bailey (nishi-nomaru)

Entrance

Though never put to the test, the castle's labyrinth of passageways and gateways in the outer zones were designed to confuse enemies.

Sangoku moat

↑ Practicing tai chi in a park in Himeji overlooked by the castle

↑ The castle grounds covered in blush-pink blooms during cherry-blossom season

💬 INSIDER TIP
Castle of Light

Every May, during the Himeji Castle Festival, the main donjon is illuminated by a light show. Visit the castle complex the week after Golden Week (May) to view this spectacle, where the old and new world seem to collide in a riot of color.

Must See

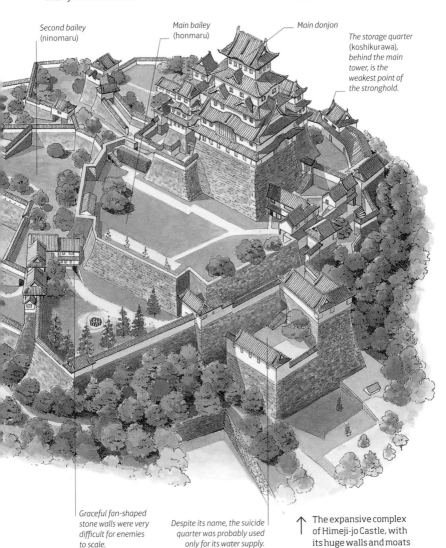

Second bailey (ninomaru)

Main bailey (honmaru)

Main donjon

The storage quarter (koshikurawa), behind the main tower, is the weakest point of the stronghold.

Graceful fan-shaped stone walls were very difficult for enemies to scale.

Despite its name, the suicide quarter was probably used only for its water supply.

↑ The expansive complex of Himeji-jo Castle, with its huge walls and moats

5

HIROSHIMA PEACE MEMORIAL PARK

広島平和記念公園

🅰B5 🚉Hiroshima Prefecture ✈Hiroshima 25 miles (40 km) E 🚉Hiroshima, then bus to Genbaku-Domu-mae 🚌🚋Genbaku-Domu-mae ⏰Peace Memorial Museum: 8:30am–6pm daily (to 5pm Dec–Feb; to 7pm Aug) 🌐visithiroshima.net

For the worst of reasons, Hiroshima needs no introduction. Each year millions of visitors are drawn to the city where so many people were wiped out in one instance of apocalyptic destruction. Built in the 1950s, this poignant park remembers this earth-shattering event.

The half-melted wreckage of the A-Bomb Dome – the former Industrial Promotion Hall – stands at the hypocenter of the blast. By the northern entrance to the park are the Peace Bell and the Memorial Mound, which contains the ashes of tens of thousands of people cremated here. Farther into the park is the Children's Peace Monument, depicting a girl with a crane. A victim of the bomb, this girl believed that she would recover if she made 1,000 paper cranes. She did not survive, but fresh paper cranes sent by school children adorn the memorial. Across the road is the Flame of Peace, which will only be extinguished when nuclear weapons have been eliminated, and the Cenotaph. Designed by Kenzo Tange for the victims of the bomb, this chest contains the names of all those who died, together with an inscription that reads "Rest in peace. We will never repeat the error." The centerpiece of the park is the Peace Memorial Museum. Poignant exhibits include a half-melted bronze Buddha, a mangled tricycle, and the imprint of a dark shadow on the granite steps of the Sumitomo Bank building – the sole remains of someone.

THE BOMBING OF HIROSHIMA

As World War II dragged on into the summer of 1945, the US decided to deploy an entirely new weapon to force Japan to surrender. On August 6 a B-29 bomber sent the first atomic bomb down on Hiroshima, a city that had seen little conventional bombing. It exploded at 8:15am, 1,900 ft (580 m) above the city center. Tens of thousands of people were killed instantly by the blast, and the death toll rose to 300,000 over the following years as after-effects took hold. Nagasaki (p266) suffered a similar fate three days later.

↑ Paying respect to the victims at the curved Cenotaph

→
Strings of paper cranes hanging on the Children's Peace Monument

303,195
Names contained in the chest of the Cenotaph.

↑ A cherry tree in bloom in front of the haunting twisted girders of the A-Bomb Dome

MIYAJIMA ISLAND

宮島

A B5 **N** Hiroshima Prefecture **R** From Hiroshima to Miyajima-guchi, then ferry **F** From Hiroshima Port or Miyajima-guchi Stn **i** At ferry terminal; www.miyajima.or.jp/english

Miyajima, as this sacred place is commonly known, means shrine island, although its official name is Itsukushima. A UNESCO World Heritage Site, it is symbolized by Itsukushima Shrine's prominent vermilion Otorii (grand gate) rising from the sea during high tide, and enchanting visitors for centuries.

The shrine sits in a beautiful setting. Felling trees is forbidden so the island has maintained its virgin forest and provides a home to a variety of flora and fauna, while tame deer roam freely. Nature trails snake up Momijidani Park, which towers behind Itsukushima Shrine.

Acclaimed as one of Japan's three most scenic views, the torii of Itsukushima Shrine appears to float in the water. To maintain the island's purity, pilgrims were not allowed to set foot on its ground. Instead, their boats would pass through this gate to reach the shrine, which had a pier into the water. The warlord Taira no Kiyomori, who funded the shrine, built the first Otorii in the 12th century, but the present 50-ft- (16-m-) high structure dates from 1875.

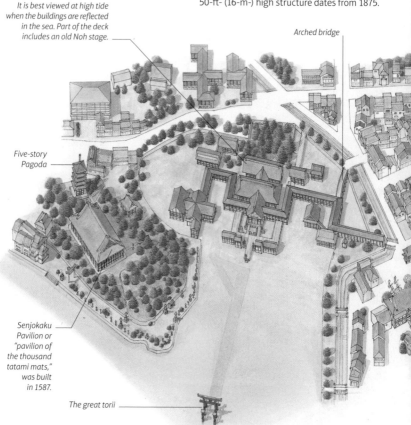

Itsukushima Shrine, founded in 593, is built on stilts over a cove. It is best viewed at high tide when the buildings are reflected in the sea. Part of the deck includes an old Noh stage.

Arched bridge

Five-story Pagoda

Senjokaku Pavilion or "pavilion of the thousand tatami mats," was built in 1587.

The great torii

1. The Otorii's four-legged *(yotsuashi)* construction grants it stability.

2. On a bluff overlooking Itsukushima Shrine is the Goju-no-to, a five-story pagoda built in 1407.

3. *Komainu*, or "lion-dogs," often guard the entrance or *honden* of Shinto shrines.

Did You Know?

To maintain the island's sacredness, no births or burials are permitted here.

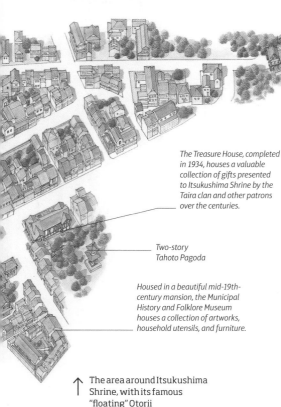

Daisho-in Temple is a delightful complex with an eclectic mix of Buddhist statuary. It is blissfully peaceful, away from the crowds of the waterfront and Itsukushima Shrine.

The Treasure House, completed in 1934, houses a valuable collection of gifts presented to Itsukushima Shrine by the Taira clan and other patrons over the centuries.

Two-story Tahoto Pagoda

Housed in a beautiful mid-19th-century mansion, the Municipal History and Folklore Museum houses a collection of artworks, household utensils, and furniture.

↑ The area around Itsukushima Shrine, with its famous "floating" Otorii

PICTURE PERFECT
Tidal Pull

The best time to take a photograph of the great torii of Miyajima is at high tide, when the gate appears to float above the waves. At low tide, you can walk to the foot of the Otorii, which is said to mark the boundary between the spirit and the human worlds.

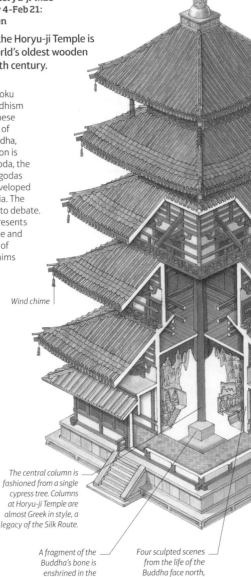

⑦ ⚲

HORYU-JI
TEMPLE

法隆寺

🅰D5 🅝Nara Prefecture 🅡Horyu-ji 🚌From Kintetsu Nara Stn or Kintetsu Tsutsui Stn to Horyu-ji-mae ⏰Feb 22–Nov 3: 8am–5pm daily; Nov 4–Feb 21: 8am–4:30pm daily 🅦horyuji.or.jp/en

The cradle of Japanese Buddhism, the Horyu-ji Temple is thought to contain some of the world's oldest wooden structures, dating from the early 7th century.

The temple was erected by Prince Shotoku (573–621) in his effort to entrench Buddhism alongside Shinto as a pillar of the Japanese belief system. Some exceptional works of art, including ancient images of the Buddha, are housed here. Horyu-ji's star attraction is the 105-ft- (32-m-) high five-story pagoda, the oldest of its kind in Japan. Japanese pagodas originated in China, where they had developed from the Buddhist stupa in ancient India. The symbolism of such buildings is subject to debate. Some say that a five-story pagoda represents the elements, as shown; others disagree and say that pagodas have an odd number of floors because Chinese numerology claims that this make them lucky.

The nine rings (kurin) of the finial are made of bronze.

Four scythes, a feature unique to Horyu-ji Temple's pagoda, are said to stop it from being destroyed by lightning.

Wind chime

The central column is fashioned from a single cypress tree. Columns at Horyu-ji Temple are almost Greek in style, a legacy of the Silk Route.

A fragment of the Buddha's bone is enshrined in the central pillar's base.

Four sculpted scenes from the life of the Buddha face north, south, east, and west.

↑ A bodhisattva sitting beside the Buddha at Horyu-ji Temple

EXPERIENCE Western Honshu

HIDDEN GEM
Temple Treasures

Although many of Horyu-ji's artifacts are housed in the Tokyo National Museum *(p128)*, the Gallery of Temple Treasures still houses Kudara Kannon, a slender Buddha.

Level 5: Sky

Level 4: Wind

Level 3: Fire

Level 2: Water

Level 1: Earth

Ornamental roof clays are made of bronze.

↑ Horyu-ji Temple's historic five-story pagoda, with its symbolic floors

8 Asuka Plain
飛鳥地方

🅰D5 🏠Nara Prefecture 🚉Asuka 🛈www.asukamura.jp/english

The Asuka Plain is scattered with excavation sites from the proto-capital Asukakyo, which flourished in the 5th to 7th centuries. The best way to explore the various tombs and temples is by bicycle.

One of the best-known sites, Takamatsuzuka Kofun contains murals of stars and mythological animals. Notable images elsewhere include Sakabune Ishi, a concentric stone that may have been used to make sake; Kame and Saru Ishi, turtle and monkey-shaped statues; and Nimen Seki, a stone with faces carved on each side.

Asuka-dera was Japan's first Buddhist temple. The Asuka-Daibutsu statues are influenced by various East Asian cultures.

9 Koka Ninja Village
甲賀の里忍術村

🅰D5 🏠394 Kokacho Oki, Koka, Shiga Prefecture 🚉Koka, then free shuttle from north entrance 🕙10am–4pm Tue–Sun 🌐koka.ninpou.jp

Shiga Prefecture once hosted one of Japan's most secretive sects – the ninja *(p235)*. Today, visitors can learn the arts of espionage, sabotage, and infiltration at this ninja village. In the grounds are a museum dedicated to ninja techniques, a house full of traps and secret panels, and a *shuriken* throwing-star dojo, as well as the Mizugomo Water Spider Pond, where you can attempt to get across the water using two floating rings and a rope. Visitors can experience ninja training for themselves and can even dress up to better understand the ways of these stealthy assassins.

↑ Delicate paintings on the ceiling of Asuka-dera Temple, in Asuka village

10

Yoshino
吉野

🅐 D5 🅝 Nara Prefecture
🅡 Yoshino ℹ (0746) 32-3081

This attractive village, its multistoried houses built on the side of a remote mountain, is one of Japan's most popular cherry-blossom-viewing spots. The Yoshinoyama area boasts 30,000 cherry trees planted at different altitudes. Each level blooms in succession, extending the viewing period to almost three weeks.

The Yoshinoyama area stretches from the south banks of the Kii River to the north end of the Omine mountain range. A UNESCO World Heritage Site, the region is dotted with many temples, including Kinpusen-ji Temple, Kinpu Shrine, Yoshimizu Shrine, and Yoshino Mikumari Shrine. There is also a pilgrimage route across the mountains. Chikurin-in Temple is known for its stroll garden, designed by the tea master Sen no Rikyu. Visitors can take advantage of the perfect vistas afforded by Mount Yoshino to view cherry blossom trees, as well as hot springs that are present in the area.

11

Mount Koya
高野山

🅐 D5 🅝 Wakayama Prefecture 🅡 Nankai line from Osaka, then cable car from Gokurakubashi Stn ℹ Nr Senjuinbashi bus stop; www.eng.shukubo.net

Set amid clumps of black cedar at an altitude of 3,000 ft (900 m) in the heart of the Kii Peninsula, Mount Koya, or Koya-san, is Japan's most venerated Shingon-Buddhist site. Saint Kukai (774–835) established a monastic retreat here in 816. There were almost 1,000 temples on the mountain by the Edo period, but typhoons and fire have since reduced the number to 117.

The western part of Koya-san contains the grandest and most revered structures. Kongobu-ji Temple, built in 1593 by Hideyoshi Toyotomi, is Koya-san's chief temple. Its rhododendrons and the sliding doors of its inner chambers, painted in the 16th century by artists of the Kano School, are among its attractions. The nearby Danjogaran complex includes the Fu-do (Fudo Hall), built in 1197, and the Konpon Dai-to, a two-story vermilion-and-white pagoda.

Rebuilt in 1937, the pagoda is regarded as the symbol of Koya-san.

The aptly named Reihokan (Treasure House), opposite the complex, displays over 5,000 paintings, statues, and mandalas in two separate buildings. The Daimon (great gate), the traditional main

---

STAY

Eko-in Temple
Sample vegetarian food, join the morning rituals, or relax in a hot spring at this Mount Koya temple.

🅐 D5 🅝 497 Koyasan, Koyacho 🅦 ekoin.jp/en/

Shojoshin-in Temple
Founded in 824, this Mount Koya temple offers simple rooms, as well as more luxurious quarters.

🅐 D5 🅝 566 Koyasan, Koyacho 🅦 shojoshinin.jp

A pagoda in front of the Nachi-no-taki waterfall, on the Kii Peninsula

entrance to Koya-san, lies a little west of here on the edge of the plateau. It affords matchless views.

In the eastern half of Koya-san are a vast necropolis and the Okuno-in (inner sanctum), Kukai's mausoleum. The stone-paved approach to Okuno-in is flanked with statues and tombs housing the remains of Japan's most illustrious families. In front of Kukai's mausoleum is the Toro-do (Lantern Hall). Day and night 11,000 lanterns burn here, including two that are said to have remained lit since the 11th century.

12
Kii Peninsula
紀伊半島

🗺️ D6 🏢 Wakayama, Mie, and Nara Prefectures 🚆 Nanki-Shirahama 🚉 JR Kinokuni line 🌐 kansai guide.jp/exciting/kii

The Kii Peninsula, with densely forested mountains at its center and craggy headlands,

←
Cherry trees at various stages of blossoming in the hills around Yoshino

pine-covered islands, and coves along its shoreline, has largely avoided the industrial development that scars much of Japan's Pacific coastline.

From the small port town of Shingu, on the east coast, you can take a bus to Shiko, then a 50-minute boat trip along the Kumano River to Doro Valley, a spectacular gorge. From May to June rhododendrons and azaleas bloom on the river's banks.

After a 40-minute local train from Shingu to Nachi, and a 20-minute bus inland, you reach Nachi-no-taki, Japan's highest waterfall. A stone path parallel to the falls leads to the ancient Nachi Taisha Shrine. With Hongu Taisha Shrine and Hayatama Taisha Shrine, this is one of three "grand" shrines in the region, called the Kumano Sanzan. These sites are linked by the millennia-old Kumano Kodo pilgrimage trails – now a UNESCO World Heritage Site. The next port south of Shingu is Katsuura, a pine-studded bay with several picturesque islets.

Farther south, the resort of Kushimoto is known for Hashi-gui-iwa, a chain of 40 rocks that seem to march out to sea, connecting the town to the island of Oshima. The peninsula's southernmost point is marked by Shio-no-misaki, a headland with a white lighthouse dating from 1873. One of the three

oldest hot springs in Japan, Shirahama Onsen, on the west coast, also has one of the area's finest beaches.

13
Iga-Ueno
伊賀上野

🗺️ D5 🏢 Mie Prefecture 🚉 Ueno-shi ℹ️ 1st Floor, Haito-Pia Bldg, in front of Ueno-shi Stn; www. iga-travel.jp

This castle town was the birthplace of Japan's revered haiku poet Matsuo Basho and home to the Iga ninja, the most inventive and feared spies of Japan's feudal era. The main attraction for most visitors is the **Ninja Museum of Igaryu**, a clan farmhouse that served as the secret headquarters of these spies and assassins. The well-restored building retains hidden panels, spy holes, secret escape routes, and trapdoors intended to repel night attacks from enemy warlords and rival ninja groups. Ninja methods are demonstrated by guides and in regular ninja shows.

Ninja Museum of Igaryu
🎟️ 🏠 117 Ueno Marunouchi 🕐 9am–5pm daily 🌐 iganinja.jp/en

THE NINJA

Ninjutsu, the "art of stealth," was developed during the bloody clan warfare of Japan's feudal era. The ninja elevated their profession of spying and assassination into a sophisticated discipline by practicing mountain asceticism and studying such subjects as astronomy, herbalism, medicine, and nutrition. They developed ingenious devices to outwit enemies, including lock picks, collapsible floats for crossing water, clothing designed to conceal swords and knives, and over 30 different kinds of *shuriken*, deadly throwing stars made of metal.

Okayama

岡山

⛰C5 ⓘOkayama Prefecture ✈🚃Okayama ℹOutside JR station; www.okayama-japan.jp/en

The former center of a domain ruled by the feudal Ikeda family, Okayama today is a vibrant modern city. Japanese tourists come to marvel at the Seto Ohashi Bridge, linking Okayama with Shikoku, which is over 8 miles (13 km) long.

The **Koraku-en Garden**, one of Japan's "famous three" gardens, was commissioned by Lord Ikeda and completed in 1700. Though a classic stroll garden, it was the first in Japan to have large expanses of lawn. The garden has three sections and features bamboo, pine, plum, cherry trees, and tea bushes. The nearby castle is incorporated into the design.

Okayama Castle is called the "Crow's Castle" due to its black walls. Destroyed in World War II, the exterior of the 16th-century castle was rebuilt in 1966. The interior displays samurai helmets, swords, and the like. More items owned by the Ikeda clan are on view at the **Hayashibara Museum of Art**, just south of the castle.

To the northeast, the **Orient Museum** traces how Near-Eastern art reached Japan via the Silk Route. The **Okayama Prefectural Museum of Art** has a collection of mostly 20th-century Japanese paintings and a few works by older artists.

Koraku-en Garden

⊘ 🏠1-5 Korakuen 🚌Koraku-en-guchi ⏰Mar 20–Sep: 7:30am–6pm daily; Oct–Mar 19: 8am–5pm daily 🅦okayama-korakuen.jp

Okayama Castle

⊘ 🏠2-3-1 Marunouchi ⏰9am–5:30pm daily

Hayashibara Museum of Art

⊘ 🏠2-7-15 Marunouchi ⏰10am–5pm Tue–Sun

Orient Museum

⊘ 🏠9-31 Tenjincho 📞(086) 232-3636 ⏰9am–5pm Tue–Sun

Okayama Prefectural Museum of Art

⊘ 🏠8-48 Tenjincho ⏰9am–5pm Tue–Sun 🅦okayama-kenbi.info

 Imbe

伊部

⛰C5 ⓘOkayama Prefecture 🚃Imbe ℹIn Imbe JR Stn; www.okayama-japan.jp/en/spot/1067

The home of Bizen pottery, Inbe is full of shops, galleries, and kilns. Originating in the Kamakura period, Bizen-ware is earthy, unglazed, and prized by tea-ceremony enthusiasts. The **Bizen Pottery Traditional and Contemporary Art Museum** displays superb examples from the Muromachi, Momoyama, and Edo periods.

Bizen Pottery Traditional and Contemporary Art Museum

⊘ 🏠1659-6 Imbe 📞(0869) 64-1400 ⏰9am–5pm Tue–Sun

→ Punting along a peaceful canal in the well-preserved Edo-era town of Kurashiki

 16

Kurashiki
倉敷

C5 Okayama Prefecture Kurashiki Kurashikikan building; www. kurashiki-tabi.jp/for/en

The Edo-period mercantile town of Kurashiki is beautifully preserved. Kurashiki means "storehouse village," a reference to the dozens of granaries (kura) with mortar and black-tiled walls that dot the town. In the heart of the old city, the Bikan Historical Area just south of the station, 200-year-old kura flank a canal lined with willows. Many of the kura have been converted into galleries, restaurants, inns, and shops and boutiques.

In the old district the finest museum is the **Ohara Museum of Art**. The collection was commissioned by industrialist Ohara Magosaburo in 1930 on the premise that great art should be accessible – even to the people of a relative

backwater such as Kurashiki. It includes rare works by the likes of Matisse, Renoir, Picasso, Degas, and Gauguin, and genuine masterpieces, like El Greco's The Annunciation. The annex houses an outstanding collection of works from Japan's mingei (or folk craft) scene.

The small **Kurashiki Archaeological Museum** occupies an old kura and includes items excavated in the region. In the **Kurashiki Museum of Folk Craft** you'll find folk crafts housed in connecting kura. The **Japanese Folk Toy Museum** has an extensive display of traditional old toys from around the world.

Ohara Museum of Art
 1-1-15 Chuo 9am–5pm Tue–Sun ohara.or.jp

Kurashiki Archaeological Museum
1-3-13 Chuo 9am–5pm Wed–Sun kurashiki-koukokan.com

Kurashiki Museum of Folk Craft
1-4-11 Chuo 9am–5pm Tue–Sun kurashiki-mingeikan.com

Japanese Folk Toy Museum
1-4-16 Chuo 10am–5pm daily english.gangukan.jp

EAT

Katsudon Nomura
Try the Okayama specialty here: demikatsu-don – rice with cabbage and deep-fried pork cutlets in a thick sauce.

C5 1-10 Heiwacho, Kita, Okayama (086) 222-2234

¥¥¥

Azuma Sushi Sansute
This Okayama sushi restaurant serves an Edo-era dish, barazushi – sushi rice topped with seafood and vegetables.

C5 2F Sansute Okayama, 1-1 Ekimotomachi, Kita, Okayama (086) 227-7337

¥¥¥

Café Moni
Try the chiffon cakes, at this café in Okayama.

C5 10-22 Honmachi, Kita, Okayama industries-moni.com

¥¥¥

← Strolling around the central pond in Koraku-en Garden, Okayama

The Sahara-like landscape of the Tottori sand dunes along the San-in coast

17 Tottori Sand Dunes
鳥取砂丘

⚠C4 🏛Tottori Prefecture 🚉Tottori 🚌From stn 🛈At Tottori Stn; (0857) 22-3318

A huge expanse of brown and yellow undulations, the Tottori sand dunes stretch for 10 miles (16 km) along the San-in coast. To the Japanese, the towering dunes, some rising to 300 ft (90 m), and the shifting patterns and shadows formed across the sand, are lyrical reminders of the human condition. Kobo Abe's powerful existential novel *The Woman in the Dunes* (1962) is set here. Commercialization has inevitably hit the area – head east across the dunes or rent a bike for a quieter experience.

18 Fukiya
吹屋

⚠C5 🏛Okayama Prefecture 🚌From Bitchu Takahashi Stn 🌐okayama-japan.jp/en/spot/953

A boom town at the center of the 19th-century copper and red-ocher mining industry, Fukiya is now a rustic hamlet tucked into mountain countryside. Well-to-do merchants and mine owners built grand houses here. Characterized by white plaster walls and red-ocher latticework windows and

doors, these buildings are the village's main cultural asset. Several are open to the public, including the former house of the Katayama family, now the **Local History Museum**, and a plaster-and-tile schoolhouse.

Just outside the village is a copper and ocher mine, which can be visited. The **Hirokane-tei**, an unusual Edo-period home resembling a fortified chateau, is about 2 miles (4 km) outside the town.

Local History Museum
🎫 🏠699 Fukiya ⏰Apr-Nov: 9am-5pm daily; Dec-Mar: 10am-4pm daily

Hirokane-tei
🎫 🏠2710 Nakano ⏰Apr-Nov: 9am-5pm daily; Dec-Mar: 10am-4pm daily

19 Amanohashidate Sandbar
天橋立

⚠D4 🏛Kyoto Prefecture 🚉Amanohashidate 🛈At Amanohashidate Stn; (0772) 22-8030

One of the highlights of Miyazu Bay, along the San-in coast, is Amanohashidate, the "bridge of heaven." The 2-mile (4-km) pine-studded sandbar separates the bay from Asokai lagoon. According to Japanese mythology, this is the spot where the gods conceived the Japanese islands. Visitors usually take the boat across the lagoon from the pier near the station, then a cable car from the

→
Cherry trees framing Hikone Castle, whose keep *(inset)* offers views of Lake Biwa

GREAT VIEW
Upside Down

It is easy to see how Amanohashidate got its heavenly name when you bend over and look at the sandbar upside down from the summit of Kasamatsu. From here, the sand spit appears to be literally reaching into the sky from the sea.

base of Kasamatsu Park to its hilltop summit – the best viewing point of the sandbar.

20

Lake Biwa
琵琶湖

 D5 🚉 Shiga Prefecture
🚉 Otsu, Hikone ℹ️ Outside Otsu Stn; en.biwako-visitors.jp

With a total area of 263 sq miles (674 sq km), Biwa-ko, Japan's largest lake, covers an area greater than Tokyo. The lake is named after the *biwa*, a musical instrument whose outline it is said to resemble. In the 15th century the high-lights of Lake Biwa were named Omi Hakkei, "the eight views of Omi." Development has changed some of these views radically, but the lake remains a beautiful place, its shore fringed with shrines, temples, and modest B&Bs. **Lake Biwa Museum** gives visitors a chance to learn more about this ancient lake.

Otsu, on the southwest edge, is the lake shore's largest city. Visitors come here to see Onjo-ji Temple, with its huge gates, and Ishiyama-dera Temple, which has some 8th-century buildings. Murasaki Shikibu, author of *The Tale of Genji*, is believed to have used one of the chambers of the Main Hall in which to write her 11th-century masterpiece.

Hikone, on the lake's eastern shore, is home to the 17th-century **Hikone Castle**. From the top floor of the keep is a superb view of Lake Biwa.

Lake Biwa Museum
♿ 🏠 1091 Oroshimocho, Kusatsu 🕙 10am–4:30pm Tue–Sun

Hikone Castle
♿ 🏠 1-1 Konkicho, Hikone 🕙 8:30am–5pm daily

DRINK

Kagoya
In addition to Scottish and Japanese whiskies, this cocktail bar by the river in Matsue also has seasonal fruit cocktails and warming winter concoctions on the menu.

🄰 C5 🏠 2-4 Higashihon-machi, Matsue 📞 (0852) 61-8456

Oideyasu Okiniya
One of the best *izakaya* in Matsue, with a great selection of beer and sake, as well as tasty snacks. Try the *maitake* (mushroom) tempura.

🄰 C5 🏠 13 Suetsugu Hon-machi, Matsue 📞 (0852) 24-8839

Bar E.A.D.
This cool riverside hangout offers a stylish space to enjoy a drink while taking in the view of Matsue at sunset. In summer, the rooftop is open and live bands keep the crowd going well into the night.

🄰 C5 🏠 36 Suetsugu Hon-machi, Matsue 📞 (0852) 28-3130

㉑ 🎋

Uji
宇治

🅰D5 🏛Kyoto Prefecture
🚉Uji, Keihan-Uji

In addition to some of the best green tea grown in Japan, the small city of Uji boasts **Byodo-in Temple**, which is featured on the 10-yen coin. The temple's Phoenix Hall and Amida Nyorai image inside are marvelous remnants of one of Japan's greatest epochs.

Manpuku-ji Temple was established in 1661 by Ingen, a priest who fled China after the fall of the Ming dynasty. Ingen introduced *sencha* (leaf green tea).

A 20-mile (35-km) drive east, in Shigaraki, is the **Miho Museum**, which has some fine Japanese treasures such as Buddha statues and handscrolls.

Byodo-in Temple
 🏠116 Uji Renge
🕐8:30am–5:30pm daily

Manpuku-ji Temple
⊗ 🏠34 Gokasho Sanban-wari 🕐9am–5pm daily

Miho Museum
⊗🍴♿♨ 🏠300 Tashiro Momodani, Shigaraki, Shiga
🕐10am–5pm Tue–Sun
🌐miho.or.jp

LAFCADIO HEARN

Lafcadio Hearn (1850–1904) arrived in Japan in 1890. He published several books, such as *Glimpses of Unfamiliar Japan* and *In Ghostly Japan*, which allowed the Japanese to view their culture through the eyes of a foreigner for the first time. Hearn's first Japanese home was Matsue. He married the daughter of a local samurai family and later acquired Japanese citizenship, changing his name to Koizumi Yakumo.

㉒

Matsue
松江

🅰C5 🏛Shimane Prefecture
✈Yonago and Izumo
🚉Matsue 🛈At Matsue JR Stn; www.visit-matsue.com

Situated at the intersection of Lake Shinji with Miho bay and Nakaumi lagoon, Matsue is also known as the "water city" and is rarely explored by international visitors.

Matsue is referred to at length in *Glimpses of Unfamiliar Japan* (1894) by Lafcadio Hearn, a journalist of Irish-Greek descent who spent 15 months in the town. Hearn described **Matsue Castle** as "a veritable architectural dragon, made up of magnificent monstrosities." It was built in 1611 of pine and stone, then partially reconstructed 31 years later. Its five-story keep is Japan's tallest.

Within a short walk are two more modest architectural gems. The **Buke Yashiki** is a mansion built in 1730 by the Shiomi family, who were chief retainers at the castle, and the **Meimei-an Teahouse** (1779) is one of Japan's oldest and best preserved. On the same street is the **Tanabe Art Museum**, with a collection of tea bowls and other tea-related objects. Just north of the castle, the **Lafcadio Hearn Residence** is beautifully preserved, and the **Lafcadio Hearn Memorial Museum** displays Hearn's manuscripts, desk, and pipes.

↑ The interior of the Miho Museum, designed by I. M. Pei, inspired by traditional temples

Matsue Castle

 🏯 1-5 Tonomachi 🚎 Kencho-mae 📞 (0852) 21-4030 🕐 Apr–Sep: 8:30am–6pm daily; Oct–Mar: 8:30am–5pm daily

Buke Yashiki

📷 🏯 305 Kitahoricho 🕐 8:30am–6:30pm daily (to 5pm Oct–Mar) 🌐 matsue-bukeyashiki.jp/en

Meimei-an Teahouse

📷 🏯 278 Kitahoricho 📞 (0852) 21-9863 🕐 Apr–Sep: 8:30am–6:30pm daily; Oct–Mar: 8:30am–5pm daily

Tanabe Art Museum

📷 🏯 310-5 Kitahoricho 📞 (0852) 26-2211 🕐 9am–5pm Tue–Sun

Lafcadio Hearn Residence

📷 🏯 315 Kitahoricho 📞 (0852) 23-0714 🕐 Apr–Sep: 8:30am–6:30pm daily; Oct–Mar: 8:30am–5pm daily

Lafcadio Hearn Memorial Museum

📷 🏯 322 Okudanicho 📞 (0852) 21-2147 🕐 8:30am–5pm daily (to 6:30pm Apr–Sep)

23

Yamaguchi
山口

🅰 B5 🏯 Yamaguchi Prefecture 🚉 Yamaguchi 🅘 Yamaguchi Stn, 1st floor; www.visit-jy.com/en

Laid out in the 14th century, Yamaguchi was modeled on Kyoto. When the Jesuit Francis Xavier visited here in 1550 he found a city of great wealth and sophistication; the Xavier Memorial Chapel, built in 1952, marks the 400th anniversary of the priest's stay. The painter Sesshu (1420–1506) designed a garden for the temple of Joei-ji, while Ruriko-ji Temple has a Japanese cypress-wood, five-story pagoda. Nearby is a set of tombs belonging to the influential Mori clan.

 Rock formations in the Akiyoshido Cave in the Akiyoshi-dai Tablelands

24

Akiyoshi-dai Tablelands
秋吉台

🅰 B5 🏯 Yamaguchi Prefecture 🚎 From Yamaguchi 🅘 At bus stn; (0837) 62-0305

Akiyoshi-dai is a plateau of grassland and rocky outcrops, which tour buses pass on their way to **Akiyoshido Cave**, one of the largest limestone grottos in Asia. The cave is 6 miles (10 km) long, only half a mile (1 km) of which is open to the public. Passageways are well lit, and a clear map is provided.

Akiyoshido Cave

📷 📞 (0837) 62-0115 🕐 Mar–Nov: 8:30am–5:30pm daily; Dec–Feb: 8:30am–4:30pm daily

---

25

Izumo
出雲

🅰 C5 🏯 Shimane Prefecture 🚉 Izumo 🅘 At Taisha-mae Stn; www.izumo-kankou.gr.jp/en

Alive with myths, legends, and tales of the supernatural, Izumo, known until the 3rd century as the "eightfold-towering-thunderhead land," has an enthralling heritage.

The town is well known throughout Japan for the **Izumo Taisha Grand Shrine**, one of the most revered and oldest Shinto shrines in the country. It is dedicated to Okuninushi-no-Mikoto, a deity who is closely associated with agriculture and medicine, as well as marriage – the latter explaining the popularity of the shrine for wedding ceremonies. The entrance to the shrine, through 11 torii (gates), is impressive. Unusually tall, the Honden (main hall) is not open to the public, although the Treasure House can be visited. The shrine's environs are sacred and therefore ecologically pristine, with towering cryptomeria trees surrounding the main compound. Just east of the shrine are a number of old houses occupied by priests who serve here. Note the traditional clay and stone walls.

Just past the shrine, on Route 431 to Okuni, there is a monument to a nun who is said to have danced on the banks of the Kamo River in Kyoto to raise money for the shrine. The dance was developed into the Kabuki theatrical form (p115).

Izumo Taisha Grand Shrine

📷 🏯 195 Taishacho Kizukihigashi 📞 (0853) 53-3100 🕐 Daily

26
Iwakuni
岩国

B5 **Yamaguchi Prefecture** **Iwakuni, Shin-Iwakuni** **At 2F bus terminal near Iwakuni Stn; (0827) 21-6050**

This city's main draw is the Kintai-kyo, or "brocade sash" Bridge, named for the rippling effect created by its five linked arches. The original structure, built in 1673, was destroyed by a typhoon in 1950. This almost exact replica depends on first-rate joinery and an invisible quantity of reinforced steel.

Kikko Park is home to samurai houses, including **Mekata House**. Iwakuni Art Museum has an impressive display of armor and weapons. A cable car climbs to Iwakuni Castle, a faithful 1962 reconstruction of the 1608 donjon.

Mekata House
2-6 Yokoyama **9am-4:30pm Tue-Sun**

Iwakuni Art Museum
 2-10-27 Yokoyama **Mar-Nov: 9am-5pm daily; Dec-Feb: 9am-4pm daily** **iwakuni-art-museum.org**

27
Hagi
萩

B5 **Yamaguchi Prefecture** **Hagi** **3537-3 Tsubaki; www.hagishi.com/en**

Hagi was a minor fishing port until Terumoto Mori fortified it in 1604. Mori samurai helped spark off the anti-Tokugawa revolt in the mid-1800s, and many of Meiji Japan's founding fathers came from Hagi. Today it is best known for its pottery-making tradition. Hagi's charm is in the details: its mossy cemeteries, teahouses, and the tiny, purple bloom of bush clover (*hagi*). The central Teramachi district contains old temples and shrines. Jonen-ji Temple is noted for its carved gate, Hofuku-ji Temple for its bibbed Jizo statues, and Toko-ji Temple for an atmospheric cemetery. Camellias and *natsu mikan* (summer oranges) hanging over whitewashed mud walls typify the samurai quarters to the west of Teramachi. Several residences are located here, including **Kikuya House**, a merchant villa with a small museum. Wealthy merchants appointed by the Mori clan once owned the fine collection in the **Kumaya Art Museum** to the north of here. It includes tea-ceremony utensils, paintings, and screens. Outside the town is the **Yoshika Taibi Memorial Museum** with rare Hagi-yaki pottery collection.

HAGI'S CERAMIC ARTS

Hagi's first kilns date from the Heian period, but the town's reputation for refined tea vessels and other wares began in the 16th century with the introduction of apprentice potters from Korea. A distinguishing mark of Hagi-yaki (Hagi-ware) is its translucent glaze *(right)*. Hagi-yaki improves with age, the muted pinks and pastels of the stoneware softening to beiges as tannin from the tea soaks through the porous glaze.

← The graceful arches of the Kintai-kyo Bridge over the Nishiki River in Iwakuni

Kikuya House

⊛ ⌂1-1 Gofukumachi
🕐10am–5pm daily

Kumaya Art Museum

⊛ ⌂47 Imauono, Tanamachi
🕐9am–4pm Tue & Sat

Yoshika Taibi Memorial Museum

⊛ ⌂426-1 Chinto 🕐9am–5pm Thu-Tue

 28

Tsuwano
津和野

🅰B5 ⌂Shimane Prefecture
🚆🚌Tsuwano 🄳Next to Tsuwano Stn; tsuwano-kanko.net/en

This tiny 700-year-old former castle town, tucked into a river valley deep in the mountains, has a large number of well-preserved samurai houses. Thousands of carp inhabit the town's brooks, outnumbering the residents, it is said, by ten to one. The hillside Taikodani Inari Shrine is one of the most important Inari (fox) shrines in Japan. It is reached through a tunnel of vermilion torii (gates), 1,174 in all. A chairlift goes up the other side of the slope to the scant remains of Tsuwano Castle, and there's a stunning view from the top.

Amane Nishi (1829–97), a Meiji-period statesman and philosopher, was born here. **Nishi House**, now a museum, is on a quiet street in the south of town. Opposite is another notable home – **Mori Ougai House**, a museum to Tsuwano-native Ougai Mori (1862–1922), author of novels such as *The Wild Geese* and *Vita Sexualis*.

Nishi House

⌂64-6 Ushiroda 🄲(0856) 72-1771 🕐9am–5pm daily

Mori Ougai House

⊛ ⌂238 Machida
🄲(0856) 72-3210
🕐9am–5pm Tue–Sun

→ Ceremony at Tsuwano's Taikodani Inari Shrine, an important fox temple

The unique Meoto Iwa, or "wedded rocks," at Futamigaura Beach ↑

A TOUR OF
ISE PENINSULA

Distance 70 miles (110 km) **Stopping-off points** Goza-shirahama Beach, Futamigaura Beach, Kashikojima
Difficulty The area has excellent bus and train services

On this tour, you'll take in the peninsula's main sites, including the city of Ise, its Grand Shrine – the most sacred in Japan – and the Ise-Shima National Park, as well as off-the-beaten track gems, from the jagged coast, where cultured oyster pearls are grown, to the undulating evergreen-clad hills inland – the habitat of monkeys, wild boars, and flying squirrels.

Locator Map
For more detail see p212

0 kilometers   5

0 miles   5

N ↑

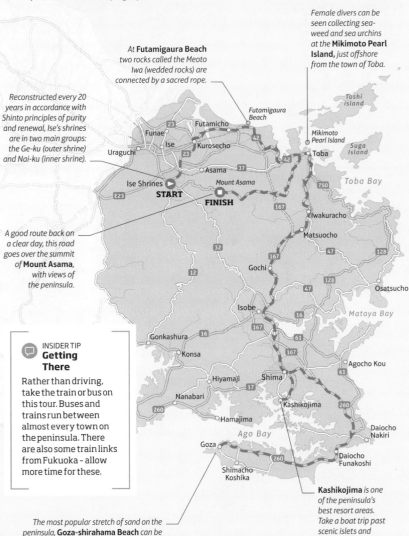

Female divers can be seen collecting seaweed and sea urchins at the **Mikimoto Pearl Island,** *just offshore from the town of Toba.*

At **Futamigaura Beach** *two rocks called the Meoto Iwa (wedded rocks) are connected by a sacred rope.*

Reconstructed every 20 years in accordance with Shinto principles of purity and renewal, Ise's shrines are in two main groups: the Ge-ku (outer shrine) and Nai-ku (inner shrine).

A good route back on a clear day, this road goes over the summit of **Mount Asama,** *with views of the peninsula.*

INSIDER TIP
💬 **Getting There**

Rather than driving, take the train or bus on this tour. Buses and trains run between almost every town on the peninsula. There are also some train links from Fukuoka – allow more time for these.

The most popular stretch of sand on the peninsula, **Goza-shirahama Beach** *can be reached by road or by boat from Kashikojima.*

Kashikojima *is one of the peninsula's best resort areas. Take a boat trip past scenic islets and oyster rafts.*

245

SHIKOKU

Late Paleolithic sites and *kofun* (burial mounds) dating from the 3rd century AD are evidence of early human activity on Shikoku. The Dogo Onsen Honkan in Matsuyama is referred to in the *Kojiki*, Japan's oldest chronicle, written in 712. Despite such ancient sites, however, Shikoku has mainly been on the margin of Japanese history. The island's most famous figure is Kukai, who was born into a poor aristocratic family in 774. This Buddhist priest, who has been called the Father of Japanese Culture, visited 88 of the island's temples in a pilgrimage that has been imitated by others for more than a thousand years.

In 1183, as chronicled in the *Tale of the Heike*, the war between the Taira and Minamoto clans for dominance of Japan spilled over into the Inland Sea and Shikoku. Some of the defeated Taira went into hiding in a gorge in central Shikoku, where many of their descendants still live.

Farmland and mountains continue to dominate Shikoku's landscape, although agriculture employs only 3 per cent of the island's four million residents. Assembly of cars and manufacture of electronic goods, particularly in the ports along the Seto Inland Sea, are the most important industries. Other industries include fruit farming (mandarin oranges in particular), seaweed and pearl cultivation, and food and chemical processing.

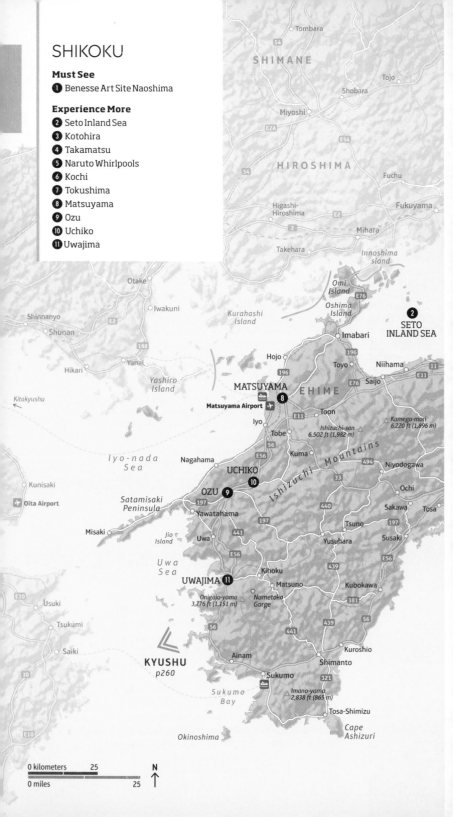

WESTERN HONSHU
p210

1 BENESSE ART SITE NAOSHIMA

4 TAKAMATSU

3 KOTOHIRA

5 NARUTO WHIRLPOOLS

7 TOKUSHIMA

6 KOCHI

Pacific Ocean

SHIKOKU

BENESSE ART SITE NAOSHIMA

ベネッセアートサイト直島

△C5 **⊙Kagawa Prefecture** **⊜Takamatsu or Uno** **⊙Hours vary, check website for individual museums** **ⓦbenesse-artsite.jp/en**

One of the 3,000 islands dotting the Seto Inland Sea (p252), Naoshima was once a desolate and depopulated industrial outpost of Japan's rustbelt. Now completely reborn, Benesse Art Site Naoshima brings together the best in contemporary art and architecture.

Naoshima's incredible transformation into an international art destination began in 1987, when Soichiro Fukutake, the chairman of Benesse Holdings – an education and publishing company – purchased the south part of the dilapidated island. Working with the leading Japanese architect Tadao Ando, a specialist in cutting-edge concrete buildings, and responsible for the famous Church of Light in Osaka, Benesse turned Naoshima into one of the world's premier art destinations.

In 1992, Benesse House, Ando's first permanent structure, opened on the site. Now formed of four buildings, it encompasses both guest accommodations and a museum housing a collection of contemporary artworks by the likes of Hiroshi Sugimoto.

The next museum to open was the Chichu Art Museum in 2004, designed to encourage visitors to reflect on the relationship between mankind and nature. Inside, five paintings from Monet's *Water Lilies* series are showcased

→

George Rickey's *Three Squares Vertical Diagonal* (2007) at Benesse House

TADAO ANDO

Ando's designs are known for their zen-like simplicity, which are said to be as evocative as haiku. On Naoshima, he crafted Benesse House, the Chichu Art Museum, and the Lee Ufan Museum out of crude concrete. For his work, the boxer-turned-architect won the prestigious Pritzker Prize in 1995.

← One of Yayoi Kusama's iconic pumpkin sculptures sitting on a pier

under natural light. Art and the natural environment are in harmony throughout the island, with Yayoi Kusama's spotted pumpkins perched on piers interrupting the horizon.

Every three years, some of the museums that are part of the Benesse Art Site Naoshima serve as venues for the Setouchi Triennale art festival, attracting almost a million extra visitors to the already popular island. The festival also takes place on other islands in the area, such as Shodoshima and Ogijima.

↑ Benesse House's light and airy restaurant, overlooking the beach

💬 INSIDER TIP
Guest Privileges

Guests staying at Benesse House benefit from after-hours access to the museums, away from the crowds, until 11pm. The hotel has four buildings: Museum, Oval, Beach, and Park.

EXPERIENCE MORE

 2

Seto Inland Sea
瀬戸内海

C5 **Setonaikai-kisen (Inland Sea cruises); www. setonaikaikisen.co.jp**

The Seto Inland Sea, Japan's most beautiful body of water, is not landlocked, as its name suggests, but seems almost so with its serene waters and over 3,000 islands. Donald Richie, in his classic travelogue *The Inland Sea* (1971), sets the scene of a boat journey westward through the narrow defiles of water: "On the left are first the sharp and Chinese-looking mountains of the island of Shikoku, so different that it appears another land, and then the flat coasts of Kyushu. This shallow sea is a valley among these mountainous islands."

You can cycle along a path that stretches from Onomichi to Imabari. Bridges, local ferries, and cruise boats provide access to the 750 or so inhabited islands. The remote fishing villages on these islands, with their salt-weathered wooden houses and black ceramic-tiled roofs, seem to hail from a different era. Among the most visited are Awaji, the largest island, Omishima, and Shodoshima, a beautiful island that, with its olive and orange groves, seems to belong more to the Mediterranean than here. But our favorite island is Naoshima, which serves as a haven for groundbreaking art (*p250*).

3

Kotohira
琴平

C5 **Kagawa Prefecture** **Kotohira, Kotoden Kotohira** **my-kagawa.jp/ en/sightseeing/ sightseeing02**

Kotohira is the home of the famous shrine complex Kotohira-gu, also affection-ately known as Konpira-san, the spiritual guardian of seafarers. The target of pilgrimages for centuries, the shrine now attracts four million visitors per year and is believed to bestow good luck upon fishermen and sailors.

A 785-stair climb (or ride in one of the palanquins

available) takes visitors up the rugged mountainside to the shrine, set in beautiful grounds. Within the complex, the Asahi Shrine is built of zelkova, a rock-hard wood that forms an excellent medium for carved relief work. The nearby Omote Shoin and Oku Shoin have celebrated screen paintings by Okyo Maruyama. The first presents burly tigers bristling with Zen energy, the second includes a waterfall flowing across a corner of the room.

The oldest Kabuki theater in Japan, the Kanamaru-za, can also be found in the town.

 PICTURE PERFECT
For Shore

Head to Chichibuga Beach, 12 miles (20 km) west of Kotohira, to get an Instagram-ready post. Stand on the sand at sunset, strike a pose, and get someone to capture your silhouette reflected in the mirror-like stretch of water.

A wooden bridge crossing one of the ponds in the Ritsurin Garden, Takamatsu

4

Takamatsu
高松

C5 Kagawa Prefecture Takamatsu At JR station; www.art-takamatsu.com

The capital of the tiny Kagawa Prefecture on the Inland Sea, Takamatsu is the main hub between Shikoku and the outside. Nonetheless, it maintains a local charm with its neighborhood shops and historic landmarks. The town grew after Ikoma Chikamasa erected Takamatsu Castle in 1588, the remains of which can still be seen. The castle has a unique seawater moat. Instead of koi fish, visitors can see bream, flounder, and sometimes even puffer fish. When the Tokugawa shoguns assumed power in 1600, they granted the town, castle, and surrounding fiefdom to their relatives, the Matsudaira clan. The family

The Akashi Kaikyo Bridge, linking Kobe to the island of Awaji in the Seto Inland Sea

devoted nearly a century to landscaping the six ponds and 13 artificial hillocks that make **Ritsurin Garden** the city's most famous landmark. Visit on New Year's Day or March 16 (the anniversary of the garden's opening) for free admission.

Takamatsu's location as an entry port for Shikoku made it the setting for such historic battles as the one between the Minamoto and the Taira clans in 1185. The **Takamatsu Heike Monogatari Wax Museum** offers a surprisingly effective re-creation of the story's high points, which are also the subject matter of the classic No play *Yashima*.

At Yashima volcanic plateau, **Shikoku Mura** is a village where immaculately preserved buildings and other artifacts of rural life display Shikoku craftsmanship.

Ritsurin Garden
1-20-16 Ritsurincho Jan & Dec: 7am–5pm daily (Feb: to 5:30pm; Nov: from 6:30am); Mar: 6:30am–6pm daily; Apr, May & Sep: 5:30am–6:30pm daily (Jun–Aug: to 7pm); Oct: 6am–5:30pm daily my-kagawa.jp/en/ritsurin

Takamatsu Heike Monogatari Wax Museum
3-6-38 Asahicho (087) 823-8400 9:30am–5:30pm daily

Shikoku Mura
91 Yashima Nakamachi (087) 843-3111 Kotoden Yashima Stn Apr–Oct: 8:30am–6pm daily (Nov–Mar: to 5:30pm)

⑤ Naruto Whirlpools

鳴門の渦潮

🅐D5 🚉Tokushima Prefecture 🚃Naruto, then bus to Naruto Park 🚢Uzushio line ferry; www.uzusio.com/en

Where the tip of Awaji Island nearly touches Shikoku, the tidal pull of two distinct bodies of water – the Seto Inland Sea and the Pacific Ocean – creates large disparities spawning powerful currents and whirlpools. Navigating the churning waters of this 1-mile (1.6-km) strait has been a part of local lore for over a millennium – there is even a manga named after the whirlpools.

Sightseeing boats now ply the 13-mph (20-km/h) currents, and provide startling views of the Onaruto suspension bridge, part of a system linking Shikoku and Honshu via Awaji Island. When the northern end of the system was completed in 1998, it had stretched 3 ft (1 m) as a result of ground shifts caused by the Kobe earthquake.

↑ A small shrine overlooking the coast at Katsurahama Park in the town of Kochi

At the Awaji end of the bridge, the **Uzunooka Onarutokyo Memorial Hall** explains the whirlpool phenomenon and offers a view of Onaruto suspension bridge and the swirling whirlpools from its terrace.

Uzunooka Onarutokyo Memorial Hall

⊗ 🏠936-3 Fukura Hei, Minamiawaji ⏰9am-5pm Wed-Mon 🌐kinen. uzunokuni.com

⑥ Kochi

高知

🅐C6 🚉Kochi Prefecture ✈🚉Kochi 🛈At JR station; visitkochijapan.com/en

Kochi city offers a rare blend of sandy beaches, mountain views, and well-preserved historic sites.

The Kochi region, formerly called Tosa, is known for its

forging of cutlery, and shops selling knives line the street in front of **Kochi Castle**, constructed in 1603, but rebuilt between 1729 and 1753 following a fire. A startlingly long sword, over 5 ft (1.5 m) in length, is among the weapons on display inside. Look out of the windows on the top floors for breathtaking views.

At Katsurahama, a beautiful white-sand beach area in the southern part of the city, the **Sakamoto Ryoma Memorial Museum** is devoted to the Tosa patriot admired for his part in the overthrow of the shogunate and restoration of the emperor in the 1860s. He was assassinated in 1867. Most Japanese visitors make a point of paying homage to a bronze statue of the man looming over the beach. From Kochi, take a day trip to Cape Muroto at the southeast tip of Shikoku

AWA-ODORI DANCING

Tokushima's celebrations for O-Bon, the festival of the dead on August 12–15, are the liveliest in Japan. Special dances, called Awa-Odori, are meant to welcome ancestral spirits on their yearly visit to the land of the living. Nicknamed "the fool's dance" because the refrain "you're a fool whether you dance or not, so you might as well dance" is sung, the Awa-Odori allegedly originated when rice wine was passed out to the townspeople of Tokushima to celebrate completion of a castle.

Did You Know?

The anime character Naruto Uzumaki, an adolescent ninja, takes his name from the whirlpools.

or Cape Ashizuri to the southwest. Both have views of the Pacific Ocean and some unusual rock formations.

Kochi Castle

⊛ 🏯 1-2-1 Marunouchi
🕘 9am–5pm daily
🚫 Dec 26–Jan 1

Sakamoto Ryoma Memorial Museum

⊛ 🏯 830 Urado-shiroyama
🕘 9am–5pm daily 🌐 ryoma-kinenkan.jp/country/en

Tokushima
徳島

🅰 D5 🚉 Tokushima Prefecture 🚌🚉 Tokushima
🛈 In front of Tokushima Stn; www. discover tokushima.net/en

The city of Tokushima forms the gateway into the island

←
The churning waters of the Naruto Whirlpools under the Onaruto suspension bridge

of Shikoku from the Kansai region of Honshu and is the traditional point of entry for those who set out to duplicate Kukai's pilgrimage *(p258)*. The old name of the province, Awa, gives its name to the town's Awa-Odori celebration in mid-August, a dancing festival that is broadcast nationwide.

South of Tokushima, the Anan coast is known for its charming fishing villages, pleasant beaches, and the sea turtles that lay and hatch eggs during the summer months (June to August).

 HIDDEN GEM
Chiiori House

Dating from around 1720, this house and inn in Tokushima province is typical of old Iya construction, with its wooden floors and *irori* (floor hearths). The beams and rafters are black from centuries of fires burning in the floor hearths *(www. chiiori.org)*.

❽ Matsuyama
松山

🅐C6 🚉Ehime Prefecture ✈🚆Matsuyama ℹAt JR station; en.matsuyama-sightseeing.com

The capital of Ehime Prefecture and a castle town since 1603, Matsuyama has many powerful associations for the Japanese.

The **Dogo Onsen Honkan**, a famous hot-spring spa, has been in use for over a millennium, and has a fine 19th-century bathhouse. Deeper into the mountains behind the historic bathhouse is Oku-Dogo Onsen, which is a much newer hotel resort area.

Natsume Soseki, an author whose portrait appears on old ¥1,000 bills, moved to the town in 1895 and later wrote about Matsuyama in his autobiographical novel *Botchan* (1906). The **Shiki Memorial Museum** is devoted to Soseki's friend Shiki (1867–1902), a Matsuyama native held by many to be Japan's greatest modern haiku poet, as well as a fine painter. The collection includes manuscripts, paintings, and photographs of Shiki and Soseki.

Matsuyama Castle is an extensive complex on a bluff overlooking the city and Seto Inland Sea. Plaques offer intelligent commentary on the castle's strategic features.

Dogo Onsen Honkan
◈ 🏠5-6 Dogoyunomachi 🚋Dogo Onsen 📞(089) 921-5141 🕑6am–11pm daily

GREAT VIEW
Capture the Castle
Matsuyama's castle stands on a hill. A former defensive feature, today it provides a great view out over the Seto Inland Sea. In spring, when the cherry trees are in bloom, the panorama is even more spectacular.

Shiki Memorial Museum
◈🅰 🏠1-30 Dōgo-kōen; 3-min walk from Dogo Onsen Honkan 🕑9am–6pm Wed-Mon (to 5pm Nov–Apr)

Matsuyama Castle
◈ 🏠1 Marunouchi 🚋Kencho-mae stop, then steep walk, or Okaido stop, then 5-min walk to cable car or lift 📞(089) 921-4873 🕑9am–5pm daily

❾ Ozu
大洲

🅐B6 🚉Ehime Prefecture 🚆Ozu ℹNear City Hall (20-min walk from JR station); (0893) 24-2664

A castle town built where the Hiji River snakes in an S-curve through a valley rimmed by picturesque bluffs, Ozu is known to insiders as the "little Kyoto" of Ehime Prefecture. Whereas it could be argued that Kyoto offers well-preserved relics of Japan's past, Ozu offers a past that is still alive. The riverfront is lined by quaint, narrow streets of tile-roofed bars and restaurants with sliding wood shutters. A riverside villa called **Garyu Sanso**, built in 1907, is one of the most spectacular buildings. On the river itself, shallow-bottomed skiffs shunt

→

Terraced fields overlooking the harbor and mountainous landscape in Uwajima

cormorant fishermen back and forth through the river breezes. Traditional culture is still the norm in Ozu, where raw silk, dairy products, and vegetables form the basis for the local economy. The town's restaurants serve eel and other fish caught in nearby rivers.

The panorama of seasonal change is especially vivid in the wooded hillsides of Ozu. August is marked with a festival of fireworks launched from an islet in the river.

Garyu Sanso
◈ 🏠411-2 Ozu 📞(089) 324-3759 🕑9am–5pm daily

⑩ Uchiko
内子

🅰C6 🏠Ehime Prefecture
🚉Uchiko 🛈 www.we-love-uchiko.jp

Located in a small valley where the Oda River splits into three branches, the town of Uchiko is famous for its historic Kabuki theater, the **Uchiko-za**, and its sloping street of two-story wooden buildings with whitewashed walls, tiled roofs, and broad fronts. In 1982 the government moved to ensure the preservation of these structures, which date from the mid-19th century. Several are open to the public, and others function as craft shops and restaurants. The area is often used for locations in historical films and television dramas.

Uchiko-za
 🏠2102 Uchiko
📞(089) 344-2840
🕐9am–4:30pm daily

←
Dogo Onsen Honkan in Matsuyama, the inspiration for *Spirited Away*

⑪ Uwajima
宇和島

🅰B6 🏠Ehime Prefecture
🚉Uwajima 🛈5-min walk from station; uwajima-tourism.org/en

Uwajima, a harbor town with a castle, old temple district, and mountain setting, is probably best known for its bullfighting, where the bulls are ranked in the same way as sumo wrestlers. Two curious sites attract visitors. The **Taga-jinja Shrine** houses sexually explicit statues and other objects associated with fertility. Next door, the **Taga-jinja Sex Museum** has similarly provocative statues from around the world.

In the mountains northwest of Uwajima, the **Nametoko Gorge** is noted for its waterfall and fine views.

Taga-jinja Shrine
1340 Fujie 🕐8am–5pm daily

Taga-jinja Sex Museum
🕐8am–5pm daily

Nametoko Gorge
🚉Matsumaru then taxi to Nametoko

EAT

Bakushukan
The perfect place in Matsuyama for a cold beer and a snack.

🅰C6 🏠20-13 Dogoyunomachi, Matsuyama
🌐dogobeer.jp

Nikitatsuan
This Matsuyama restaurant uses fresh local produce.

🅰C6 🏠3-18 Dogokita-machi, Matsuyama
📞(089) 924-6617

Kappo Kotobuki
Try the abalone at this sushi restaurant in Matsuyama.

🅰C6 🏠1-3-12 Nibancho, Matsuyama 🌐kappou-kotobuki.net

A LONG WALK
THE 88-TEMPLE PILGRIMAGE

Distance About 745 miles (1,200 km) **Time** 6-8 weeks
Difficulty Some tricky terrain; signage is mostly in Japanese

When pilgrims retrace the route of Kukai, the founder of Shingon Buddhism who made a pilgrimage of 88 of the island's minor temples in the 9th century, they are honoring a cultural icon. Those who hope to atone for a grave error complete the pilgrimage in reverse order, believing that they will encounter the saint as they walk or in their dreams. About 100,000 pilgrims complete the circuit each year, and countless others follow part of it. Pilgrims can collect a series of stamps as they visit each temple, many of which offer lodgings and meals. If the circuit is too much, you can walk part of it or take a week-long bus tour.

Did You Know?

There are actually 108 temples on this pilgrimage route.

Popular with tour groups, Temple 51, also known as **Ishite-ji**, is associated with the legend of a very rich man breaking Kukai's begging bowl.

Imabari

Hojo

Toyo

Niihama

Saijo

EHIME

Matsuyama

Toon

Iyo

Tobe

Ishizuchi-san
6,502 ft (1,982 m)

Nagahama

Kuma

Ishizuchi Mountains

Uchiko

Ozu

Ochi

Yawatahama

Tsuno

Susaki

Satamisaki Peninsula

Jio
Island

Uwa

Yusuhara

Uwa Sea

Uwajima

Kihoku

Matsuno

Kubokawa

*Onigajo-yama
3,776 ft (1,151 m)*

Ainam

Shimanto

Kuroshio

Sukumo

*Imano-yama
2,838 ft (865 m)*

Sukumo Bay

Tosa-Shimizu

Okinoshima

Cape Ashizuri

↑ A stone statue of Jizo bodhisattva at Kannon-ji, Temple 16

0 kilometers   25
0 miles   25

N
↑

Temple 1, **Ryozen-ji**, near Naruto, is the start and end of the pilgrimage, though devout pilgrims will extend the start and end to Mount Koya (p234) on Honshu, the head-quarters of the Shingon sect. Sign the book of completion here.

The name of Temple 2, **Gokuraku-ji**, refers to the Pure Land, or Western Paradise, of the Amida Buddha, a fundamental concept in Shingon Buddhism.

The birthplace of Kukai is marked by Temple 75, **Zentsu-ji**, one stop from Kotohira.

Sakaide

Takamatsu

Sanuki

Marugame

Hiketa

Mitoyo

KAGAWA

Kan-onji

Kotohira

Naruto

Waki

Iyomishima

Awa

Tokushima

Kawanoe

Yoshino-gawa

Komatsushima

Miyoshi

Kamiyama

Tsurugi   Mountains

Katsuura

Ochiai

TOKUSHIMA

Anan

Tsurugi-san
6,414 ft m (1,955 m)

Naka

Otoyo

Tosa

Minami

Monobecho
Befu

KOCHI

Umaji

Mugi

Kochi

Kainan

Between temples 11 and 12 is an uphill trek notorious as the "pilgrim crusher."

Nankoku

Aki

Kitagawa

Yasuda

Toyo

Tosa

Nahari

Temple 31, **Chikurin-ji**, was built in 724 by order of Emperor Shomu. Kukai received his training at this temple.

Muroto

Cape Muroto

The main hall of **Shinsho-ji**, Temple 25, is home to thousands of small statues of Jizo bodhisattva holding a ship's wheel. Jizo is thought to save sailors caught in storms.

→ A striking golden domed subtemple at Ishite-ji, Temple 51 of the pilgrimage

KYUSHU

Organized communities settled in Kyushu in the Jomon period (14,500–300 BC). According to legend, it was from Kyushu that the first emperor of Japan, Jimmu, set out in the 6th century BC on his campaign to unify the country. And it was through Kyushu in the 4th century AD that Chinese and Korean culture, including Buddhism and the Chinese writing system, first infiltrated Japan. Not all foreign incursions were welcomed, however. The natives of the island repelled several Mongolian invasions, the last and most formidable in 1274 only by the intervention of a powerful storm, the *kamikaze* (divine wind), which scuttled the Mongolian fleet.

In the 16th century, Christianity, firearms, and medicine were introduced through the port cities of Nagasaki and Kumamoto by the merchants and emissaries of Portugal, Spain, and Holland. Later, during the two centuries of Japan's self-imposed isolation, the tiny island of Dejima off the coast of Nagasaki was the country's sole entrepôt for Western trade and learning. The city grew because of this contact with the rest of the world but, four centuries later, Nagasaki was devastated by an atomic bomb detonated by the US in 1945.

Today, the island is characterized by volcanic activity. Kagoshima lies in the shadow of Sakurajima, which daily belches ash; Mount Aso is one of the world's largest calderas; and steaming fissures and fumaroles are found at Beppu, Unzen, and other spa towns.

O-shima

Katsumoto
Iki Island
Gonoura

FUKUOKA ①
Fukuoka Airport

Yobuko
Itoshima
Kasuga
385

Karatsu

Hirado
Matsuura
Taku
203
YOSHINOGARI RUINS
⑭

Hirado Island
Imari
SAGA
Saga
Okawa

Takeo
Kashima
YANAGAWA ⑫

Sasebo
E35
Matsubara
Omuta

NAGASAKI
Ariakekai

Arikawa
Nishi-Sonogihanto
Nagasaki Airport
207
Arao

Goto-retto
Nakadori Island
Omura
Isahaya
SHIMABARA PENINSULA
⑬

Narao
206
NAGASAKI ②
E34
57
Mount Unzen
4,875 ft (1,486 m)
Misumi

Fukue
251

Fukue Island
Nomo-zaki
Kuchinotsu

Hondo

Amakusa Island

Ushibuka
Minamata

Naga-shima

Izumi

Akune
Satsuma

Koshiki Island
Sendai
①

Kushikino
E3A

Hioki

270

Kaseda
CHIRAN ㉑

Satsuma-hanto
Makurazaki

Amami Oshima Island,
Yakushima Island ↙

KYUSHU

Must Sees
① Fukuoka
② Nagasaki

Experience More
③ Yufuin
④ Kokura
⑤ Usa
⑥ Beppu
⑦ Usuki Stone Buddhas
⑧ Kurume
⑨ Onta
⑩ Dazaifu
⑪ Kumamoto
⑫ Yanagawa
⑬ Shimabara Peninsula
⑭ Yoshinogari Ruins
⑮ Mount Aso
⑯ Takachiho
⑰ Nichinan Coast
⑱ Kirishima-Kinkowan National Park
⑲ Kagoshima
⑳ Amami Oshima Island
㉑ Chiran

KYUSHU

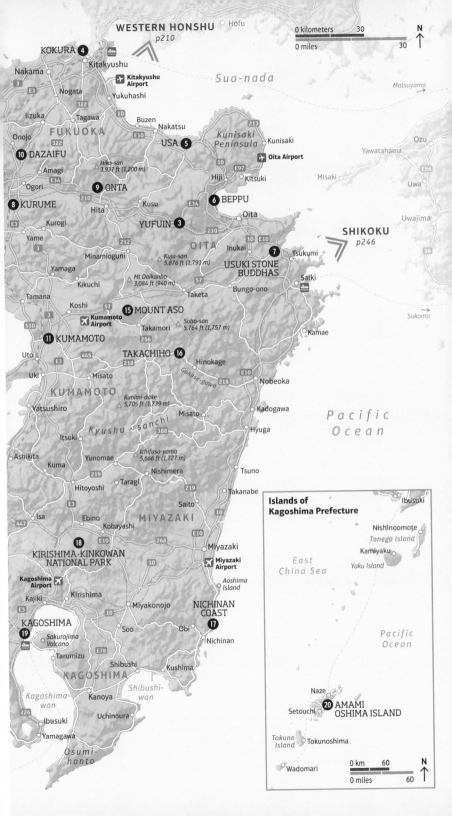

Fukuoka's neon-lit buildings reflected in the mirror-like Naka River at nighttime ↑

FUKUOKA

福岡

AA6 **Q**Fukuoka Prefecture **✈**Fukuoka **Q**Hakata **i**Hakata Stn; 1F Solaria Terminal Bldg, Tenjin; yokanavi.com/en

Strikingly modern, Fukuoka bills itself as the gateway to southern Japan. The closest city to mainland Asia, it has, for at least a millennium, been the country's main port of entry for Chinese and Korean culture. This has lent it an attractive international flavor, both culturally and on its restaurant menus.

①

Fukuoka City Museum

A3-1-1 Momochihama **S**Nishijin **O**9:30am-5:30pm Tue-Sun **C**Dec 28-Jan 4 **W**museum.city.fukuoka.jp/en

This museum traces the relationship between Fukuoka and its Asian neighbors from the Ice Age to the city's modern waterfront developments. The museum utilizes four generations of a fictitious local family to bring this history to life.

The primary artifact in the collection is a gold 3rd-century Chinese seal, which was discovered on Shika Island, across the bay from the city, in 1784. It is believed to have been gifted to envoys from an early Japanese kingdom by Emperor Guangwu of China.

②

Fukuoka Tower

A2-3-26 Momochihama **S**Nishijin **O**9:30am-10pm daily **W**fukuoka tower.co.jp

The city's tallest structure, at an impressive 768 ft (234 m) tall, dominates the waterfront Momochi district. Resembling a mirrored sail, the tower boasts the highest seaside observation deck in Japan, as well as shops and restaurants.

Fukuoka Tower is also a spectacle from the ground – every evening, on the hour, it is illuminated by a light installation reflecting the time of year.

③

Ohori Park

A1 Ohorikoen **S**Ohorikoen **O**Fukuoka Art Museum: 9:30am-5:30pm Tue-Sun (Jul-Oct: to 8pm Fri & Sat) **W**Fukuoka Art Museum: fukuoka-art-museum.jp

Located in the west of the city, Ohori Park is a popular green space, with pathways, pavilions, and islets connected by traditional bridges. The park is also home to the Fukuoka Art Museum, which houses an impressive collection of modern art.

INSIDER TIP
Use Your Noodle

Fukuoka is celebrated for its *yatai*. These sit-down food stalls are legendary, with their colorful, lamp-lit stands serving steaming bowls of ramen and open-pot stews. Head to Nakasu Island to find them.

④
Fukuoka Asian Art Museum

📍 3-1 Shimokawabatamachi
🚇 Nakasu-Kawabata
🕐 9:30am–6pm Sun-Tue & Thu, 9:30am–8pm Fri & Sat 🌐 faam.city.fukuoka.lg.jp

An expansive collection of contemporary Asian art is found at this museum. From Pakistan to the Philippines, works from 23 countries are housed here, and the museum claims to represent the distinct cultures found across the continent. Folk art and traditional art are displayed alongside contemporary works, showing the influence of cultural heritage.

⑤
Shofuku-ji Temple

📍 6-1 Gokushomachi
🚇 Gion, Gofukumachi

Despite its modernity, Fukuoka also has sights of antiquity. Shofuku-ji Temple, northwest of Hakata Station, is said to be the oldest Zen Buddhist temple in Japan. It was founded in the late 12th century by the priest Yosai, who introduced both Zen and tea to Japan. The Kushida Shrine, just to the west, dates from the 8th century.

---

⑥
Hakata Machiya Folk Museum

📍 6-10 Reisenmachi
🚇 Gion 🕐 10am–6pm daily
🌐 hakatamachiya.com

The exhibits and dioramas in this traditional building celebrate the area's heritage. You can watch local artisans at work here, including demonstrations of Hakata silk weaving.

←
Weaving cloth on a loom at the Hakata Machiya Folk Museum

EAT

Hakata Issou
Made from pork from local farms, the rich and silky *tonkotsu* broth served here has been nicknamed the "pork bone cappuccino" by local ramen lovers.

📍 3-1-6 Hakataekihigashi
📞 (092) 472-7739

¥¥¥

Ganso Hakata Mentaiju
Mentaiko (spiced herring roe), a specialty in this city, is served here with both rice and *tsukemen* (ramen and soup served in two separate bowls). Dip the noodles into the spicy *mentaiko* soup – the result is out of this world.

📍 6-15 Nishinakasu
📞 (092) 725-7220

¥¥¥

The glowing lights of the buildings lining Nagasaki's historic harbor at dusk ↑

2

NAGASAKI

長崎

🅰A6 🏛Nagasaki Prefecture ✈🚉Nagasaki ℹIn Nagasaki JR Stn; www.travel.at-nagasaki.jp/en

A history of contact and interaction with Europe, even after foreign powers were expelled elsewhere in the country in the 17th century, its tragic fate as victim of the second atomic bomb in 1945, and miraculous resurgence since the war have made Nagasaki one of the most cosmopolitan and eclectic cities in Japan.

①

Shrine to the 26 Martyrs

🅰7-8 Nishizakamachi
🚉🚏Nagasaki 🕐Museum: 9am-5pm daily

Christianity was officially banned in 1597 by the shogun Toyotomi Hideyoshi, who feared that conversions would lead to the undermining of the state by foreign powers. In that year, to emphasize the point, 26 defiant Christians were crucified on Nishizaka Hill, the first of over 600 documented martyrdoms in the Nagasaki area alone. A stone relief, a small chapel, and a museum honor the martyrs who, in 1862, were declared saints by the Pope. Without a clergy or a single chapel to worship in, Christianity, astonishingly, managed to survive covertly for another 200 years until the end of Japan's isolationism.

→ The simple stone relief depicting the 26 Christian martyrs of Nagasaki

②

Spectacles Bridge

🅰8 Uonomachi
🚏Meganebashi Bridge

One of the most photographed sights in Nagasaki is the curious Megane-bashi, or Spectacles Bridge, a Chinese bequest to the city. Built by the Zen priest Mozi in 1634, it remains the oldest stone bridge in Japan. It earned its name because the curve of the bridge reflected in the Nakashima River resembles a pair of glasses.

③

Dejima

🅰6-1 Dejimamachi
🚏Dejima 🕐8am-9pm daily
🌐nagasakidejima.jp

After the Portuguese were expelled from Japan in 1638, the Dutch, confined to the tiny island of Dejima, were the only foreign power permitted to

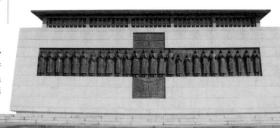

remain in the country. Dejima was once surrounded by mud walls, and the only Japanese people allowed to enter were traders, prostitutes, and monks collecting alms. Dejima Museum, housed in Japan's first Protestant seminary, and Dejima Dutch Factory Historic Site next door contain historical artifacts from excavations on the site.

---

④ Suwa Shrine

📍 18-15 Kaminishiyama-dori 🚊 Suwa Jinja

Located in a wooded hilltop precinct at the top of 277 stone steps, Suwa Shrine affords fine views. The original buildings were destroyed by fire in 1857 but later beautifully restored. The purpose of this popular shrine, home to the city's pantheon of Shinto gods, was to promote Shintoism and eradicate the last vestiges of Christianity from the area. The autumn festival, Kunchi Matsuri, is celebrated here, with blazing floats and dragon dances.

⑤ Sofuku-ji Temple

📍 7-5 Kajiyamachi 🚊 Sofukuji
🕐 8am–5pm daily

The Chinese provenance of this temple is shown by the entrance gate, which depicts the gateway that, according to legend, is seen in the Chinese undersea paradise. The temple also has a second gate known as First Peak Gate, dating from the late Ming period.

Sofuku-ji Temple is one of the three largest Chinese places of worship in Nagasaki. The temple was founded, with the help of local Chinese residents, by a monk in 1629. The cooking pot in the grounds was used to make gruel to feed over 3,000 people each day during one of Nagasaki's worst famines in 1682.

---

⑥ Kofuku-ji Temple

📍 4-32 Teramachi
🚊 Shimenkaikan 🕐 9am–5pm daily

Kofuku-ji Temple, in the heart of the Teramachi district, was Japan's first Obaku Zen Buddhist temple. Founded by a Chinese priest in 1623, the building is also known as the Nanking Temple and is often visited by residents from that city. The main buildings, including the Buddha hall, are constructed in Chinese style.

⑦
Oura Catholic Church

📍 5-3 Minamiyamatemachi 🚉 Oura Tenshudo ⏰ 8am–6pm daily

This white church was built in 1864 under the direction of Bernard Petitjean, a French priest who became the first Bishop of Nagasaki. It was erected in order to serve the foreign community that settled in Nagasaki after the new trade treaties were signed but, soon after its foundation, Petitjean was approached by a group of Japanese Christians who had been practicing their faith in secret since it was outlawed.

Classed as a National Treasure, Oura is one of the oldest churches in Japan and the country's earliest Gothic wooden structure. A wooden building beside the church contains items connected with the persecution of Nagasaki's early Christians.

⑧
Atomic Bomb Museum

📍 7-8 Hiranomachi 🚉 Atomic Bomb Museum ⏰ 8:30am–5:30pm daily (to 6:30pm May–Aug) 🌐 nagasakipeace.jp

> This museum is a must for anybody

↑ Examining photographs and artifacts at the Atomic Bomb Museum

visiting the city. Displays depict Nagasaki before and after the explosion. It traces with great objectivity and fairness the events leading up to the bombing, the history of nuclear weapons, and the evolution of the international peace movement. Photographs, artifacts, videos, and dioramas vividly recreate the tragedy. A clock, frozen at the moment the bomb exploded, is one of the most poignant items.

⑨
Peace Park

📍 9 Matsuyamamachi 🚉 Heiwa-koen ⏰ 24 hours daily

A black stone pillar marks the spot where the US detonated its second atom bomb at 11:02 on

August 9, 1945, three days after the bombing of Hiroshima. The intended target was the nearby shipyards. The blast killed an estimated 75,000, and 75,000 more were injured in its wake. Small wonder that the citizens of Nagasaki have become staunch advocates of world peace, erecting several monuments in the park, including a 30-ft (9-m) tall Peace Statue. A 1959 reconstruction of the Urakami Catholic Church, which stood at the epicenter, stands near the park.

⑩
Confucius Shrine

📍 10-36 Ouramachi 🚉 Oura Tenshudo ⏰ 8:30am–5pm daily

Vibrant yellow roof tiles and vermilion walls instantly announce this building as a shrine dedicated to the scholar Confucius. Built by the city's Chinese community in 1893, the repairs and extensions accorded the shrine after it was damaged in the atomic bombing included the addition in 1982 of a National Museum of Chinese History. The antiquities on display are on loan from the Chinese National Museum and the prestigious Palace Museum in Beijing.

← Seibo Kitamura's towering Peace Statue in Nagasaki's poignant Peace Park

⑪ Glover Garden

8-1 Minamiyamatemachi
Oura Tenshudo
9:30am-6pm daily
glover-garden.jp

With the reopening of the port to Westerners in the 19th century, Nagasaki flowered as a prosperous international city. Suitable housing was required for the sudden influx of foreigners and many of the comfortable stone and clapboard residencies that were built during this period survive today, preserved in Glover Garden.

The best-known European-style residence here is Glover House. It was built in 1863 for Thomas Glover, an extraordinary British entrepreneur whose ventures included bringing the first steam locomotive to Japan, coal mining, a tea import house, ship repair yards, and the founding of a beer company, the forerunner of today's Kirin Beer.

Other notable buildings in the park include Ringer House, standing on foundation stones brought from Vladivostok, and Walker House, which displays the colorful floats used in the city's annual Kunchi festival. The Old Hong Kong and Shanghai Bank Building houses displays tracing Nagasaki's contact with Western ideas.

FOREIGNERS IN NAGASAKI

The Portuguese and Dutch were the first to arrive when Nagasaki's harbor opened to international trade in 1571, followed by Chinese merchants, who established their own community. The Portuguese brought Catholicism to the city, but this minority soon faced religious persecution. When Japan became a closed country in 1634, only the Dutch were allowed to trade here. After the port reopened in 1853, British, American, French, German, and Prussian trade missions came to the city. The legacy of this extraordinary foreign contact survives in some of the local festivals and cuisine, like the Portuguese *castella,* an egg-and-flour-based sponge cake.

⑫ Hollander Slope

2 Higashiyamatemachi
Medical Center

A pleasant cobblestone street built by the Dutch, the Slope was once the center for the city's expatriate community. For a time, all Westerners, irrespective of nationality, were called "Hollanders" by the Japanese. Some of the wooden houses along the Slope are open to the public. One of the most imposing, the 1868 Junibankan, was once the Prussian Legation building.

⑬ Huis Ten Bosch

1-1 Huistenboschmachi, Sasebo **Huis Ten Bosch** **9am-9pm daily** **huistenbosch.co.jp**

Built in 1992 at the staggering cost of US$1.75 billion, Huis Ten Bosch is a reproduction of a traditional Dutch village. Replete with churches, houses, shops, windmills, a farmhouse, and canals, it is one of the largest theme parks in Japan. Replicas of the royal palace and of Holland's tallest church tower are highlights. As you travel through the park by horse-drawn carriage, old-fashioned taxi, or canal boat, you'll soon forget that you aren't in the Netherlands.

↓ A reconstruction of a historic Dutch windmill in Huis Ten Bosch

EXPERIENCE MORE

3

Yufuin
湯布院

🅰B6 🏛Oita Prefecture
🚉Yufuin 🚹At JR stn;
(0977) 84-2446

Known for picturesque wisps of morning mist, Yufuin sits at the foot of Mount Yufudake. The resort prides itself on country inns, boutiques, summer concerts, and a host of museums, including the **Sueda Art Museum** and the **Trick 3D Art Yufuin Museum**.

JR Yufuin Station, built in 1990 has a sooty exterior resembling a locomotive's boiler. It displays art in its exhibition hall, and the floors are heated by an underground hot spring.

A walking and cycling path follows the shore of Lake Kinrin. Shitan-yu, an old outdoor bath with a thatched roof, is beside the lake. The bathing is mixed, as baths were before the arrival of Americans and Europeans.

Sueda Art Museum
🏛1834 Kawakami
📞(0977) 85-3572
🕐9am-5pm daily

Trick 3D Art Yufuin Museum
🏛3001-8 Kawakami
🕐9:30am-5:30pm daily

4

Kokura
小倉

🅰B5 🏛Fukuoka
Prefecture 🚉Kokura
🚹At JR station; www.
gururich-kitaq.com/en/

Gateway to northern Kyushu, Kokura is a modern city. This is embodied in the designs by Arata Isozaki, especially **Chuo Toshokan Kitakyushu** library (1974), which has been used as a set for many movies. The city and its environs – including Dan no Ura battlefield, where the Taira clan were defeated, and straits of Shimonoseki – can be seen from here. Next to the castle is the **Kokura Castle Japanese Garden**, which surrounds a samurai house.

Chuo Toshokan Kitakyushu
🏛4-1 Jonai 🕐Tue-Sun

Kokura Castle Japanese Garden
♿ 🏛2-1 Jonai 🕐Apr-Oct: 9am-6pm daily (Nov-Mar: to 5pm) 🌐kokura-castle.jp

5

Usa
宇佐

🅰B6 🏛Oita Prefecture
🚉Usa 🚌Sightseeing bus
tour recommended

The center of Tendai-sect sanctuaries and shrines

Did You Know?

The god of war, Hachiman was held to be the guardian of the samurai.

dedicated to Hachiman, the god of war, the area around Usa and the Kunisaki Peninsula is believed to have been the nucleus of ancient Buddhist sites. These religious places are of Korean inspiration and origin. The most famous site, Usa Jingu Shrine, dedicated to the ancient Japanese deities, is also identified with the influential figure of Hachiman.

On the peninsula, to the east of Usa, are stone tombs, Heian-period statues, and, at Kumano Magaibutsu, the largest carved rock-face reliefs in Japan. The ancient ambience of the peninsula can be sensed near the summit of Mount Futago, where stone guardians mark the approach to

→

Traditional torii marking the entrance to the famous Usa Jingu Shrine

↑ The main shopping street in the spa town of Yufuin, surrounded by mountains

TOP 5 BEPPU SPAS

Tanayu
🅦 suginoi-hotel.com
Outdoor pools offer great city views at this vast complex.

Takegawara
Famed for its black-sand baths.

Beppu Beach Sand Bath
📍 9 Shoningahamacho
Enjoy a sand bath with a view of Beppu Bay.

Myoban Hot Spring
A quiet *onsen* option.

Onsen Hoyo Land
📞 0977 66-2221
Both mud and steam baths are available here.

Futago-ji Temple. Twin avatars of the mountain are enshrined at the temple hall here, built into the side of a cliff. The oldest wooden structure in Kyushu, the main hall of Fuki-ji Temple, dating from the Heian period, has faint, eerily beautiful frescoes of the Buddhist paradise.

6 Beppu
別府

📍 B6 📍 Oita Prefecture
🚆 Oita 🚉 Beppu 🚌 From Tokyo, Osaka, Kobe, and Hiroshima 🚉 Beppu Stn; www.city.beppu.oita.jp

If you can accept its brazen commercialism, Beppu, a glitzy, neon-strung hot-spring resort, constitutes an amazing thermal and entertainment roller coaster.

**INSIDER TIP
Be Footloose**

Dotted around Beppu are *ashiyu - onsen* for your feet. Usually found in public places, these small hot water pools are the perfect place to rest weary feet and are often free of charge.

The city's porous skin is punctured by a number of vents from which steam continuously rises. Scalding water surfaces at the 3,750 hot springs and 168 public baths, and is also piped into private homes to heat rooms and fuel ovens.

Beppu offers interesting variations on the theme of a hot bath. Visitors can soak in a series of tubs of graded temperatures, plunge into thermal whirlpools, be buried in hot black sand, or sit up to the neck in steaming mud.

The most famous sights are the **Boiling Hells** (Jigoku) – pools of mineral-colored water and bubbling mud. The eight pools are within walking distance of each other in Beppu's Kannawa and Shibaseki districts. Each has a different function, color, and mineral property. For example, the waters of Ocean Hell (Umi Jigoku) are the color of a tropical sea, while Blood Pond Hell (Chi-no-Ike Jigoku) takes its color from dissolved red clay.

Many baths are attached to hotels but also open to the public. The hugely popular **Suginoi Hotel** on the western fringes of town, is an irresistible hot-spring fantasy. Built in 1879 just inland from Beppu Bay, **Takegawara Bathhouse** is one of Beppu's oldest public baths, in which

visitors are buried in black sand before plunging into adjacent hot pools. Up in the hills north of Kannawa, **Myoban Hot Spring** is a quieter place to which Japanese people have been coming for well over a thousand years for curative baths. For an overview of Beppu, climb the 410-ft (125-m) Global Tower, between the station and Suginoi Hotel.

Boiling Hells
♿ 📍 559-1 Kannawa
📞 (0977) 66-1577
🕐 8am–5pm daily

Suginoi Hotel
♿ 📍 1 Kankaiji 🕐 9am–11pm daily 🅦 suginoi-hotel.com

Takegawara Bathhouse
♿ 📍 16-23 Motomachi
📞 (0977) 23-1585 🕐 6:30am–10:30pm daily (from 8am for sand bath)

Myoban Hot Spring
♿ 📍 Myoban 🕐 8:30am–5:30pm daily 🅦 jigoku-prin.com

Some of the carved Usuki Stone Buddhas, about which little is known

Usuki Stone Buddhas
臼杵石仏

A B6 **Q** Oita Prefecture **Q** Usuki, then JR bus to Usuki-Sekibutsu **O** 6am–7pm daily (Oct–Mar: to 6pm)

Despite the dissemination of images of Oita's Seki Butsu (stone Buddhas) throughout Japan, the site itself is only a minor tourist area. Though it is probable that the work was begun during the late Heian period and completed in the early Kamakura era, there appears to be no consensus regarding the origin of the site, who commissioned or executed the dozens of carvings, or why such a large, relatively remote area was dedicated for the images.

All of this adds a great deal of mystery and charm to the place. Late afternoon is very atmospheric, when sculptured sunlight draws out the earth hues from the faces and torsos of these mysterious and peaceful stone Buddhas.

SHOP

Head to the town of Arita, in Saga Prefecture, to visit ancient pottery studios producing beautiful porcelain.

Koransha
A A6 **Q** 1-3-8 Kobira, Arita **W** koransha.co.jp

Fukagawa Seiji
A A6 **Q** 1-1-8 Kobira, Arita **C** (0955) 42-5215

Arita Porcelain Lab
A A6 **Q** 340-28 Toya, Arita **W** arita-touki.com

8
Kurume
久留米

A A6 **Q** Fukuoka Prefecture **Q** Kurume **i** At JR stn; www.welcome-kurume.com/en

The sprawling city of Kurume is the center of *kasuri* textiles. These employ a distinctive ikat weaving style, in which the threads have been tie-dyed before weaving; unlike Southeast Asian forms of ikat, both the warp and weft are patterned. The **Kurume Regional Industry Promotion Center** sells these textiles. *Rantai-shikki* is a local basket-weaving style whereby layers of lacquer are applied to bamboo to produce basketware. Examples can be bought at Inoue Rantai-Shikki, opposite the Honmachi-yon-chome bus stop. The **Ishibashi Bunka Center**, a ten-minute bus ride from the station, has an art museum and Japanese garden.

Many artisans work in the villages of Hirokawa and Yame, a 40-minute bus ride from Kurume. In Hirokawa, visit the **Moriyama Kasuri Workshop**, which employs a 16th-century technique to make paper, using mulberry-tree fibers.

Kurume Regional Industry Promotion Center
Q 2F Jibasan Kurume Center, 5-8-5 Higashi Aikawa **C** (0942) 44-3700 **O** 10am–5pm daily

Ishibashi Bunka Center
Q 1015 Nonakamachi **C** (0942) 33-2271 **O** 9am–5pm Tue–Sun

Moriyama Kasuri Workshop
Q 109 Niishiro, Hirokawa-machi **C** (0943) 32-0023 (reservation required) **O** 9am–4pm Mon–Sat

Did You Know?

Students visit Dazaifu Tenman-gu Shrine to pray for success in their exams.

9

Onta
小鹿田

🅐 B6 ⬛ Oita Prefecture
🚉 Hita, then bus to
Sarayama 🛈 At Hita Stn;
(0973) 22-2036

Tucked into a wooded mountain valley, this tiny village has been producing Onta-ware since a group of Korean potters set up their kilns here in 1705. Later luminaries of the *mingei* (folk craft) movement, such as Yanagi Soetsu and Bernard Leach, praised Onta-ware for its unpretentious quality. The kilns, dug into the hillside and water-powered, are still used.

↓ The ornate exterior of Dazaifu Tenman-gu Shrine

The simple, functional objects are characterized by marked, dribbled glazes in earth colors. The Onta Folk Pottery Festival takes place on the second weekend of October.

10

Dazaifu
大宰府

🅐 A6 ⬛ Fukuoka Prefecture
🚉 Dazaifu 🛈 At Dazaifu
Stn; (092) 925-1880

Dazaifu was of great military importance under the Yamato government *(p211)* and an administrative center in the later Nara period. Today, most visitors come for **Dazaifu Tenman-gu Shrine**. Located in a tranquil district close to the station, the shrine is dedicated to the calligrapher, scholar, and poet Sugawara Michizane. The guardian of learning, Michizane, who died in AD 903, is also known by his divine name of Tenjin. The Treasure House can be visited, and just behind it is a hall displaying curious tableaux of Hakata clay dolls representing scenes from Michizane's life.

 PICTURE PERFECT
Time Travel

After going through the torii at Dazaifu Tenman-gu Shrine, pause at the pond in the shape of the Japanese character for "heart." Take a picture of the bridges linking the three islands, representing the past, present, and future.

The **Kyushu National Museum** focuses on the interaction of Japan with other Asian nations. Exhibits include 75 hand-drawn Edo period *Um sum* cards depicting customs.

The **Dazaifu Government Ruins** is a spacious park with a scattering of medieval ruins.

Dazaifu Tenman-gu Shrine
🎫🕐 🏠 4-7-1 Saifu 📞 (092)
922-8225 🕐 Treasure House:
9am–4:30pm Tue–Sun

Kyushu National Museum
🎫🎟🕐 🏠 4-7-2 Ishizaka
🕐 9:30am–5pm Tue–Sun
🌐 kyuhaku.jp

Dazaifu Government Ruins
🏠 4-6-1 Kanzeonji 📞 (092)
922-7811 🕐 24 hours daily

Kumamoto
熊本

🄰A6 🚇Kumamoto Prefecture ✈Aso Kumamoto 🚉Kumamoto 🛈www.kumamoto-guide.jp/en

Kumamoto was an important seat of power during the Tokugawa shogunate (1603–1868). Its star attraction, one of the largest castles in Japan, dates from this period. The city's main sights are found in an area south of the castle.

The longevity of Kumamoto's residents (the city has several centenarians) is ascribed to a passion for living and a healthy diet. The latter includes *karashi renkon* (deep-fried lotus root stuffed with mustard miso) and various brands of sake made from water supposedly purified by the area's rich volcanic soil.

🔍 HIDDEN GEM
World in Miniature

Kumamoto's Suizen-ji Joju-en Garden *(8-1 Suizenjikoen)* recreates the 53 post stations – including Mount Fuji and Lake Biwa – of the old Tokaido highway, the road that connected Edo with Kyoto during the Edo period.

Dominating the center of the city from an imposing hill, **Kumamoto Castle** was constructed on the orders of Kato Kiyomasa, a warrior who fought alongside Ieyasu Tokugawa at the decisive Battle of Sekigahara in 1600. He was rewarded for his loyalty with lands encompassing most of present-day Kumamoto. The castle was completed in 1607. Unlike more decorative castles such as Himeji *(p224)*, Kumamoto's citadel is rigorously martial in appearance, with steep, nearly impregnable walls. The original structure had 49 towers and 29 gates, but it was almost completely destroyed during the Satsuma Rebellion in 1877. Although the main keep was reconstructed on a smaller scale in 1960, it is a highly effective replica, successfully evoking the fearsome magnificence of the original. Due to damage from the 2016 earthquake, the castle is currently closed, but the imposing structure can still be viewed from the outside, and there is a reconstruction tour route.

Gyobu-tei, an 18th-century residence once owned by the powerful Hosokawa clan, is located a little northwest of the castle grounds. It presents insights into the way the feudal elite lived during the Edo period. This building also suffered serious damage in 2016 and is currently closed.

The family possessions of the powerful Kato and Hosokawa clans can be found near the castle in the **Kumamoto Prefectural Art Museum**, a distinctive modern building with a pleasant tearoom. The museum also has interesting replicas of ancient burial mounds and archaeological finds from the region.

Kumamoto is renowned for its crafts, especially damascene inlay designs, Amakusa pearls, and Yamaga lanterns. These lanterns, made from gold paper, are a feature of the city's festival in August. The **Kumamoto Traditional Crafts Center** has a good selection of these local crafts.

Kumamoto Castle
♿ 🄰1-1 Hommaru
🔒For restoration 🌐castle.kumamoto-guide.jp/en

Gyobu-tei
♿ 🄰3-1 Furugyocho
📞(096) 352-6522
🔒For restoration

Kumamoto Prefectural Art Museum
♿⊙ 🄰2-2 Ninomaru
📞(096) 352-2111 🕘9:30am–5:15pm Tue–Sun

Kumamoto Traditional Crafts Center
♿ 🄰3-35 Chibajomachi
📞(096) 324-4930
🕘9:30am–5:30pm Tue–Sun

A sightseeing cruise on one of the canals in the town of Yanagawa

Mount Unzen, thought to be dormant until one of its peaks erupted in 1990, can be climbed or partly ascended by ropeway from the Nita Pass.

 Yoshinogari Ruins
吉野ケ里遺跡

🅰 A6 🏠 Saga Prefecture **🚃 Yoshinogari-koen or Kanzaki, then 15-min walk or take taxi** **🕐 9am–5pm daily** **🌐 yoshinogari.jp/en**

Pit dwellings and hundreds of burial urns excavated at Yoshinogari point to the existence of a sophisticated Yayoi-period society (300 BC–AD 300) in the region. Smart irrigation systems and rice cultivation were begun in this period, laying the pattern for later Japanese society. The area is believed by some to be the home of Queen Himiko, mentioned in 3rd-century Chinese annals. Watchtowers and Yayoi-period homes have been reconstructed here.

 Yanagawa
柳川

🅰 A6 🏠 Fukuoka Prefecture 🚃 Nishitetsu Yanagawa 🛈 www.yanagawa-net.com/eng

The Stone Quays of Yanagawa are not as busy as they used to be, but the canals and old moats that run through this former castle town are still vital to its economy, and eel remains the local delicacy. Visitors can board *donkobune* (gondolas) for a *kawakudari* (river cruise). As you float along the restored canals, you'll glide past old samurai villas and storehouses. The canals are at their best during sakura season in spring.

Other Yanagawa sights include Suiten-gu, a pretty shrine used by the same sect as the shrine in Kurume; Kyu Toshimake Jyutaku, an Edo-period tea garden; and a house-museum, **Hakushu Kinenkan**, the birthplace of Hakushu Kitahara (1885–1942), a prolific writer best known for children's poems.

Hakushu Kinenkan

♿ 🏠 55-1 Okinohatamachi 📞 (0944) 72-6773 🕐 9am–5pm daily

The formidable bulk of Kumamoto Castle, built in the early 17th century

 Shimabara Peninsula
島原半島

🅰 A6 🏠 Nagasaki Prefecture 🚃 Shimabara 🚌 From Kumamoto 🛈 Unzen Spa (0957) 73-3434; Shimabara Peninsula Tourism Association (0957) 62-0655

Ruled by the Christian Lord Arima until 1616, Shimabara Peninsula is known as the site of anti-Christian pogroms ordered by the Tokugawa shogunate. Later, in the 1880s, Unzen Spa became a resort for Westerners. At an altitude of 2,300 ft (700 m) and surrounded by pine forests, the spa was an ideal retreat from the summer heat. Thousands of azaleas bloom on the peninsula in spring, and in autumn the maple leaves turn brilliant shades of red. In 1934 the Unzen-Amakusa National Park, one of Japan's first such protected areas, was created.

Most hotels in Unzen Spa have their own hot-spring baths. Away from the resorts, visitors can see the notorious Hells (Jigoku): scalding sulfurous cauldrons in which 30 Christians were boiled alive after the outlawing of Christianity in Japan. As a demonstration of the ferocity of the waters, elderly ladies in smocks lower eggs placed in baskets into the pools and sell them hard-boiled to tourists.

DRINK

Kuma Shochu Museum

Shochu – made from sweet potato, rice, or barley – is drunk on the rocks, or mixed with water. Learn about its production and sample the spirit at this museum in Kumamoto.

🅰 A6 🏠 Gonoharumachi 461-7, Hitoyoshi, Kumamoto 🌐 denshogura.jp

↑ Steam rising from a crater on Mount Aso, Japan's largest active volcano

 15

Mount Aso
阿蘇山

🅰B6 🚉Kumamoto Prefecture 🚃Aso, then bus 🚌Kyushu Odan sightseeing bus from Beppu or Kumamoto 🌐asocity-kanko.jp/en

Actually a series of five volcanic cones, Mount Aso is one of the world's largest calderas, with a circumference of 80 miles (130 km). Of the five peaks, Mount Takadake, at about 5,220 ft (1,590 m), is the highest. Mount Nakadake is still active, emitting sulfurous fumes and hot gases, earning Kumamoto the epithet *hi-no-kuni* ("the land of fire").

Below these peaks, the caldera is dotted with towns set among forests, grasslands, bamboo groves, and hot springs. Arriving tour buses

> **INSIDER TIP**
> **Onsen Hopping**
>
> Kurokawa, the town at the base of Mount Aso, is considered one of Japan's best *onsen* locations. A pass gives access to several hot springs at a discounted rate (*www.kurokawa onsen.or.jp*).

pass a curious, grass-covered mountain resembling an inverted rice bowl, aptly named Komezuka (Rice Mound), and often stop at the pretty Kusasenri Meadow.

A bus service runs to the top of Nakadake, providing, on clear days, awesome views into the depths of the crater and its malodorous green lake. Hikers can follow a path to the summit for a closer look. A popular hiking route starts at the very top of the ropeway, proceeds to Mount Takadake around the crater rim, and descends to Sensui Gorge. Access to the crater is constantly under review depending on volcanic activity, so be sure to check the website in advance for an update.

The **Mount Aso Volcanic Museum**, at the base of Nakadake, offers a fascinating preview of the mountain even when the crater is closed due to a high level of dangerous, sulfuric fumes. Two cameras on the crater wall relay continuous images of the cone's volcanic activity.

Mount Aso Volcanic Museum
♿ 🏠1930-1 Akamizu
🕐9am–5pm daily

 16

Takachiho
高千穂

🅰B6 🏠Miyazaki Prefecture 🚌From Kumamoto and Miyazaki 🌐takachiho-kanko.info/en

The Takachiho mountain region, a place of homage for those with an affection for Japan's ancient pantheon of gods and goddesses, is alive with the resonances of legend. Most of the sights are connected with Japan's rich mythology. Kagura, a mime-dance said to have been first performed by the Sun Goddess, Amaterasu Omikami, is thought to have originated here. The cave into which Amaterasu vanished, casting the world into a contemporary gloom until she could be lured out, faces Ama no Iwato Shrine,

↑ Rowing boats under a pretty waterfall in Takachiho Gorge

 Vermilion entrance to Udo Jingu Shrine, built into a cave along the Nichinan coast

a pavilion-style shrine noted for a sacred tree that stands in its grounds. A short walk from here is Ama no Yasugawara, the grotto where the gods are supposed to have convened in order to devise a way to entice the Sun Goddess from her lair. The entrance to the cavern is next to a clear, pebble-strewn river. Many visitors have placed miniature cairns there in the hope that, by association, some of the wisdom and power of the gods will rub off on them.

The area's main shrine, Takachiho Jinja is famous for its ancient cryptomeria trees, a common feature of Japanese shrines and temple grounds. It was founded by the 11th emperor of Japan around 1,900 years ago. The shrine stages nightly extracts of kagura lasting one hour, providing a rare opportunity to witness a performance in richly atmospheric surroundings. Visitors usually try to

> **North of Udo Jingu is Sun-Messe Nichinan, where perfectly reproduced statues of Moai, officially approved by Easter Island, are displayed.**

factor into their itinerary a rowboat trip along Takachiho Gorge, with its scenic rock formations and waterfalls.

🔟 Nichinan Coast
日南海岸

🅰️ B7 🚩 Miyazaki Prefecture 🚉 Nichinan line from Miyazaki 🌐 kankou-nichinan.jp/english

The Nichinan coastal landscape is known in Japanese as Onino Sentakuita, the "devil's wash-board," an apt description for the eroded, rippled effect presented by the rock shelves.

The gateway to the coast is Aoshima Island, barely a mile in circumference and connected to the mainland by a walkway. An attractive vermilion shrine stands at the center of this densely forested islet, which can get crowded in summertime. Miyazaki city, to the north, is known for its year-round flowers.

Udo Jingu Shrine, another striking vermilion-colored shrine about 20 miles (32 km) south of Aoshima, stands in a cave beside the ocean. The shrine is dedicated to Emperor Jimmu's father, who is believed to have been washed there at birth, and

serves as a catalyst for propitious marriages and fertility. The water dripping from breast-shaped rocks is compared to mother's milk, and milk candies are sold at the shrine shop. North of Udo Jingu is Sun-Messe Nichinan, where perfectly reproduced statues of Moai, officially approved by Easter Island, are displayed. One stop farther on the Nichinan line lies Obi, an old castle town, where the ruins of the castle and samurai houses may be visited. Farther south is Ishinami Beach, which is a stretch of fine white sand.

EAT

Iroha
This is one of the best restaurants in Kumamoto (p274) to sample local dishes, including basashi, a horse-meat sashimi.

🅰️ A6 🏠 4-21 Suizenjikoen, Chuo, Kumamoto

18 Kirishima-Kinkowan National Park
霧島錦江湾国立公園

🅰A7 🔲Miyazaki and Kagoshima Prefectures 🔲Kobayashi (JR Kitto line), then Miyazaki Kotsu bus to Ebino Highland

This region, identified with Japanese foundation myths, centers on the volcanic plateau of Ebino-Kogen (Shrimp Meadow), which is surrounded by volcanoes, crater lakes, and hot springs. The Ebino-Kogen Nature Trail is the best of several hiking routes, going past three ponds, two of which are cobalt blue. The climb up to the peak of Mount Karakunidake is popular in summer. There are many steaming hot springs in the area; some of the best are the Iodani, Arayu, Hayashida, and Sakura *onsen*.

This is an active volcanic area, and some parts of the park may be off-limits for safety reasons at any one time. This can also result in closures of roads and hiking trails.

Did You Know?

When it rains, an amazing azure lake forms in Mount Karakunidake's crater.

19 Kagoshima
鹿児島

🅰A7 🔲Kagoshima Prefecture ✈🚆Kagoshima 🚢From Tokyo, Nagoya, Osaka, and Nagasaki ℹ At Kagoshima-Chuo Stn; www.kagoshima-kankou.com

Kagoshima looks out across the broad sweep of a bay to the brooding silhouette of Sakurajima, an active volcano that sometimes showers the city in a blanket of volcanic ash.

Historically, Kagoshima enjoyed an unusual degree of independence. Center of the feudal domain of Satsuma, Kagoshima's Shimazu clan ruled Okinawa for eight centuries, absorbing much of the culture of China and Southeast Asia transmitted through the islands. The legacy of that contact is evident today in a cuisine that relies on sweet potatoes rather than rice, and in its typically Okinawan preference for pork dishes.

Shochu, Kagoshima's liquor made mostly from sweet potatoes (although it can be made from rice or barley), is believed to have passed through Okinawa from China or Korea. There are over 120 *shochu* distilleries in Kagoshima alone. Local craft traditions, particularly ceramics and fine silk brocades, reflect an aesthetic of Asian provenance.

Kagoshima's sultry climate is apparent at the former stately home of **Sengan-en**,

 HIDDEN GEM
Sand Baths

A sand bath at Ibusuki, 17 miles (28 km) SE of Chiran, consists of being buried in sand that is naturally heated by rising steam. After staying buried for ten to 20 minutes, guests wash off the sand and enter hot-spring baths.

The waterfront city of Kagoshima, with Sakurajima volcano in the background ↑

SAKURAJIMA VOLCANO

A dramatic eruption of Sakurajima in 1914 deposited three billion tons of lava in the narrow strait between the mountain and the peninsula, thus joining the island to the mainland. One of Japan's foremost writers, Shusaku Endo, is said to have had himself lowered by helicopter into the smoking crater of Sakurajima, the model for his 1959 novel *Kazan (Volcano)*.

↑ Crystal-clear waters at a rock-dotted beach on Amami Oshima island

where semitropical plants grow alongside plum trees and bamboo groves. The garden's centerpiece is a pond and small waterfall.

On an artificial island in the harbor is the Kagoshima Aquarium, with species from local waters and the coral reefs around the Nansei islands, southwest of Kyushu. One of the city's best attractions is the **Kagoshima City Museum**

of Art, with its displays of Satsuma ceramics.

The city is also associated with Saigo Takamori (1827–77), who led the ill-fated Satsuma Rebellion. Japanese visitors pay their respects to him in a cave on Shiroyama Hill where he committed ritual suicide.

Sengan-en

🏛️🍵🖼️🎁 🕐9700-1 Yoshinocho 🕘9am–5pm daily 🌐senganen.jp/en

Kagoshima City Museum of Art

🏛️🍵 🕐4-36 Shiroyamacho 🕘9:30am–6pm Tue–Sun 🌐city.kagoshima.lg.jp/ artmuseum

---

Amami Oshima Island
奄美大島

🅰️D2 🏛️Kagoshima Prefecture ✈️From Tokyo, Osaka, Fukuoka, Kagoshima, Naha 🚢From Kagoshima to Naze 🌐amami-tourism. org/en

Subtropical Amami is home to a wealth of flora and fauna. The coral reefs and offshore islets of Setouchi, in the south, are part of a protected marine park offering excellent diving, snorkeling, and boat trips.

The Oshima Tsumugi Mura is an artisan village set aside for the production of *tsumugi*, a delicate handwoven silk fabric used to make kimonos.

Chiran
知覧

🅰️A7 🏛️Kagoshima Prefecture 🚌From Kagoshima 🛈(0993) 83-1120

Tucked into the green folds of tea plantations and wooded hills, exquisite Chiran was one of 113 castle towns built to protect the feudal lords of Satsuma. Seven preserved samurai houses and gardens on Samurai Lane can be visited with a single entrance ticket. Sata combines a dry-landscape garden, an expanse of white raked sand, and mountains used as "borrowed scenery." Hirayama is composed almost entirely of hedges, clipped into the illusion of undulating hills blending seamlessly with a backdrop of mountains. A hill above the village was the site of a World War II training ground for kamikaze pilots. Cherry trees are dedicated to 1,026 men who flew their fatal missions from Chiran.

Selecting porcelain from
a laden stall at Arita's
ceramics market

A DRIVING TOUR
SAGA POTTERY TOWNS

Locator Map
For more detail see p262

Length 50 miles (80 km) **Stopping-off points** Arita, Imari, Karatsu **Difficulty** Easy; roads are in good condition

Ceramics enthusiasts will thoroughly enjoy Saga Prefecture, where pottery towns have been producing high-quality wares for at least 500 years. This tour takes in the three main pottery towns – Arita, Imari, and Karatsu – which are all within convenient distances of each other. Stop off at these towns to admire the craftsmanship of the area's potters.

Yobuko's daily produce market includes stalls devoted to reasonably priced ceramics.

Karatsu's wares are often used in tea ceremonies. The Nakazato Taroemon Kiln is run by descendants of the town's first Korean potters.

*With its 2,500-year-old ceramics, the **Yoshinogari Ruins** (p275) is a good starting point for the tour.*

FINISH Yobuko

Chinzei

204

Karatsu

Takashima Island

Mitsusemura

323

Fukushima Island

204 E35 Yamamoto

Fujicho

263

385 E34

Kiyama

Tosu

3

34

Matsuura

Okawano

Taku

SAGA

E34

Ogi

Yoshinogari Ruins

START

Kurume

Imari

498

Kanzaki

498

Arita

Takeo

34

Saga

385

E3

Chikugo

Sasebo

Okawa

Miyama

E35

E34

Shiroishi

444

208

Yanagawa

Kashima

*A small town, **Arita** has a shrine to potters and dozens of kilns. Pop into the Kyushu Ceramic Museum for an overview of the region's pottery.*

Imari porcelain was exported by the Dutch East India Company to Europe in the 17th century where it was highly prized. Today, Imari-ware is produced in the kilns of Okawachiyama.

*The 236,000-strong prefectural capital, **Saga City** hosts an annual hot-air balloon competition in November.*

Did You Know?

Korean potters were brought to Kyushu in the 1590s and given sovereign control over the kilns.

0 kilometers 15

0 miles 15

N ↑

OKINAWA

An exotic coral bar slicing through the Pacific Ocean and East China Sea, the Okinawa archipelago was a vassal of China from the 14th century; its masters named it Liu-chiu (Ryukyu in Japanese). Under the Chinese, and later under the suzerainty of the Satsuma domain, the islands assimilated diverse influences, creating a unique culture that still sets them apart from mainland Japan.

Okinawa, the largest and busiest island in the group, gives its name to the prefecture, which united these 160 islands into one administrative group in 1879. In the closing stages of World War II, during the Battle of Okinawa, this was the scene of fierce fighting and the mass suicide of thousands of civilians. Naha, the main city, was damaged in the battle but has since become a heady mix of refined civilization and neon glitz. Art galleries and teahouses stand alongside red-light bars, snake restaurants, and karaoke cabins. Ceramic *shisa* lions, topping the red-tiled roofs of traditional Okinawan houses, add to the eclectic mix of war memorials, sacred groves, flower-covered coral walls, craft shops, and luxury hotels.

OKINAWA

Experience

Amami Island, Kyushu

IE ISLAND ⑦

NAKIJIN CASTLE RUIN ⑪

Nakijin

OCEAN EXPO PARK ⑧ Motobu

Minnashima

84 72

505

Sesoko Island

Yae-take 1,486 ft (453 m)

449

58

Nago

East China Sea

Nago Bay

329

Inbu Beach

E58

58

Moon Beach

Onna

329

Ginoza

E58

Kin

Zanpamisaki Cape

Nakadomari

58

Ishikawa

Kin Bay

Ikei Island

329

Yomitan

Uruma

Miyagi Island

Kadena

Gushikawa

58

E58

10

Okinawa

Katsurenzaki Cape

Chatan

330

Ukibaru Island

⑥ NAKAMURA HOUSE

Ginowan

⑤ NAKAGUSUKU CASTLE RUIN

Tsuken Island

58

Urasoe

Nishihara

329

NAHA CITY ①

Yonabaru

Kume Island

Naha Airport ✈

Haebaru

Azama

Tomigusuku

E58

Chinen

Kudaka Island

② THE FORMER JAPANESE NAVY UNDERGROUND HQ

331

77

507

④

Nanjo

331

Itoman

Yaese

GYOKUSENDO CAVE

Himeyuri Peace Museum

Mabuni Hill

③ OKINAWA BATTLE SITES

Cape Kyan

0 kilometers   8

0 miles   8

N

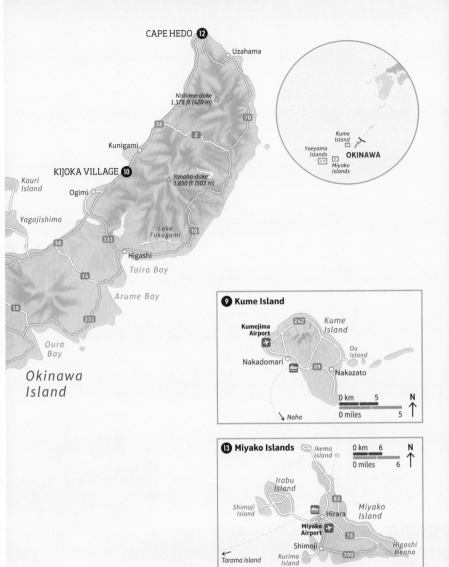

CAPE HEDO **12**

Uzahama

Nishime-dake
1,378 ft (420 m)

Kunigami

KIJOKA VILLAGE **10**

Yonaha-dake
1,650 ft (503 m)

Ogimi

*Kauri
Island*

Yagajishima

*Lake
Fukugami*

Higashi

Taira Bay

Arume Bay

*Oura
Bay*

*Okinawa
Island*

OKINAWA

*Kume
Island*

*Yaeyama
Islands*

*Miyako
Islands*

9 Kume Island

**Kumejima
Airport**

*Kume
Island*

Nakadomari

*Ou
Island*

Nakazato

0 km   5

0 miles   5

N

↘ *Naha*

13 Miyako Islands

0 km   6

0 miles   6

N

*Ikema
Island*

*Irabu
Island*

*Shimoji
Island*

Hirara

**Miyako
Airport**

Shimoji

*Miyako
Island*

*Higashi
Henna*

Tarama Island

*Kurima
Island*

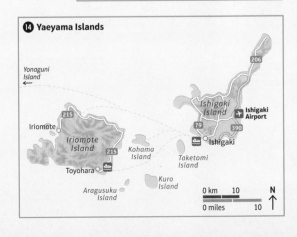

14 Yaeyama Islands

*Yonaguni
Island*
←

Iriomote

*Iriomote
Island*

*Kohama
Island*

*Ishigaki
Island*

**Ishigaki
Airport**

Ishigaki

*Taketomi
Island*

Toyohara

*Aragusuku
Island*

*Kuro
Island*

0 km   10

0 miles   10

N

EXPERIENCE

❶ Naha City

那覇市

🅐F7 🅞Okinawa Island ✈🚌Naha 🛈Airport 1F; otic.okinawa

Shuri, the most historical settlement in Okinawa, was its capital until the islands became part of Japan in 1879, after which Naha was declared the capital. The two cities have since expanded and merged. Naha prospered through its seaborne trade with other parts of Asia and, eventually, the West. The city that emerged from the ruins of World War II is a bustling center, with the archipelago's best restaurants, nightlife, and shopping.

A long thoroughfare in central Naha, Kokusai-dori (International Street) typifies the new city, with its boutiques and craft shops. The atmosphere along Heiwa-dori market street (to the south, off Kokusai-dori) harks back to an older Naha. Started by widows who had lost their husbands in the Battle of Okinawa, the market is full of Asian aromas, crowded alleys, and stalls selling Okinawan art, crafts, bric-a-brac, and exotic foods.

To the east, along Himeyuri-dori, is the pottery quarter of Tsuboya, which dates from the late 17th century. Over 20 workshops still produce wine flasks, tea bowls, and *shisa* (statues of a legendary lion, used all around the island as propitious roof ornaments). You can see examples at the **Tsuboya Pottery Museum**.

Also of interest in central Naha are the Sogen-ji Ishimon gates. The temple itself, originally a 16th-century memorial to the Ryukyu kings, was destroyed in the war; three of the original arched stone gates have been restored.

The Commodore Perry Memorial by Tomari port marks the point where the commander of the American "black ships" landed on June 6, 1853.

Shuri, the 16th-century former capital, lies 4 miles (6 km) east of central Naha. It contains various shrines, temples, ceremonial gates, and fortifications – a reminder of the sophistication of the Ryukyu kingdom. *Ryusen* and *bingata* (p290) fabrics are made, exhibited, and sold at the **Shuri Ryusen**, where the materials are dyed. With over 4,000 exhibits, the **Okinawa Prefectural Museum & Art Museum** highlights the area's art and culture, and has the original bells from Shuri Castle and Engaku-ji Temple.

Shuri Castle was the headquarters of the Japanese high command during the war, resulting in its total destruction. Shurei-mon, the castle's ceremonial entrance gate, was rebuilt in 1958.

Naha City's imposing Shurei-mon (inset) leading to Shuri Castle, with its richly decorated Seiden (main hall) ↓

Photographs of victims of the Battle of Okinawa at the Himeyuri Peace Museum

Natural disasters and war have led to the constant rebuilding of the 16th-century Benzaiten-do temple, north of the castle park.

Tsuboya Pottery Museum

 1-9-32 Tsuboya
(098) 862-3761 ⏰10am-6pm Tue-Sun

Shuri Ryusen

1-54 Shuri Yamagawacho
⏰9am-6pm daily shuri-ryusen.com

Okinawa Prefectural Museum & Art Museum

3-1-1 Omoromachi
⏰9am-6pm Tue-Sun (to 8pm Fri & Sat) okimu.jp/en

---

② The Former Japanese Navy Underground HQ

旧日本海軍司令部壕

F7 3 miles (5 km) S of Naha From Naha bus terminal to Tomigusuku Koen-mae or Uebaru danchi-mae ⏰8:30am-5pm daily (to 5:30pm Jul-Sep) kaigungou.ocvb.or.jp

Parts of the subterranean rooms and tunnels where the Japanese Navy conducted the closing stages of World War II are open to the public. The Imperial Navy Admiral was one of over 4,000 men who committed suicide here on June 13, 1945. Many of the officers killed themselves by *seppuku* (ritual disembowelment); others used hand grenades – scorch marks can still be seen on tunnel walls.

---

③ Okinawa Battle Sites

沖縄戦跡国定公園

F7 9 miles (15 km) S of Naha Bus tour from Naha recommended

At the southern end of the island are various battle sites and memorials to victims and those who committed suicide rather than surrender to advancing American forces.

Cape Kyan saw some of the fiercest exchanges. Many locals jumped to their deaths here. To the northeast, the Himeyuri no To Monument and the Himeyuri Peace Museum are memorials to a group of young women who died while working as volunteer nurses during the Battle of Okinawa. A total of 136 people died inside a cave while trying to escape from the carnage. Most perished from the effects of a gas bomb fired into the cavern, others committed suicide. Konpaku no To, 1 mile (2 km) south, is a cliffside memorial where 35,000 unknown soldiers and civilians were interred.

One of the heaviest losses of life was on Mabuni Hill. Now a memorial park, it is dotted with monuments dedicated to both military and civilian dead. Photos, memorabilia, and personal accounts of the battle can be seen at the nearby **Peace Memorial Museum**.

Peace Memorial Museum

614-1 Mabuni, Itoman
⏰9am-5pm daily Dec 29-Jan 3 peace-museum.pref.okinawa.jp/english

---

THE BATTLE OF OKINAWA

Few conflicts in modern history have been fought with such ferocity as the Battle of Okinawa. It began when five American divisions landed on the island on April 1, 1945. Although outnumbered, the Japanese fought hard, utilizing flame-throwers, grenades, bayonets, and kamikaze pilots (Japanese suicide bombers). By the end of the 82-day battle, 13,000 American soldiers and 250,000 Japanese soldiers and civilians had died.

↑ A walkway among the rock formations at the vast Gyukusendo Cave

 4

Gyokusendo Cave
玉泉洞

F7 **19 miles (30 km) SE of Naha**

Featuring over 460,000 stalactites, this cave system is negotiated with the help of rather slippery pathways and wooden walkways. The stalactites at Gyokusendo Cave have been likened to giant bamboo, wine glasses, organ pipes, and even statues by Rodin.

The cave can be viewed by visiting **Okinawa World**, a park and museum with a large snake collection, including Okinawa's most poisonous reptile, the *habu*.

Okinawa World

 1336 Tamagusuku Maekawa, Nanjo **9am–5:30pm daily** **gyokusendo.co.jp/okinawaworld**

HIDDEN GEM
Beach Time

Located east of Gyokusendo, Mibaru beach is a pristine 1-mile (2-km) stretch of sand. With shallow water, it's ideal for paddling. There's a reef off-shore so consider taking a trip on a glass-bottom boat to see it.

 5

Nakagusuku Castle Ruin
中城城跡

F7 **9 miles (13 km) NE of Naha City, 10-min walk from Nakamura House** **8:30am–5pm daily (May–Sep: to 6pm)** **nakagusuku-jo.jp/en**

Built by Lord Gosamaru in the mid-1400s, Nakagusuku was one of the first stone castles in Japan. The views along the east coast of central Okinawa are excellent. The walls are the only structures to survive the ravages of time and the 1458 Amawari Rebellion. Passages link three main compounds, each enclosed by high, fortified walls.

 6

Nakamura House
中村家

F7 **9 miles (13 km) NE of Naha City** **9am–5:30pm Wed–Mon** **nakamurahouse.jp**

A visit to this 18th-century farmhouse, now a museum with exhibits about Okinawan

→ A perfect reconstruction of a Japanese home at Traditional Okinawan Village

daily life, offers rare insights into a more refined style of rural architecture. It consists of five buildings around a courtyard. A stone enclosure, with a barrier to repel evil spirits – a typical Okinawan feature – faces the entrance.

7

Ie Island
伊江島

F6 **From Motobu port**

Ie is a picturesque little island ideal for bicycling. Bike rentals are plentiful, and the whole island can be explored in under 8 hours. The north

> The stalactites at Gyokusendo Caves have been likened to giant bamboo, wine glasses, organ pipes, and even statues by Rodin.

terminates in steep cliffs, while the interior is an expanse of sugarcane, tobacco, and pineapple fields. Gusukuyama, Ie's only hill, provides a first-rate view.

During World War II, Niya-Thiya, a cave in the southwest, was used as a shelter by locals. The Ernie Pyle Monument is dedicated to the US war correspondent who died when his jeep was blown up on the island only a few weeks before the end of the conflict.

8

Ocean Expo Park
海洋博記念公園

A F6 **A** 12 miles (20 km) NW of Nago **B** Kinenkoen-mae **C** 8am–7pm (to 8:30pm in summer); some attractions close earlier **W** oki-park.jp/kaiyohaku

The Okinawa International Ocean Exposition was held here in 1975; since then, several new attractions have been added to this coastal park. The Okinawa Churaumi Aquarium houses more than 700 species of fish in three sections (tropical, ocean, and deep sea) and the Oceanic Culture Museum relates the development of the Okinawan people to the maritime culture of Oceania through fishing and navigation exhibits.

The Traditional Okinawan Village is a faithful reconstruction of 17th- and 18th-century dwellings, featuring sacred springs and forest, places of worship, storehouses, and an arboretum with native plants. On the coast close by is the Tropical Dream Center, a complex of high-tech greenhouses and botanical gardens.

About 19 miles (30 km) to the south of the park, you'll find breathtaking beaches along the coast of Nago Bay. Between Cape Busena and Inbu Beach, **Busena Marine Park** is one of the world's best underwater observatories.

Busena Marine Park
A 1744-1 Kise, Nago **C** 9am–6pm daily (to 5:30pm Nov–Mar) **W** busena-marinepark.com

DRINK

Bar Spade
This Naha City dive bar attracts a mixed crowd of all ages with its 600-yen drinks, free popcorn, and open pool table.

A F7 **A** Yonaha Building 2F, 3-23-10 Kumoji, Naha City **W** barspade.com

Ukishima Brewing
Serving its own locally made craft brews, ranging from IPAs to wheat beers, this Naha City bar is a must for any beer fan.

A F7 **A** 3-3-1 Makishi, Naha City **W** ukishima brewing.com/tap-room.html

The Smuggler's Irish Pub
This is a great place to enjoy a pint of Guinness and watch the football in Naha City. The staff are attentive and the crowd friendly.

A F7 **A** 1-9-1 Matsuo, Naha City **C** (098) 862-0124

Tatami-ishi, a rock mosaic resembling a tortoise shell, on Ou Island off Kume

9

Kume Island
久米島

🗺 D2 🚗 56 miles (90 km) W of Okinawa Island ✈ From Naha ⛴ From Naha Tomari port ℹ (098) 985-5288

Volcanic Kume is famous for its sugarcane and pineapple plantations, and Kumejima-*tsumugi*, an exquisite silk pongee. Buses serve many of the island's sights.

The village of Nakadomari, in the southwest, boasts one of the oldest houses in Okinawa, Uezu-ke, which was built in the 1700s in the Okinawan samurai style. An extraordinary tree, the Goe-da Pine, whose five separate trunks span upwards, is just a short walk from the house. Rice-planting rituals and prayers for rain are still conducted at Chinbei-donchi, the island's foremost shrine, north of Nakadomari. Nearby,

the sacred Yajiya-gama Caves were used for burials 2,000 years ago.

The 650-ft- (200-m-) high Hiyajo Banta cliff to the north affords good views toward the Aguni and Tonaki islands and the barrier reef below.

Nakazato village, in the east of the island, is one of its most traditional settlements, with several well-preserved buildings. You can see women weaving and dyeing Kumejima-*tsumugi* here. Nearby Eef Beach is Kume's largest resort.

Tiny Ou Island is well worth the 20-minute walk across a bridge from Nakazato's Tomari port. In the southwest is a mosaic of over 1,000 pentagonal stones, called the Tatami-ishi, which resemble flattened tortoise shells.

OKINAWAN ARTS AND CRAFT

Okinawan artists and craftsmen are honored as masters or, in a few rare cases, Living National Treasures. The island's textiles are among the finest in Japan, especially the linen-dyed *bingata* and *ryusen* fabrics, *bashofu*, and *kasuri*, a high-quality cloth made from the finest natural fibers. Equally, the glossy, black Okinawan lacquerware has been made for over 500 years, using the wood of the indigenous *deigo* tree as a base. New crafts have appeared since the war, most notably glassware, its vibrant colors reflecting Okinawa's sparkling coral seas.

→ Delicately decorated lacquered box

10

Kijoka Village
喜如嘉村

🗺 G6 🚗 16 miles (25 km) NE of Nago 🚌 67 from Nago to Daiichi Kijoka

The main reason for a visit to Kijoka Village, in Ogimi, is to watch the making of *bashofu*,

indication of the original size of Nakijin Castle. It was built in the 14th century by King Hokuzan, founder of the North Mountain Kingdom, an esoteric and short-lived domain.

The entrance, with its flat stone ceiling, is still intact. Because the castle faced the sacred island of Iheya, three wooden shrines were built here to allow the local priestesses to conduct rituals, but none has survived. There are stunning views across the East China Sea toward several other offshore islands, including the Amami and Yoron groups.

 12

Cape Hedo
辺戸岬

🅐G6 🅐31 miles (50 km) NE of Nago 🚌67 from Nago to Hentona

The remote, northernmost point of Okinawa Island is a wild and breathtaking area of outstanding natural beauty and, mercifully, few tour buses. A grassy plateau runs to the edge of a steep, 330-ft- (100-m-) high cliff, beyond which are coral reefs. The views of distant Yoron, Iheya, and Izena islands are magnificent. The road to Hedo Point

a rare lightweight textile made of plantain fiber, which is used to make Okinawan kimonos. The stages involved in producing this increasingly scarce linen can be seen at the **Bashofu Hall**, a well-known workshop.

Bashofu Hall

🅐454 Kijoka ⏰10am–5:30pm Mon–Sat (to 5pm Nov–Mar) 🚫Obon, Dec 29–Jan 3 🔗bashofu.jp

---

 11

Nakijin Castle Ruin
今帰仁城跡

🅐G6 🅐11 miles (18 km) NW of Nago 🚌65 or 66 from Nago or express from Naha Airport to Nakijin-jo Ato Iriguchi ⏰8am–6pm daily (to 7pm May–Aug) 🔗nakijinjoseki-osi.jp

The foundations, gate, and 4,900-ft (1,500-m) stretch of remaining wall give some

→

The monumental stone remains of the 14th-century Nakijin Castle, near Nago

passes through a number of traditional villages, such as Ogimi, renowned for producing a unique pale yellow *bashofu* cloth. A short distance south of Hedo Point, the site of Uzahama-iseki features the remains of a prehistoric settlement.

13 Miyako Islands
宮古諸島

🅐D2 🏠200 miles (330 km) SW of Okinawa Island 🛫From Tokyo, Osaka, Naha, and Ishigaki Island 🛈At airport; en.miyako-guide.net

Set amid coral reefs in an emerald sea, Miyako consists of eight perfectly flat islands. Unique customs and a distinct dialect set the inhabitants of Miyako apart from Okinawan mainlanders. Spared the devastation of World War II, traditional houses are one-story buildings with red-tiled roofs and surrounding coral walls that serve as shelters against typhoons.

Hirara town, a former city now merged with other towns in the area to make up the city Miyakojima, is Miyako Island's main area. North of the port is Harimizu Utaki Shrine, dedicated to the two gods who are believed to have created the island. The mausoleum of the 15th-century chieftain Nakasone Toimiya has graves and tombs that combine local styles with the far more elaborate Okinawan style.

The **Miyakojima City**

Did You Know?

Anyone taller than 4 ft 7 in (140 cm) had to pay taxes, according to the Nintozeiseki stone.

Botanical Garden, northeast of Hirara, contains over 40,000 tree and almost 2,000 plant species from around the world.

In the backstreets of Hirara, women dry strips of Miyako-*jofu* indigo cloth. Just north of Hirara is the Nintozeiseki, a 55-in (1.4-m) stone, which was used during the suzerainty of the Satsuma domain in the 17th century.

At the tip of Higashi Henna cape on the east coast you can look out over the Pacific Ocean to the left and the East China Sea to the right. On the southwest coast, facing Kurima Island, Yonaha Maehama Beach, a 2-mile (4-km) stretch of pristine white sand, offers swimming, fishing, and diving.

Mostly set aside for sugarcane plantations, Kurima is of interest to ornithologists as sea hawks rest here for a few days in October on their way to the Philippines. The main sight on Ikema, off

the far north of Miyako, is the Yaebishi (or Yabiji) reef, which emerges in all its splendor during low spring tides. Both Kurima and Ikema can be reached via a road bridge.

Off the west coast, and accessible by boat from Miyako Island, is Irabu, linked by six bridges to neighboring Shimoji. On Shimoji, two deep green lakes called Tori-ike are connected to the sea by an underground river and tunnel.

Miyakojima City Botanical Garden

🏠1166-286 Higashinaka-sonezoe, Hirara 📞(0980) 73-2690 ⏰10am–6pm daily

14 Yaeyama Islands
八重山諸島

🅐D2 🏠270 miles (430 km) SW of Okinawa Island 🌐visit okinawa.jp/destinations/yaeyama-region

The Yaeyamas are Japan's most southerly islands. Some of the finest scuba diving in Asia is found here.

Ishigaki Island's airport and harbor serve the outlying islands in the group. Glimpses of the unique Yaeyama culture can be seen at the **Yaeyama Museum**, near the harbor,

↑ The lighthouse at Higashi Henna, where the Pacific and the East China Sea meet

↑ Glass-bottomed boats at Kabira Bay and scuba diving *(inset)* in the waters off Ishigaki, one of the Yaeyama Islands

which contains Yaeyama-*jofu* textiles, and Polynesian-style canoes. Not far away is **Miyara Dunchi**, a 19th-century noble-man's home. Shiraho Reef, off the southeastern tip of the island, is the world's largest expanse of blue coral. Kabira Bay, on the north shore, is full of small islets and supports a cultured black pearl industry.

Meaning "prosperous bamboo," **Taketomi Island** is a quiet, unspoiled island. Its neatness stems from an old custom by which it was, and still is, the responsibility of all householders to sweep the street in front of their own property. The island can easily be explored on foot or by bike.

To the west, Kondoi is the island's finest beach; Kaiji Beach has star-shaped sand – the fossilized skeletons of tiny sea animals. The aquamarine waters here support bountiful tropical sea life, and brilliantly colored butterflies swarm around the beach.

As much as 90 per cent of **Iriomote Island** is forest and jungle. Visitors can take cruises along its two main rivers, the Nakama and Urauchi, where black oyster beds, mangroves, and tropical trees can be seen. The island is the last habitat of the Iriomote wild cat.

Yonaguni offers swordfish and bonito fishing, and Japan's strongest spirit – *hanazake*.

Ishigaki Island

☒ From Tokyo, Osaka, Nagoya, Naha, and Miyako *i* (0980) 87-0971

Yaeyama Museum

⊗ ⌂ 4-1 Tonoshiro, Ishigaki 🕻 (0980) 82-4712 ⊙ 9am-5pm Tue-Sun

Miyara Dunchi

⊗ ⌂ 178 Okawa, Ishigaki 🕻 (0980) 82-2767 ⊙ 9am-5pm Wed-Mon

Taketomi Island

⛴ From Ishigaki *i* (0980) 85-2488

Iriomote Island

⛴ From Ishigaki *i* (0980) 84-7320

Yonaguni Island

⛴ From Ishigaki ✈ From Naha and Ishigaki *i* (0980) 87-2402

EAT

Goya

This Miyakojima eatery's namesake is a green bitter gourd. Here, *goya* is deep fried, pickled, and even made into ice cream.

⌂ D2 ⌂ 570-2 Hirara Nishizato, Miyakojima 🕻 (0980) 74-2358

¥¥¥

NORTHERN HONSHU

The backcountry reputation of Northern Honshu belies its rich history. Long ago, it was home to indigenous people, who may have been from the Ainu ethnic group. In the 12th century, Hiraizumi was the capital of the Northern Fujiwara clan, rivaling Kyoto in splendor, and during feudal times, Morioka, Tsuruoka, Hirosaki, and Aizu Wakamatsu were thriving castle towns. Foremost, though, was Sendai, ruled by the north's most powerful clan. Despite these significant settlements, when haiku poet Matsuo Basho set out in 1689 on his five-month trek to northern Japan, he likened it to going to the back of beyond. Three centuries later, *shinkansen* lines and expressways provide easy access, and the north is as much a part of the information age as the rest of Japan.

On March 11, 2011, a 9-magnitude earthquake and subsequent tsunami hit this northern part of the country. More than 18,000 people lost their lives and much of the area was devastated, with some coastal areas completely destroyed. The Fukushima Daiichi nuclear plant was also badly damaged by the tsunami, and although much of Northern Honshu has been rebuilt the long-term effects of the nuclear disaster are still unclear.

Oma

Sai

SHIMOKITA PENINSULA ⑲

Mutsu

Wakinosawa

338

279

Rokkasho

Hiranai

Noheji

⑳ **AOMORI**

AOMORI

Misawa

Towada-Hachimantai NP (Towada Section)

E4A

Hachinohe

Lake Towada

E45

Taneichi

103

Kazuno

Ninohe

Kuji

E4A

Kuzumaki

Fudai

⑰ **TOWADA-HACHIMANTAI NATIONAL PARK**

Iwaizumi

E4

46

⑯ **MORIOKA**

Miyako

4

106

Todoga-saki

IWATE

Yamada

Hanamaki

45

Ou-sanmyaku

⑮ **TONO**

Kamaishi

E46

Kitakami

Mizusawa

Ofunato

⑧ **HIRAIZUMI**

Rikuzen-Takata

Ichinoseki

Kesennuma

45

Shizugawa

Osaki

MIYAGI

Ishinomaki

E4

⑦ **MATSUSHIMA**

⑫ **SENDAI**

Natori

✈ **Sendai Airport**

Iwanuma

E6

Soma

Haramachi

6

Namie

Otakine-yama 3,914 ft (1,193 m)

Tomioka

E6

Iwaki

Kitaibaraki

Pacific Ocean

0 kilometers   50

0 miles   50

N

NORTHERN HONSHU

Must See

① Nikko

Experience More

② Nikko National Park
③ Mashiko
④ Kitakata
⑤ Bandai-Asahi National Park
⑥ Aizu Wakamatsu
⑦ Matsushima
⑧ Hiraizumi
⑨ Tsuruoka
⑩ Sado Island
⑪ Dewa Sanzan
⑫ Sendai
⑬ Kakunodate
⑭ Yamadera
⑮ Tono
⑯ Morioka
⑰ Towada-Hachimantai National Park
⑱ Oga Peninsula
⑲ Shimokita Peninsula
⑳ Aomori
㉑ Hirosaki

↑ Looking over Lake Chuzenji from the Futara-san Shrine

❶

NIKKO

日光

🗺 F4 ⚑ Tochigi Prefecture 🚉 Nikko 🚌 Nikko, Tobu Nikko ℹ At Tobu Nikko Stn; www.visitnikko.jp

Written with characters that mean "sunlight," the mystical town of Nikko has become a Japanese byword for splendor. In 766, the formidable Buddhist priest Shodo Shonin founded Rinno-ji Temple here. This was the first of many and Nikko became a renowned Buddhist-Shinto religious center.

①
Takino-o Shrine

⚑ 2310-1 Sannai 📞 (0288) 54-0535 🚌 Taiyuin Futarasan-jinja-mae 🕐 24 hours daily

Possibly dedicated to a female deity, this shrine draws women and those looking for love. Toss a stone through the top of the torii and into the grounds and your wish could come true.

②
Shinkyo Bridge

🚌 Shinkyo

This red-lacquered wooden bridge, just to the left of the road bridge, arches over the Daiya River where, legend has it, Shodo Shonin crossed the water on the backs of two huge serpents. The original bridge, which was built in 1636 for the exclusive use of the shogun and imperial messengers, was destroyed by a flood. The current bridge dates from 1904.

③
Futara-san Shrine

⚑ 2307 Sannai 🚌 Taiyuin Futarasanjinja-mae 🕐 8am-5pm daily (Nov-Mar: to 4pm) 🌐 futarasan.jp

Founded by Shodo Shonin in 782, this shrine is dedicated to the gods of the mountains: Nantai (male), Nyotai (female), and Taro, their child. It is actually the main shrine of three; the other two are at Lake Chuzenji and on Mount Nantai. The bronze torii here has been designated an Important Cultural Property. But the shrine's most interesting feature for visitors is a tall bronze lantern, nicknamed the "ghost lantern," which is said to take the shape of a monster at night. The gashes in the lamp are from the sword of a terrified samurai who attacked it when the flame started to flicker in a peculiar way. A vermilion fence now protects the lantern from attack.

④
Rinno-ji Temple

⚑ 2300 Sannai 🕐 8am-5pm daily

The first temple founded at Nikko, by Shodo Shonin in 766, Rinno-ji was originally called Shihonryu-ji. When it became a Tendai-sect temple in the 17th century it was renamed. Its Sanbutsu-do (Three Buddha Hall) is the largest hall at Nikko. The three gilt images, of Amida Buddha,

Senju (thousand-armed) Kannon, and Bato (horse-headed) Kannon, enshrined in the hall correspond to the three mountain deities enshrined at Futara-san Shrine. Beyond the hall, the nine-ringed bronze pillar, Sorinto, contains 1,000 volumes of sutras (Buddhist scriptures) and is a symbol of world peace.

The beautiful Treasure Hall (Homotsuden) houses a large and fascinating array of temple treasures, mainly dating from the Edo period. Behind it is the Shoyoen, a lovely Edo-style 19th-century stroll garden that has been carefully landscaped so that it is at its best for every season. The enchanting path through the garden meanders around a large pond, over stone bridges, and past mossy stone lanterns.

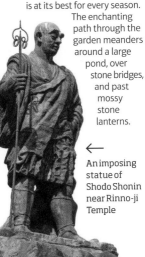

← An imposing statue of Shodo Shonin near Rinno-ji Temple

⑤ Kanman-ga-Fuchi Abyss

 Nishisando

Lava flows from an old eruption of Mount Nantai combine with the limpid waters of the Daiya River to make these unusual scenic pools. It is not hard to see why the abyss is a spot sacred to Buddhism. About 70 stone statues of Jizo, the bodhisattva of children, line the path by the river. They are known as phantom statues because their numbers appear to change every time you look.

⑥ Nikko Botanical Gardens

📍1842 Hanaishicho
 Nikko Shokubutsuen
🕒9am–4:30pm Tue–Sun
🔒Dec 1–Apr 14 🌐bg.s.u-tokyo.ac.jp/nikko/eng

Some 2,200 varieties of plants and flowers from Japan and around the world are at these gardens, a branch of the Koishikawa Botanical Gardens of the University of Tokyo. Flora from Nikko National Park are showcased. April to July, when skunk cabbages and irises bloom, is a lovely time to visit.

EAT

Nikko Yuba Zen

This restaurant, which seats just ten people, offers a modern twist on Nikko's famous *yuba* (tofu skins).

📍1007 Kamihatsuishimachi 🔒Tue nikkoyuba makizen.gorp.jp

¥¥¥

Hippari Dako

Funky *izakaya* serving *yakitori* (succulent meat skewers), fried noodles and other Japanese soul food.

📍1011 Kamihatsuishimachi, Nikko, Tochigi 📞0288-53-2933

¥¥¥

Gyoshintei

Surrounded by a forest, this charming building serves refined *shojin-ryori* (vegetarian) meals.

📍2339-1 Sannai, Nikko, Tochigi meiji-yakata.com/en/gyoshin

¥¥¥

(8) ⚐

TOSHO-GU SHRINE

東照宮

⚐ 2301 Sannai 🚉 Omotesando 🕐 8am–5pm daily
(to 4pm Nov–Mar) 🌐 toshogu.jp/english

Iemitsu Tokugawa set out to dazzle with this mausoleum-shrine for his grandfather Ieyasu Tokugawa. For two years, some 15,000 artisans from all over Japan worked, building, carving, gilding, painting, and lacquering, to create this flowery, gorgeous Momoyama-style complex.

Although designated a Shinto shrine in the Meiji period, Tosho-gu retains many of its original Buddhist elements, including the sutra library, which chronicles the temple's history, the Niomon Gate, and the unusual five-story pagoda with a suspended pillar. The famed *sugi-namiki* (Japanese cedar avenue) leading to the shrine was planted by a 17th-century lord, in lieu of a more opulent offering. The shrine is undergoing major renovation work, which is scheduled to be completed in 2024, though most of it is still open to visitors. Don't miss the Tokugawa armor in the Treasure Hall or the painted doors in the Museum of Art.

→

The embellished structures
making up the Tosho-gu
Shrine complex

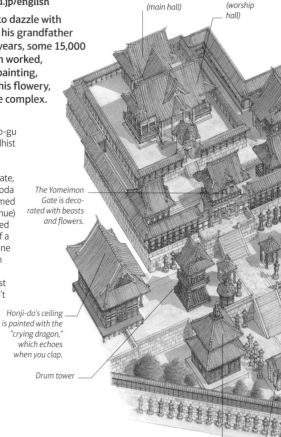

Honden (main hall)

Haiden (worship hall)

The Yomeimon Gate is decorated with beasts and flowers.

Honji-do's ceiling is painted with the "crying dragon," which echoes when you clap.

Drum tower

The Rinzo contains a sutra library of Buddhist scriptures set within a revolving structure.

The sacred fountain is covered with an ornate Chinese-style roof. The granite basin (1618) is used for ritual purification.

IEYASU TOKUGAWA

Ieyasu (1543–1616) was a wily strategist and master politician who founded the dynasty that would rule Japan for over 250 years. Born the son of a minor lord, he spent his life accumulating power before becoming shogun in 1603, when he was 60. He built his capital in the swampy village of Edo (now Tokyo), and his rule saw the start of the flowering of Edo culture. After his death, he was enshrined and given his posthumous name: Tosho-Daigongen, "the great incarnation illuminating the East."

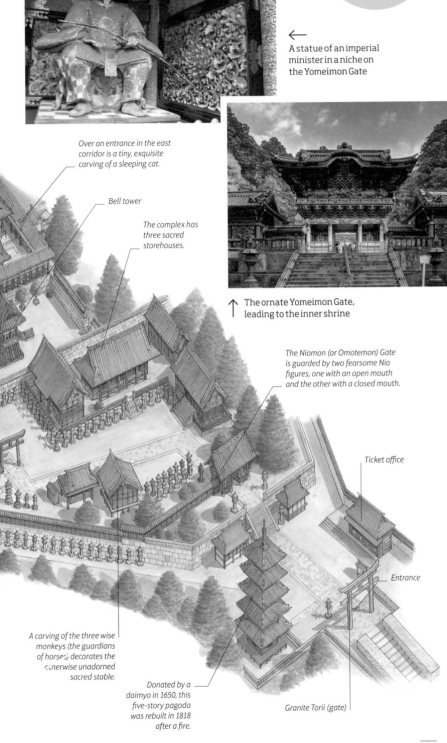

← A statue of an imperial minister in a niche on the Yomeimon Gate

Over an entrance in the east corridor is a tiny, exquisite carving of a sleeping cat.

Bell tower

The complex has three sacred storehouses.

↑ The ornate Yomeimon Gate, leading to the inner shrine

The Niomon (or Omotemon) Gate is guarded by two fearsome Nio figures, one with an open mouth and the other with a closed mouth.

Ticket office

Entrance

A carving of the three wise monkeys (the guardians of horses) decorates the otherwise unadorned sacred stable.

Donated by a daimyo in 1650, this five-story pagoda was rebuilt in 1818 after a fire.

Granite Torii (gate)

TAIYUIN-BYO SHRINE

大猷院廟

📍2300 Sannai 🚃Taiyuin Futarasanjinja-mae 📞(0288) 53-1567
🕐8am–5pm daily (to 4pm Nov–Mar)

If Tosho-gu is splendid, Taiyuin-byo is sublime. It was built modestly so that it would not eclipse Tosho-gu, a sign of deep respect to Ieyasu Tokugawa. Despite this restraint, it is still an ornate tomb reflecting the power of the imperial family.

Finished in 1653, Taiyuin-byo is the mausoleum of Iemitsu Tokugawa (1604–51), the powerful third shogun and grandson of Ieyasu Tokugawa, who closed Japan to foreign commerce and isolated it from the world for over 200 years. Tayuin is his posthumous Buddhist name. As with Tosho-gu, Taiyuin-byo has retained many of its Buddhist elements, despite being reconsecrated as a Shinto shrine in the Meiji period. Set in a grove of Japanese cedars, it has a number of ornate gates ascending to the Haiden (worship hall) and Honden (main hall). You can admire the grand interior of the Haiden, which has coffered ceilings and carvings, but the Honden is usually closed to the public. The shogun's ashes are entombed beyond the sixth and final gate.

The Honden holds a gilded Buddhist altar with a wooden statue of Iemitsu Tokugawa.

Decorated with carvings of dragons, the Haiden also has some famous 17th-century lion paintings.

Did You Know?

To stop him seizing power, Iemitsu forced his brother Tadanaga to commit seppuku.

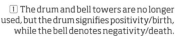

Entrance

① The drum and bell towers are no longer used, but the drum signifies positivity/birth, while the bell denotes negativity/death.

② As well as being inlaid with peonies, the Yashamon Gate is also ornamented with four statues of Yasha, a fierce guardian spirit.

③ Marking the main entrance to the shrine, a powerful red-faced Nio warrior god stands guard on either side of the Niomon Gate, frightening away evil spirits.

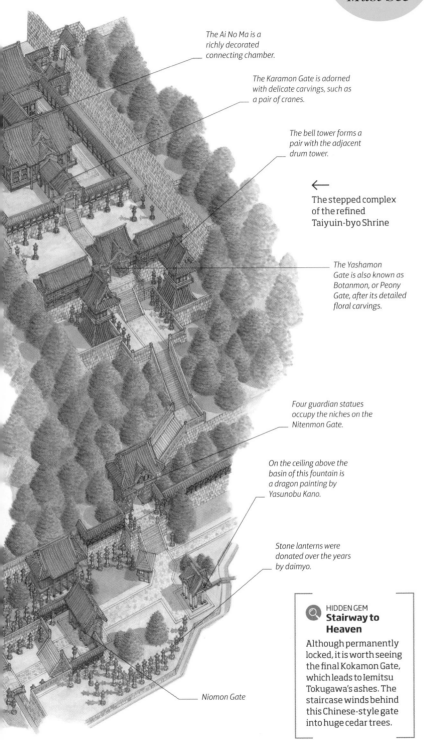

The Ai No Ma is a richly decorated connecting chamber.

The Karamon Gate is adorned with delicate carvings, such as a pair of cranes.

The bell tower forms a pair with the adjacent drum tower.

← The stepped complex of the refined Taiyuin-byo Shrine

The Yashamon Gate is also known as Botanmon, or Peony Gate, after its detailed floral carvings.

Four guardian statues occupy the niches on the Nitenmon Gate.

On the ceiling above the basin of this fountain is a dragon painting by Yasunobu Kano.

Stone lanterns were donated over the years by daimyo.

Niomon Gate

HIDDEN GEM
Stairway to Heaven

Although permanently locked, it is worth seeing the final Kokamon Gate, which leads to Iemitsu Tokugawa's ashes. The staircase winds behind this Chinese-style gate into huge cedar trees.

EXPERIENCE MORE

2

Nikko National Park
日光国立公園

F4 Tochigi, Fukushima, and Gunma Prefectures From Nikko Stn 1404-1 Kinugawaonsen Ohara, Nikko; www.visitnikko.jp

The magnificent national park that includes Tosho-gu and its environs is largely a mountainous volcanic plateau, studded with lakes, waterfalls, and hot springs. For a taste of Oku-Nikko, the mountainous interior, take the bus west to Lake Chuzenji. The hairpin curves of Irohazaka, along the old ascent to the sacred Mount Nantai, start at Umagaeshi (horse return), where pilgrims had to give up their horses and walk. At the east end of the lake, the Kegon Falls cascade 315 ft (96 m) to the Daiya River below. An elevator through the cliff runs to an observation deck at the base of the falls.

3

Mashiko
益子

F4 Tochigi Prefecture Mashiko From Tobu-Utsunomiya Stn Next to Mashiko Stn; www.mashiko-kankou.org

Home to the famous potter Shoji Hamada (1894–1978), a founder of the *mingei* (folk art) movement, Mashiko is full of pottery workshops. The **Mashiko Sankokan Museum** contains Hamada's studio, and his eclectic collection of ceramics. The vats of the eighth-generation **Higeta Dyeworks** are sunk in the floor of a thatched workshop.

Mashiko Sankokan Museum

3388 Mashiko
(0285) 72-5300
9:30am-5pm Tue-Sun

Higeta Dyeworks

1 Jonaizaka (0285) 72-3162 8:30am-5pm Tue-Sun

 PICTURE PERFECT
Flaming Bridge

Built in 1636, Shinkyo Bridge in the Nikko National Park is among the finest in Japan. Its gorgeous burnt-red span makes a great focal point for a snap, set as it is against the dramatic mountain scenery and lush foliage.

4

Kitakata
喜多方

F3 Fukushima Prefecture Kitakata At JR station; www.kitakata-kanko.jp

Mud-walled *kura* (storehouses) were long used to keep sake, miso, rice, and other provisions from fire, theft, and vermin. Kitakata has more than 2,600, including a *kura*-style temple. South of the **Kai Honke**, a handsome sake merchant's

← The Kegon Falls, surrounded by beautiful fall foliage, in the Nikko National Park

 Praying at the grave site of the Byakkotai samurai on Iimoriyama, near Aizu Wakamatsu

house, is a *kura*-lined lane. The **Yamatogawa Sake-Brewing Museum** runs tasting tours. Kitakata is also known for its *oki-agari* dolls, which roll upright when knocked over.

Kai Honke
Ⓐ Ⓑ ⓐ1-4611 Kitakata
Ⓒ(0241) 22-0001 Ⓓ10am–
5pm daily ⒺDec–Mar

Yamatogawa Sake-Brewing Museum
ⓐ4761 Teramachi Ⓓ9am–
4:30pm daily (book ahead)
Ⓦyauemon.co.jp

 5

Bandai-Asahi National Park
磐梯朝日国立公園

ⒶF3 ⒶYamagata, Niigata, and Fukushima Prefectures ⒶTo Fukushima, Tsuruoka, or Inawashiro, then bus ⒶAt Yamagata and Aizu-Wakamatsu Stns

On July 15, 1888, Mount Bandai erupted, killing 477 people. Dammed streams formed hundreds of lakes and marshes, creating the lush natural beauty of the Bandai-Asahi National Park. Crisscrossed by five scenic toll roads, including the Bandai-Azuma Skyline (open April 22 to November 5), the park is studded with hot springs and camping grounds. The best way to explore is by car or bus.

Goshikinuma (five-colored marshes) is a 2-mile (4-km) trail starting at the Goshikinuma or Bandai-kogen bus stops.

6

Aizu Wakamatsu
会津若松

ⒶF3 ⒶFukushima Prefecture ⒶAizu-Wakamatsu ⒶAt Tsuruga-jo Castle; www.samurai-city.jp/en

Once home to the north's second most powerful clan, Aizu Wakamatsu takes pride in its samurai past. With ties to the Tokugawas, the Matsudaira clan bitterly resisted the 19th-century movement to reinstate the emperor. In the 1868 Boshin War, the Byakkotai (White Tigers), a band of teenage samurai fighting against imperial forces, mistakenly thought the castle had fallen and committed mass suicide on Iimoriyama, the hill (east of the station) where they are now buried.

Aizu Wakamatsu's top sights are fairly spread out so buy an all-day bus pass at the bus station office. **Tsuruga Castle**, the heart of the city for over 600 years, was last rebuilt in 1965 as a museum. To the east is the **Samurai Residence** (Buke-yashiki), a good reproduction of a 38-room samurai manor. Nearby, the **Oyakuen** (medicinal herb garden) of a 17th-century villa contains over 200 herbs.

For shopping, head to Nanukamachi-dori, which is lined with old shops.

Tsuruga Castle
Ⓐ Ⓑ ⓐ1-1 Otemachi
ⓦTsurugajo Iriguchi Ⓒ(0242) 27-4005 Ⓓ8:30am–5pm daily

Samurai Residence
Ⓐ ⓐ1 Higashiyamamachi Ishiyama ⓦAizu Bukeyashiki-mae Ⓒ(0242) 28-2514 ⒹApr–Nov: 8:30am–5pm daily; Dec–Mar: 9am–4:30pm daily

Oyakuen
Ⓐ ⓐ8-1 Hanaharumachi
ⓦOyakuen-mae Ⓒ(0242) 27-2472 Ⓓ8:30am–5pm daily

↑ Buying fresh oysters at the Shiogama Wholesale Fish Market, in Matsushima

7 Matsushima
松島

 G3 **Miyagi Prefecture** **Matsushima-Kaigan** **By Matsushima sight-seeing boat pier; www.matsushima-kanko.com**

Take a hint from Matsuo Basho's 1689 visit to the bay of Matsushima and make Shiogama your starting point. The busy Shiogama Wholesale Fish Market, active from early morning until about 1pm, is known for its huge tuna auctions. Make time to lunch at one of Shiogama's superb sushi restaurants before taking the ferry to Matsushima.

Although the tsunami of March 2011 caused widespread destruction along Japan's northeast coast, Matsushima was spared thanks to the many islands in its bay. These pine-covered islets are the reason Matsushima became renowned as one of Japan's "three famous views." The best way to see the bay is on one of Matsushima's many sightseeing boats. Within walking distance of the port are other highlights, including Zuigan-ji Temple, which was built in the early 1600s for the warlord Masamune Date, and dozens of small restaurants serving local seafood, such as Matsushima's prized oysters.

8 Hiraizumi
平泉

 G2 **Iwate Prefecture** **Hiraizumi** **Next to JR station; (0191) 46-2110**

Nine hundred years ago, the Northern Fujiwara clan, under Fujiwara Kiyohira, made this small town into a cultural and economic capital, second only to Kyoto. Three generations later, Hiraizumi was in ruins. Yoshitsune, Japan's archetypal tragic hero, had sought refuge here from Yoritomo, his jealous brother and Japan's first shogun, but was betrayed by Yasuhira, the last Fujiwara leader, and killed. Yoritomo then turned against Yasuhira and had the clan wiped out.

At its peak, Hiraizumi had a population of 100,000. Wishing to create a Buddhist paradise on earth, Kiyohira enriched the 9th-century temples Chuson-ji and Motsu-ji. Chuson-ji is five minutes by bus from the station, followed by a long climb lined with towering Japanese cedars. Only two of its many original buildings remain: the small Golden Hall, splendid with gold leaf, lacquer, and mother-of-pearl, where the first three Fujiwara leaders are buried; and the Sutra Hall. In the Treasure Hall are precious artifacts from the Fujiwara coffins and the temple.

All that remains of the original Motsu-ji (a ten-minute walk from the station) are its foundations and beautiful Heian-period paradise garden, the best in Japan.

9
Tsuruoka
鶴岡

 F2 **Yamagata Prefecture** **Tsuruoka** **In front of JR station; (0235) 25-7678**

Tsuruoka was the Sakai clan's castle seat. Best of this

HIDDEN GEM
For Sake's Sake

Niigata, set across the water from Sado Island, is known as the home of sake. Founded in 1767, Imayotsukasa offers a free tour that illustrates the history of sake and its production process, and, of course, a tasting at the end *(www.imayotsukasa.co.jp/en)*.

friendly town's attractions is the **Chido Museum**, west of the former castle grounds. It includes a *kabuto-zukuri* (helmet-style) farmhouse, and marvelous folk objects such as lacquered sake caskets, bamboo fishing poles, and decorative straw *bandori* (backpacks). Southeast of the castle is the **Chidokan**, a school for young samurai.

Chido Museum

⊛ ⌂10-18 Kachushinmachi ℂ(0235) 22-1199 ⊙Mar–Nov: 9am–5pm daily; Dec–Feb: 9am–4:30pm Thu–Tue

Chidokan

⌂11-45 Babacho ℂ(0235) 23-4672 ⊙9am–4:30pm Thu–Tue

Sado Island

佐渡島

🅰E3 ⌂Niigata Prefecture 🚢Ferry or hydrofoil from Niigata (city) to Ryotsu 🛈2F Ryotsu port; www. visitsado.com/en

Though it receives more than a million visitors a year, Sado Island still feels remote. For centuries, this mellow island 37 miles (60 km) off Honshu's northwest coast was home to

Kodo, one of the most dynamic *taiko* drumming groups, is known for performances of drum, flute, song, and dance. Kodo means both "children of the drum" and "heartbeat." The throbbing heart of Kodo is the *o-daiko*, a convex wooden drum used in Japanese folk festivals. Kodo spends much of the year performing in Japan and world-wide, and hosts an annual three-day Earth Celebration, when international musicians come to Sado to perform.

political exiles, including the emperor Juntoku in 1221, the priest Nichiren in 1271, and Zeami, the Noh actor and playwright, in 1433. Of the 88 Noh theaters once here, about 35 are left. In 1601 the discovery of gold in Aikawa brought an influx of convicts who were forced to work in the mines. Buses connect the island's small towns, and tour buses stop at major sites. In the main port of Ryotsu in the east, outdoor Noh performances are held at the Honma No Stage. In Aikawa, on the west coast, the touristy **Sado Kinzan Gold Mine** has

mechanical dolls recreating the harsh mining conditions.

The **Kodo** drumming group is the island's most famous attraction. Based in Ogi, in the southwest, the group has put Sado firmly on the map.

Sado Kinzan Gold Mine

⊛ ⌂1305 Shimoaikawa 🚌To Aikawa Eigayosho ⊙Apr–Oct: 8am–5:30pm daily; Nov–Mar: 8:30am–5pm daily 🌐sado-kinzan.com

Kodo

⌂148-1 Kaneta Shinden 🌐kodo.or.jp

↑ The wild natural landscape of Sado Island, with jagged rocks lining the coast

↑ The five-story Buddhist pagoda on Mount Haguro, Dewa Sanzan

Dewa Sanzan

出羽三山

🅰F2 **🚩**Yamagata Prefecture **🚌**From S Mall bus terminal, near JR Tsuruoka Stn **ℹ️**In front of Tsuruoka Stn; data. yamagatakanko.com

Dewa is the old name for this region, and Sanzan are its three mountains – Haguro-san (Mount Black Wing), Gassan (Mount Moon), and Yudono-san (Mount Bath) – opened for religious purposes 1,400 years ago by Hachiko, an imperial prince turned wandering priest. The three are sacred to *yamabushi*, mountain ascetics of the Shugendo sect.

The route to the peak of **Mount Haguro** is a climb up the 2,446 stone steps of the Japanese cedar-lined path. Take the bus to Haguro Center to start the climb. At the second stage is a teahouse with a view of the Mogami River valley. A side path goes to the ruins of a temple where poet Matsuo Basho stayed. At the top is the Dewa Sanzan

Shrine, which has the largest thatched roof in Japan, Hachiko's tomb. After the 1868 Meiji Restoration, all Shugendo temples were turned into Shinto shrines. The only true Buddhist structure left is the five-story pagoda at the foot of the stone steps.

Mount Gassan, also topped by a shrine, offers alpine flowers and summer skiing. It's a 3-mile (5-km) trek to the top from the Hachigome bus stop. The shrine on **Mount Yudono**, a 2-mile (2.5-km) hike from the Yudonosan Hotel bus stop, has a sacred hot spring. Mummified priests, examples of *sokushin jobutsu* (living Buddhas), can be seen at the temples of Dainichi-bo and Churen-ji, on the way to Mount Yudono.

Mount Haguro
🕐Apr–Nov: 8:30am– 4:30pm daily; 9:30am– 4pm daily

Mount Gassan
🕐Jul 1–Oct

Mount Yudono
🕐Late Apr–early Nov

Sendai

仙台

🅰G3 **🚩**Miyagi Prefecture **🚄🚍**Sendai **ℹ️**At 2F JR Sendai Stn; www.sendai-travel.jp

Laid out in a grid pattern in the 1600s by the dynamic lord Masamune Date, Sendai is the north's largest city. Osaki Hachiman Shrine is a black lacquer architectural beauty in the northwest of the city. Overlooking the ruins of Aoba Castle from 1602 is a statue of the warrior Masamune, nicknamed the "one-eyed dragon." The ruins are set in a park that is a bus ride to the west of the station. Nearby, the ornately carved Date mausoleums at Zuihoden, rebuilt after the war, are replicas of Momoyama-period architecture.

On the western outskirts of the city, the quiet Akiu Onsen area is home to traditional *ryokan* inns and natural hot-spring baths, making it the perfect place to base yourself while exploring the surrounding area.

BASHO AND HAIKU

Poet Matsuo Basho (1644–94) perfected the form that came to be known as haiku. A classical haiku is 17 syllables (written 5-7-5), includes a seasonal word, and refers to an objective image in the present. Basho spent most of his life traveling and writing haiku. His travel journal *The Narrow Road to the Deep North* details his five-month pilgrimage in 1689, and has since inspired many people to make the journey for themselves.

BUDDHIST SECTS

In the course of 1,500 years or so, since the first priests from mainland Asia brought Buddhism to Japan in the 6th century, usurping the native Shinto, hundreds of separate Buddhist movements, sects, and subsects developed in the country.

Contrasting beliefs appealed to different groups of nobility, samurai, and commoners, who each adapted practices to their own ends. In the eyes of many visitors today, Zen, one-time favorite of the samurai, is the quintessential religion of Japan, but it is just one of several major movements originating in China, and is itself subdivided into various sects. Of the other movements that flowered in Japan after World War II, the Tendai and Shingon sects of esoteric Buddhism still have millions of devotees.

↑ A man relaxing in the garden of a Buddhist temple

BUDDHIST MOVEMENTS

Zen Buddhism
This school developed during the Kamakura period (1185–1333). There are three main sects: Soto, Rinzai, and Obaku. All place emphasis on *zazen* (sitting meditation) and self-help.

Shingon
Founded in Japan in the 9th century by the monk Kukai, this branch incorporates Hindu elements, such as hand gestures *(mudra)* and the chanting of mantras.

Tendai
Brought to Japan in the 9th century by the monk Saicho, Tendai places emphasis on selfless devotion. From its base at Mount Hiei, Tendai spawned the Jodo, Jodo Shin, and Nichiren sects.

Shugendo
This offshoot of Shingon combines Buddhism and Shinto beliefs, and promotes ascetic practices in mountain retreats.

↑ The contemplative bronze figure of the Great Buddha in Kamakura

↑ Blossoming cherry trees skirting the Hinokinaigawa River banks in Kakunodate

EAT

Pairon
This eatery in Marioka is the original home of *jajamen* noodles, served with fried *niku-miso* (miso with mince). After eating the noodles, break an egg into the broth and slurp that, too.

G2 **5-15 Uchimaru, Morioka** **pairon. iwate.jp/**

Azumaya
Morioka is home to the noodle-eating tradition of *wanko-soba*. At Azumaya patrons eat as many single mouthful bowls as possible. The local record is 570 bowls.

G2 **17-40 Uchimaru, Morioka** **wankosoba.jp**

13
Kakunodate
角館

G2 **Akita Prefecture** **Kakunodate** **At JR stn; (0187) 54-2700**

Though it does not have many of its original samurai houses left, this town still evokes the past. More than 150 weeping cherries in the Uchimachi district, brought from Kyoto about 300 years ago, are National Natural Treasures now.

This district is home to many samurai houses that are open to the public. The **Aoyagi-ke** features ceilings painted with waves as protection from fire. At the **Ishiguro-ke**, known for its garden, the transoms between rooms project shadows by candlelight. Also in Uchimachi, the **Denshokan Museum** has exhibits and demonstrations of local crafts, including *kabazaiku* (objects of polished cherry bark) and *itayazaiku* (baskets and folk objects woven of split maple).

Aoyagi-ke
3 Omotemachi-Shimocho **Apr-Oct:**

9am-5pm daily (Nov-Mar: to 4pm) **samuraiworld. com/english**

Ishiguro-ke
1 Omotemachi-Shimocho **(0187) 55-1496** **9am-5pm daily**

Denshokan Museum
10-1 Omotemachi-Shimocho **(0187) 54-1700** **Apr-Nov: 9am-5pm daily (Dec-Mar: to 4:30pm)**

14
Yamadera
山寺

G2 **Yamagata Prefecture** **Yamadera** **4495-15 Yamadera; data.yamagata kanko.com/english/sight seeing/yamadera.html**

When haiku master Matsuo Basho *(p308)* visited the temple of Yamadera in 1689, he penned one of his classics: "silence / sinking into the rocks / the shrill of cicada."

Literally "mountain temple," but officially Risshaku-ji, the foot of Yamadera is the site of temple buildings, a statue of

Basho, and a stone inscribed with his Yamadera haiku.

The temple's main hall is reached by climbing about 1,000 steps up the mountainside, passing moss-covered stone statues, and tiny shrines along the way. It's an atmospheric climb that's capped with views of the valley below.

While Basho took months to hike around northern Honshu, for today's travelers Yamadera is a day trip from either Sendai or Yamagata cities.

 15

Tono
遠野

G2 **Iwate Prefecture**
Tono **By JR stn; www.tonojikan.jp**

In Tono people still live in rhythm with nature, and observe old traditions. Much has changed, though, since folklorist Kunio Yanagita compiled the *Legends of Tono* in 1910. Few of the *magariya* (L-shaped houses, shared by people and horses) are left, but the mountains ringing the Tono basin are still beautiful.

Tono's attractions are best reached by car or bicycle, both of which can be rented at the station. The **Municipal Museum** in the town center introduces local culture. At Denshoen, local experts teach traditional crafts. A short walk away are Kappabuchi stream and Joken-ji Temple, both traditionally the home of *kappa* (water imps). Northwest of the railroad station, Tono Furusato Village has six *magariya*, where you can see traditional craftwork being made. Hayachine Shrine, a 30-minute drive from the station, is known for its kagura (sacred dances), and Mount Hayachine is popular with climbers.

$\rightarrow$

Bright-red fall leaves surround the poignant ruins of Marioka's castle

---

Municipal Museum

⌖ **3-9 Higashidatecho**
☎ (0198) 62-2340 ☐ Apr-Oct: 9am-5pm daily (Nov-Mar: Tue-Sun) ☒Last day of month May-Oct, Nov 24-30, public hols

---

16

Morioka
盛岡

G2 **Iwate Prefecture**
Morioka **2nd flr, JR stn; www.morioka-hachimantai.jp**

Once the center of the Nanbu domain, Morioka is now Iwate's capital and a transportation hub for the north, known for its Nanbu *tetsubin* (iron kettles) and Mount Iwate, the volcano that overlooks it. In October, salmon run up the Nakatsu River, one of three rivers that divide the city.

Near the ruins of Morioka Castle is a cherry tree, over 350 years old, that has grown from a crevice in a boulder. Over Nakatsu River is the **Suzuki Morihisa Iron Studio**, which has superb iron pieces on display. For folk crafts, such as cute *kokeshi* dolls, head for Konya-cho (dyers' street) and Zaimoku-cho (lumber street).

Suzuki Morihisa Iron Studio
☐ 1-6-7 Minamiodori
☐ 9am-5pm Mon-Sat
☒ suzukimorihisa.com

Towada-Hachimantai National Park

十和田八幡平国立公園

G1 Akita, Aomori, and Iwate Prefectures Morioka, Aomori From stations to Lake Towada or Hachimantai At Lake Towada; (0176) 75-1015

This national park is in two sections, with the mountainous Hachimantai section 37 miles (60 km) south of the Towada section. The best way to get around the park is by car: trains are limited and buses not available in winter.

Hachimantai offers hiking and ski trails aplenty, frozen lava flows, alpine flora, and mountain views. A favorite with Japanese tourists, it has scenic toll roads, hot-spring and ski resorts, and a variety of tourist facilities. Good stopping places include Goshogake *onsen*, and the Hachimantai Resort ski complex.

In the Towada section highlights include the lovely Lake Towada. Its symbol, a statue of two maidens (1953) by Kotaro Takamura, is on the southern shore. More dramatic is the 6-mile (9-km) Oirase Gorge to the east of the lake. North of the lake are some atmospheric spa inns, such as the excellent Tsuta Onsen.

Oga Peninsula

男鹿半島

F1 Akita Prefecture Oga Next to JR stn; (0185) 24-4700

Kicking 12 miles (20 km) into the Sea of Japan (East Sea), this foot-shaped peninsula has a rocky coastline, little fishing villages, good seafood, and hills with Akita cedar. The lookout on Mount Kanpu offers a panoramic view of mountains, sea, and rice fields. The peninsula is known for the Namahage Festival on New Year's Eve, when men in horned masks and straw coats go from house to house, scaring children into being good and idlers into working. A tourist version of the festival, the Namahage Sedo Matsuri in February, is held at Shinzan Shrine, in Oga city.

Shimokita Peninsula

下北半島

G1 Aomori Prefecture Ominato Next to JR Shimokita Stn en-aomori.com/aomoristory/shimokita.html

This peninsula offers unspoiled beauty. In the interior is the Osorezan (Mount Dread), one of three Japanese mountains sacred to spirits of the dead, with a crater lake and sulfur hot springs. It is open from May to October and blind mediums communicate with the spirits July 20–24. Take the ferry from Sai along the west coast to Hotoke-ga-ura (Buddha Coast), past sea-worn cliffs and rock formations. In the southwest the port of Wakinosawa is home to snow monkeys. A ferry runs from here to Aomori.

Aomori

青森

G1 Aomori Prefecture Shin-Aomori, Aomori JR bus stn bldg; www.en-aomori.com

Aomori is home to the riotous Nebuta Matsuri in early August and **Sannai-Maruyama**, a Jomon-period site. Since its discovery in 1993, the site has yielded relics and ruins from 4,000 to 5,500 years ago, including a woven pouch, red lacquerware, and clay figures. Most impressive are the reconstructed pit dwellings and a standing-pillar building.

Sannai-Maruyama

3 miles (5 km) SW of city center From Shin-Aomori & Aomori Stns to Sannai-Maruyama Iseki-mae Jun-Sep: 9am-6pm daily (Oct-May: to 5pm) sannaimaruyama.pref.aomori.jp

Hirosaki

弘前

F1 Aomori Prefecture Hirosaki Hirosaki Stn; www.hirosaki-kanko.or.jp/en

The cultural and educational center of Aomori, Hirosaki is a

←

Atmospheric waterfall in an autumnal setting in the Oirase Gorge

The moat-surrounded Hirosaki Castle, the former home of the Tsugaru family ↑

delight. Most streets lead to Hirosaki Park, the old castle grounds of the Tsugaru lords. The castle was destroyed by lightning but its picturesque 1810 keep, some smaller towers, several gates, and three moats remain. Kamenoko-mon, the imposing main gate, is on the northside, where historic samurai houses still stand. Nearby is the **Tsugaruhan Neputa Mura**, displaying the Neputa floats used in Hirosaki's refined summer festival. Visitors can try making local crafts and take *shamisen* lessons.

The wooded castle park is famous for its cherry blossoms, at their best in late April. The **Hirosaki City Museum**, inside the park, has local history exhibitions. Twenty-two temples line the approach to **Chosho-ji Temple**, the Tsugaru family temple, on a bluff overlooking

the Hirosaki plain and Mount Iwaki. Its two-story gate has extra-deep eaves because of the heavy snows in the area. A side hall contains polychrome statues of the Buddha's 500 disciples. The main hall has the naturally mummified body of the 12th Tsugaru lord.

The streets around the castle were designed to twist and turn to confuse enemy forces. The large Kankokan (municipal information center) just south of the park is a good place to get oriented. It also displays local crafts. Other craft outlets include Tanakaya, on the corner of Ichiban-cho, with its traditional and modern Tsugaru lacquerware. Miyamoto Kogei, on Minami Sakura-cho, sells baskets of *akebi*, a wild vine fruit from the mountains.

Tsugaruhan Neputa Mura

🎨 👘 🏠 61 Kamenokomachi
🕐 9am–5:30pm daily
🌐 neputamura.com/en

Hirosaki City Museum

🎨 🏠 1-6 Shimoshiroganecho
📞 (0172) 35-0700 🕐 9:30am–4:30pm daily

Chosho-ji Temple

🎨 🏠 1-23-8 Nishi-Shigemori
📞 (0172) 32-0813 🕐 Apr-Nov: 9am–4pm daily, by appt Dec-Mar

🔍 HIDDEN GEM
Rice Work!

Inakadate village near Hirosaki is famous for its rice paddy artworks. Perspective drawing methods are used to make the images look their best when seen from the 72-ft (22-m) observation platform.

DRINK

Ichinosuke

This *izakaya* (pub) specializes in Aomori's traditional food and *jizake*, or local artisan-made sake.

🅰 G1 🏠 1-5-19 Yasukata, Aomori 📞 (050) 3462 034

Tsugaru Joppari Isariya Sakaba

This farmhouse-style *izakaya* in Aomari hosts live *shamisen* music.

🅰 G1 🏠 2-5-14 Honcho, Aomori 🌐 maruto misuisan.jpn.com/ isariya-tugaru

A-Factory

Learn all about apple-cider brewing at this hip space in Aomari, which combines a factory and a bar.

🅰 G1 🏠 1-4-2 Yanakawa, Aomori 🌐 jre-abc.com/ wp/afactory

HOKKAIDO

First settled 20,000 years ago, this remote northern island became the homeland of the indigenous Ainu people after the 12th century. The Japanese made early forays to Yezo, as the island was called, in ancient times, but it was perceived as remote, inhospitable, and cold. For centuries only the persecuted Ainu, refugee warriors, and banished criminals lived there. In the late 1860s, however, the new Meiji government decided officially to develop the island. Thereafter it became known as Hokkaido, or "north sea road."

Since then, the population has risen to just under 6 million. The few Ainu left number somewhere between 24,000 and 60,000. Fishing, farming, forestry, and mining are the main industries, but tourism draws several million visitors north each year. The lively capital of Sapporo attracts visitors with its spectacular festivals, while the island's many national parks offer boundless opportunities for outdoor enthusiasts, including camping, hiking, and hot-spring bathing.

HOKKAIDO

Experience

Rebun Island
Kafuka
Wakkanai
Sarufutsu
Wakkanai Airport
238
Rishiri Island
7
RISHIRI-REBUN-SAROBETSU NATIONAL PARK
Toyotomi
Hamatonbetsu
E5
Horonobe
Teshio
232
Nakagawa
Enbetsu
Otoineppu
Hako-dake 3,704 ft (1,129 m)
40
Shosanbetsu
Bifuka
Haboro
Uryu-ko
Nayoro
275
Tomamae
Shibetsu
232
239
Obira
Horokanai
Wassamu
E5
Rumoi
275
Mashike
E62
Numata
Asahikawa
Shokanbetsu-dake 4,891 ft (1,491 m)
Fukagawa
Asahikawa Airport
Hamamasu
Takikawa
E5
Akabira
Atsuta
Sunagawa
38
231
Bibai
Furano
Shakotan
Tsukigata
Yobetsu-dake 4,258 ft (1,298 m)
Yoichi
Otaru
Tobetsu
12
Iwamizawa

Sea of Japan (East Sea)

Kamoenai
5
E5A
Ebetsu
E5
274
Oiwake
E38
Iwanai
SAPPORO 5
E5
36
NISEKO SKI RESORT 2
Kutchan
230
Eniwa
Hidaka
Suttsu
Yotei-zan 6,227 ft (1,898 m)
Eniwa-dake 4,331 ft (1,320 m)
Chitose
237
Kimobetsu
4
New Chitose Airport
Kuromatsunai
SHIKOTSU-TOYA NATIONAL PARK
Lake Shikotsu
Biratori
Kariba-yama 4,987 ft (1,520 m)
37
Toyoura
36
Tomakomai
229
Oshamanbe
Lake Toya
Shiraoi
235
Setana
Kunnui
Date
E5
Shizunai
Yakumo
Noboribetsu
E5
Taisei
Muroran
Kumaishi
5
Mori
Okushiri
Shikabe
Esashi
Nanae
3 ONUMA QUASI-NATIONAL PARK
Kaminokuni
Kamiiso
5
Minami-Kayabe
HAKODATE 1
Hakodate Airport
Kikonai
228
Fukushima
228
Matsumae

NORTHERN HONSHU
p294

Aomori
Imabetsu

0 kilometers   40

0 miles   40

N

Sea of Okhotsk

Esashi

Omu

Okoppe

Setouchi

Monbetsu

238

Yubetsu

Takinoue

Tokoro

Engaru

Abashiri

Shirataki

Aibetsu

E39

Kitami

39

Rubeshibe

39

Sounkyo

*Asahi-dake
7,513 ft (2,290 m)*

Asahidake

△

**DAISETSU-ZAN
NATIONAL PARK**

△ *Tokachi-dake
6,814 ft (2,077 m)*

Rikubetsu

242

241

273

Kamishihoro

Ashoro

E61

H O K K A I D O

Honbetsu

Shintoku

241

Shimizu

E38

Obihiro

38

Ikeda

Makubetsu

Nakasatsunai

★ **Tokachi-Obihiro
Airport**

E60

236

*Horoshiri-dake
6,732 ft (2,052 m)*

△

Taiki

Hidaka Mountains

Hiroo

Mitsuishi

236

Samani

Erimo

Bihoro

Tsubetsu

243

*Lake
Kussharo*

**AKAN
NATIONAL PARK**

Shari

Tokoro-gawa

39

244

8

*Lake
Akan*

△ *O-Akan-dake
4,918 ft (1,499 m)*

Lake Mashu

Teshikaga

243

Shibecha

240

Akan

**KUSHIRO
WETLANDS
NATIONAL PARK**

9

✈ **Kushiro
Airport**

E38

Shiranuka

Onbetsu

Urahoro

Kushiro

391

Utoro

**SHIRETOKO
NATIONAL PARK**

13

*Rausu-dake
5,446 ft (1,660 m)*

334

Rausu

△

R U S S I A

335

244

Shibetsu

Nakashibetsu

Bekkai

**NEMURO
PENINSULA**

10

44

Hamanaka

Akkeshi

Nemuro

LAKE FUREN

11

12 **AKKESHI BAY**

*Pacific
Ocean*

HOKKAIDO

EXPERIENCE

1

Hakodate
函館

🅰 A3 🄷 Hokkaido Prefecture ✈🄼🚌 🄷 Hakodate 🄸 JR station; www.hakodate.travel/en

Once an island, the fan-shaped city of Hakodate now straddles a low sandbar that links it to the mainland. In 1854, the city was designated one of the first treaty ports in Japan. Fifteen years later the city was the scene of the last battle in Japan before World War II.

Within easy reach of the center is Mount Hakodate, the peak of which can be reached by cable car, road, or on foot. From here, you can see the sea, the mountains, and the unique shape of the city below.

The quiet Motomachi district, nestling beneath Mount Hakodate in the south of the city, is the most attractive area. Western-style buildings are a feature here, a legacy of the treaty-port status. They include the Old Public Hall, with its stately blue-and-yellow clapboarding; the Russian Orthodox Church with its spire and onion domes; and, nearby, the Old British Consulate.

In the north, Goryokaku Park provides a peaceful haven for strolling, and its more than 1,500 cherry trees

The star-shaped Goryokaku Fort in Hakodate and the Former Magistrate Office *(inset)*

↓

create a popular springtime spectacle. The pentangle-shaped Goryokaku Fort was completed in 1864 to defend against the Russians, but it fell to imperial forces in 1869. The Former Magistrate Office sits at the center of the fortress.

Hot-spring enthusiasts will want to stay at the *onsen* resort of Yunokawa, 15 minutes from the center. About an hour's drive to the east of the city is the active Mount Esan volcano with nearby azalea gardens and forested slopes.

 2

Niseko Ski Resort
ニセコスキーリゾート

A3 Hokkaido Prefecture Niseko niseko.ne.jp/en/niseko

Some of Japan's best skiing can be found in the Niseko mountains. Snowboarders and skiers alike favor this area for its long, cold winter season, numerous slopes, and quality off-piste powder. In summer it offers adventure-sports vacations. Four major resorts are connected at the top of the same mountain and shuttle buses link them at the base. A single pass can be used for all the resorts.

The town of Hirafu is very popular among visitors, and during the skiing season it takes on the character of a lively alpine village.

3

Onuma Quasi-National Park
大沼国定公園

A3 Hokkaido Prefecture Onuma-Koen Next to station; (0138) 67-2170

Three large, islet-studded lakes – Onuma, Konuma, and Junsainuma – are surrounded by forest and form the Onuma Quasi-National Park. Deer and foxes inhabit the forests, and the lakes support many kinds of waterfowl, particularly during the spring and fall migrations. Wildflowers are abundant in summer, and among the rare birds that come to Onuma are the ruddy kingfisher, the white-tailed eagle, and Steller's sea eagle. The graceful form of Mount Komagatake provides a stunning backdrop to the north. An easily followed hiking trail from the north side of Lake Onuma to the upper mountain provides a fabulous view of south-western Hokkaido.

↑ Downhill skiing on the powdery slopes of Niseko Ski Resort

4

Shikotsu-Toya National Park
支笏洞爺国立公園

A3 Hokkaido Prefecture Toya Toyako Onsen 142-5 Toyako Onsen, Toyako; www.toyako-vc.jp/en

The disjointed Shikotsu-Toya National Park is like an open-air museum to vulcanology. It contains the 6,230-ft- (1,900-m-) high Mount Yotei, two crater lakes, and the spa towns of Jozankei in the north and Noboribetsu in the south.

Beside Lake Shikotsu is the popular hot-spring resort of Shikotsu Kohan, as well as the remarkable moss-covered Kokenodomon gorge. The lake is dominated to the north by the rugged peak of Mount Eniwa, and to the south by Mount Fuppushi and Mount Tarumae, with its cinder cone.

Lake Toya, 25 miles (40 km) farther southwest, contains the picturesque group of islands known as Nakajima. Nearby stands Japan's youngest volcano, the bare-sloped Showa Shinzan (it formed between 1943 and 1945), beside the extremely active Mount Usu.

The mountains in the park make for rewarding hikes; trails are well defined, and the views from the tops of Eniwa and Tarumae are superb.

EAT

Hakodate Morning Market

This famous market (open Jan–Apr: 6am–2pm; May–Dec: 5am–2pm) is packed with stalls selling fish, salmon roe, sea urchin, crab, and more. Pick anything and have it placed on one of the charcoal grills that dot the street.

A3 9-19 Wakamatsucho, Hakodate hakodate-asaichi.com

Umizora No Haru

Based on a traditional Ainu house, this Sapporo restaurant has thatched walls and textiles on loan from Shiraoi's Ainu Museum. The food includes salmon tataki, grilled venison, and dumplings topped with salmon eggs, plus a millet sake.

A2 5-8 Minami 4 Jo Nishi, Chuo, Sapporo umizoranoharu.com

❺ Sapporo
札幌

 A2 ☐ **Hokkaido Prefecture** ✈ **Shin-Chitose, Okadama** 🚌 ℹ️ **Sapporo International Communication Plaza, opposite Sapporo Clock Tower; www.plaza-sapporo.or.jp/en**

Capital of Hokkaido, the modern city of Sapporo lies on the Ishikari plain, straddling the Toyohira River. Four subway lines, streetcars, and a well laid-out grid structure make getting around fairly straightforward. At Sapporo's heart lies the long Odori Park, dominated at the east end by the metal television tower and at the west by a view to the mountains. One block north, opposite the wooden Tokei-dai clock tower, is the Sapporo International Communication Plaza, an essential stop for information on Hokkaido, with friendly staff to help with planning and booking. The city gives its name to the famous local beer; its brewing is shown at the **Sapporo Beer Garden and Museum** northeast of the station. Nightlife is focused on the Susukino area, with thousands of restaurants and bars. Local specialties include "Genghis Khan" – mutton

↑ Sapporo's Odori Park, site of the annual Yuki Matsuri (Snow Festival)

and vegetables grilled at the table on a charcoal-fired griddle.

A large collection of Ainu artifacts is displayed at the Exhibition Room of Northern Peoples in the **Botanic Gardens**. The gardens themselves are a refreshingly quiet spot, with a representative collection of Hokkaido's flora. The large-scale outdoor sculptures at the **Sapporo Art Park** make for an interesting hands-on excursion.

Lying 9 miles (14 km) east of the city, the **Historical Village of Hokkaido** commemorates the official settlement of the island in the 1860s. This cluster of late 19th- and early 20th-century buildings has been gathered from around Hokkaido. Some have displays of traditional life inside.

Sapporo Beer Garden and Museum
🏠 9-1-1 Kita 7-Jo Higashi
🕐 11am–9pm daily
🌐 sapporobeer.jp/brewery/s_museum

Botanic Gardens
🎟️ 🏠 Kita 3 Higashi 8
🕐 9am–4pm Tue–Sun
🌐 hokudai.ac.jp/fsc/bg/index_e.html

SAPPORO SNOW FESTIVAL

Sapporo's annual Snow Festival (Yuki Matsuri) transforms Odori Park and Makomanai Park into a fairy-tale land of ice sculptures in early February. Watching the making of these carvings (from about a week before the start of the festival) is fascinating. This popular event overlaps with Sapporo White Illumination (mid-Nov–mid-Feb), when strings of white lights adorn Odori Park and Ekimae-dori.

Sapporo Art Park

⌂ 2-75 Geijutsunomori
🕐 Jun-Aug: 9:45am-5:30pm daily (Sep-May: to 5pm daily)
🚫 Nov 4-Apr 28: Mon 🌐 art park.or.jp/en

Historical Village of Hokkaido

♿ ⌂ 50-1 Konopporo, Atsubetsu 🕐 May-Sep: 9am-5pm daily (Oct-Apr: to 4:30pm Tue-Sun) 🌐 kaitaku.or.jp

---

⑥

Daisetsu-zan National Park

大雪山国立公園

📍 B2 🏛 Hokkaido Prefecture 🚆 Tokachi-Obihiro, Asahikawa 🚌 Obihiro, Asahikawa 🚌 Sounkyo, Kamikawa; www.daisetsu zan.or.jp/english

At 890 sq miles (2,310 sq km), Daisetsu-zan is Japan's largest national park. A huge raised plateau ringed with peaks, right in the center of Hokkaido, the park was established in 1934. Asahikawa to the northwest or Obihiro to the south make the best starting points for visiting the park, with easy car access by routes 39 and 273. Buses connect the major *onsen* resorts of Sounkyo, Asahi-dake, and Tenninkyo. The Sounkyo Gorge, with the cascading Ryusei and Ginga waterfalls, is best explored by bicycle or on foot. The ropeway at Sounkyo and the cable car at Asahi-dake tend to be packed but offer quick access; away from the top stations people become scarcer and the views more spectacular.

In Ainu legend the peaks of the Daisetsu mountains are the dwelling places of benevolent but powerful god-spirits who, in human form, helped in times of need. A network of trails across these mountains provides everything from day hikes to week-long tramps, and it is worth taking the time to hike or go by cable car up from the low access roads to the higher levels for the breathtaking views. The dramatic, conical, steam-venting peak of Mount Asahi (or Asahi-dake), Hokkaido's highest at 7,500 ft (2,290 m), offers an uplifting panorama across the high plateau. June and July bring alpine flowers, while fall colors are at their best in late August and September. En route, you may see bears and pika (a rodent), as well as rubythroats and nutcrackers in the trees, among other species.

An excellent route for the fit day-hiker starts from Sounkyo *onsen*. From there take the rope way and cable car, then hike southwest over Mount Kurodake, continuing along the trails to Mount Asahi. From the top, descend via the cable car to Asahi-dake *onsen*. It should take around seven hours.

Located 30 miles (50 km) west of the park, near the pretty town of Biei, the Blue Pond is an unbelievable color.

DRINK

Bow Bar Sapporo

For whisky aficionados, Bow Bar is a must-go spot when in Sapporo. The selection of rare whiskies here is unparalleled, and a glass is bound to warm you up.

📍 A2 🏛 Hoshi Building 8F, 2-7-5 Minami 4-jo Nishi, Chuo, Sapporo 🕐 7pm-2am Mon-Sat 🌐 thebowbar-sapporo.com

Bar Yamazaki

This iconic Sapporo bar was managed for more than 50 years by the legendary bartender Ichiro Yamazaki. His apprentices still serve cocktails in Yamazaki's signature style.

📍 A2 🏛 3-3 Minami 3-jo Nishi, Chuo, Sapporo 🕐 6pm-12:30am Mon-Sat 🌐 bar-yamazaki.com

↑ Trekking in the mountains of Japan's largest national park, Daisetsu-zan

⑦

Rishiri-Rebun-Sarobetsu National Park

利尻礼文サロベツ国立公園

🅰A1 🏛Hokkaido Prefecture ✈🚉Wakkanai 🚢From Wakkanai to both islands

Consisting of the Sarobetsu coast and the two islands of Rishiri and Rebun, this park is within sight of the Russian island of Sakhalin. The coastal meadows in the Sarobetsu area and the shores of the

↑ Taking a break on Mount Rishiri, Rishiri-Rebun-Sarobetsu National Park

shallow lagoons in the coastal plain are carpeted with flowers in summer, including yellow-orange lilies, white cotton grass, white rhododendrons, and purple irises.

About 12 miles (20 km) offshore on the island of Rishiri, the startling 5,650-ft- (1,720-m-) high conical peak of Mount Rishiri (Rishiri-Fuji) appears to rise straight from the sea. A road runs around its coastline, making for incredibly scenic cycling and linking the various settlements including Oshidomari, the main port, and Kutsugata, the second port on the west side. Trails to the top of Mount Rishiri thread through a host of alpine summer flowers. Those less inclined to hike may choose to fish or simply relax and enjoy the excellent fresh fish at local restaurants.

Rebun, Rishiri's partner and Japan's northernmost island, is lowly in comparison but is renowned as the "isle of flowers." Kafuka is its main port; the fishing village of Funadomari is at the opposite, north end of the island. There's great hiking (sometimes hard going), especially on the west coast; the island's youth hostel organizes guided walking groups.

⑧

Akan National Park

阿寒国立公園

🅰C2 🏛Hokkaido Prefecture ✈Memanbetsu (Abashiri), Kushiro 🚉Minami-Teshikaga, Kawayu-Onsen 🚌From Kushiro 🅹Akanko Onsen; en.kushiro-lakeakan.com

This enormous national park in east-central Hokkaido is possibly the most beautiful in Japan. Travel around the park is limited; there are tour buses, but cycling or rental car are better options.

The western portion, around Lake Akan, is dominated by a pair of volcanic peaks: in the southeast is the 4,500-ft (1,370-m) Mount O-Akan while in the southwest is the still-active Mount Me-Akan, at 4,920 ft (1,500 m). The day hike up Me-Akan from Akan Kohan *onsen* and down the other side on a well-trodden trail to attractive Lake Onneto affords marvelous views in any season, but especially in fall.

East of Akan lies Lake Kussharo, in a huge caldera with a 35-mile (57-km) perimeter. Beautiful all year, this vast lake freezes over

 ←
Winter sun rising over large, volcanic Lake Kussharo, in Akan National Park

 Kushiro Wetlands National Park
釧路湿原

🅰C2 🏠Hokkaido Prefecture 🚅🚌 🚆Kushiro 🚉JR Kushiro Stn; en. kushiro-lakeakan.com

If any creature represents Japan, it is the *tancho*, or red-crowned crane, regarded as a symbol of happiness and long life. A large peat swamp, an expanse of undulating reed beds crisscrossed by streams, the Kushiro Wetlands National Park is one of the main homes of these enormous and graceful birds, which stand 4 ft 6 in (1.4 m) high.

In the early 1900s, the cranes were pushed to the verge of extinction in Japan by hunting and loss of habitat, but now protection and provision of food for them during the winter months has boosted the population to around 1,250 birds.

From December to March, the cranes forage along streams and marsh edges, or fly to one of three major feeding sites north of Kushiro: two in Tsurui village and one in Akan village. These sites offer the best opportunities

for viewing the cranes year round. On late winter days, the birds display, calling and dancing to one another in the snow as they prepare for the breeding season ahead.

In summer (May to September), the cranes are territorial, occupying large, traditional nesting grounds where they usually raise just one chick, or occasionally two.

Did You Know?

The harmonics created by pressure in the ice make Lake Kussharo sound as if it is singing.

TOP 5 **HOKKAIDO FOODS**

Kaisen don
A fishy dish, *Kaisen don* is a bowl of rice topped with salmon roe and sea urchin.

Hairy Crab
The hairy crab is famed for its sweet flesh and creamy, buttery roe.

Sapporo-Style Soup Curry
A curry-flavored soup served with chicken and flash-fried vegetables.

Sapporo Miso Ramen
Hokkaido's hearty ramen is miso-based and includes sweet corn.

Yubari Melon
Sweet Yubari melons can cost as much as ¥20,000 each.

---

almost entirely in winter. Thermal vents keep tiny portions ice-free; here flocks of whooper swans remain throughout the winter.

Farther east again lies Lake Mashu. The crater's steep cliffs rise 650 ft (200 m), the water is astonishingly clear, and the lake has no inlets or outlets. The panoramic view from the crater rim takes in Mount Shari to the north, the Shiretoko Peninsula to the northeast, and Lake Kussharo and beyond to the Akan volcanoes in the west.

The park's forests are home to woodpeckers and other birds, red foxes, sika deer, and Siberian chipmunks. There are outdoor hot-spring pools at Akan Kohan, on Lake Akan's south shore, and Wakoto, on Lake Kussharo's south shore.

 →
Elegant red-crowned cranes in the snow at Kushiro Wetlands National Park

PICTURE PERFECT
Here Comes the Sun

Cape Nosappu, on the Nemuro Peninsula, is the perfect spot to celebrate *hatsuhinode* – the first sunrise of the year. Hot drinks are served free of charge, and a folk performance ushers in the New Year.

10

Nemuro Peninsula
根室半島

🅐C2 🏠Hokkaido Prefecture 🚗Nemuro-Nakashibetsu 🚌Nemuro 🅘In front of Nemuro Stn; (0153) 24-3104

The low-lying Nemuro Peninsula, a coastal plateau carved by streams into steep-sided gullies, is well loved by naturalists. The best way to explore the area is by car.

The red fox is common here and, in forests around Onneto, there are also many sika deer. In summer, lilies, fritillaries, and other wildflowers are plentiful, while in winter, both white-tailed and Steller's sea eagles can be seen. Offshore and in the many sheltered bays, there are flocks of sea ducks, particularly scoters and harlequins, and many other seabirds can be spotted.

11

Lake Furen
風蓮湖

🅐C2 🏠Hokkaido Prefecture 🚗Kushiro 🚌Nemuro

Situated on Hokkaido's east coast, beautiful Lake Furen is the seasonal haunt of hordes of birds: migrating waterfowl in spring and fall, swans in late fall, sea eagles in winter, and red-crowned cranes in summer.

Nearly 12 miles (20 km) long and up to 2 miles (4 km) wide, the lagoon is only 6 ft (2 m) deep or less in places. It is fringed by forests of fir and spruce, with alder and birch scrub in wetter areas. Some easy forest walks start from the south end of the lake, at Hakuchodai and Shunkunitai,

offering a wealth of great bird-watching opportunities and plenty of wildflowers en route. In winter, the frozen lagoon and adjacent areas are good for cross-country skiing.

12

Akkeshi Bay
厚岸湾

🅐C2 🏠Hokkaido Prefecture 🚗Kushiro 🚌Akkeshi 🅘1st Floor, Akkeshi Gourmet Park, 2-2 Suminoe, Akkeshi; (0153) 52-4139

Akkeshi's sheltered tidal lagoon is renowned for its oysters. The bay is extensively farmed, and there is a shrine to the oysters on a rocky islet. Throughout the winter, and during spring and fall migration, whooper swans gather in the inner bay, while in summer red-crowned cranes breed upriver and at the nearby Kiritappu wetland. The scenic coastal road from Akkeshi around to Kiritappu is well worth driving for an insight into the fishing and seaweed-harvesting lifestyles of some of the local people. Walking at the cape beyond Kiritappu is exhilarating, but early summer mornings are best avoided because this is when a sea mist is most likely to conceal the view.

> Lake Furen is the seasonal haunt of hordes of birds: migrating waterfowl in spring and fall, swans in late fall, sea eagles in winter, and red-crowned cranes in summer.

← Sailing on the icy waters of the Strait of Nemuro, off the Nemuro Peninsula

 A walkway in the Five Lakes area, Shiretoko National Park

⓭

Shiretoko National Park
知床国立公園

🅰C2 🏠Hokkaido Prefecture ✈Memanbetsu (Abashiri) or Nakashibetsu 🚉Shiretoko-Shari ℹShiretoko Shizen center; (0152) 24-2114

This rugged finger of land jutting into the Okhotsk Sea was named Shiretoko ("the end of the earth") by the Ainu. Now a World Heritage Site, Shiretoko National Park consists of a well-forested ridge of volcanic peaks dominated by the 5,450-ft (1,660-m) Mount Rausu. The peninsula supports one of the healthiest populations of brown bears left in Hokkaido. Sightings are rare, though the boat ride from Utoro north to the cape during the summer is one possible way of seeing them as they forage along the coastal strip.

Minke whales, dolphins, and porpoises may be seen in summer, too, along with birds such as spectacled guillemots, Japanese cormorants, and short-tailed shearwaters. White-tailed sea eagles nest along the peninsula. In winter their numbers are swollen by hundreds more arriving from Russia. Despite their numbers, they are overshadowed by the arrival of pairs of the world's largest eagle: Steller's sea eagle. Both types of eagle are best seen in winter north of Rausu on the southeast coast.

North of Utoro lie the pretty Shiretoko Five Lakes, reflecting Mount Rausu. An easy 1-mile (2-km) trail starts beyond the visitor center, and *onsen* fans will not want to miss the hot Kamuiwakka waterfall, northeast of here. The high pass from Utoro to Rausu (Route 334) is open from May to October, and the view east from here to Kunashiri Island is dramatic. From near the pass, a hiking trail strikes off south for Lake Rausu and Mount Onnebetsu, while another heads north for Mounts Rausu, Io, and Shiretoko, and the cape beyond. Mount Rausu is a day hike along a good trail. The journey to the cape, however, requires several days and careful planning. Note that hiking is possible only from June to September.

STAY

Akan Tsuruga Besso Hinanoza
This elegant lakeside inn in Akan National Park offers organic food, a tree-trunk bar, and hot-spring baths.

🅰C2 🏠2-8-1 Akanko Onsen, Akan, Kushiro 🌐hinanoza.com/en

¥¥¥

Kushiro Prince Hotel
With views of Lake Kussharo, this hotel is ideal to explore Akan National Park.

🅰C2 🏠7-1 Saiwaicho, Kushiro 🌐princehotels. co.jp/kushiro

¥¥¥

Hotel Nemuro Kaiyoutei
The rooms of this Nemuro hotel are clean, roomy, and modern. A great base to explore the peninsula.

🅰C2 🏠2-24 Tokiwacho, Nemuro 🌐n-kaiyoutei.co.jp

¥¥¥

NEED TO KNOW

A bullet train speeding past Mount Fuji

BEFORE
YOU GO

Things change, so plan ahead to make the most of your trip. Be prepared for all eventualities by considering the following points before you travel.

AT A GLANCE

CURRENCY
Japanese Yen (¥)

AVERAGE DAILY SPEND

SAVE	SPEND	SPLURGE
¥10,000	¥20,000	¥40,000

BOTTLED WATER	COFFEE	BEER	DINNER FOR TWO
¥100	¥300	¥400	¥5,000

ESSENTIAL PHRASES

Hello	Konnichiwa
Goodbye	Sayonara
Please	Onegaishimasu
Thank you	Arigato gozaimasu
Do you speak English?	Eigo o hanasemasuka?
I don't understand	Wakarimasen

ELECTRICITY SUPPLY

Power sockets are type A and B. Standard voltage is 100v and the frequency is 50 Hz (east) and 60 Hz (west).

Passports and Visas

For entry requirements, including visas, consult your nearest Japanese embassy or check the **Ministry of Foreign Affairs** website. EU nationals and citizens of the UK, US, Canada, Australia, New Zealand, and many other countries do not need a visa for stays of up to three months. Citizens of some countries may extend this stay by another 90 days at immigration offices in Japan (at least 10 days before the expiration date).
Ministry of Foreign Affairs
🅦 mofa.go.jp

Government Advice

Now more than ever, it is important to consult both your and the Japanese government's advice before traveling. The **UK Foreign and Commonwealth Office**, the **US State Department**, the **Australian Department of Foreign Affairs and Trade**, and Japan's **Ministry of Health, Labor and Welfare** offer the latest information on security, health, and local regulations.

Each year, Japan experiences over 1,000 earthquakes. The government has issued a useful **Disaster Preparedness Manual** with safety guidelines in the event of strong tremors.
Australian Department of Foreign Affairs and Trade
🅦 smartraveller.gov.au
Disaster Preparedness Manual
🅦 metro.tokyo.jp/english/guide/bosai/index.html
Ministry of Health, Labor and Welfare
🅦 mhlw.go.jp/english
UK
🅦 gov.uk/foreign-travel-advice
US
🅦 travel.state.gov

Customs Information

You can find information on the laws relating to goods and currency taken in or out of Japan on the **Customs and Tariff Bureau**'s website.
Customs and Tariff Bureau
🅦 customs.go.jp/english/index.htm

Insurance

We recommend that you take out a comprehensive insurance policy covering theft, loss of belongings, medical care, cancellations, and delays, and read the small print carefully.

Vaccinations

No inoculations are needed for Japan, but it is advisable to be vaccinated against encephalitis if you are planning on staying for over a month or are visiting rural areas.

Booking Accommodations

As well as Western-style hotels, Tokyo offers a few idiosyncratic options. *Ryokans* are traditional inns, which may have an on-site *onsen*, while capsule hotels are made up of inexpensive sleeping pods. For help with booking hotels, visit the **Japan National Tourism Organization, Rakuten Travel,** or **Japanican.**

Japanican
w japanican.com/en
Japan National Tourism Organization
w jnto.go.jp
Rakuten Travel
w travel.rakuten.com

Money

Japan has traditionally had a cash-based economy. The move to contactless is accelerating but it's still wise to carry around some cash at all times. Cards can be used at major stations to buy JR train tickets and are accepted by most taxis.

Tipping is not part of the culture in Japan. Attempts to do so could lead to confusion, with servers doing their best to return the money.

Travelers with Specific Requirements

The visually impaired are well provided for, but people in wheelchairs occasionally have issues at small stations and pedestrian over- and underpasses, despite a 2008 law requiring barrier-free access. **Accessible Tokyo** provides information about disabled access and facilities.
Accessible Tokyo
w accessible.jp.org

Language

Japanese is the official language spoken in Japan. Cities are well signposted in English, and it is not hard to get around. Away from the cities, few locals are comfortable with speaking English.

Opening Hours

> **COVID-19** The pandemic continues to affect Japan. Some museums, tourist attractions, and hospitality venues are operating on reduced or temporary opening hours, and require visitors to make advance bookings for a specific date and time. Always check ahead before visiting.

Monday Many tourist attractions close for the day; when Monday is a bank holiday, they often close on Tuesday instead.
Weekends Banks, post offices, and offices are closed. Department stores may have reduced opening hours on Sunday.
Public holidays Many places are closed.

PUBLIC HOLIDAYS

1 Jan	New Year's Day
2nd Mon, Jan	Coming of Age Day
11 Feb	National Foundation Day
23 Feb	Emperor's Birthday
20/21 Mar	Vernal (Spring) Equinox
29 Apr	Showa Day
3 May	Constitution Memorial Day
4 May	Greenery Day
5 May	Children's Day
3rd Mon, Jul	Marine Day
11 Aug	Mountain Day
3rd Mon, Sep	Respect for the Aged Day
22/23 Oct	Autumnal Equinox
2nd Mon, Oct	Sports Day
3 Nov	Culture Day
23 Nov	Labor Thanksgiving Day

GETTING AROUND

Whether you're visiting for a short city break or traveling around the islands, discover how best to reach your destination and travel like a pro.

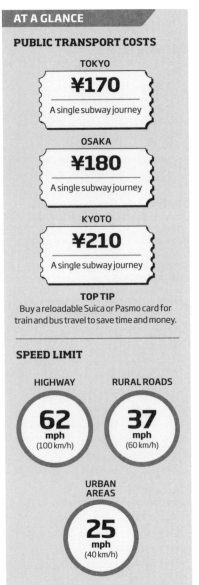

AT A GLANCE

PUBLIC TRANSPORT COSTS

TOKYO

¥170

A single subway journey

OSAKA

¥180

A single subway journey

KYOTO

¥210

A single subway journey

TOP TIP
Buy a reloadable Suica or Pasmo card for train and bus travel to save time and money.

SPEED LIMIT

HIGHWAY

62 mph (100 km/h)

RURAL ROADS

37 mph (60 km/h)

URBAN AREAS

25 mph (40 km/h)

Arriving by Air

The main international gateways to Japan are **Narita International Airport**, located at some distance from Tokyo, **Haneda Airport**, which is smaller but closer to the center, and Osaka's **Kansai International Airport**. Other airports handling international flights (mainly from Asia) include Naha in Okinawa; Fukuoka and Nagasaki in Kyushu; Hiroshima, Nagoya, Niigata, and Sendai in Honshu; and Sapporo in Hokkaido.

Haneda Airport
W tokyo-haneda.com
Kansai International Airport
W kansai-airport.or.jp/en
Narita International Airport
W narita-airport.jp/en

Train Travel

Japan's rail system is one of the best in the world in terms of safety, efficiency, and comfort. The Japan Railways Group (JR) is the main operator and runs over 12,400 miles (20,000 km) of tracks, as well as the *shinkansen*. Often, multiple lines run between the same places. As well as the bullet trains, there are *tokkyu* ("limited express," the next fastest), *kyuko* ("express"), *kaisoku* (misleadingly called "rapid"), and *futsu* ("local").

The **Japan Rail Pass** is recommended for those planning to travel extensively, but there are also a whole host of regional rail passes, such as the **JR East Rail Pass** covering northeast Honshu. There are two types of **JR West Rail Pass**: the Sanyo Area Pass covers Osaka, Okayama, Hiroshima, and Hakata, while the Kansai Area Pass includes Osaka, Kobe, Kyoto, Himeji, and Nara.

Tickets and seat reservations for longer trips can be bought at JR stations, as well as from authorized travel agents. Seat reservations, which are charged at a small extra fee, are recommended for long-distance trips.

Japan Rail Pass
W japanrailpass.net
JR East Rail Pass
W jreast.co.jp
JR West Rail Pass
W westjr.co.jp

GETTING TO AND FROM THE AIRPORT

Airport	Bus	Taxi	Train	Express
Tokyo (Narita)	¥1,000 (90 mins)	¥20,000 (60 mins)	¥1,200 (90 mins)	¥3,070 (50 mins)
				¥2,520 (36 mins)
Tokyo (Haneda)	¥950 (55 mins)	¥8,000 (30 mins)	¥470 (30 mins)	None
Osaka (Kansai)	¥1,600 (60 mins)	¥15,000 (50 mins)	¥1,100 (70 mins)	¥2,500 (50 mins)

RAIL JOURNEY PLANNER

Plotting the country's main long-distance rail routes, this map is a handy reference for traveling between Japan's main towns and cities by train. Journey times, usually by *shinkansen,* are listed below.

Tokyo to Niigata	2.5 hrs
Tokyo to Nagoya	1.5 hrs
Tokyo to Osaka	2.5 hrs
Tokyo to Kyoto	2 hrs
Kyoto to Kanazawa	2.5 hrs
Kyoto to Matsue	4 hrs
Tokyo to Sapporo	8 hrs
Tokyo to Sendai	1.5 hrs
Sendai to Hakodate	3 hrs
Hakodate to Sapporo	3.5 hrs
Hakodate to Kushiro	7.5 hrs
Osaka to Hiroshima	1.5 hrs
Hiroshima to Fukuoka	1 hr
Fukuoka to Nagasaki	2 hrs
Fukuoka to Kumamoto	1 hr
Fukuoka to Beppu	2 hrs
Kumamoto to Kagoshima	1 hr

••• Direct train routes

Kushiro

Sapporo

Hakodate

Niigata

Sendai

Kanazawa

Kyoto

Nagoya

Tokyo

Matsue

Hiroshima

Osaka

Fukuoka

Beppu

Nagasaki

Kumamoto

Kagoshima

Long-Distance Bus Travel

The efficiency and extent of the rail network means that few visitors use long-distance coaches, but the bus network is comprehensive, and for those without a Japan Rail Pass, a bus is a much cheaper option than the train. While styles and services vary, coaches are uniformly comfortable, and often have toilets. For timetable details contact a local information centers or see **JR Bus Kanto**.

JR Bus Kanto
W jrbuskanto.co.jp.e.wn.hp.transer.com

Boats and Ferries

It is possible to travel to Japan by ferry from some parts of Asia, including Pusan in South Korea and Shanghai in China. The Far Eastern Shipping Line also connects Japan to Russia.

Ferries and boats are a great way to get around the island nation of Japan. Tickets for boats can be bought at the ferry terminal on the day of departure. Usually there is a form to fill in, which enables the ferry company to compile a list of passengers. The **Japan National Tourism Organization** (JNTO) produces a travel manual detailing the main services.

Japan National Tourism Organization
W japan.travel/en

Public Transportation

Most cities operate multiple transport services, comprising subway systems, buses, and even streetcars. Safety and hygiene measures, timetables, ticket information, transport maps, and more can be obtained at tourist information centers, stations, and municipal websites.

Tickets

Basic fare tickets for short distances are normally bought from ticket machines at stations. At major transportation hubs, these machines will have an English-translation button, and accept credit and debit cards. Most machines accept ¥1,000 and ¥5,000, some take ¥10,000 notes, and all give change. Many stations have maps in English, indicating the fares to destinations. If in doubt about the cost of a trip, simply buy a cheap ticket and pay any excess at the destination using the fare adjustment machine near the exit barrier. This machine will supply you with a new ticket. If there is no such machine, station staff will work out the additional charge; you will not be penalized for having the wrong-value ticket.

Many cities have their own special tickets, and local tourist information centers can provide information and advice. In Tokyo, there are a variety of options, including the "Free Kippu,"

which allows unlimited travel on most of the subway, bus, and streetcar lines in the city center for 24 hours. But, unless you are planning on making a lot of journeys in one day, use a Suica, or Pasmo, card instead. These electronic cards can be purchased from vending machines at many stations, as well as on the Japan Rail Pass website (p330). You can top them up, using cash, at these machines or on buses. These cards are valid on most forms of city transport. To use, simply hold your card up against the reader.

Subway

The Tokyo subway system is extensive with color-coded maps matching the color of the subway cars. Other cities, including Osaka, Nagoya, Kobe, Sendai, Yokohama, Fukuoka, Kyoto, and Sapporo, also have subway systems, but their modes of operation differ slightly.

The Japan Rail Pass cannot be used on any subway system. If you do not have a valid pass or reloadable card, buy a ticket from either a vending machine or a ticket window. If you are in any doubt about how much to pay, then simply buy the cheapest ticket and pay the excess at the end of your journey.

Station names are often displayed on platform signboards in romanized form as well as Japanese. All mass-transit systems stop running at around midnight until about 5am.

Streetcars

Modern and old-fashioned streetcars still run in quite a few Japanese cities, including Hiroshima, Nagasaki, Kumamoto, and Sapporo. Tokyo has two streetcar lines, and the Enoden Railway in Kamakura, south of Tokyo, is also classed as a streetcar. Fares and systems for paying on streetcars differ from city to city; some charge a flat fare irrespective of the distance traveled, while others have specific charges for different routes. The fare machine is sometimes manned separately. Follow the example of other passengers as to when to pay, and whether to pay the fare collector or put money into a box.

Bus

Bus depots (basu noriba) are often located outside of train stations in cities. The method of paying fares varies. Some buses are boarded at the front, and the fare – often a flat rate – is deposited into a slot beside the driver but most have card readers next to this slot. Exit from the door in the middle of the bus. A second system invites passengers to step aboard toward the center or back of the bus, where a machine distributes numbered tickets. The number on this ticket appears on a screen at the front of the bus, which corresponds to the fare to be paid. Before you disembark, drop the indicated amount and your ticket into the box beside the driver.

Taxis

Taxis come in various colors, but all have a "taxi" sign on the roof. A red sign to the left of the driver indicates that the taxi is available. You can flag a taxi on the street or look for a stand: they are invariably located near main stations. They are expensive, with rates starting at around ¥600–¥700 for the first mile. Fares increase per mile, and are higher at night and on weekends. Drivers operate taxi doors from inside so you do not need to bother opening and closing them. Few taxi drivers speak much English, so it is best to carry a map marked with instructions in Japanese and the phone number of your destination.

Driving

Japan is an enjoyable and safe country in which to take to the road. In the countryside, renting a car is usually the best way to get around.

Driving in Japan

Road surfaces are usually good, and rental cars are very well maintained. The main problem foreign drivers in Japan will face is navigation. It can be difficult trying to find one's way around Japan's towns and cities, which often have complex networks of one-way streets. Only main thoroughfares have names, and although rented cars are usually equipped with sat-nav systems, these are in Japanese.

Visitors must produce an international driver's license (International Driving Permit), but Japan does not recognize international driving permits from Switzerland, Germany, or Taiwan. However, drivers from these countries are instead allowed to drive in Japan for up to one year with an official Japanese translation of their license, which is available from the **Japan Automobile Federation**, or at their country's embassy or consulate in Japan.

Japan Automobile Federation
w jaf.or.jp/e

Car Rental

Vehicles are available for rental at ports of entry, major train stations, and local dealers. Car rental companies are generally not used to dealing with customers in English. Two companies more likely to have English-speaking staff are **Toyota Rent a Car** and **Nippon Rent-A-Car**. There is also a greater chance of finding English-speaking staff with international car agencies, such as **Avis, Budget** and **Hertz**.

Avis
w avisrentacar.jp
Budget
w budgetrentacar.co.jp/en
Hertz
w hertz.com

Nippon Rent-A-Car
w nrgroup-global.com/en
Toyota Rent a Car
w rent.toyota.co.jp/eng

Parking

Public parking is available but it tends to be expensive – and the parking fee rises as you move closer to a city center. There are cheaper car parks in neighborhoods on the city fringes, but these may be hidden away on backstreets and difficult to find. On-street parking is not permitted in Japan, and parking meters are a rarity. To overcome the problem of a lack of sufficient space, the Japanese have developed various innovative parking solutions, such as lifts and rollover systems.

Rules of the Road

For visitors who wish to acquaint themselves with driving conditions in Japan, the Japan Automobile Federation publishes "Rules of the Road" in five languages. This can be purchased for ¥1,000 from its regional offices, which are listed on its website.

The Japanese drive on the left side of the road. Drivers may not turn left on a red light. Drivers tend to be considerate while on the road, but although most drivers adhere to the laws, some tailgate, speed, and have a habit of driving over intersections after a light has turned red. It is not a good idea to follow suit. Vehicles to the front and rear should be observed carefully when approaching traffic lights.

Cycle Hire

As indicated by the often large bicycle parks outside big stations and the huge numbers of bikes parked on the streets of Japan's cities, cycling is an extremely popular way of getting around. There are often bicycle-rental companies in tourist areas. A good option in the capital is **Tokyobike Rentals**.

Sidewalks are frequently used by cyclists, despite the fact that it is illegal to do so. However, this is not strictly enforced and some towns prefer cyclists to use sidewalks rather than roads.

Tokyobike Rentals
w tokyobikerentals.com/en

Walking

From epic pilgrimages to city strolls, Japan rewards traveling on foot. Trails are maintained and well signposted. In cities, many sights are within walking distance. As you explore on two feet, you can absorb the streetlife, take in the architectural details, and peek into any café, shop or bar that catches your interest.

PRACTICAL INFORMATION

A little local know-how goes a long way in Japan. Here you will find all the essential advice and information you will need during your stay.

AT A GLANCE

EMERGENCY NUMBERS

GENERAL EMERGENCY

119

COAST GUARD

118

FIRE AND AMBULANCE

119

POLICE

110

TIME ZONE
JST
There is no daylight saving time.

TAP WATER
Unless stated otherwise, tap water in Japan is safe to drink.

WEBSITES AND APPS

Japan Times
Visit www.japantimes.co.jp for Japan's leading English-language newspaper.

Yomiwa App
Simply take a picture of any Japanese text and this clever app will translate it, no Internet connection needed.

HyperDia App
A travel planning app, providing up-to-date information for Japan's rail network.

Personal Security

Japan is a relatively safe country to visit. Thefts and muggings are rare, but there are sporadic incidents of bag-snatching and pick-pocketing in crowded areas. It is generally safe to walk around at night, but be careful in Tokyo's Roppongi and Kabukicho entertainment districts.

If you have anything stolen, report the crime within 24 hours to the nearest police station and take ID with you. Contact your embassy if you have your passport stolen, or in the event of a serious crime or accident.

As a rule, the Japanese are very accepting of all people, regardless of their race, gender, or sexuality, but even the cities aren't particularly multicultural, and staring is commonplace.

Homosexuality was criminalized in Japan in 1872, but the law was repealed seven years later. Despite this historic acceptance, same-sex marriages are still not legally recognized.

LGBT+ travelers are unlikely to encounter any problems in Japan. Public displays of affection between both straight and same-sex couples are frowned upon by some Japanese people, but less so in Tokyo. **Utopia Asia** is a comprehensive guide to Japan's LGBT+ scene.
Utopia Asia
w utopia-asia.com

Health

Japan has a world-class health system, but medical expenses can be extremely high. It is therefore important to arrange comprehensive medical insurance before traveling. If you are sick while in Japan, consult a doctor at a local clinic; for minor problems, see a pharmacist. For medical services in Tokyo, see **Himawari**, which is run by the Metropolitan Government.
Himawari
w himawari.metro.tokyo.jp

Smoking, Alcohol, and Drugs

Japan has a zero-tolerance policy toward the possession of even small amounts of narcotics. The punishment is a jail sentence and heavy fine.

Japan has a strict limit of 0.03 per cent BAC (blood alcohol content) for drivers. If a driver exceeds this limit, they will face a heavy fine and up to five years in prison.

In many Tokyo wards, smoking on the street is banned (sometimes punishable by on the spot fines, although a warning is more common), except in designated areas. Smoking is banned on buses and trains (except for some long-distance trains, such as *shinkansen*, which have smoking cars), as well as in stations, schools, hospitals, and public institutions, but smoking is still permitted in many bars and restaurants.

ID

You must carry your passport or residence card with you at all times. A photocopy of your passport photo page (and visa if applicable) should suffice.

Local Customs

The traditional greeting in Japan is a bow, its depth reflecting the relative status of participants. Visitors, however, rarely need to bow; a handshake is fine. In many situations, bows are part of the service, for instance in elevators, stores, restaurants, and hotels. They can be met with a brief smile. If you feel the need to bow, hold your arms and back straight, bend from the waist, and pause for a moment at the low point.

Shoes are an important element of etiquette. The principle is not to bring dirt from outside into the interior. If shoes are prohibited somewhere, there will usually be a lowered *genkan*, or entryway area in front of the door, where you take off your shoes and put on slippers. If no slippers are provided, or if they are too small, you can wear socks. As a general rule, no footwear – even slippers – should be worn on tatami matting.

Historically, tattoos have been associated with *yakuza* (mafia) and some *onsen* don't allow people with tattoos. In the run up to the Rugby World Cup and the Olympics, the Japanese government implemented measures to ensure that people with tattoos would be able to use hot springs and public baths, but it's still good to check with individual *onsen* before visiting.

There are several rules for table manners to be observed when using chopsticks. If you touch food in a communal dish with your chopsticks, you must then take it. Gesturing and pointing with them is seen as bad manners. It is taboo to pass food directly from one set of chopsticks to another as this is associated with funerary rites, although it is acceptable to use them to place food on another's plate. For similar reasons, inserting both chopsticks vertically into a bowl of rice is also taboo.

Bodily emissions are considered very rude, though anything drawn inward is acceptable – therefore, sniffing is fine, but blowing your nose in public is not.

Visiting Temples and Shrines

The atmosphere in Buddhist temples and Shinto shrines is informal, and there are no clothing restrictions. Visitors should show respect, and not be noisy, but there are few of the taboos found in some other Buddhist nations. Remember to remove your shoes when you enter sacred buildings.

Cell Phones and Wi-Fi

Foreign cell phones may not work in Japan. Check with your cell operator before traveling. If you aren't covered, you can rent a cell phone, SIM card, or Wi-Fi router from companies such as **Softbank Global Rental**. Some cafés offer free or inexpensive WiFi.
Softbank Global Rental
W softbank-rental.jp

Post

Post offices (*yubin-kyoku*) and mailboxes are identified by the character looking like a "T" with an extra horizontal bar across the top. Stamps are also sold at convenience stores.

Taxes and Refunds

Visitors must pay a ¥1,000 tourist departure tax. A consumption tax of 10 per cent is charged on goods and services. Claiming back this money is relatively simple. There is no need to show customs your products and receipts at the airport; instead, you can apply for a cash refund as soon as you have made a purchase at one of the tax refund counters found in shopping centers and malls.

INDEX

Page numbers in **bold** refer to main entries.

21st Century Museum of Contemporary Art (Kanazawa) **166**
88-Temple Pilgrimage (Shikoku) 60, **258-9**

PHRASE BOOK

The Japanese language is related to Okinawan and is similar to Altaic languages such as Mongolian and Turkish. Written Japanese uses a combination of three scripts: Chinese ideograms, known as *kanji*, and two syllable-based alphabet systems known as *hiragana* and *katakana*. These two latter are similar, *katakana* mainly to transcribe non-Japanese words. Traditionally, Japanese is written in vertical columns from top right to bottom left, though the Western system is increasingly used. There are several romanization systems; a simplified version of the Hepburn system is used as the base for this guide. To simplify romanization, macrons (long marks over vowels to indicate longer pronunci-ation) have not been used. Japanese pronunciation is fairly straightforward, and many words are "Japanized" versions of Western words. This phrase book gives the English word or phrase, followed by the Japanese script, then the romanization.

GUIDELINES FOR PRONUNCIATION

When reading the romanization, give the same emphasis to all syllables. The practice in English of giving one syllable greater stress may render a Japanese word incomprehensible.

Pronounce vowels as in these English words:

a	as the "a" in "cap"
e	as in "red"
i	as in "chief"
o	as in "solid"
u	as the "oo" in "cuckoo"

When two vowels are used together, give each letter an individual sound:

ai	as in "pine"
ae	as if written "ah-eh"
ei	as in "pay"

Consonants are pronounced as in English. The letter *g* is always hard as in "gate," and *j* is always soft as in "joke." *R* is pronounced something between r and l. Similarly, *f* is pronounced somewhere between *f* and *h*. Whereas "*SI*" always becomes "*shi*," and *V* in Western words (e.g. "video") becomes *b*. If followed by the consonants b, p, or m, *n* usually becomes *m*, although there are some exceptions to this rule.

All consonants except *n* are always either followed by a vowel or doubled; however, sometimes an *i* or *u* is barely pronounced.

DIALECTS

Standard Japanese is used and understood throughout Japan by people of all backgrounds. But on a colloquial level, there are significant differences in both pronunciation and vocabulary, even between the Tokyo and Osaka-Kyoto areas, and rural accents are very strong.

POLITE WORDS AND PHRASES

There are several different levels of politeness in the Japanese language, according to status, age, and situation. In everyday conversation, politeness is largely a question of the length of verb endings (the longer *masu* ending is, as a rule, more polite), but in formal conversation you will notice that entirely different words and phrases (*keigo*) are used. As a visitor, you may find that people try to speak to you in formal language, but there is no need to use it yourself; the level given in this Phrase Book is neutral yet polite.

IN AN EMERGENCY

Help!	助けて！	Tasukete!
Stop!	止めて！	Tomete!
Call a doctor!	医者を 呼んでください！	Isha o yonde kudasai!
Call an ambulance!	救急車を 呼んでください！	Kyukyusha o yonde kudasai!
Call the police!	警察を 呼んでください！	Keisatsu o yonde kudasai!
Fire!	火事！	Kaji!
Where is the hospital?	病院はどこに ありますか？	Byoin wa doko ni arimasu ka?
police box	交番	koban

COMMUNICATION ESSENTIALS

Yes/no.	はい／いいえ	Hai/iie.
... not ...	・・・ない／・・・ません	... nai/ ... masen
I don't know.	知りません。	Shirimasen.
Thank you.	ありがとう。	Arigato.
Thank you very much.	ありがとう ございます。	Arigato gozaimasu.
Thank you very much indeed.	どうもありがとう ございます。	Domo arigato gozaimasu.
Thanks (casual).	どうも。	Domo.
No, thank you.	結構です。	Kekko desu.
Please (offering).	どうぞ。	Dozo.
Please (asking).	お願いします。	Onegai shimasu.
Please (give me or do for me).	・・・ください。	... kudasai.
I don't understand.	わかりません。	Wakarimasen.
Do you speak English?	英語を 話せますか？	Eigo o hanesemasu ka?
I can't speak Japanese.	日本語は 話せません。	Nihongo wa hanasemasen.
Please speak more slowly.	もう少しゆっくり 話してください。	Mo sukoshi yukkuri hanashite kudasai.
Sorry/Excuse me!	すみません。	Sumimasen!
Could you help. me please? (not emergency)	ちょっと手伝って いただけませんか？	Chotto tetsudatte itadakemasen ka?

USEFUL PHRASES

My name is	私の 名前は・・・です。	Watashi no namae wa ...desu.
How do you do, pleased to meet you.	はじめまして、 どうぞよろしく。	Hajimemashite, dozo yoroshiku.
How are you?	お元気ですか？	Ogenki desu ka?
Good morning.	おはようございます。	Ohayo gozaimasu.
Hello/good afternoon.	こんにちは。	Konnichiwa.
Good evening.	こんばんは。	Konbanwa.
Good night.	おやすみなさい。	Oyasumi nasai.
Good-bye.	さよなら。	Sayonara.
Take care.	気をつけて。	Ki o tsukete.
Keep well (casual).	お元気で。	Ogenki de.
The same to you.	そちらも。	Sochira mo.
What is (this)?	(これは) 何 ですか？	(Kore wa) nan desu ka?
How do you use this?	これをどうやって 使いますか？	Kore o doyatte tsukaimasu ka?
Could I possibly have ...? (very polite)	・・・をいただけますか？	... o itadakemasu ka?
Is there ... here?	ここに・・・が ありますか？	Koko ni ... ga arimasu ka?
Where can I get ...?	・・・はどこに ありますか？	... wa doko ni arimasu ka?
How much is it?	いくらですか？	Ikura desu ka?
What time is ...?	・・・何時ですか？	... nanji desu ka?
Cheers! (toast)	乾杯！	Kampai!
Where is the restroom/toilet?	お手洗い／おトイレは どこですか？	Otearai/otoire wa doko desu ka?
Here's my business card.	名刺をどうぞ。	Meishi o dozo.

USEFUL WORDS

I	私	watashi
woman	女性	josei
man	男性	dansei

wife	奥さん	okusan
husband	主人	shujin
daughter	娘	musume
son	息子	musuko
child	子供	kodomo
children	子供たち	kodomotachi
businessman/	ビジネスマン／	bijinessuman/
woman	ウーマン	wuman
student	学生	gakusei
Mr./Mrs./Ms. ...	・・・さん	...-san
big/small	大きい／小さい	okii/chiisai
hot/cold	暑い／寒い	atsui/samui
cold (to touch)	冷たい	tsumetai
warm	温かい	atatakai
good/	いい／	ii/
not good/	よくない／悪い	yokunai/warui
bad		
enough	じゅうぶん／結構	jubun/kekko
free (no charge)	ただ／無料	tada/muryo
here	ここ	koko
there	あそこ	asoko
this	これ	kore
that (nearby)	それ	sore
that (far away)	あれ	are
what?	何？	nani?
when?	いつ？	itsu?
why?	なぜ／どうして？	naze?/doshite?
where?	どこ？	doko?
who?	誰？	dare?
which?	どちら？	dochira?

SIGNS

open	営業中	eigyo-chu
closed	休日	kyujitsu
entrance	入口	iriguchi
exit	出口	deguchi
danger	危険	kiken
emergency	非常口	hijo-guchi
exit		
information	案内	annai
restroom, toilet	お手洗い／手洗い／	otearai/tearai/
	おトイレ／トイレ	otoire/toire
free (vacant)	空き	aki
men	男	otoko
women	女	onna

MONEY

Could you	これを円に	Kore o en ni
change this into	替えてください？	kaete kudasai?
yen please?		
I'd like to cash	この	Kono
these travelers'	トラベラーズチェック	toraberazu
checks.	を現金にしたいです。	chekku o genkin ni shitai desu.
Do you take	クレジットカード／	Kurejitto-kado/
credit cards/	トラベラーズチェックで	toraberazu-chekku
travelers'	払えますか？	de haraemasu ka?
checks?		
bank	銀行	ginko
cash	現金	genkin
credit card	クレジットカード	kurejitto-kado
currency	両替所	ryogaejo
exchange office		
dollars	ドル	doru
pounds	ポンド	pondo
yen	円	en

KEEPING IN TOUCH

Where is a	電話はどこに	Denwa wa doko ni
telephone?	ありますか？	arimasu ka?
May I use your	電話を使っても	Denwa o tsukatte
phone?	いいですか？	mo ii desu ka?
Hello, this is ...	もしもし、・・・です。	Moshi-moshi, ...desu.
I'd like to make	国際電話、	Kokusai denwa,
an international	お願いします。	onegaishimasu.
call.		
airmail	航空便	kokubin

e-mail	イーメール	i-meru
fax	ファックス	fakkusu
postcard	ハガキ	hagaki
post office	郵便局	yubin-kyoku
stamp	切手	kitte
telephone booth	公衆電話	koshu denwa
telephone card	テレフォンカード	terefon-kado

SHOPPING

Where can I	・・・はどこで	... wa doko de
buy ...?	買えますか？	kaemasu ka?
How much does	いくらですか？	Ikura desu ka?
this cost?		
I'm just looking.	見ているだけです。	Mite iru dake desu.
Do you have ...?	・・・ありますか？	... arimasu ka?
May I try this	着てみても	Kite mite mo
on?	いいですか？	ii desu ka?
Please show me	それを	Sore o
that.	見せてください。	misete kudasai.
Does it come in	他の色も	Hoka no iro mo
other colors?	ありますか？	arimasu ka?
black	黒	kuro
blue	青	ao
green	緑	midori
red	赤	aka
white	白	shiro
yellow	黄色	kiiro
cheap/expensive	安い／高い	yasui/takai
audio equipment	オーディオ製品	odio seihin
bookstore	本屋	honya-ya
boutique	ブティック	butikku
clothes	洋服	yofuku
department store	デパート	depato
electrical store	電気屋	denki-ya
fish market	魚屋	sakana-ya
folk crafts	民芸品	mingei-hin
ladies' wear	婦人服	fujin fuku
local specialty	名物	meubutsu
market	市場	ichiba
menswear	紳士服	shinshi fuku
newsstand	新聞屋	shimbun-ya
pharmacist	薬屋	kusuri-ya
picture postcard	絵葉書	e-hagaki
sale	セール	seru
souvenir shop	お土産屋	omiyage-ya
supermarket	スーパー	supa
travel agent	旅行会社	ryoko-gaisha

SIGHTSEEING

Where is ...?	・・・はどこですか？	... wa doko desu ka?
How do I get	・・・へは、どうやって	... wa doyatte
to ...?	いったらいいですか？	ittara ii desu ka?
Is it far?	遠いですか？	Toi desu ka?
art gallery	美術館	bijitsukan
reservations	予約窓口	yoyaku-madoguchi
desk		
bridge	橋	hashi/bashi
castle	城	shiro/jo
city	市	shi
city center	町の中心	machi no chushin
gardens	庭園／庭	teien/niwa
hot spring	温泉	onsen
information	案内所	annaijo
office		
island	島	shima/jima
monastery	修道院	shudo-in
mountain	山	yama/san
museum	博物館	hakubutsukan
palace	宮殿	kyuden
park	公園	koen
port	港	minato/ko
prefecture	県	ken
river	川	kawa/gawa
ruins	遺跡	iseki
shopping area	ショッピング街	shoppingu-gai

shrine	神社／神宮／宮	jinja/jingu/gu
street	通り	tori/dori
temple	お寺／寺	otera/tera/dera/ji
tour, travel	旅行	ryoko
town	町	machi/cho
village	村	mura
ward	区	ku
zoo	動物園	dobutsu-en
north	北	kita/hoku
south	南	minami/nan
east	東	higashi/to
west	西	nishi/sei
left/right	左／右	hidari/migi
straight ahead	真っ直ぐ	massugu
between	間に	aida ni
near/far	近い／遠い	chikai/toi
up/down (top/bottom)	上／下	ue/shita
new	新しい／新	atarashii/shin
old/former	古い／元	furui/moto
upper/lower	上／下	kami/shimo
middle/inner	中	naka
in	に／中に	ni/naka ni
in front of	前	mae

GETTING AROUND

bicycle	自転車	jidensha
bus	バス	basu
car	車	kuruma
ferry	フェリー	feri
baggage room	手荷物一時預かり所	tenimotsu ichiji azukarijo
motorcycle	オートバイ	otobai
one-way ticket	片道切符	katamachi kippu
return ticket	往復切符	ofuku kippu
taxi	タクシー	takushi
ticket	切符	kippu
ticket office	切符売場	kippu uriba

TRAINS

What is the fare to ...?	・・・まで いくらですか？	... made ikura desu ka?
When does the train for... leave?	・・・行きの電車は、何時にでますか？	... yuki no densha wa nanji ni desu ka?
How long does it take to get to ...?	・・・までの時間は どのくらい かかりますか？	... made jikan wa dono gurai kakarimasu ka?
A ticket to ..., please.	・・・行きの切符を ください。	... yuki no kippu o kudasai.
Do I have to change?	乗り換えが 必要ですか？	Norikae ga hitsuyo desu ka?
I'd like to reserve a seat, please.	席を 予約したいです。	Seki o yoyaku shitai desu.
Which platform for the train to ...?	・・・行きの電車は、何番ホームですか？	... yuki no densha wa nanban homu desu ka?
Which station is this?	ここは、どの駅ですか？	Koko wa dono eki desu ka?
Is this the right train for ...?	・・・へは、この電車で いいですか？	... e wa kono densha de ii desu ka?
bullet train	新幹線	shinkansen
express trains:		
"limited express" (fastest)	特急	tokkyu
"express" (second)	急行	kyuko
"rapid" (third)	快速	kaisoku
first-class	グリーン車／一等	gurinsha/itto
line	線	sen
local train	普通／各駅電車	futsu/kaku-ekidensha
platform	ホーム	homu
train station	駅	eki
reserved seat	指定席	shitei-seki
second-class	二等	nito

subway	地下鉄	chikatetsu
train	電車	densha
unreserved seat	自由席	jiyu-seki

ACCOMMODATIONS

Do you have any vacancies?	部屋がありますか？	Heya ga arimasu ka?
I have a reservation.	予約を してあります。	Yoyaku o shite arimasu.
I'd like a room with a bathroom.	お風呂付の部屋 お願いします。	Ofuro-tsuki no heya, onegaishimasu.
What is the charge per night?	一泊 いくらですか？	Ippaku ikura desu ka?
Is tax included in the price?	税込みですか？	Zeikomi desu ka?
Can I leave my luggage here for a little while?	荷物をここに ちょっと預けても いいですか？	Nimotsu o koko ni chotto azuketmo ii desu ka?
air-conditioning	冷房／エアコン	reibo/eakon
bath	お風呂	ofuro
check-out	チェックアウト	chekku-auto
hair drier	ドライヤー	doraiya
hot (boiled) water	お湯	oyu
Japanese-style inn	旅館	ryokan
Japanese-style room	和室	washitsu
key	鍵	kagi
front desk	フロント	furonto
single/ twin room	シングル／ ツイン	shinguru/ tsuin
shower	シャワー	shawa
Western-style hotel	ホテル	hoteru
Western-style room	洋室	yoshitsu

EATING OUT

A table for one/two/three, please.	一人／二人 三人、 お願いします。	Hitori/futari/ sannin, onegaishimasu.
May I see the menu?	メニュー、 お願いします？	Menyu, onegaishimasu?
Is there a set menu?	定食が。 ありますか？	Teishoku ga arimasu ka?
I'd like	私は・・・が いいです。	Watashi wa ... ga ii desu.
May I have one of those?	それをひとつ、 お願いします？	Sore o hitotsu, onegaishimasu?
I am a vegetarian.	私は ベジタリアンです。	Watashi wa bejitarian desu.
Waiter/waitress!	ちょっと すみません！	Chotto sumimasen!
What would you recommend?	おすすめは 何ですか？	Osusume wa nan desu ka?
How do you eat this?	これは、どうやて 食べますか？	Kore wa, doyatte tabemasu ka?
May we have the check please.	お勘定、 お願いします。	Okanjo, onegaishimasu.
May we have some more ...	もっと・・・、 お願いします。	Motto ..., onegaishimasu.
The meal was very good, thank you.	ごちそうさまでした、 おいしかったです。	Gochiso-sama deshita, oishikatta desu.
assortment	盛り合わせ	moriwase
boxed meal	弁当	bento
breakfast	朝食	choshoku
buffet	バイキング	baikingu
delicious	おいしい	oishii
dinner	夕食	yushoku
to drink	飲む	nomu
a drink	飲み物	nomimono
to eat	食べる	taberu

food	食べ物／ごはん	tabemono/gohan
full (stomach)	おなかがいっぱい	onaka ga ippai
hot/cold	熱い／冷たい	atsui/tsumetai
hungry	おなかがすいた	onaka ga suita
Japanese food	和食	washoku
lunch	昼食	chushoku
set menu	セット／定食	setto/teishoku
spicy	辛い	karai
sweet, mild	甘い	amai
Western food	洋食	yoshoku

PLACES TO EAT

Cafeteria/canteen	食堂	shokudo
Chinese restaurant	中華料理屋	chuka-ryori-ya
coffee shop/cafe	喫茶店／カフェ	kissaten/kafe
local bar	飲み屋／居酒屋	nomi-ya/izakaya
noodle stall	ラーメン屋	ramen-ya
restaurant	レストラン／料理屋	resutoran/ryori-ya
sushi on a conveyor belt	回転寿司	kaiten-zushi
upscale restaurant	料亭	ryotei
upscale vegetarian restaurant	精進料理屋	shojin-ryori-ya

FOODS

apple	りんご	ringo
bamboo shoots	たけのこ	takenoko
beancurd (tofu)	豆腐	tofu
bean sprouts	もやし	moyashi
beans	豆	mame
beef	ビーフ／牛肉	bifu/gyuniku
beefburger (patty)	ハンバーグ	hanbagu
blowfish	ふぐ	fugu
bonito, tuna	かつお／ツナ	katsuo/tsuna
bread	パン	pan
butter	バター	bata
cake	ケーキ	keki
chicken	とり／鶏肉	tori/toriniku
confectionery	お菓子	okashi
crab	かに	kani
duck	カモ	kamo
eel	うなぎ	unagi
egg	卵	tamago
eggplant/aubergine	なす	nasu
fermented soybean paste	みそ	miso
fermented soybeans	納豆	natto
fish (raw)	刺身	sashimi
fried tofu	油揚げ	abura-age
fruit	くだもの	kudamono
ginger	しょうが	shoga
hamburger	ハンバーガー	hambaga
haute cuisine	会席	kaiseki
herring	ニシン	nishin
hors d'oeuvres	オードブル	odoburu
ice cream	アイスクリーム	aisu-kurimu
jam	ジャム	jamu
Japanese mushrooms	まつたけ／しいたけ／しめじ	mats'take/shiitake/shimeji

Japanese pear	梨	nashi
loach	どじょう	dojo
lobster	伊勢海老	ise-ebi
mackerel	さば	saba
mackerel pike	さんま	samma
mandarin orange	みかん	mikan
meat	肉	niku
melon	メロン	meron
mountain vegetables	山菜	sansai
noodles:		
buckwheat	そば	soba
Chinese	ラーメン	ramen
wheatflour	うどん／そうめん	udon (fat)/somen (thin)
octopus	たこ	tako
omelet	オムレツ	omuretsu
oyster	カキ	kaki
peach	桃	momo
pepper	こしょう	kosho
persimmon	柿	kaki
pickles	漬物	tsukemono
pork	豚肉	butaniku
potato	ジャガイモ	jagaimo
rice:		
cooked	ごはん	gohan
uncooked	米	kome
rice crackers	おせんべい	osembei
roast beef	ローストビーフ	rosutobifu
salad	サラダ	sarada
salmon	鮭	sake
salt	塩	shio
sandwich	サンドイッチ	sandoichi
sausage	ソーセージ	soseji
savory nibbles	おつまみ	otsumami
seaweed:		
laver (dried)	のり	nori
kelp (chewy)	こんぶ	kombu
shrimp	海老	ebi
soup	汁／スープ	shiru/supu
soy sauce	しょうゆ	shoyu
spaghetti	スパゲティ	supageti
spinach	ほうれん草	horenso
squid	いか	ika
steak	ステーキ	suteki
sugar	砂糖	sato
sushi (mixed)	五目寿司	gomoku-zushi
sweetfish/smelt	鮎	ayu
taro (potato)	里芋	sato imo
toast	トースト	tosuto
trout	鱒	masu
sea urchin	ウニ	uni
vegetables	野菜	yasai
watermelon	すいか	suika
wild boar	ぼたん／いのしし	botan/inoshishi

DRINKS

beer	ビール	biru
coffee (hot)	ホットコーヒー	hotto-kohi
cola	コーラ	kora
green tea	お茶	ocha
iced coffee:		
black	アイスコーヒー	aisu-kohi
with milk	アイスオーレ	kafe-o-re
lemon tea	レモンティー	remon ti
milk	ミルク／牛乳	miruku/gyunyu
mineral water	ミネラルウォーター	mineraru uota
orange juice	オレンジジュース	orenji jusu
rice wine (non-alcoholic)	酒（甘酒）	sake (ama-zake)
tea (Western-style)	紅茶	kocha

tea with milk	ミルクティー	miruku ti
water	水	mizu
whisky	ウイスキー	uisuki
wine	ワイン／ぶどう酒	wain/budoshu

HEALTH

I don't feel well.	気分が よくないです。	Kibun ga yokunai desu.
I have a pain in …	･･･が痛いです。	… ga itai desu.
I'm allergic to …	･･･アレルギーです。	… arerugi desu.
asthma	喘息	zensoku
cough	咳	seki
dentist	歯医者	haisha
diabetes	糖尿病	tonyo-byo
diarrhea	下痢	geri
doctor	医者	isha
fever	熱	netsu
headache	頭痛	zutsuu
hospital	病院	byoin
medicine	薬	kusuri
Oriental medicine	漢方薬	kampo yaku
pharmacy	薬局	yakkyoku
prescription	処方箋	shohosen
stomachache	腹痛	fukutsu
toothache	歯が痛い	ha ga itai

NUMBERS

Number	Japanese	Romaji
0	ゼロ	zero
1	一	ichi
2	二	ni
3	三	san
4	四	yon/shi
5	五	go
6	六	roku
7	七	nana/shichi
8	八	hachi
9	九	kyu
10	十	ju
11	十一	ju-ichi
12	十二	ju-ni
20	二十	ni-ju
21	二十一	ni-ju-ichi
22	二十二	ni-ju-ni
30	三十	san-ju
40	四十	yon-ju
100	百	hyaku
101	百一	hyaku-ichi
200	二百	ni-hyaku
300	三百	san-byaku
400	四百	yon-hyaku
500	五百	go-hyaku
600	六百	roppyaku
700	七百	nana-hyaku
800	八百	happyaku
900	九百	kyu-hyaku
1,000	千	sen
1,001	千一	sen-ichi
2,000	二千	ni-sen
10,000	一万	ichi-man
20,000	二万	ni-man
100,000	十万	ju-man
1,000,000	百万	hyaku-man
123,456	十二万三千 四百五十六	ju-ni-man-san-zen- yon-hyaku-go- ju-roku

TIME

Monday	月曜日	getsuyobi
Tuesday	火曜日	kayobi
Wednesday	水曜日	suiyobi
Thursday	木曜日	mokuyobi
Friday	金曜日	kinyobi
Saturday	土曜日	doyobi
Sunday	日曜日	nichiyobi
January	一月	ichi-gatsu
February	二月	ni-gatsu
March	三月	san-gatsu
April	四月	shi-gatsu
May	五月	go-gatsu
June	六月	roku-gatsu
July	七月	shichi-gatsu
August	八月	hachi-gatsu
September	九月	ku-gatsu
October	十月	ju-gatsu
November	十一月	ju-ichi-gatsu
December	十二月	ju-ni-gatsu
spring	春	haru
summer	夏	natsu
fall/autumn	秋	aki
winter	冬	fuyu
noon	正午	shogo
midnight	真夜中	mayonaka
today	今日	kyo
yesterday	昨日	kino
tomorrow	明日	ashita
this morning	今朝	kesa
this afternoon	今日の午後	kyo no gogo
this evening	今晩	konban
every day	毎日	mainichi
month	月	getsu/tsuki
hour	時	ji
time/hour (duration)	時間	jikan
minute	分	pun/fun
this year	今年	kotoshi
last year	去年	kyonen
next year	来年	rainen
one year	一年	ichi-nen
late	遅い	osoi
early	早い	hayai
soon	すぐ	sugu

ACKNOWLEDGMENTS

DK would like to thank the following for their contribution to the previous edition: Masumi Kamozaki, Helen Peters, Simon Scott, Matthew Wilcox

The publisher would like to thank the following for their kind permission to reproduce their photographs:

Key: a-above; b-below/bottom; c-centre; f-far; l-left; r-right; t-top

123RF.com: 126-7t; Steve AllenUK 65br; Leonid Andronov 214t; Nattee Chalermtiragool 152t; David Crane 71c; Diego Grandi 186bl; jaimax 268bl; kawamuralucy 114tl; liligraphie 40-1b; Sanchai Loongroong 309tr; Luciano Mortula 186crb, 217bl; mtaira 173bl; oleandra 82-3; ookinate23 39crb; Sean Pavone 235tl; PaylessImages 41crb; Chan Richie 286crb; Pandech Saleewong 34tl; Sompob Tapaopong 253t; tomas1111 132c; Yiu Tung Lee 220tr; tupungato 32cr; yusukerf 43tr.

4Corners: Massimo Borchi 136; Maurizio Rellini 326-7.

Alamy Stock Photo: Stuart Abraham 43cl; AF archive 47cl; Aflo Co. Ltd. 11br, 55tr, 59crb, 62b, 66-7t, / Hiroyuki Sato 28cr, / Nippon News 255tr / Ben Weller 70br; age fotostock / Javier Larrea 201b; All Canada Photos 38-9t; ART Collection 73cb, 224fbl; Askanioff 216clb; David Ball 310t; Mark Bassett 13br; Patrick Batchelder 8cl; Blue Jean Images 254tr, 308tl; Tibor Bognar 160br, 162bl, 242br; Dominic Byrne 322-3t; Pocholo Calapre 36tc; Nano Calvo / © 2010 Olafur Eliasson Colour activity house, 2010 166-7t; Jui-Chi Chan 119t; David Cherepuschak 175tr; Chon Kit Leong 202-3t; Trevor Chriss 74cb; Chronicle 75tr, 75cr, 240tr; Classic Image 73br, 74-5t; coward_lion 46-7b, 170c, 195t, 198tl; Terry Donnelly 324b; Paul Dymond 291br; EDU Vision 141bl, 241tr, 300bc, 308br; Ei Katsumata - FLP 244; Robert Evans 4, 134br; Everett Collection Historical 76tl; F1online digitale Bildagentur GmbH / D.Fernandez & M.Peck 323br; Malcolm Fairman 73tl, 190bl; FantasticJapan 157tr; Food for Thought 140bl; Fabio Formaggio 61cl; Granger Historical Picture Archive 74tl; Harry Green 87cra; Hemis 93br, 111crb, 194clb, 306tl; Brent Hofacker 61br; Camilla Hohmann 290bc; Horizon Images / Motion 231ca, 279tr; Peter Horree 111cr; Image navi - QxQ images 43crb, 140cl, 293t; imageBROKER 193tr; JeffG 88clb; Haiyun Jiang 72bc; jirobkk 312bl; John Frost Newspapers 76cr; Jon Arnold Images Ltd 320bc; Juite Wen 172t; Yoshiyuki Kaneko 311br; Keystone Pictures USA 86tr; Hideo Kurihara 111bl, 114br; Lebrecht Music & Arts 47tr, 73tr, 76bc; Chu-Wen Lin 318clb; Cseh Loan 197bl; LOOK Die Bildagentur der Fotografen GmbH 159b, / Axel Schwab 168b; Ivan Marchuk 72br; Iain Masterton 61tr, 63br, 107, 235br, 240b; Michael Matthews 226bl; mauritius images GmbH 22t, 92t, 196b, / Jose Fuste Raga 116-7b; Mint Images Limited 54-5b, 55br; Trevor Mogg 237tr; Moonie's World 119cra; Tuul and Bruno Morandi 243br; Geoffrey Morgan 265cl; myLAM 92bl; paolo negri 307cra; Newscom 44br, 106clb, 110–111t, / BJ Warnick 196cr; Nic Cleave Photography 233br; Niday Picture Library 72t; Old Paper Studios 75clb; Panther Media GmbH / Pius Lee 171bl; Alberto Paredes 184tr; Sean Pavone 12-3b, 118br, 135, 170t, 188bl, 190-1t, 194bl, 198-9b, 238-9b, 256br, 274b, 278-9b, 313t, 318b, 320t; Miguel A. Muñoz Pellicer 121t; Photononstop 25tr, / © Estate of George Rickey / VAGA at ARS, NY and DACS, London 2019 Three Squares Vertical Diagonal, 2007 250-1b; Prisma by Dukas Presseagentur GmbH 76crb, 130tl, 219tr, / Raga Jose Fuste 145b; PUMPKIN at Benesse Art Site Naoshima / Akira Suemori 68tl; QEDimages 200bl; Alex Ramsay 198c; Cheryl Rinzler 67cla; Magda Rittenhouse 69br; robertharding 67crb, 276tl, 325t; Ian Robinson 259br; Thomas Kyhn Rovsing Hjørnet 52-3t; Ralph Rozema 159c; Pietro Scòzzari 287tl; Alex Segre 130-1b; Skye Hohmann Japan Images 174cr; SOURCENEXT 13t, 56-7t, / MIXA 97clb; dave stamboulis 321bl, 322clb; John Steele 97b, 258clb; StockFood Ltd. 140cla; StockShot 319tr; Jeremy Sutton-Hibbert 52bl, 65cl; TCD / Prod.DB 46tl; The Picture Art Collection 68-9b, 73cla, 128crb; Top Photo Corporation 269b; Travel 53br; travelbild-asia 128-9t; Jorge Tutor 131tr; Leisa Tyler 30crb; Lucas Vallecillos 10clb, 59tr, 71br, 115t, 192b, 202bl, 231ca, 248tr; Ivan Vdovin 128bl, 131clb; Chris Willson 12clb, 280, 293cl; Peter M. Wilson 98bl; World Discovery 70bl, 109br, 113tr; World History Archive 216fclb, 224fbr, 287br; Masayuki Yamashita 45cl, 89br, 142-3; Ka Wing Yu 271tl; Philipp Zechner 311tr.

AWL Images: Jan Christopher Becke 290-1t; Marco Gaiotti 17t, 148-9; Gavin Hellier 191cra.

Bridgeman Images: Pictures from History 224bl.

Depositphotos Inc: javarman 177tr; kadsada23@gmail.com 288t; leungchopan 276br; nicholashan 30t; parody 301tl; sepavone 215cr; Torsakarin 2-3; yoshiyayo 77cb.

Dreamstime.com: Aaa187 229; Leonid Andronov 37bl; Sittichan Ausavakornthanarat 34-5ca; Kristopher Bason 21, 314-5; Beatricesirinun 24cla; Bennnn 53cl; Bennymarty 12t, 26crb, 63cl, 90t, 116tl, 155cra, 156-7b; Shubhashish Chakrabarty 169tr; Checco 228clb; Cowardlion 86-7b, 143bl, 163tl, 203clb, 302clb, 302cb, 302bc, 305tl; Leo Daphne 51br, 266br; Eudaemon 115cr; Eyeblink 292b; F11photo 309b; Ioana Grecu 36-7t; Angela Ho 41cl; Thomas Humeau 74br; Ixuskmitl 206bl, 272-3b; Jonkio4 87tl; Kan1234 57br, 270br; Thitichot Katawutpoonpun 275tl; Patryk Kosmider 204bl; Kuremo 142bl; Erik Lattwein 49bl; Chon Kit Leong 232bl; Bo Li 65tr; Lumppini 50-1b; Luciano Mortula 218-9t; Mosaymay 32crb; Mrnovel 28bl, 216crb; Roland Nagy 8cla; Naruto4836 140br; Ngo Pang Ng 286b; Thanathorn Ngammongkolwong 306-7b; Sean Pavone 10ca, 20bl, 24-5t, 36bl, 41tr, 48bl, 49crb, 64-5b, 76-7t, 100bl, 102-3, 158-9t, 164t, 165tr, 166bl, 225, 231tl, 242-3t, 252b, 264t, 266t, 288-9b, 294-5, 298t, 301cra; Phuongphoto 24tl, 144-5t; Picturecorrect 58-9t; Pipa100 228br; Platongkoh 32bl; Psstockfoto 299cl; Prasit Rodphan 48-9t; Eq Roy 64tr; Somchai Sanguankotchakorn 154t; Seiksoon 39cl; Serge001 96tl; Hsu Yu Sheng 24-5ca; Siraanamwong 185cla; Ignasi Such 160-1t; Aduldej Sukaram 77cra; Parinya Suwanitch 108bl; Tktktk 22cr, 28crb; Jens Tobiska 50tr; Torsakarin 177cra, 226-7t; Tupungato 121cr, 309cr; Vincentstthomas 44-5t; Krisada Wakayabun 42-3t; Chun-Chang Wu 251cra.

Getty Images: a-clip 10-11b; AFP / Kazuhiro Nogi 62tl, 250clb, / Martin Bureau 54tl, 57cla, / Toshifumi Kitamura 139cra, / Japan Pool 45br; Corbis Documentary / B.S.P.I. 238bc; Carl Court 77crb, 122-3; Yongyuan Dai 77tr; De Agostini Picture Library 55cl; DigitalVision / Matteo Colombo 26t; Fine Art 159tr; Glowimages 224cra; Taro Karibe 60tl; John S Lander 56b, 205cra; Moment / Marser 146-7; Denis O'Regan 216fcrb; Print Collector 75br; Raga 60-1b; Jeremy Sutton-Hibbert 193br; The Asahi Shimbun 63t, 138-9b, 139tl, 139tr.

iStockphoto.com: 10max 254-5b; 4X-image 132cl; akiyoko 11t; AlexStoen / Yayoi Kusama Pumpkin, 1994 251tl; alisonteale24 22bl; ColobusYeti 62cr; coward_lion 74cla, 115br, 174b, 236-7b; Yongyuan Dai 19br; DanielBendjy 40tl; DavorLovincic 30cr, 32t, 277t; E+ / Eloi_Omella 18, 210; electravk 309cra, 309crb; enviromantic 185cra; finallast 224br; golaizola 112-3b; gyro 178; helovi 309cl; iconogenic 272tl; japanthings 121br; JavenLin 112-3t; kanonsky 35tr; kiennews 51tr; Korkusung 22crb, 95br; Rich Legg 132cb; lisegagne 51cl; MasaoTaira 176tr; Masaru123 66b; Milkos 8clb; mrtom-uk 224crb; Tamaki Nakajima 42-3b; Nayomiee 140t; nicholashan 30bl; oluolu3 197t; paprikaworks 256-7t; Sean Pavone 6-7, 8-9, 120b, 222-3t, 234b, 238t; petesphotography 20t, 282-3; preck13 304b; Ratth 133bc; recep-bg 58bl; RichLegg 13cr; Rixipix 106br; sara_winter 207cra; SeanPavonePhoto 11cr, 19cb, 189t, 200tr, 209b, 260-1; shirophoto 28t; somchaij 26bl; spastonov 140clb; superjoseph 186-7; chee gin tan 17bl, 180-1; tanukiphoto 34-5t; thanyarat07 71bl; TommL 16, 78-9; visualspace 94-5t; VittoriaChe 26cr; whitewish 188cra; winhorse 99br.

Rex by Shutterstock: Snap Stills 47br.

Robert Harding Picture Library: Photo Japan 205t.

Shutterstock: EQRoy 69cl; witaya ratanasirikulchai 69tr.

Sound Museum Vision: 59cl.

SuperStock: age fotostock / Lucas Vallecillos 38-9b; Mauritius / Jose Fuste Raga 19tl, 246-7; Prisma / Steve Andrew Vidler 128br.

Front Flap: Alamy Stock Photo: Patrick Batchelder cb; Jui-Chi Chan cra; Sean Pavone bl; StockShot cla; AWL Images: Marco Gaiotti br; Dreamstime.com: Sean Pavone tc.

Cover images:
Front and Spine: **iStockphoto.com:** pigphoto..
Back: **Dreamstime.com:** Leonid Andronov cl; **iStockphoto.com:** E+ / petesphotography c, Sean Pavone tr, ppigphoto b.

For further information see: www.dkimages.com

Illustrators:
Richard Bonson, Gary Cross, Richard Draper, Paul Guest, Claire Littlejohn, Maltings Partnership, Mel Pickering, John Woodcock

Penguin Random House

This edition updated by
Contributor Rob Goss
Senior Editor Alison McGill
Senior Designers Tania Da Silva Gomes, Vinita Venugopal
Project Editors Parnika Bagla, Dipika Dasgupta, Rebecca Flynn
Project Art Editor Bharti Karakoti
Editor Kanika Praharaj
Assistant Editor Arushi Mathur
Picture Research Coordinator Sumita Khatwani
Assistant Picture Research Administrator Vagisha Pushp
Jacket Coordinator Bella Talbot
Jacket Designer Ben Hinks
Senior Cartographer Mohammad Hassan
Cartography Manager Suresh Kumar
DTP Designers Rohit Rojal, Tanveer Zaidi
Senior Production Editor Jason Little
Senior Production Controller Kariss Ainsworth
Deputy Managing Editor Beverly Smart
Managing Editors Shikha Kulkarni, Hollie Teague
Managing Art Editors Bess Daly, Priyanka Thakur
Art Director Maxine Pedliham
Publishing Director Georgina Dee

First edition 2000

Published in Great Britain by Dorling Kindersley Limited
DK, One Embassy Gardens, 8 Viaduct Gardens, London SW11 7BW

Published in the United States by DK Publishing, 1450 Broadway, 8th Floor, New York, NY 10018

Copyright © 2000, 2021 Dorling Kindersley Limited
A Penguin Random House Company

21 22 23 24 10 9 8 7 6 5 4 3 2 1

A CIP catalog record for this book is available from the British Library.

A catalog record for this book is available from the Library of Congress.

ISSN: 1542 1554
ISBN: 978 0 2415 2041 3

Printed and bound in Malaysia.

www.dk.com

MIX
Paper from responsible sources
FSC™ C018179
www.fsc.org

This book was made with Forest Stewardship Council™ certified paper – one small step in DK's commitment to a sustainable future. For more information go to www.dk.com/our-green-pledge

A NOTE FROM DK EYEWITNESS

The rapid rate at which the world is changing is constantly keeping the DK Eyewitness team on our toes. While we've worked hard to ensure that this edition of Japan is accurate and up-to-date, we know that opening hours alter, standards shift, prices fluctuate, places close and new ones pop up in their stead. So, if you notice we've got something wrong or left something out, we want to hear about it. Please get in touch at travelguides@dk.com